HINDI
ACTION
CINEMA

HINDI ACTION CINEMA

INDUSTRIES, NARRATIVES, BODIES

Valentina Vitali

Indiana University Press
Bloomington and Indianapolis

This book is a publication of

Indiana University Press
601 North Morton Street
Bloomington, Indiana 47404-3797 USA

www.iupress.indiana.edu

Telephone orders   800-842-6796
Fax orders   812-855-7931
Orders by e-mail   iuporder@indiana.edu

Hindi Action Cinema was originally published in 2008 by Oxford University Press, India. This reprint published by arrangement with the original publisher for sale in World outside South Asia (including Bangladesh, Bhutan, India, Myanmar, Nepal, Pakistan, and Sri Lanka)

Manufactured in India

Cataloging information is available from the Library of Congress.

ISBN 978-0-253-22222-0 (pbk.)

1 2 3 4 5 15 14 13 12 11 10

Contents

Photographs

Note on the Transliteration of Film Titles and Names

For the transliteration of Indian film titles and names, I have adopted the spelling as it appears in the *Encyclopaedia of Indian Cinema* (Rajadhyaksha and Willemen 1999). For all films, I have used the official English title whenever the film has been given one, either on release or in existing filmographies. For films which do not have an English title, I have given a literal translation of the original title, unless the title is the name of a character.

Acknowledgements

This book was written in conversation with Paul Willemen, who also helped with the research for Chapters 1 and 2. I thank him for his patient support, intellectual integrity, and invaluable practical help.

Of the many people to whom this book owes much, special thanks go to Ashish Rajadhyaksha. Without his friendship and work, and the friendship and writings of Madhava Prasad, whom I also met at the Centre for the Study of Culture and Society (Bangalore), my interest in Hindi cinema would long have waned. My friend Francesca Orsini, who encouraged my research on Hindi cinema from the beginning, also read early versions of the manuscript and offered much-needed advice on how to make my writing more accessible.

I also wish to thank Virchand Dharamsey for sharing his boundless knowledge of Indian silent cinema during long afternoons in the dusty corridors of the Asiatic Society Library, Mumbai. Vinci Wadia generously granted me access to material that enabled me to write Chapter 2. I would like to thank him here for preserving that precious material in the first place and for the time he devoted to my questions about the work and outstanding writings of his father, J.B.H. Wadia. Chapter 4 owes much to the professionalism and kind assistance of Urmila Joshi, Lakshmi Iyer, and Arti Karkhanis at the National Film Archives of India. Many thanks also go to Rachel Dwyer, who encouraged my first foray into Hindi action cinema and enabled the publication of years of research on the subject. Much of the funding for the research came from the Society for South Asian Studies, which supported the project from its inception.

Finally, I am for ever grateful to Flavia and Aleardo Vitali for the confidence they have shown in me ever since I can remember. To them and to Paul Willemen, with whom it started, I dedicate this book.

Young India Players present
Y. M. DAVE
(SUPER STUNT STAR)
Toofan Mail
तुफ़ान मेल
WITH
PADMA
&
ADI PATEL
A WADIA BROTHERS PRODUCTION

Introduction

It is not a question of presenting works in correlation
with their time,
but, rather, in the time in which they are born, of presenting the
time that knows them.
—Walter Benjamin,
'Literary History and the Study of Literature'

RAJKUMAR SANTOSHI'S *GHATAK/LETHAL* (1996) TELLS THE STORY OF KASHI NATH (Sunny Deol), the son of a nationalist hero who sets out to free the residents of a small town from the terrorizing regime of arch-villain Katya (Danny Denzongpa). *Ghatak* features several fights and nearly all of them are witnessed by a (diegetic) crowd. The final confrontation between Kashi and Katya inscribes the spectator in the viewing position of the crowd, standing by and cheering as the hero kills the other man. This type of mise en scène is very common in action cinema and there is nothing particular about this film that one cannot find in many other action movies. Except, that is, the time that knew *Ghatak* as a film. I first saw it as a newly released film in 1996. I was then living in Allahabad, in the north Indian state of Uttar Pradesh, at a time when the popularity and influence of the Bharatiya Janata Party (BJP) was fast rising in the Hindi belt. Watching the film's closing scene from my balcony seat, I remember thinking then that I was seeing a film that was part of a swelling cultural–ideological wave which would be flooding large parts of the country for a long time to come. In many ways, this book emerges from, and is an elaboration of, that impression of seeing a film, not simply as a story or as a cultural object that may or may not be a work of art, but as an integral moment of an unfolding historical process.

Conventionally speaking, one might say that this book is about the relationship between history and cinema. The problem with such a formulation is that it risks suggesting that cinema is one thing and history another, the relationship between the two being a matter for historians and film theorists to discuss in an interdisciplinary exchange. Historians have many useful observations to make about films and about cinema as a cultural form, while film scholars have written insightful things about the history of their object of study, but juxtaposing cinema and history as distinct, though related, fields of enquiry obscures the fact that cultural forms emerge from within history. The question is thus less about how a film's relation to history should be understood, than the reading and understanding of films as technologically and industrially bundled discursive constellations animated by the very substances and rhythms that we refer to as history. Films are primary sources every bit as much as statesmen's diaries, minutes of governmental meetings, or the objects and detritus that can be found on the sites of ruined cities. Just as historians have to pay serious attention to the specificities of the media in which source material is encountered, so the specificities of cinematic discourses considered by film theorists are not separate from, but are an integral part of historiography.

When films have been examined as primary sources, attention has tended to focus on two particular aspects of the indexical dimension of films.[1] The most widely practised approach has been to examine what the films' stories have to say about events or periods already defined and labelled by historians. Plots, dialogues, and their settings are scrutinized to identify historically pertinent information in what film scholars call the pro-filmic event, that is to say, in the 'reality' recorded by the camera and the microphone. Although documentaries and newsreels are the types of cinema privileged by this approach, it is generally conceded that documentary aspects may also be discerned in fiction films. For instance, in the 1950s some French critics[2] regarded feature films as quasi-documentaries about actors: a film starring Ava Gardner was seen as, among other things, a film about the actress Ava Gardner. There are merits to this proto-modernist way of reading films as being also about the materials with which they are made, but, in practice, because of the reductive understanding of a film's 'materials', this remains a rather limited approach to cinema as history.

A second, more sophisticated, way of dealing with cinema as history has been to examine a film as a historical account marked by emphases and omissions that are due to state- or self-censorship, lack of money, or psychic repression. This approach, pioneered by Marc Ferro 1988 [1977] and Pierre Sorlin (1980), involves measuring the film retrospectively against other historiographic accounts that, although not necessarily taken to be 'truthful', are nevertheless understood to be offering a fuller and more objective picture than the one presented by the analysed film. The film's emphases, omissions, or simply 'distortions' are examined by resorting to certain techniques of psychoanalysis—and especially to Freud's account of the four processes of distortion at work in dreams.[3]

The information disclosed by such an approach can provide useful clues to the way a film functions as a text-in-history, bearing the marks of the geo-temporal location, of the conditions of its production and/ or circulation, and of the institutions that regulated both. But this approach has also tended to put more emphasis on what is not in the film, rather than on assessing what is. For instance, in his analysis of Lev Kuleshov's *Po zakonu / Dura Lex / By the Law* (1926), Ferro maintained that 'the historical and social reading' of this and other films enabled historians 'to reach invisible zones in the past of societies—to reveal self-censorship or *lapses* (which remain in the unconscious of participants and witnesses) at work within a society (1977: 20). Along the same lines, Sorlin argued that cinema

underscores a way of looking; it allows the distinguishing of the visible from the invisible and thus the ideological limits of perception in a certain age. [U]nder the cover of an analogy with the sensible world, which often allows it to pass as a faithful witness, cinema creates a fictional universe by reverting to comparison, matching, development, repetition, ellipsis (1977: 242; English translation from Casetti 1999).

Psychoanalysis can have a significant role to play if we are to understand how thoughts and intuitions are transformed as they are made to migrate from one level of consciousness to another, or from one medium into another. But, as Freud once said, there are times when a cigar is just a cigar. Notions of condensation, displacement, or secondary elaboration are to be kept in mind as a useful way of tracking when the image of a cigar is not just a cigar, that is to say when it stands in as a symbol of some other preoccupation. However, it is equally important to be able to tell when a cigar is just that, what brand it is, what economic circuits must be operating for that cigar to get to that smoker in that film at that place and time, and why someone such as that smoker may want to purchase and smoke it. By attaching importance exclusively to a film's distortions, that is to the relations between the visible and the invisible (or repressed), the approach pioneered by Ferro and Sorlin overlooks many of the complexities that the visible (and the audible) itself involves: its direct and immediate (or unmediated) implications, rather than its more or less hidden associations.

Questions about the relationship between films and history and the reading of films as historical documents imply that a film is inserted into a social context and that its functioning as a text, its capacity to produce meaning, is informed and limited by that context. The story of the study of cinema has been marked by many attempts at grappling with the question of how material socio-economic arrangements shape cultural production and, through culture, modes of thinking. Conceptualizations of that interaction have informed, for instance, debates on notions of national cinema, that is to say of a cinema's connectedness with the historical constellation that generates it and which, by addressing that constellation cinematically, cinema in turn helps to shape. As Siegfried Kracauer argued in 1946: 'Through an analysis of the German films, deep psychological dispositions predominant in Germany from 1918 to 1933 can be exposed—dispositions which influenced the course of events during that time and which will have to be reckoned with in the post-Hitler era' (1974: v).

Setting out to demonstrate that there was more to cinema than a machine bound to new production, models, markets, professions, and economic values, Kracauer produced an account that successfully fused the industrial and national dimensions of cinema, better to understand how German films' cinematic characteristics sustained 'dispositions' enacted in history. Over the years, however, it was the historiographic model pioneered by, among others, Lewis Jacobs, in his *The Rise of the American Film: A Critical History* (1939), and Oskar Kalbus, in *Vom Werden Deutscher Filmkunst* (1936), that became the norm. Jacobs's book, in particular, has come to be regarded as a template for the writing of national film histories. Divided into six parts, entitled 'Fade In', 'Foundations', 'Development', 'Transition', 'Intensification', and 'Maturity', Jacobs's book chronicled both the cultural and the industrial dimensions of cinema by relying on a linear notion of history that understood both cinema and the nation to be the organic result of an evolutionary— indeed a maturational—trajectory.

While debates about film history date back to the 1920s, interest in the relationship between films and history underwent a significant resurgence in the 1970s and 1980s. To begin with, scholars began to distance themselves from traditional approaches to the history of cinema such as Jacobs's. This historiography was criticized for having focused exclusively on films (at the expense of the cinema's technological, economic, and social dimensions), for having relied on inadequate research tools (such as personal memories of stars or of the researcher) and analytical categories (such as notions of 'schools', 'movements', or 'periods'), and for having adopted a linear model of historical 'development', when, in reality, cultural–historical change follows far more contradictory patterns. One factor in this resurgence of interest in questions of film and of history was growing awareness of the problems of 'doing history' in general. As historians began to regard cinema as a historical source, film scholars began to open their object of study to political, economic, and social history (Casetti 1999: 289–91). In this context, as Kracauer's work became the object of renewed interest, the historiographic model pioneered by Jacobs and Kalbus came to be regarded as unproductive because, with its evolutionary, historicist underpinning, it forestalled the possibility of understanding how specific economic arrangements may shape cultural issues.

In Europe, the study of cinema acquired special status in the aftermath of 1968, when, engaging directly with the practices and politics of cultural activists, intellectuals used cinema as a platform to find better ways than were available in the study of literature for understanding the functioning of industrial cultural practices as processes that help to sustain or to disrupt the given economic dynamics governing social relations. The disciplinary split that followed those debates on cinema led to the opening of the first film studies departments (as separate from literary studies) in universities. At the time in which I write, the opposite movement is taking place: media studies, in which film is firmly subordinated to television, electronic media, and journalism, has emerged and achieved institutional recognition as a ground for the formation of a reserve army of labour for a limited range of (mostly) national cultural industries. The study of cinema, on the other hand, is increasingly confined to language and literature departments, where it is once again brought into line with what used to be called the 'literary sciences', that is to say into the realm of the 'high arts' and aesthetics. Within this disciplinary reshuffling, the understanding of cinema and of other media as functions of the public sphere is made seemingly irrelevant. Indeed, film students are ever more insistently being urged to devote attention to the marketing of films, while research on cinema is fine-tuned more and more closely to the study of 'consumption habits'. In this context, film authors or directors are being 'studied' as if the concept of *auteur* had never been unpacked from the humanist underpinnings that *Cahiers du Cinéma* originally gave to it, while national cinemas are 'learned' by way of lists of exemplary directors and their most 'representative' films or, worse, their box-office hits. What such canons represent, however, is rarely asked. Vague notions of context are invoked, but the conceptualization of either that context or of the films' relation to it is postponed ad infinitum. National histories tend to be presented like series of bookmarks arranged one after the other, linear trajectories from birth into maturity to which films are made to fit, retrospectively, as the natural and necessary mirrors ('reflections') of their time. The bigger the box-office earnings, the more the film reflects the *Zeitgeist*, conceived as 'what people want'.

This way of proceeding blocks the understanding of the relation between a film's strategies of narration and the socio-economic context that shaped, and which was in turn shaped by, the film because it fails to reflect, directly and critically, on the historian's operation—the time in which s/he speaks, the interests that direct his/her reading of the films, and the tools used for analysis. A framework is assumed for our reading of the films that prompts us to suppose that similar formal devices had the same narrative function 'then' as they have 'now'. Fundamental differences are overlooked in the operation of cultural forms as they are mobilized 'here' and 'elsewhere'. At worst, a historiographic-analytical model patterned on the uniquely specific development of the most powerful film industry today, located mainly in Los Angeles, is projected onto films that are produced and which circulate under differently specific cultural-historical contingencies. In this way, the coalition of interests sustaining that dominant, North American industrial-financial constellation is allowed to dictate the terms by which we relate to films that, while also made in the context of globally incubating (American-controlled) capital, are differently positioned within its expanding operation, sometimes also critically so. Past cultural series are reduced to fetishes, obsolete clusters of commodities seemingly immaterial to the understanding of the becoming of the present that we inhabit. Their study is instrumentalized, made conducive to the reproduction of the very industrial-cultural forces whose operation we originally intended to historicize.

Like the many histories of national cinemas that followed his book, Jacobs inherited his linear conceptualizations of history and of cultural series from the type of literary historiography that Walter Benjamin had attacked only a few years before in his 'Literary History and the Study of Literature'. In 1931, when he first published that essay, Benjamin described contemporary literary history as 'a kind of applied taxonomy of taste', something 'halfway between a textbook of aesthetics and a bookseller's catalogue' (1999a: 459). Four years later, he completed what he later described as an attempt to formulate a theory of cultural production that would be 'completely useless for the purposes of fascism'.

Much more modestly, but equally urgently, this book re-proposes a line of historiographic inquiry that seeks to open up the connections between the ways in which a film is made and circulated within a given socio-economic juncture, and the film's strategies of address (film as discourse) as functions of that constellation. By way of an examination of the action cinema made in Bombay, I try to demonstrate the productivity of a framework that may enable us better to analyse *how* specific interests, carried more or less consciously by historical agents (whether individuals or as social categories) work themselves into film texts that help shape our future through the filters and institutions of cultural production.

A cinema, perhaps even more directly than other industries, constitutes its audiences while constituting itself as an industry (Hozic 2001: xv). Of the few analytical tools available within film theory, the concept of genre is the most open to industrial-commercial considerations, and, to that extent, discussions of individual film genres can be, and often are, the most exposed to the kind of instrumentalization sketched above. At worst, discussions about particular bundles of films are caught in a contradictory tension between, on the one hand, genre as an empirically given, historically specific set of narrative traits and, on the other, genre as an abstract, theoretical category. To put it another way, to identify a film as belonging to a particular genre, the critic has to know what the features of that genre are, but, equally, the critic only knows those features by reference to films identified as constituting the genre (Tudor 1974: 135). Failing to resolve this conundrum, critics tend to define a genre retrospectively: having identified a set of narrative ingredients or sales points in films that are marketed under a label dictated by some sectors of the film industry, the critic undertakes a search for similar ingredients in other (older or newer) films—only finally to reproduce in the definition of the genre the marketing strategy that the industry developed to promote a particular group of films at a particular time.

There is a difference between talking about a film and talking about the ways in which the film is sold. Much writing on individual genres tries to find coherence in the marketing categories by which bundles of films are sold and, ultimately, projects onto the films those marketing categories. But genre history can provide the conceptual space where questions can be asked about the ways in which a cinema constitutes its audiences or subjects and, through them, its conditions of existence as an industry. As Christine Gledhill has written, 'in this space issues of texts and aesthetics—the traditional concern of film theory—intersect with those of industry and institution, history and society, culture and audiences—the central concerns of political economy, sociology and cultural studies' (2000: 221). In and of themselves, marketing strategies, of which genre is one, do speak of an economic fantasy, a preferred or desired horizon. A film also speaks of the specific economic constellation of which it is a part. It is worth avoiding the practice of projecting marketing categories onto films directly and, in so doing, reducing a film to a sales strategy while instructing spectators to read the film as 'just that'. Instead, this book examines action cinema as a structural category marking the site where specific social-economic factors generate cultural objects configured in particular ways and featuring determinate (and determined) modes of address. It is in such configurations that this book seeks to find the reasons why some filmmakers in certain sectors of the industry were moved to prioritize one selected narrative ingredient (action), as well as for the diverse ways this ingredient was mobilized at different times in India.

Genres are systems for the regulation and circulation of meaning. They have a public, historically specific existence. The ancient Greeks devised theoretical systems whereby fictional works were divided into genres on the basis of mode of delivery: the lyric was a work in which only the author or narrator spoke; in drama only the characters spoke; while in the epic both narrator and characters could speak (Ducrot and Todorov 1972: 198). A hierarchy obtained within this system and within the genres themselves. This is to say, genres are first and foremost modes of address or delivery designed to regulate the circulation of meaning on the basis of given (hierarchical) social relations. Existing social relations determine who speaks to whom, about what, and in which way. Steve Neale was among the first scholars to discuss film genres as processes of systematization. He argued that, on the one hand, genres are crucial to the film industry because 'they provide, simultaneously, maximum regularity and economy in the utilisation of plant and personnel, and the minimum degree of difference necessary for each individual product' to be sold (Neale 1980: 51–3). On the other hand, film texts consist of a weaving together of a multitude of discursive currents, each with their own semantic fields and implied subject positions. According to Neale, [genres] intervene between the instances of the process of subject regulation: that of mainstream narrative and that of the individual text. Genres [e]stablish a regulation of the variety of mainstream narrative across a series of individual texts, organising and systematising the difference that each text represents, filling in the gap between text and system. [G]enres function to move the subject from text to text and from text to narrative system, binding instances together into a constant coherence, the coherence of the cinematic institution. (1980: 49)

While Neale's seminal conceptualization of genre had the merit of finally opening up for film theory the possibility of tracing connections between empirical genres and the socio-economic pressures that lend bundles of films their shared traits, he stopped short of specifying the nature of the regulation imposed, presenting instead generic regulation as one more instance of narrative regulation in general, and plugging the gap with vague references to 'the cinematic institution'. But a cinema, whether as an industry or as a series of texts, is always situated in a historical context. Marketing is one of many important dimensions of that context and of the institution of cinema, but it is not always a determining one. What I am concerned about here are not just the processes of industrial transformation that led Indian filmmakers to make and market films on the basis of the action ingredient. Rather, I am interested in the manner in which one may, as it were, reverse-engineer the historical dynamics underpinning the ways in which action became (or not) a defining ingredient of cinema in India at any given time. In this way, the study of cinema may help us to illuminate the nature of the relationship between economic and cultural priorities at specific historical junctures. How does a cinema produce the conditions for its own existence and growth? What can the changes in a cinema's economic and narrative structures tell us about the conditions for the sustenance of other economic sectors, and about changes in those conditions? If one dimension of hegemony is the ability to organize fantasies, how do films produce new social spaces and, over a period of time, participate in the causation of historical change?

If, at one level, the problem lies with the ways in which the notion of film genre has been theorized and used in film studies, at a more fundamental level, it is the models of history and of culture that have tended to be deployed for the study of film genres (as also of film authors, national cinemas, and so forth) that have left important dimensions of cinema out of sight. In 'Theses on the Philosophy of History' Walter Benjamin famously imagined history as an angel with his face turned towards the past, his wings spread: 'Where a chain of events appears before us, he sees one single catastrophe, which keeps piling wreckage upon wreckage and hurls it at his feet. [A] storm is blowing [that] drives him irresistibly into the future to which his back is turned, while the pile of debris before him grows.' What we call progress, Benjamin concluded, history's forward drive, is this storm (1999a: 392). It is this ill wind that both condensed into Rajkumar Santoshi's *Ghatak* and blew through the cinema in Allahabad in 1996. Elsewhere, many other films were made then, including Hou Hsiao-hsien's *Nanguo zaijan, nanguo / Goodbye South, Goodbye* (Taiwan), Chantal Akerman's *Un divan à New York* (Belgium), and Anand Patwardhan's *Narmada Diary* (India). These films contain elements of a public sphere and social relations radically different in kind than the one addressed and, in the process, proposed by Rajkumar Santoshi's feature as 'the present' that we are supposed to inhabit. To find ways of grasping the relationship between cinema and history requires that our sense of history be opened up to the multiple and contradictory possibilities (the futures) it must have contained at the time in which these other (Hou's, Akerman's, and Patwardhan's) films were also made. Like Benjamin's storm, linear historiographies and retrospective definitions of genre leave those possibilities behind, as rubble or wreckage that historians, busy identifying 'general trends', as if always facing forward, chose not to see.

But within that rubble, cultural forms do operate that, while perhaps not setting the trend dominant at any given point in time, remain nevertheless available for scrutiny. If they survive and circulate, it is because they must have a function. This function is never simply given: the functions of cultural forms change depending on the historical forces that avail themselves of those forms or categories. In order to grasp the connection between a film and its time, understood as a forcefield where multiple and contradictory interests are always necessarily at work, our understanding of history must be drawn into the analysis of the film as the specific cluster of dynamics that lends the film's formal strategies their equally specific, multiple, and coexisting capacities of signification. For instance, a generic form may characterize a particular type of industrial production, as in the Fordist organization of man production; but it may also convey something about the way a relatively new or diversifying production enterprise seeks to position itself in an already established marketplace. In the latter case, the presence and the mode of inscription of generic features says more about the producers' 'business plan' and aspirations (their more or less realistic fantasies) as they are necessarily adjusted to the perceived 'prevailing conditions', both in the industry and in the social juncture where the products are supposed to circulate. Genre, understood as a structural category, a system that draws its capacity to regulate the circulation of meaning from given socio-economic relations, can thus play an import role in the tracing of connections between a film and its time. To remain available for such a task, however, Neale's notion of 'the cinematic institution' needs to be opened up and scrutinized in all its complexity as a historically specific set of tensions and contradictory pulls that change over time and which respond to economic, technological, social, and political pressures.

This book endeavours to explore moments in the history of a cinema in which a category that can be found in all the cinemas of the world—the 'action ingredient', as Paul Willemen called it (2005a)—acquired prominence as a narrative element and as a means to make and sell films. My objective is not to identify every instance of action cinema in Indian cinema. I have, to begin with, focused exclusively on the cinema produced in Bombay between, roughly, the 1910s and the early 2000s. Moreover, within that narrow field, the reader will find that there are many films and actors I have not discussed. There are good reasons for these self-imposed limits. Given that in the Bombay industry, cinematic moments are identifiable when the 'action' ingredient came to the foreground as a category that defined that particular cinema's dominant generic ground, the question I want to ask is: why at these times and in that way?

In order to begin to answer this question, while avoiding reductive and unproductive notions of text–context 'reflection', films are discussed here simultaneously as commodities—the products of an industry, of identifiable commercial-economic interests within it—and as clusters of narrative strategies. On the one hand, given that the economic history of Indian cinema still remains to be written, this approach forced me to piece together what little information can be gleaned from extant archival sources so as to begin to retrace the changing shape of Indian cinema as an industry that first emerged at the beginning of the twentieth century. On the other hand, to use a familiar but misleading terminology, examining films as elements of both 'base' and 'superstructure' meant addressing a problem that has plagued cultural history from its inception. In the narrower field of film historiography, that problem has manifested itself as the emergence of two distinct historiographic strands that have grown further and further apart: those that study the economy of the film industry and those that analyse the films. In any industrialized society, commodities do circulate anonymously among strangers, but they are also invested with social meanings and aspirations, desires, and horizons that are far in excess of their immediate utilitarian value. As Susan Buck-Morss (1995) has shown, within the discipline of economics, the gradual erasure of the social value of commodities can be traced back to the eighteenth-century Enlightenment in Europe. While this trajectory was already resisted and counteracted by the likes of Hegel and Marx, today, books that discuss cultural items as pertaining to both economic and aesthetic spheres are few and far between.[4]

This is, of course, not to say that cultural historians have confined themselves to various degrees of formalism. Although not directly and explicitly about the circulation of cultural items as commodities, a significant number of recent studies have addressed the crucial question of the social dimension of cultural products by turning their attention to the ways in which cultural items 'talk to us'. That is to say, to the ways in which books or films address their actual, anticipated, or unintentionally addressed readers or viewers on the one hand, and to the ways in which readers or viewers handle the ways in which they are addressed on the other hand.[5] In film theory, it is especially the work of Paul Willemen and of Philip Rosen that has drawn attention to the importance of modes of address as a way of tracking how a text modulates the forces and dynamics that constitute history as a process which, among other things, yields specific films. In line with this particular tradition of film theory, here I explore the connections between (a) the industrial considerations that generated a film, (b) its narrative strategies, and (c) the social functions of those strategies within the socio-economic juncture that made them necessary. This triple track allows me to examine the filmic devices by which viewers are positioned in certain ways vis-à-vis what they are given to see as 'the real' by the cinematic apparatus and, crucially, to understand the functioning of those positioning devices as, precisely, functions of the specific socio-economic constellation that produced them. The toolbox I relied on to identify economic-commercial interests as they work themselves into the film texts as a set of pressures resulting in particular arrangements of formal, cinematic strategies was developed in dialogue with the work of Paul Willemen, often by borrowing from, and adapting to my ends, the work of structuralist semiotics and linguistics.[6] The field that opened up as a result of this approach is vast. The task of formal textual analysis becomes a complex affair when it is opened up to a 'context' the fabric of which is not only constantly shifting, but, more importantly, the changing texture of which is conceptualized as an effect of struggles between the multitude of interests constitutive of that fabric, each pulling in different directions and resorting to different sets of cultural-industrial resources. That texture is not proposed here as a comprehensive panorama of Hindi cinema, nor is the toolkit used explicitly formulated as a tightly knit analytic framework, a set of inflexible rules. My objective is to demonstrate the feasibility of a line of inquiry the productivity of which will ultimately depend on its capacity to trigger a wider debate, both on the nature of the historical-economic factors I identify as responsible for this or that cinematic development, and on the content of the toolbox itself.

Chapters 1 to 6 are structured like a tracking movement, or a slow zoom. Given that the very diverse visions staged by the films through their narrative or formal strategies were triggered by, and responded to the economic pressures confronted by the films as products, the reader's attention is first called to that 'real' which the people who made the films thought they inhabited. Each chapter thus proceeds from international and Indian economics to the film industry as a sector of that economic constellation and, from here, to the films as products and as texts. Again, this structure is not meant to provide a comprehensive overview of India at a specific point in time, but, rather, to outline, selectively though as accurately as possible, the economic and industrial factors given to the films as their point of departure. Through the analysis of films, I show that specific economic forces can be seen to be at work and read in the films' narrative strategies. At given moments in the history of cinema in India, some economic-industrial pressures emerged that led filmmakers to prioritize the action ingredient. Many other, equally specific but different, economic-industrial factors were also at work in the Indian economy and in the film industry at the same time, but these other factors led filmmakers to prioritize narrative ingredients other than action. A film is always subject to each of the pressures at work within the film industry which produced it and, as a result, a film always contains a variety of narrative ingredients. Here I am only concerned with the action ingredient and with the pressures that led to its prioritization. For it is this changing fabric of dynamics that lent the films' formal strategies (the ways films presents 'action') their function and meanings at the time in which the films were made. The films' capacity to address the public sphere at any given time and, in this way, to constitute the conditions for their own existence is to be found in the modalities of these socio-economic configurations.

I do not argue that the cluster of commercial-industrial pressures determining a film's formal strategies is necessarily in line with the overall direction of the country's economy at the time the film was made. A film, any film, does a very broad range of things, only a fraction of which can be discussed in any single piece of writing, no matter how thorough the analysis. The purpose of my textual analysis is, first, to show how some of a film's narrative elements are directly connected to the economic conditions out of which the film resulted as a commodity, and, second, to demonstrate that such elements simultaneously refracted important forces at work in the historical-geographic place that configured the film. Through such refractions, a film inevitably distorts the contingencies that made it possible or necessary, because films work with material and with codes that pertain to a different sphere of existence than economics. Yet, precisely through such distortion processes—through the transposition or translation of a set of economic considerations into a cluster of discursive choices—a film can visualize or stage horizons of experience that differ from the one dominant at the time, giving as 'real' a set of possibilities that are not the same as the 'reality' that determined, to a large extent, the film's conditions of possibility in the first place.

A film always intervenes in the given social conditions of existence: while being shaped by economic forces that require and sustain certain social arrangements, a film, or rather, filmic discourse can position spectators in relation to what is given to be seen as the 'real' in such a way that it makes possible different positionalities. For instance, films featuring women became an element of Indian culture at a time when pre-industrial power blocs were firmly in place and managed to impose a strict taboo on public performances by women, effectively preventing low caste (or class) access to such public performances. The stunt films of the 1920s began to be made when these power blocs were dominant, but this did not prevent the films from offering views of real women moving in previously unseen ways to sections of the population to whom such views had until then not been presented in quite the same way. By opening up, through narration, new positionalities, a film does not simply intervene in social relations. In one and the same movement, by restaging ideal or anticipated social relations, a film also produces fantasies about economic horizons different from the one prevailing at the time that generated it. Such fantasies are cinematic elaborations of the very economic pressures and considerations which produced the film and which the film registers and expresses in the body of the text itself. This is not to say that, over a series of films, such pressures become dominant and the fantasy is materially realized. It simply says that films may contain elements of a public sphere significantly different in kind from the one that governed their making or that now governs our reading of such films.

Chapters 1 to 6 follow a chronological order and cover a period of just over eighty years, but they do not offer an account of the emergence, development, and culmination of Bombay's action cinema as a whole in all its details. Action films were a far more prominent a feature of Bombay cinema in the 1930s than they were in the 1950s. Each chapter, therefore, examines the industrial-commercial reasons for the prominence or not of action films at certain times in the history of Bombay cinema, the forms that were characteristic of action films in different decades, and the instrumental connections between those formal characteristics and the broader economic juncture in which the films circulated. The clusters of films examined in each chapter also present a distinct problem of film history and cultural theory. Chapter 1 opens with the 1910s, a decade in which action cinema was not a feature of Indian film production but which needs to be considered in order to trace the subsequent emergence of the action ingredient as a category in its own right, becoming, in time, constitutive of a new genre: the stunt film, which began to be made in the 1920s. Here I have focused primarily on the films produced by Sharda Film Company and on its star, Master Vithal, although Vithal was by no means the only actor specializing in such roles at the time. While I also briefly discuss Ganpatrao Bakre, who worked for Surya, many actors have been left out, such as Raja Sandow and Krishna Film Company's Nandaram. These omissions are primarily motivated by the understanding that Vithal's case is paradigmatic, the dynamics dictating his rise and decline as a stunt actor having affected and determined also the careers of his competitors. Sharda was set up in the mid-1920s, a period in which, for the first time, film production in India acquired the dimensions of an industry. Indian cinema was then characterized by extremely weak generic differentiation. Each producer active at the time covered most of the generic spectrum and Sharda, like other companies, made historical, costume, and social dramas. Unlike other companies, however, Sharda was the first to distil a narrative ingredient—stunts—from the range of available generic formats. Marking it as its own through the ex novo construction of a film star, Sharda used the stunt ingredient as a selling point in order to capitalize on the expansion of the market for cinema. In the mid-1920s, this was an urban market, confined almost exclusively to Bombay (and a handful of other cities) when the population of Bombay expanded to accommodate a growing industrial workforce.

Having been first formulated through the study of film industries—the European and the American cinemas—the economic priority of which was, from their inception, production (as opposed to distribution or exhibition), film historiography still tends to narrate the emergence and development of other national cinemas by focusing almost exclusively on production. As I have argued elsewhere (2006), in the context of the cinema in India this has created enormous problems because, as becomes clear from an analysis of Sharda's operation, it was exhibition, not production, which, in those years, dictated the terms by which films were made. By the end of World War II, when film production began to become a regular feature of India's industrial sector, exhibition networks controlled by local agents were firmly in place and shaped Sharda's and other producers' work. Sharda was therefore, in intent, an industrial-commercial operation characterized by a high yearly turnover of films. In practice, however, Sharda's market remained limited, exclusively urban and shaped by pre-industrial conditions. This led the company to create a figure, Master Vithal, whose performance in action did not display human physical energy as a marketable asset, continuing instead to carry pre-industrial connotations of hierarchical, even aristocratic, status, although with Vithal a particular image of aristocratic status was effectively commodified, transformed into a selling point designed to target the closest thing to a mass urban market Bombay cinema had, until then, addressed.

In the following decades, the interactions between the film industry's three sectors took other forms, resulting in profoundly different products. But the power relations between exhibitors, producers, and, from the 1930s, distributors, remained, in essence, the same from Sharda's time well into the following decades. In the 1930s, with the gradual introduction of synchronized film sound and the collapse of Madan Theatres' chain of cinemas, Indian exhibition opened up. The introduction of synchronized sound makes the 1930s a critical moment in the historiography of all cinemas, but in the case of Indian cinema this is especially so. Although systematic research in this area has yet to be undertaken, one thing is clear: unlike in the US and in Europe, where synchronized film sound, introduced for purposes of competition, mobilized enormous investments over an extremely short period of time, in India that kind of capital was simply not made available. As Madan Theatres' collapse suggests, film sound presented itself to the Indian film industry as the prospect of, and, simultaneously, the obstacle to, an expansion of the market. But the 1930s in India also saw the emergence and development of distribution as a distinct sector of the film industry. In Chapter 2, I suggest that in India film sound and distribution are tightly connected developments. The lack of integration that characterized the market for consumer goods (including cinema) before and after Madan's collapse enabled booking agents to become distributors by exploiting the delay between the aspiration towards, and the realization of, a national market for cinema. Finally, sound was introduced over a much longer period than in Europe and the US, at a time when other industrial sectors began to diversify and, with sectoral diversification, to decentralize. Chapter 2 thus examines the presence and function of women in action roles from the mid-1920s to the end of the 1930s: a time when, competing for the now available exhibition space, films began to be made featuring women in new types of roles. Through an analysis of the silent and sound features produced by Jamshed Boman Homi Wadia, I argue that Wadia Movietone's best-known features, starring Fearless Nadia, foreground notions of industrialization, not as a concrete project, but as a future or a horizon that the films present as highly desirable, that is to say, as an aspiration or a fantasy. The films do so not only in their representation of industrial technology, but also through their cinematic rendition of a broad range of ideal body types and movements, ideal uses of physical energy that are wrapped into a narrative held together by a device—images of a woman—that, by the 1930s, was a well-tested selling strategy. Recording the performance of a real woman moving in ways that she would normally not be seen doing by the general public and infringing established codes of modesty gave the films a commercial, competitive edge while simultaneously enabling the films to register dimensions of social modernization. The drive for industrialization that characterized the Indian economy in those years thus produced, on the one hand, figurations of the human energy that may be required to produce industrial goods and, on the other, secondary elaborations of the terms by which social relations were to be reconfigured in order to use that energy productively. Nadia met primarily the latter function.

The factors that led Bombay production to temporarily abandon this generic trend in the 1950s are discussed in a section called 'Interlude'. The generic shift of those years responded to a generalized concern over the new terms of socially acceptable behaviour, the relations that were to create India as an independent nation state. The urgent question of what kind of nation state was to be built absorbed or marginalized other preoccupations. In those years, questions of individuation or the creation of a labour force came couched in explicitly nation-building discourses, while the more radical sectors of capital, which had been responsible for action cinema in the preceding decades, were contained by a political and economic coalition with more conservative power blocs set on frustrating the new Indian state's thrust for modernization along industrial lines. Because this situation hardly changed in the following decade, Chapter 4 deals with an asynchronous moment in the history of Bombay cinema: the wrestling films of Dara Singh.

In the 1960s, Dara Singh became a very popular film star and in many years of research on Indian cinema I have yet to meet an Indian of that generation who does not remember the wrestler-star fondly. But, with the exception of Rajadhyaksha and Willemen's *Encyclopaedia of Indian Cinema* (1999), he does not feature in any of the books on Indian cinemas because many of the elements that characterize the imaginary public sphere his films addressed did not materialize as prominent features of Indian society until decades later. Dara Singh's films were produced under a peculiarly Indian set of conflictual pressures: a circumscribed and far from integrated film exhibition sector rooted in localized and, on the whole, pre-industrial financial circuits; changes in the industrial make-up of Bombay; the emergence of a suburban, working population no longer primarily employed in the cotton mills; and an increasingly fragmented film-production sector seeking to capitalize on this new market with low-budget films made to measure to circumvent the exhibitors' reluctance to expand. Dara Singh's films registered those pressures and opportunities in their commercial exploitation of presentations of physical energy. The narrativization of this energy constituted the films' and their star's most valuable asset, resulting, at times, in the fetishization of the actor-wrestler's muscles as a symbol of sheer physical energy. Nevertheless, blocking factors also governed their making and circulation, and these were also registered in the films, where they can be seen to produce inconsistent editing within fight scenes and discontinuities in camera positioning.

The preoccupation with the form of sheer physical energy, and its use, that characterizes Dara Singh's films was not a prominent feature of the Hindi action cinema of the following decade. By the mid-1970s, the socio-economic pressures that had marginalized that 1960s vision produced, in their turn, quite different films and visions of capital accumulation. As a result, Dara Singh's films were—in the 1960s and thereafter—'marginal' cinema. This is not to say that, apart from Dara Singh's films, no action film was made between the 1950s and the early 1970s in Bombay or elsewhere in India, or that Dara Singh's films were not successful. It simply means that, more so than in the case of Dara Singh's wrestling movies and urban thrillers, action films produced under those conditions were asynchronous moments, destined to fall out of historiographies intent on narrating the modalities of a cinema retrospectively as a linear succession of genre- or trend-setting films. All I can do here, given the limitations imposed by the format, is to remind the reader of the necessity for research capable of accounting also for the existence and modes of narration of these other films, for they too were a factor in the re-emergence of the action ingredient as a defining category of Bombay cinema's centre ground in the 1970s.

I discuss this decade in Chapter 5, where, as many others have done before me, I revisit the action films of Amitabh Bachchan. I have tried to resist the temptation of referring to the processes that led to this type of Bombay film as the 'mainstreaming' of action cinema. When I do so, readers should bear in mind that, to begin with, in a film industry characterized by at least three large production centres and products in some twenty languages, the notion of a single 'mainstream' is, at best, questionable. But the problem of referring to Bachchan's action films as 'the mainstream' of 1970s Hindi cinema has above all to do with the fact that the capital which began to circulate through or 'as' these films bore an extremely oblique relation to the state as the agency that, in India as in any other country, seeks to regulate the circulation of both capital and cultural production. Although in essence this was far from being an unprecedented situation (all cultural production anywhere is always in an oblique relation to the state), and while Bachchan's action movies did borrow from, among others, Dara Singh's films, they also responded to a radically different configuration than the one addressed by the earlier films. Bombay cinema in the 1970s was marked first and foremost by Indira Gandhi's new and abruptly implemented policies of credit centralization. The capital that sought to circumvent those measures found in cinema a more effective means of circulation than the nationalized networks made available by the state. Within a few years, this resulted in the production of a new star, pitted, not surprisingly, against state institutions, as well as in entirely different commercial and narrative elaborations of the action ingredient as it had been put to work in earlier films. The financial (as opposed to industrial) nature of the capital that underpinned Bachchan's films led to a comparative marginalization of images of sheer physical energy and to a mode of staging action scenes that was, on the whole, more discontinuous than was the case in Dara

Singh's films, because, by the 1970s, the action ingredient was mobilized by an advertising address: the more or less explicit promotion of a genre as central to the Bombay film industry's dominant stream, and marketed precisely as such.

I do not address this notion of 'the mainstream' directly in the chapter dedicated to the 1970s, nor in any other chapter, but the central issue underpinning it, that is the notion of film genre as a structural, rather than a marketing, category, runs like a thread throughout the book, linking the chapters and the films discussed in each of them, their strategies of narration, their production, and their circulation. Bound up with it are questions about film historiography as itself a moment of history, a present to be conceptualized and understood with our eyes as open as possible so as to make whole what has been wrecked by what we are supposed to accept unproblematically as 'progress'. Hindi action films of the 1990s and early 2000s are a good indication that it is not exactly 'progress'. I discuss examples of that more recent Bombay action cinema in Chapter 6, where I examine the interconnections between, on the one hand, real estate and the emergence, in India, of multiplex cinemas in shopping malls, and, on the other, changes in the filmic representation of urban environments, contemporary actors' bodies as sites of display, and the cinematic rendition of those bodies' movements in that changing environment. The increasing visibility of Hindi films outside India in recent years has led historians to pay greater attention than in the past to the economic circumstances that generated these and other contemporary Hindi films. I hope that what follows may help to equip the scholars now undertaking such research better to see exactly in whose interest are the bleak fantasies proposed by films that we are increasingly asked to celebrate as the pinnacles of Indian cinema.

NOTES

1. Here and in the following chapters, the terms 'indexical', 'iconic', and 'symbolic' refer to C.S. Peirce's classification of signs into icons, indexes, and symbols. An icon is a sign that represents its object mainly by its similarity to it, where the relationship between signifier and signified is one of resemblance and likeness. An index is a sign by virtue of an existential bond between the sign and its object, where the index retains within itself traces of the physical, existential connection between sign and reality. Peirce's favourite example of indexicality is the death mask: 'Both the face like a skull and the skull like a face ... one living above the other. One concealed beneath the other' (Pierce [1977]; also quoted in Willemen [2000: 8]). A symbol corresponds to Saussure's arbitrary

sign, where Peirce (1977), like Saussure, speaks of a contract whereby the symbol is understood to represent the object. See also Wollen (1998: 122–3) and Eco (1976). It is important to note that Peirce did not consider these three types of sign as mutually exclusive. On the contrary, all three modes are co-present within any one sign because all signs always depend on both intellectual cognition and sensuous perception. The difference between icon, index, and symbol is a difference in the way these two registers of experience are orchestrated.

2. Writing mainly for *Positif* and *Cahiers du Cinéma*.

3. As described by Freud in 'The Dream-Work' (1976) the four processes are condensation, displacement, secondary elaboration, and conditions of representability.

4. Among earlier attempts to relate the economic priorities of cinema as an industry, or, more specifically, film production, with that cinema's stylistic, narrative dimension is David Bordwell, Janet Steiger, Kristin Thomson's (1985) work on American cinema. Bordwell et al.'s account, however, ultimately led to a reduction of American cinema to notions of 'classical narrative' and, over time, to the institutionalization of that American model as a universal cinematic language and as a mode of historiography valid for any cinema. This is a problem because, in practice, Bordwell et al.'s object of study, the formation of the American film industry and, within it, of dominant power blocs the economic priority of which was film production, was a unique, nationally specific phenomenon. Although as a 'model' it is far from helpful for the historiography and analytical study of cinemas that grew out of entirely different historical, socio-economic conditions, Bordwell et al.'s work nevertheless continues to be used as such. It is a moot point whether this has to do with the authors' methodology or with the power of the institutions within or about which they wrote. A more recent and, in my opinion, far more convincing attempt at relating American cinema's economic priorities to its aesthetics is Philip Rosen's remarkable *Change Mummified: Cinema, Historicity, Theory* (2001). Unlike Bordwell et al., Rosen pre-empts the danger of 'universalism' by making historiography itself the object of his, the film historian's, scrutiny. Within the field of Indian cinema, attempts at tracing the interrelationship between the industrial and ideological dimensions of films were undertaken by Madhava Prasad (1998b) and Manjunath Pendakur (2003). This book draws on, and takes off from, the work of both historians.

5. See, for instance, the work of Susan Buck-Morss (2000), Jonathan Crary (1990 and 1999), Mikhail Iampolski (1998), Wlad Godzich and Jeffrey Kittay (1987), Peter Bürger (1992), and Michael McKeon (1987).

6. For a more precise articulation of these borrowings and their application to film theory, see Paul Willemen's 'For a Comparative Film Studies' (2005b).

1

The 1920s

IN 1899, HARISHCHANDRA SAKHARAM BHATAVDEKAR, ONE OF SOUTH ASIA'S earliest filmmakers, filmed a wrestling match in Bombay's Hanging Gardens. Action and stunts have since been an important ingredient of cinema in India. This is especially true of silent and early sound cinema. Together, they cover a time span of just over thirty years that can be divided into three phases. The first, from the last years of the nineteenth century until the end of World War I, sees the development of indigenous exhibition networks in a few urban centres, until then nearly exclusively showing foreign films. The second starts with the end of World War I, when we witness the beginning of regular indigenous production. The third phase does not quite coincide with the introduction of film sound, which it precedes by a few years, but with the Depression, when exhibition began to expand also outside India's main cities. This chapter focuses on the first two of these movements and with the earliest appearance of a cluster of films relying on the action ingredient. Important elements of the second phase, however, including the prominence of women in the stunt films of those years, are discussed in the next chapter, which deals primarily with the third phase and with the introduction of synchronized sound.

These three phases fed into, and resonated with, the state of affairs in other sectors of the economy and the changes that took place there largely as a result of British policies in India that responded to the rise of the US as a world economic power. But this is not to say that the emergence, development, and consolidation of the film industry in the country 'reflected' the economic situation of colonial India. As will become apparent in this and the following chapters, the relations between economic forces and cultural production are neither a matter of direct determination nor can they be traced in any linear fashion. While economic-industrial dynamics may change very quickly, whether industrial or not, cultural products have a much longer life than the marketeers of the culture industry would have us believe. Their internal logic and cultural function draw as much from immediate economic and social pressures as from cultural (iconographic, visual, aural, linguistic, etc.) habits that have developed over a much longer period, often over centuries, and the social dynamics attaching to those habits in these earlier temporalities. Elements of pre-industrial cultural forms can be found in any cinema. To grasp their socio-cultural function in an industrial configuration means accounting for resonances that imply delays and asynchronicities as well as correspondences. The problem, as Walter Benjamin put it, is 'to deploy a mode of analysis that can blast open the continuum of history' (Benjamin 1973: 264), working not with periods as such, but with dialectical junctures that enable us to explore 'the potential of the gap created by a historically changed constellation' (Hansen 1983: 155–6), and thus consider the possibility that the films it produced at any one time may have contained elements of a public sphere radically different in kind than the one that now governs our reading of films.

The meanings of any cultural form change over time. A crucial implication of the non-linear historiographic model used here is that it becomes possible to grasp the functioning of cultural forms such as a film's narrative strategies only if we are aware of the time in which those forms were or are active—of the forces and dynamics that are constitutive of that time and which, ultimately, ascribe(d) functions and meanings to the cultural stock available to them. Which economic pressures were at work when cinema arrived in South Asia? How did these pressures shape the film industry there? An understanding of the functioning of early Indian stunt films both as clusters of narrative strategies and as constitutive of India's socio-cultural fabric at the time cannot be achieved independently from an identification of the economic factors and considerations that led to the production of those films. It is to these factors that I devote large sections of this chapter. They are meant to provide an outline of the structural conditions that led to the gradual prioritization of one narrative ingredient, stunts, and to its transformation into a generic feature of Bombay film production from the mid-1920s. It has not been my intention to offer, in this outline, an overview of Indian economics at the time, but to point only to those factors that will enable us to catch a glimpse of the instrumental function of the action ingredient and its use as a crucial factor in, or as a mechanism for, the reproduction of the very material, historically specific conditions that produced the films as commodities in the first place.

THE 1910s

From the beginning of British rule until the late 1920s, colonial economic policy in India was fully geared towards the fuelling of British industrialization. This meant that over a period of 130 years and more, the colonial administration effectively fostered and, to some degree, reformatted along the lines of English landlordism, an economy and social relations that were fundamentally feudal, to the advantage of British industry. Colonial economic policy until well after the end of World War 1 focused on agricultural exploitation and the extraction of primary materials, as well as, in the nineteenth century, on the import of British industrial goods, such as Lancashire cotton.[1] As has been amply documented by Indian historians, the growth of indigenous industry in India was, for the most, hindered by a plethora of colonial taxes and other forms of administrative-financial measures. During the first half of the nineteenth century, when industrialization was taking deep hold in Britain and other parts of the North Atlantic region, in India new industrial technology and novel processes had only trifling impact. The outbreak of World War 1 had some initially disruptive effects, but its general impact was favourable to Indian industry, if limited. India became the supply centre for all Allied operations east of the Suez canal, a fact that sharply increased aggregate demand in India. At the same time, foreign competition declined sharply and Central Powers ceased taking about 14 per cent of India's exports (of agricultural raw materials). But while Indian industries benefited from the curtailment of foreign competition and by the reduction of foreign demand for factory inputs, they were unable to extend existing capacity or the variety of industrial activity much. Although there was significant engineering capacity, no machine-building facilities of any consequence existed. Virtually all plant, equipment, stores, and prime movers came from abroad. The economy was also desperately short of skilled labour, technicians, and supervisory skills (Morris 2005: 600–1). As a result of these factors, at least until 1921, the growth of indigenous industry remained sluggish.

Large-scale private factory enterprise between 1850 and World War 1 was associated almost entirely with three industries: jute, which was based around Calcutta and was exclusively controlled by British capital; cotton, which was essentially Indian in origin, controlled by Indian investors and based in Bombay and the nearby town of Ahmedabad; and iron and steel, which, although controlled by Indians, initially struggled for lack of local demand and, at least until 1900, of support from the colonial administration. Indian industrial economic life was centred nearly exclusively in or around the two cities of Calcutta and Bombay. This created a situation of extreme polarization between, on the one hand, the two urban centres and, on the other, a large territory dotted with villages and small towns sustained by small, often family-based agricultural units. The railways linked the cities to other parts of the country, but slow development of industry and two successive waves of influenza epidemics during 1918–20 caused migration to the cities to remain comparatively low.[2] The direct impact of the industrial developments of the colonial period on the occupational distribution of the Indian labour force was minuscule. Average daily employment in registered factories increased more than fivefold between 1900–1 and 1946–7 (from 537,000 to 2,654,000) but even on the eve of Independence it still amounted to less than 2 per cent of the Indian labour force (Morris 2005: 642).[3] In 1891 the urban population represented no more than 9.4 per cent of the total population of undivided India; in 1911, urbanization remained at exactly the same rate as twenty years earlier (Visaria and Visaria 2005: 519).

This situation made for a peculiar cinema. In America, the Edison monopoly and the counter-trust led the film industry to become a fully corporate venture, the economic priority and operational emphasis of which was, at least until the late 1960s, film production.[4] This has never been the case in India, not even today.[5] From the beginning, cinema in India was shaped by poor access to technology—the colonial administration imposed heavy duties on all imports and to this day all equipment and film stock are imported—and, more crucially, by the lack of an integrated national market. Like in much of the rest of the world, cinema first reached India with the Lumière Brothers in 1896. Two years later, Hiralal Sen, one of India's first filmmakers (Rajadhyaksha and Willemen 1999: 210), started making films, but regular Indian film production did not actually take off until 1919, when as many as eleven films were made. By then, Indian-controlled exhibition networks were firmly in place. Figures for the first years of the twentieth century are not available, but, in India as elsewhere, films were first exhibited in a variety of venues that were already in use for other purposes (in theatres and fairgrounds as well as in tents near religious and wrestling sites), where they were shown as part of a larger, non-cinematic programme by exploiting the dimension of 'technological novelty' of the new medium. The first entrepreneurs to exhibit films were thus agents who dealt in a variety of other equipment, including electrical parts and gramophones.

Initially, the colonial administration issued licences for the use of the equipment, not the site of projection, but from 1910 measures were introduced to phase out tent shows and force exhibitors to make arrangements for more permanent, licensed exhibition spaces. India's first permanent cinema, the Elphinstone, was opened in Calcutta in 1905 by Madan Theatres, followed by the Minerva and the Star in 1907. By 1921, India counted 148 cinemas (Dharap 1978: E-3) for a population of 305.7 million (Visaria and Visaria 2005: 488). Although separate figures for permanent and travelling cinemas are not available, we know that permanent cinemas were located almost exclusively in the country's few urban centres; travelling cinemas catered for the rest of the country. In Bombay cinemas first opened in the European area of the Fort (the Excelsior and the Empire on Ravelin Street) and, between 1911 and 1917, in the bazaar area of Sandhurst Road in Native Town (the American-India in 1911, the Coronation in 1912, and, a few years later, the Alhambra, the Olympia and the Globe). By 1918, Sandhurst Road cinemas were more or less phased out by smarter venues, including some converted bungalows, that opened in Grant Road (the El Dorado, which opened in 1917, the Majestic and Precious in 1918, as well as the Imperial and the Royal, which opened soon after) and Lamington Road (the Royal Opera House opened in 1915, the Novelty in 1922, the West End in 1924), near the cafes, bars, and colleges that had also sprung up in residential and commercial areas within a Native Town increasingly populated by growing numbers of white-collar workers and students (Bhaumik 2001: 20–4).

Most of the cinemas at this time almost exclusively showed foreign films. In any single year between 1912 and 1918, no more than four Indian films were made (five if we include films below 1500 feet), but, lack of equipment notwithstanding, the scarcity of local production is more likely to have been an effect, rather than the cause, of the exhibitors' preference for foreign films. Until 1922 all foreign films were imported via London (Thompson 1985), from where colonial trade routes were exploited. Foreign films destined for India were shipped to Bombay and travelled across the country via the railways, which charged film (but not theatre) companies for the transport. The films imported were primarily American features and serials and Italian, French, and some British films. Although the urban film market—the only market to have more than one venue—did not stratify into first-, second-, and third-run venues until the 1920s, in the 1910s two quite clearly defined types of foreign films circulated, depending on the location of, and the kind of audience patronizing, the venue. The first type was the prestigious and recent feature production which was distributed by foreign companies like Pathé with some delay and which could be seen in what, from 1916, came to be known as 'picture palaces'. The second type was constituted by run-down copies of old films, primarily American serials, which could be acquired cheaply on the London market and which were circulated fast in many of the Native Town cinemas, such as the Globe, generating quick profits for the Indian exhibitor.

Distribution rights of an American film for India, Burma, and Ceylon could be purchased for as little as Rs 2000 (*Indian Cinematograph Committee: Evidence*, henceforth *ICC*, 1928: III, 435). Although on average they cost more, foreign films were still much cheaper to exhibit than local productions because by the time the copy of an American or European film reached the Indian market, the film had already recovered its cost of production and generated a profit on the American and European markets, a point I return to later. The point here is that, by contrast, Indian films were expensive. They were expensive to make and, as a result, they had to be billed for longer to recover their cost. For instance, the capital at Dada Saheb Phalke's disposal when he made *Raja Harishchandra/King Harishchandra* (1913) was Rs 15,000 (ibid.: 878). The film drew large crowds when it was first released in Bombay in 1913, and its 1917 remake continued to do so for years thereafter. According to an article in the *Modern Review* of May 1918, it brought to its director

more than Rs 70,000 as revenue up to now and still more demands for the hire of this film are pouring in from all parts of India which he is unable to meet all at once. Whenever his films have been exhibited the receipts at the box-office have always averaged Rs 800–900. (p. 518)

But Phalke could charge 'between Rs 12,000 and Rs 60,000' to rent the film for one year. Very few cinemas could afford to pay that much, or, what amounts to the same thing, to bill the film for that long, because very few cinemas, and especially those located outside the main urban centres, could count on a sufficiently large audience to recover the hiring and transport costs.

Phalke's films registered this polarization between the industrializing centre, where they were made, and the larger, essentially rural, territory they addressed. They expressed this paradox as a polarization at the level of the text. The son of a Sanskrit scholar and trained in architecture and landscape painting, Phalke worked as a photographer, as a stage make-up man, as an assistant to a German illusionist, and as a magician. After opening an art printing and engraving workshop in 1908, he became interested in cinema. After a short spell in London, where he familiarized himself with the technology of cinema and bought the necessary equipment, Phalke opened Phalke Films on Dadar Main Road in Bombay in 1912, for which he made five films. It was not until 1918 that he was able to raise the finance to set up Hindustan Cinema Films in Nasik, south-west of Bombay, the first purely indigenous film production company with corporate shareholding (Rajadhyaksha and Willemen 1999: 176–7). One of Hindustan's financiers, Mayashankar Bhatt, was a landlord and businessman with significant interests in the textile and coal industries who later also became the main financial backer of Sharda Film, which I will discuss in detail shortly, and, in the early 1930s, the president of the Motion Picture Society of India.

Despite the artisanal mode of production that characterized Phalke Films, from the beginning Phalke intended his film operation to be a fully commercial enterprise. He hired out the films on a commercial basis and promoted himself as the 'Pioneering Cine-Artist of the East' (as on a title at the beginning of *Kaliya Mardan/The Slaying of Kaliya*, 1919). Accordingly, the article in the *Modern Review* of 1918 profiled the director as one of the contemporary Indian figures who were 'establishing new industries and venturing in the uncharted sea of commercial exploration' (p. 516). With its emphasis on the manufacturing of the films, their cost, the revenues they generated, their comparatively widespread circulation, and their mass popularity, the article also stressed the industrial and ultimately modern dimension of Phalke's operation. In his unpublished biography, *Those Were the Days*, J.B.H Wadia reminisces about seeing Phalke's *Lanka Dahan/Lanka Aflame* (1917) as a young man:

It was [i]n my school days that I had seen my first Indian film. It was Dadasaheb Phalke's memorable *Lanka Dahan* tagged to an American feature film at the old West End Cinema of Seth Rustomji Domahji [*sic*] Wellington situated just behind the Girgaum Police Court. The roadside and the compound of the cinema used to be chockfull with bullock carts in which devoted people from small towns and villages nearby Bombay came to have a 'darshan' of their beloved gods, Shree Ram and Shree Hanuman. As a Westernised Parsi youngster I had a hearty laugh at the sight of a muscular Seeta played by a male artiste (Salunke), as also the all-powerful tail of Shree Hanuman made of rope. But I was stunned by the spectacular burning of Lanka and the thrilling flight of Ram Bhakt in the sky with every shot of the divine flier become progressively smaller and smaller to heighten the effect of the sequence. (Wadia 1978: ch. 7.)[6]

As young J.B.H. Wadia's reactions on seeing *Lanka Dahan* also indicate, at one level Phalke's films capitalized precisely on that element of novelty and modernity that is common to early cinema the world over.[7] He did so through the ostentatious use of special effects, as in *Shri Krishna Janma / The Birth of Shri Krishna* (1918), by occasionally filming industrial processes, as in the shorts *Glass Factory at Talegaon* (1915) and *How Films are Made* (1917), or by eventually casting women in female roles. Importantly, his casting of women as actresses broke with a long tradition, not only of the stage, of looking down upon, and at times squarely banning, public performances by women.

At the same time, Phalke's films glaringly reneged on their modernity. To begin with, as no woman agreed to be cast and in spite of Phalke's original intentions, in the 1913 version of *Raja Harishchandra* female roles were played by men. More crucially, Phalke's feature films centred exclusively on themes borrowed from Hindu mythology. *Lanka Dahan*, for one, was based on a story from the Ramayana that had been a very popular subject for chromolithography before Phalke (Pinney 2004: 73) and the film appears to have been Phalke's most popular (Dwyer 2005: 23).[8] So, as the *Modern Review* of September 1917 put it,

[Mr Phalke] believes that in our Puranas there is an inexhaustible mine for the film-producer and it is his experience that films which depict stories from the Puranas are more popular with the cinema-goers than his other films of scenes of Indian life. The Puranic stories are familiar to all, the incidents need little explanation and the films that incorporate these stories grip the audience as no other films will do. (p. 287)

The reality, as Indian exhibitors knew only too well, was of course somewhat different. By 1917 foreign films starring real women like Helen Holmes and featuring altogether more secular myths also fared very well indeed at the box office. But the point here is that unlike American movies and, if in a different way, more like Italian historicals of the 1910s and 1920s, the films of Phalke and of his contemporaries—figures like Baburao Painter, Kanjibhai Rathod, and Suchet Singh, all of whom plucked from Hindu mythology for their film subjects[9]—suggest that Hindu mythology was perceived not in tension with notions of Indian modernization, but as a factor instrumental to its realization.

Mythological themes were deemed to be good business. At one level, mythological subjects enabled filmmakers to cut costs, at least to the extent that narrative short cuts could be taken. Well into the late 1920s, in some cinemas showing foreign films there would be a 'translator', 'demonstrator', or 'lecturer', who, as a Telugu exhibitor put it to the ICC, 'kn[ew] all about the story' and, 'as soon as one scene [was] on, explain[ed] the whole thing' (*ICC* 1928: III, 251). As in the early American cinema of attraction, so in India, moments of stories believed to be 'familiar to all' could be presented as tableaux the linking of which '[n]eed[ed] little explanation'. So, as late as 15 September 1928, the *Bombay Chronicle* advertised United Picture Syndicate's 'Mythological Production *Kichak Vadha* or *Sairandhri*' (director unknown 1928) as

> A Glorious Chapter from the popular epic Mahabharata.
> See How Bhima the human giant restrains his anger to obey the orders
> of his elder brother Dharmaraja.
> See How Sairandhri persuades queen Sudeshna to refrain from sending
> a married woman to serve a drunken man.
> See How Bhima kills Kichaka and many other wonderful Scenes.[10]

And yet a great deal of effort and expense went into the shooting of scenes deemed to deserve special attention:

> The story of the burning of Lanka by Hanuman [in *Lanka Dahan*] is cleverly put on the screen and this film has entailed heavy expenses on Mr Phalke in its production. In order to put this scene on the screen actual houses had to be erected to order and burnt and this alone cost a pretty sum. A whole staff of builders, masons and artists were busy for several months carrying Phalke's behest into execution. The work of the man who played the role of the Monkey-God Hanuman [Ganpat Shinde] in this film is so realistic that as he was performing his part in the scenes in a jungle at Nasik before the camera he had to be rescued from the attacks of several monkeys who infested the jungle and who took him for one of themselves. (*Modern Review* April 1918: 518)

That it should be this very scene, featuring the performance of Hanuman, Rama's right arm, that the *Modern Review* writer selected to highlight the production of the film is in itself revealing. But mention of 'builders, masons, and artists' is followed by the description of a composite and multi-layered figure, a god represented in a realistic manner by an athletic-looking man who is magically transformed into an animal. I return to this cluster of contradictory trajectories at a later stage in the chapter. For the moment it is enough to observe that these tensions were manifest in the cinema of this and the following decade at many levels. In 1924, for instance, the *Bombay Chronicle* advertised Phalke's Krishna trilogy for Hindustan Films as an invitation to come and pay obeisance to Lord Krishna—a promotional strategy that, while exploiting the novelty of cinema as a new technology and mode of representation, simultaneously encouraged the abolition of representational distance. That is to say, for all their technological innovations, special effects, and comparatively high production cost, Phalke's films, unlike the best of American and European early cinema, were characterized by the use of discursive and representational strategies rooted in ideologies of mimesis that preceded modernity while presenting the results—the films themselves—as evidence and celebrations of Indian modernity. Mythological narratives were choreographed for the camera as they had been staged since the nineteenth century in theatre presentations while simultaneously claiming that it was the very modernity of the cinematic medium that allowed the distance to be abolished between presentation and representation. The fact of mechanical reproduction—and the modifications this brought about to a narratorial position that had relied on the live performance of story construction—was both acknowledged and denied. Significantly, when the prints of the *Raja Harishchandra* he had made in 1913 had been played to destruction, Phalke simply remade it in 1917, shot by shot (Schulze 2003), and sold it as the same film (Rajadhyaksha and Willemen 1999: 243). While European and American films of that period also manifest a similar tendency to value industrial modernity's potential to reactivate and reanimate pre-modern ideologies of mimesis, in India this tension remained a characteristic feature well into the following decades and, arguably, into the twenty-first century. More than ten years after *Raja Harishchandra*, the *Bombay Chronicle's* advertisement for Hindustan's *Bhakta Damaji/Damaji the Devotee* (D. Phalke 1928)—a 'brand new historical and mythological film' released in Bombay at the Novelty cinema in Lamington Road—thus urged the public not to miss 'this immortal episode in Maratha history on screen' (21 November 1928: 2). The advertisement incorporated into an industrial medium the divinely revealed and 'immortal' character ascribed to scriptures and myths, and projecting it onto secular notions of 'history', capitalized on that characteristic by exploiting it as a marketing device: revealed history as the star of a film show.

This yoking together of the industrial, commercial, and technological nature of the medium with narrative strategies rooted in pre-industrial temporalities and social systems, and the tension between concepts and ideas that we now understand as complementary, such as the mythic, the magic, and the real or realistic, is typical of the Indian films of the 1910s and continued well into the next decade. For instance, on 2 February 1929 the *Bombay Chronicle* advertised a programme at the Krishna cinema in which a 'devotional picture' called *Tarun Tapaswini/Young Ascetic* (Prafulla Ghosh 1929) was accompanied by 'cycle-tricks by Mr Narimo and Mr Mohidin on the stage—along with the film'. But by then, the simultaneous cinematic mobilization of elements pertaining to very different worlds had become, as a rule, more layered, the elements intertwined and fused within more nuanced narrative grids. In the 1910s, the polar opposites of modernity and the pre-modern coexisted side by side in an undiluted manner, registering in the Indian cinema of this decade the polarized cultural-economic geography within which that cinema circulated. Caught between the industrial nature of the medium and the reality of equipment shortage, artisanal modes of production, and localized financial networks rooted in a patchwork of small industrial and landed capital, the films registered and internalized the paradox of an unprecedented potential for reproducibility in the absence of a uniformly urbanized or semi-urbanized integrated national market in which to realize it. In the process, the films referred back to the polarized social reality that produced them with strategies that inscribed their addressees into essentially pre-industrial social relations, a place where modern technology could be seen at work but remained other-worldly and unavailable. After the end of World War 1 things began to change. In isolated areas, different economic pressures began to surface that led to a new kind of cinema. It is at this point that 'action' first made its entry in Indian films.

THE 1920s

The economic and social forces constitutive of the time that knew early Indian action or stunt cinema were not the same as those governing the narrative strategies of Phalke's early films. A film industry had developed since Phalke had made *Raja Harishchandra* that produced this action cinema. This industry was not only radically different from Phalke's operation, it could emerge only because of the profoundly changed state of affairs in other sectors of the Indian economy. What follows is an account of that new industry, Bombay cinema, and of the broader economic factors that made it what it became in the mid- to late 1920s, that is to say in the years in which Sharda Film Company emerged as one of India's earliest producer of stunt films.

At the end of World War I Britain had to renegotiate the position of its currency in relation to the gold standard and colonial priorities for India began to shift, but it was not until the years immediately preceding the Depression that the colonial administration began to promote the growth of indigenous industry. In spite of this, and even if industrial capacity could not expand much until the end of World War I, during the War the profits of existing enterprises rose substantially, particularly in the last half of the conflict and for a few years thereafter. A boom psychology stimulated entrepreneurial expectations and encouraged plans to expand old companies and form new ones as soon as hostilities ended (Morris 2005: 602). During the inter-War period, when the world's largest economies experienced sharp falls in industrial activity, Indian manufacturing output grew at a rate well above the world average, faster than that of the US, the UK, and Germany. Although this growth really took off in the following decade, the first signs of it were already apparent in isolated areas in the 1920s.

Partly due to a significant drop in the mortality rate, between 1921 and 1931 the population of undivided India showed a massive increase (of 10.6 per cent, from 305.7 million to 338.3 million). The rate of growth between 1921 and 1941 (1.2 per cent per year) was the highest recorded for India and added, over two decades, nearly eighty three million people to the country's population. The urban population increased somewhat (it represented 10.2 per cent of the total population in 1921 and 11.1 per cent in 1931), but the rate of urbanization did not accelerate significantly in the ten years after World War I. In the 1910s, the textile industry had gradually begun to move outside the city of Bombay and a large number of mills had opened elsewhere in Bombay Presidency. But the geographical polarization that had characterized that decade, a polarization between a few industrialized centres and the rest of the country, continued into the 1920s. It was not until the 1930s, when the composition of India's manufactured output began to change, that this polarization was significantly dented. In 1921 the city of Bombay witnessed the highest levels of immigration recorded between 1881 and 1931 and its population crossed the one million mark. Census records reveal that this influx of immigrants was constituted primarily by men in the age group between 15 and 45 (Kosambi 1986: 54–7). Although the population of the city began to decrease, if only temporarily, throughout the remaining part of the decade, and although the wartime boom of Bombay's textile mills lasted only until 1922, the sharp increase in the city's population during the first two decades of the century and the unprecedented influx of immigrant men in the latter part of the 1910s and first years of the 1920s provided a radically new impetus for the cinema produced there.

By 1925, twenty-one new cinemas had opened in Bombay Presidency, bringing the total number of venues in the area to seventy-five (Bhaumik

2001: 36). Although most of these were located outside Bombay city itself, the figure acquires special significance when we compare it to the slow increase in the number of cinemas across the rest of the country. Undivided India had 148 cinemas in 1921; in 1927 the number of venues had increased by 50 per cent, to 346 (309 of which were permanent and thirty-seven touring cinemas), only to fall rather sharply in the following year to 275 (241 of which were permanent and thirty-four touring cinemas; Dharap 1978: E-3). Calcutta, Madras, and Delhi each had thirteen, nine, and six cinemas respectively, while a very limited number of other cities had three or four each (*ICC* 1928: IV, 351–65). By the mid-1920s, stratification had also begun to take place between cinemas for different classes of people. In Bombay, when the Gaiety was re-opened as The Capitol in 1928 after being 'internally rebuilt and redecorated on a lavish scale' to be transformed into 'Bombay's most comfortable and luxurious film centre', the *Bombay Chronicle* of 14 January of that year announced that

[t]he management have set the comfort and convenience of the patrons as their foremost ideal, together with the presentation of only films of outstanding merit. [T]he most important alteration is the provision of a new main entrance facing Victoria Terminus which will give direct access to the seats in the dress circle whose patrons will be cut off entirely from the floor of the house in which the cheaper seats will be located. Entrance to the latter will be obtained through two other doors, one in Wandby Road and the other in Murzhan [*sic*] Road. (pp. 4, 7)

The film selected for the Capitol's opening, which was attended by the governor of Bombay and his wife, was 'the Magnificent All-British *The Flag Lieutenant*' (Maurice Elvey 1926). Bombay's first smart cinema for Indian films, the Krishna, in Charni Road, did not open until 1925. By then, however, away from the picture palaces of the Fort, and from the cinemas of Grant and Lamington Road which catered primarily for the white-collar workers and students living in that area, new cinemas had begun to open also in the mill areas of the city, in Parel, Sewri, and Dadar (the Venus and Laxmi in 1924, the Saraswati in 1927, the Kohinoor, and the Surya soon after) (Bhaumik 2001: 36). In 1927, when the colonial administration set up the ICC to inquire into the state of cinema in the country, Bombay had a total of twenty-one cinemas, seven of which had been newly built or converted into cinemas after 1923.[11] This expansion of the exhibition sector, confined primarily to the country's few main cities, was not symptomatic of an emerging integrated national market for films. It did, however, lead to the production of a kind of Indian cinema that was radically different from the cinema made in the previous decade.

In 1918 only one Bombay cinema 'specialized' in Indian films (Barnouw and Krishnaswamy 1980: 48). In the early part of the 1920s about half of India's permanent cinemas were controlled by Madan Theatres. In 1919 Madan Theatres floated on the stock market, incorporating Elphinstone Bioscope and Excelsior Theatre Company, an exhibitor that had been funded by a building concern, Bombay Building Company, which had made large profits during the city's building boom of the 1910s. Madan filled a large part of its theatres with second-hand copies of foreign films which, until 1919, it hired from the Eastern Express Film Hire Service in London (Bhaumik 2001: 51). In that year, however, Madan also became Pathé, United Artists and Metro's distributor for India (Rajadhyaksha and Willemen 1999: 139), the country's largest, rivalling Universal. As a distributor, in 1927 it demanded between 20 and 25 per cent of the box office or a fixed flat fee. The nearest to a vertically integrated corporate structure that the Indian film industry was ever to see, throughout the 1920s Madan Theatres was not only one of the largest importers of foreign films, but also the only Indian company to have the semblance of a full fledged industrial structure (with some foreign capital), producing Indian films and operating the only chain of cinemas that spanned the country as a whole. In 1927 Madan Theatres (directly or indirectly) controlled about 100 of India's 346 cinemas. Outside Calcutta Madan Theatres never exhibited its own (Indian) films in the cinemas it controlled directly, all of which showed foreign films only for fear of losing its habitual, that is to say upper- and middle-class audience. The company did, however, indirectly control several 'associated' cinemas which were bound by contract to show Madan productions.

In Bombay Presidency, Madan Theatres controlled three cinemas in Pune, one in Surat, one in Ahmedabad, and, in Bombay itself, the Excelsior and the Empire in the Fort and the Empress, the Edward, and, indirectly, the Crown and the Globe on Sandhurst Road. The other cinemas of the city were either controlled by offshoots of foreign distributors (like Pathé's Royal Opera House on Lamington Road), by companies that had opened in the immediate post-War period and which had gradually expanded into film production (Kohinoor Film's Imperial cinema and Imperial Film's Majestic cinema, both on Grant Road, or Krishna Film's Krishna cinema on nearby Charni Road), or by independent exhibitors, like the Parsi entrepreneurs Seth Rustomji and Seth Ruttonshaw Dorabji, who controlled the West End on Lamington Road, the Wellington and the Venus in Parel and, from 1930, the Super on Charni Road, as well as a few cinemas in other parts of the country (like the New Elphinstone and the Wellington in Madras). Independent exhibitors like the Dorabjis were not direct importers of films. They either financed agents to provide films for their cinemas or finally gave in to Madan Theatres, obtaining their whole programme from that monopoly. Bombay's prime venues for imported 'quality' films were the Empire and the Excelsior in the Fort, Pathé's Royal Opera House on Lamington Road, and the Dorabjis' Wellington, but most of the cinemas in the city and the country at this time showed primarily, if not exclusively, foreign films. According to an independent witness to the ICC, J.D. Khandhadia, these included the West End, the Empress, the Edward, and Universal Picture House, which showed 'light literature films' (*ICC* 1928: I, 548–9).

Between 1922 and 1927 foreign production imports into India increased by 138 per cent. According to the ICC's *Report*, 85 per cent of the pictures released in India in 1926 were foreign and most of these were American (p. 188). Such a flooding of the Indian market worried the colonial administration and if the British government ever concerned itself the cinema in India it was not to monitor indigenous production, but the circulation of American films. A common argument against American films from colonial quarters was that they could have 'a bad influence' on Indian subjects because, ostensibly depicting Western society as having few or no moral standards, they could call into question the legitimacy of British rule in India. The real concern of the colonial administration, in relation to cinema as to other industrial products, was, however, that the US was making great inroads into a market that Britain still considered its own. Hence the decision to set up a commission to inquire into the state of the film industry in the colony and, in the ICC documents themselves, the relentless pressure to adopt 'Imperial Preference', that is to say essentially to accord priority to British films. But by the 1920s British film production had more or less collapsed,[12] leaving very little to import apart from newsreels. London had lost its role as the world's film exchange centre and American films were imported into India directly from the US. For the American industry, the foreign market was then a fairly marginal consideration since American films amply recovered their cost and more on the domestic market. Of all foreign markets available to American distributors, India was one of the most insignificant, not least because of the shortage of cinemas and the country's low buying power. Whatever returns India generated for American distributors were a marginal bonus and, as a result, copies of American films could be acquired at extremely low cost. Moreover, it was becoming the policy of American companies to 'cultivate markets' by flooding countries short of currency with copies of American films for a nominal price, in the process also avoiding high import duties. The witnesses of the ICC confirm all of this. In 1927, D. Bhavani of Imperial Studio told the committee that 'buying a second-hand copy of a foreign film cost £20 or £30 [or an average of] 4 annas a foot' (*ICC* 1928: I, 179–80), while Alex Hague, 'sole proprietor of Pathé India' observed that 'about 25 per cent of all importers are small importers importing cheap films produced by small companies. One can get these films for about US$75 royalty from the US' (ibid.: 529). In some cities, like Bombay, Surat, Ahmedabad, Karachi, Madras, and Calcutta, the importer or, in the case of Indian films, the producer, would take between 30 and 40 per cent of the box office, but in smaller places a flat hire fee of Rs 40–60 per night was agreed upon.

Screening cheaply acquired foreign films enabled Indian exhibitors to run cinemas at a profit in spite of the lack of a nationally integrated consumer market. Madan Theatres maintained a nationwide chain of theatres which was centrally managed from Calcutta. As the sole Indian distributor for a number of large foreign companies, Madan Theatres rented the foreign films cheaply and used the distribution and exhibition revenues to finance its own production programme. But even so, high transport costs, low disposable incomes, and no notions of leisure time outside the main urban centres made running a cinema profitable only in towns with at least 25,000 inhabitants. Ranging between Rs 3000 and Rs 4000 in the late 1920s, the weekly box office for a first-rate foreign film was lower than that of an Indian film, which could generate as much as Rs 7000 during the first week in Bombay and in a few other cities. But a European or an American film was not only cheap to hire, in 1927 it also circulated in 73 per cent of the country's cinemas, where it cashed in at least the minimum fixed hire fee, while an Indian film would circulate in only 27 per cent of the country's venues, and most of these were cinemas in locations where the average box office would not amount to more than Rs 40 or Rs 50 a day. In these cinemas, cheaply acquired or hired old foreign films dominated until sound cinema arrived. At one level, as a number of exhibitors invited to testify in front of the ICC clearly stated, showing cheap foreign films enabled small venues to survive in spite of Madan's monopolistic practices. At another, more fundamental level, these revenue figures suggest that cheap foreign films dominated because in India at this time the audience available to cinema was small and quickly exhausted. While a good foreign film in a city centre cinema could rely on a larger and higher class audience and thus easily stay on the programme for more than one week, in the mofussil (towns and suburban areas outside city centres) the programme of cheap and old foreign films changed twice a week. In 'small stations' the exhibitor had to 'change the programme every two days' (*ICC* 1928: I, 169, 561–2).

The polarization between a handful of urban centres and a large but essentially rural territory, that is to say the absence of a nationally integrated consumer market, is the reason why distribution did not emerge as a distinct sector until the following decade (see Chapter 2). Many of the Indian producing companies active in the 1920s had emerged from exhibition concerns that had diversified into production and tended to distribute their own films only. This was of course the case for Madan Theatres, but also for companies like Sharda Film, Imperial Films, Hindustan Cinema Films, Krishna Film, and Kohinoor Film. The role of a so-called distributor or 'booking agent' was to 'receive enquiries for the booking of the films, [d]istribute these films upcountry, collect the hire, get back the picture, and pay the income to the producer each week after deducting [the distributor's] dues' (*ICC* 1928: I, 577). It is not clear from the ICC document how much such 'dues' amounted to, but witnesses testify that 'production [of Indian films] on the scale sufficient to make distribution a viable trade ha[d] not occurred yet' (ibid: 576). In reality it was not so much production as exhibition that was the problem. Sometimes, as in the case of Kohinoor, a booking agent advanced part of one or more companies' capital for production. However, at this stage at least, individual producers were still in a position to—and did—bind their agent to handling their productions on an exclusive basis. Irrespective of how many other companies an agent had invested in, he could distribute the films of one producer only. While on first impression this would suggest that production, or rather the shortage of Indian films, was the crux of the matter, in reality shortage of production only constitutes a problem in the presence of demand. In other words, it was not enough for the booking agent to advance the money to become a significant player in the industry, a distributor in the current sense of the term. For distribution to emerge as a distinct sector and, over the years, for distributors to acquire the importance they have been ascribed—in, for instance, the 1951 *Report of the Film Enquiry Committee*—a more integrated market, a high supply of films and a shortage of exhibition space would also have to be in place. As I argue in Chapters 4 and 5, when these conditions materialized some decades later, it was exhibitors that emerged as the sector capable of dictating the terms according to which distributors and, through them, producers had to operate. But most of these conditions did not begin to surface until well into the 1930s, and even then, they did so only after the influx of immigrants in and around Bombay city led to the opening of cinemas in the mill areas.

In 1923, one year before the opening of the cinemas in the mill areas, two of the Grant Road cinemas, Imperial Film's Majestic cinema and Kohinoor Film's Imperial cinema, switched from foreign to Indian films. The Globe, Sandhurst Road's prime venue for American serials, also switched to showing Indian films in the same year. It was followed by Dorabji's Venus in Parel four years later, and by the Novelty on Lamington Road. And yet, in 1927 only six of Bombay's twenty-one cinemas primarily or exclusively screened Indian films. Notwithstanding the small number of Bombay venues devoted to the screening of Indian films and in spite of the sharp rise in imported productions, the 1920s saw the emergence of a sizeable production sector in Bombay. In 1919 Indian film production moved for the first time into double figures (eleven films). Crucially buttressed by the influx of immigrants to the city and the surrounding region, and by the subsequent opening of cinemas in the areas around the mills, in the following years film production expanded exponentially. In 1922 sixty-three films were made, rising sharply to eighty-eight in 1925, ninety-two in 1926, 114 in 1928, 140 in 1929, 194 in 1930, and 237 (twenty-eight of which were sound films) in 1931. This latter figure was surpassed for the first time only in 1947, when 280 films were made (Rajadhyaksha and Willemen 1999: 32–3). The immediate post-World War I period witnessed not only the opening of Phalke's Hindustan Cinema Films (1918), but also of Kohinoor Film, India's largest and most influential film company of the silent period, and of Star Films, which, under the different names of Majestic (in 1923), Royal Art Studio (in 1925), and finally Imperial Films (in 1926), lasted well into the sound period. By 1924, when Kohinoor began to decline, smaller and often short-lived production companies began to proliferate. The most successful among them were Krishna Film, which opened in 1924 as an offshoot of Kohinoor, and Sharda Film. With the exception of Imperial, which was located near Lamington Road, most of the production companies of this period were based around Dadar and Tardeo.

In the mid- to late 1920s, production costs for a single film ranged between Rs 7000 and Rs 25,000. Witnesses to the ICC state that the capital required to run a production company was Rs 200,000 to Rs 300,000 (2 to 3 lakhs), but it is not clear how reliable these figures actually are. When

Sharda Film tried to float on the stock market, the company's prospectus boasted that the company's estimated value was Rs 1,500,000 (15 lakhs) and that current partner Mayashanker Thacker was prepared to invest Rs 50,000 to begin with and a further Rs 50,000 at a later stage (*Bombay Chronicle*, 4 May 1929: 3), but, no financier having come forward, Mayashanker Thacker finally bought the company 'outright for about 5 lakhs [500,000]' (*Indian Cinematograph Year Book*, henceforth *ICY*, 1938: 19–20]. The most stable among the companies of this period each made about ten films a year. With a few exceptions, each of these companies controlled (that is to say leased) their own exhibition venue, the programme of which, however, they did not manage to fill, forcing them to sub-lease out their cinema to another producer. Krishna Film, for instance, made its own films and exhibited them at the Krishna cinema, which it controlled, but it also contracted Sharda Film which, in the allocated weeks, in addition to showing its own films was also responsible for the rest of the programme, including the provision of a live show. Cinemas had exclusive rights of exhibition, whether the film was their own production (as for Krishna's films at the Krishna cinema) or that of the leasing company. Contracts between exhibitors and independent producers bound both the producer to supply the cinema with the whole of its yearly output, as well as the exhibitor to screen it all. Each company also operated its own printing laboratory and, significantly, between three and six copies were made of each Indian film. The Sharda Film floatation prospectus stated that three copies were required for the Bombay market, two each for Bangalore and Lahore, one for Calcutta (where Madan Theatres ruled), and one for Africa. Although perhaps a little too optimistic, the prospectus is nevertheless indicative of the importance of some markets as opposed to others. With the cost of a copy at Rs 1000 (for a 10,000 foot film), Sharda's estimated revenue from the three Bombay copies was Rs 20,000, as opposed to the Rs 6000 expected from the two copies sent to Bangalore, the Rs 4000 from the two copies for Lahore, and the Rs 1000 from the one for Calcutta.

Whether these figures are reliable or not, the point here is another. Give or take one or two films, an average of ten films a year is not a negligible rate of production, certainly not for a company today, and reliable data exist to confirm that a large number of films began to be made in Bombay in the 1920s. More important than the reliability of the figures mentioned in the ICC and other contemporary documents is the fact that, in spite of both the exponential increase in production and the scarcity of venues for Indian films, complaints about shortage of films are advanced from all quarters. This is because, as also stated by the ICC witnesses, in order to remain a profitable proposition for exhibitors, films had to be circulated at an extremely fast pace, thus effectively shortening the exploitable life of an individual production and generating increasing demand. As the representative of Pathé put it to the ICC, 'there are not enough theatres in the country at present which would give adequate returns on a picture in which a considerable amount of money is invested' (*ICC* 1928: I, 507), or, which amounts to the same thing, audiences in non-urban areas were too small to let the film run long enough to recover the investment. Which is why, outside urban centres, a film would not run for more than two days. But even in the cities, the ICC witnesses stated that while a good foreign film in a city centre cinema could stay on the programme for more than one week, in other areas the programme had to be changed twice a week. This state of affairs is corroborated by exhibitors' advertisements in the dailies of the time. Many of the mofussil cinemas were 'corrugated iron. In some there are no chairs and people sit on the ground. The ground slopes in one place and is high in another. Corrugated iron is considered best. Some mofussil cinemas are housed in tents and there are also gunny bag theatres' (ibid.: 578). But even in the better cinemas of the urban areas of Parel and Dadar, a film would not run for more than a week unless the exhibitor had failed to secure a replacement. Moreover, whereas in Bombay's best cinema tickets could cost as much as Rs 12 for a box for four people, in mill areas cinemas prices could be as low as 1 anna for a third class ticket. The speed at which the programme in these cinemas changed suggests that even at this price and even in densely inhabited areas with a population with some disposable income, available audiences, although on the increase, were still quickly exhausted. Conditions in the cities and in the rest of the country thus meant that it could take as long as two years for a company to recover the cost of production, and few investors were prepared to wait that long. With no fully fledged distributor to sell the finished film outright, production companies of the 1920s were permanently plagued not so much by low capitalization, as by the lack of revolving credit.

THE ACTION INGREDIENT

In the mid-1920s, a few years after the opening of the cinemas near the mills in and around Bombay, some companies began to produce films that were designed to meet this situation. Sharda Film was not the only company to do so, but it was one of the first to strike the winning formula. Sharda Film was set up in 1925 under the direct financial control of Mayashankar Bhatt, the landowner, merchant, textile-mills and carbon industrialist who, in the previous decade, had financed the Hindustan and the Star Film companies. By 1920, he also dealt in Agfa and Gevaert stock and film distribution. Two factors enabled Sharda Film to overcome the obstacle of a limited, non-integrated national market: low production costs and the securing of exhibition in Bombay. By exploiting a market— the mill and mofussil areas—and generic ingredients that companies like Madan Theatres, which catered for the upper end of the urban market, did not touch, Sharda Film was able to recover its production costs and generate good profits through one-week screening in Bombay and in a couple of other cities.

Publicity was not an alien concept to the producing companies of the 1920s. For instance, the top scenarist of the silent period, Mohanlal Gopaldas Dave, started his career as a publicist for Imperial and Kohinoor (Rajadhyaksha and Willemen 1999: 83). In his autobiography, J.B.H Wadia writes that

[Dave] must have turned out one story a month in the silent film era, at least. He was also the Gujarati publicist of American films. He would see [the films] in advance and write out their advertisements in different formats for the papers. Over and above that he would also write out their story-content for free distribution as handouts in theatres for the benefit of cinegoers. (Wadia 1978: ch. 15)

By the time Sharda was launched, films were regularly advertised in the daily press by the exhibitor. Illustrated film booklets had also begun to be used to promote the films, but a common complaint among producers, who generated this and other promotional material, was that exhibitors did not avail themselves of it. In order to add to the speed at which the invested capital circulated, Sharda thus resorted to three devices: the use of generic ingredients deemed to sell especially well in the cinemas frequented by the 'mill-hand', the film star, and women.

After the success of Phalke's *Raja Harishchandra*, mythological films continued to be made in (relatively) large numbers in the following decades,[13] but in the mid-1920s, when production increased sharply, Indian cinema was characterized by weak generic differentiation. Although this feature became extreme in the 1950s, when the social drama was Hindi cinema's all-encompassing genre, it can be seen to be already in place in the 1920s and 1930s, especially when compared with the American cinema of the same decades. Most Indian films made in the silent period were either mythologicals or devotionals, or fell within the broadly defined categories of costume (historical) and social (contemporary) dramas. All Indian producers covered most of the generic spectrum because genre was quite simply not used as a marketing category, certainly not to the same degree that American studios used it.[14] Like other companies of the period, Sharda made historical, costume and social dramas, and mythologicals. Unlike other companies, however, Sharda was the first to specialize in what has retrospectively been defined as the action film genre. In practice, Sharda's films became distinctive because of their greater reliance on the 'stunts' ingredient and, equally importantly, because Sharda marked that ingredient as its own through the construction of an action star, Master Vithal.

Film historians have tended to explain away the choice of stunts or action as the preferred generic ingredient and a distinctive selling point of some Indian cinema (of the 1920s as much as of the 1970s) as an effect of foreign (read American) influence. In reality, this is a discourse that dates back to the mid-1920s. On the Indian front, it voiced a conservative reaction to notions of social modernization that could be found also in the rearguard of the nationalist movement: the belief that colonialism had opened the way to a wave of modernization that, destroying (an idealized) Indian tradition, corrupted Indian mores and, with that, the hierarchical allocation of resources and pleasures. In colonial discourses on culture, notions of American influence expressed the fear of losing the Indian market to American manufacturers—a fear that, from the mid- to late 1920s, was more than justified. In 1927, an inquirer on the ICC thus asked film director N.G. Deware whether, when making films 'suitable to the Indian market', he found it necessary to adopt 'American methods' to make them 'sensational':

Deware: Not particularly. But in social pictures we have got some stunts just to attract and keep the liveliness in the picture all the time. [T]hey do like to see certain stunts in the story.

Inquirer: Well, what Americans call giving pictures a certain amount of pep. Have you found your audience requiring pep and is the type you have got to give the American type of pep or your own?

Deware: We have our own type. (*ICC* 1928: I, 588)

Deware, the son of a photographer and originally a photographer himself, was then working for Kohinoor as cameraman, director, and translator of intertitles (into English) for a monthly salary of 'Rs 550 in all' (ibid.: 583). One year after this interview, he helped finance and worked on the first film of J.B.H. Wadia, the director who, in the early 1930s, was to make India's most popular and profitable action films featuring women. To take Deware's succinct reply lightly would be a mistake. To begin with, American films were not the only films circulating in India at the time. Italy's 'film of the age, the unique spectacular colossal' *Maciste alpino / Maciste as a Mountaineer* (Giovanni Pastrone 1916) was released at the El Dorado cinema on Lamington Road on 29 September 1917, and was followed, in the 1920s and in other cinemas, by more features starring former dockworker Bartolomeo Pagano in the popular role of strongman Maciste, like *Maciste atleta / Maciste as an Athlete* (Giovanni Pastrone 1917), *Maciste e la figlia del re della plata / Maciste and the Silver King's Daughter* (Luigi Romano Borgnetto 1922), *Maciste imperatore / Maciste Emperor* (Guido Brignone 1924), *Maciste nella gabbia dei leoni / Maciste in the Lion's Cage* (Guido Brignone 1926), *Maciste contro lo sceicco / Maciste against the Sheikh* (Mario Camerini 1926) and *Maciste all' inferno / Maciste in Hell* (Guido Brignone 1926). Along with Douglas Fairbanks' Zorro and Eddie Polo's Tarzan films, 1920s audiences could watch productions featuring a variety of muscular, athletic, or acrobatic heroes, including *Attila il flagello di Dio / Attila the Scourge of God* (Febo Mari 1917), *Sansone contro i Filistei / Samson amongst the Philistines* (Domenico Gaido 1918), and *Spartaco / Spartacus* (Giovanni Enrico Vidali 1913). Italian acrobat Luciano Albertini was a regular presence under his stage name of Sansonia 'the Hercules of the screen' (*Bombay Chronicle* 12 May 1928) and appeared in Bombay in *Il Ponte dei sospiri / The Bridge of Sighs* (Domenico Gaido 1921), *Eine Minute vor Zwölf / One Minute to Twelve* (Nunzio Malasomma 1925), *Rinaldo Rinaldini* (Max Obal 1927), and *Der Abgrund des Todes / The Modern Ulysses or the Death Cheat* (Max Obal 1927)—'not a picture depending on one stunt or on several small ones!'—as well as in *La Spirale della morte / Once aboard the Lugger* (Filippo Castamagna and Domenico Gambino 1917) as 'the speed-king'. The 'world's strongest man' Carlo Aldini featured in *Wer Hat Bobby Gesehen? / Who Has Seen Bobby?* (Rolf Randolf 1930) while, from the French side, in the 1920s Gaumont and Pathé imported, among others, Louis Feuillade's *Judex* (1916) and Eclair's popular *Protéa* series (1913–17) with Josette Andriot in the roles of thief or spy. Houdini was also a frequent presence, as in the film *The Grim Game* (Irving Willat 1919).

But the problem with attempts to explain away the emergence of Indian action heroes and heroines as derivative of American serials is not so much that American serials were hardly the only films of this type circulating in India at the time, but that such an explanation implies a sense of direct determination which is ahistorical and misplaced. The circulation of generic categories cannot be understood in anthropomorphic terms, as if a film, like an individual, could 'influence' another. Of course, individuals copied and, at times, quite simply recycled whole sequences of American films, but the question is which bits or aspects of these films were borrowed and why? Precise material conditions determine the circulation of films, and generic facets of cultural forms can take root 'elsewhere' because they respond to structural conditions that are economically and socially pertinent in that 'elsewhere'. In short, specific aspects of foreign cultural production are borrowed and restyled because they are deemed capable of conveying important meanings about the particularities of the situation at home.[15] Notions of cultural influence block the understanding of the social function of these action films in India, that is to say of the relation between their strategies of representation and the socio-economic context that shaped, and which was in turn shaped by, the films. A frame is imposed on our reading of the films that prompts us to look for similarities and to assume that similar formal devices must necessarily have the same narrative function in Indian as they do in American films. The 'influence' approach thus overlooks fundamental differences, and, ultimately, projects onto the Indian cinema a historiographic model patterned on the uniquely specific historical development of the American film industry.

In 1920s India, the use of action and stunts as a preferred generic ingredient and marketing device resonated, first and foremost, with contemporary discourses on physical culture and with physical performance shows that had been popular, in India as much as elsewhere, before the invention of cinema. The latter continued to be performed well into the twentieth century and, in Bombay at least, spectacles of this type often accompanied film screenings. On 6 November 1926, for instance, a *Bombay Chronicle* advertisement announced that the opening of *Maciste in the Lion's Cage* at the Globe would be accompanied by a live show:

> See: American Dancing Girls, English Clowns, Sudanese Acrobats,
> Russian and Hungarian Half-Breeds,
> Well-Known athlete Maciste in the Lion's Cage
> An alternation of feminine charms with the expansion of powerful
> masculine muscles.
> Next week: *Maciste Against the Sheikh*

Advertisements for this type of live show always appeared on the same page of Indian dailies along with advertisements for various physical health improvement products, like 'Clarke's blood mixture, for that ulcerated leg' or 'Dr DeJongh's light-brown cod liver oil' (*Bombay Chronicle*,

26 December 1926), as well as with advertisements for films. The market for physical culture education was thriving and many of the events that were advertised next to the cinemas' advertisements were intended both as a commercial venture and as demonstrations of the effectiveness of various training methods. In the *Bombay Chronicle* of 10 July 1926, the caption to a picture of a Mr K.G. Rao, director of the National Physical Culture Institute, bare-chested, arms bent with his hands clasped together in front of his midriff, thus read:

Exercise for self-defense. Health for longivity [*sic*]. The most patronized Institute in Bombay, where instruction is imparted with clock-work regularity, by a staff of competent teachers. Join our Institute and be fit.

while two weeks later a brief news item in the *Bombay Chronicle* (31 July 1926) entitled 'Physical Culture Demonstration' announced that

an interesting lecture on Physical Culture was given at the Hall of the Samaj by D.M. Kalyanpurkar, founder and conductor of the Bombay Gymnastic Institute. Mr Kalyanpurkar emphasized the supreme necessity of physical culture for young India. He deplored the apathy shown by the so-called educated class to the glorious field of building a healthier and stronger physique and finished with a moving appeal for a wider interest in this great department of national well-being.

A year earlier, the *Modern Review* of May 1925 (pp. 585–6) had already published an article entitled 'From a Weakling to a Hercules' which accompanied a profile of the internationally known athlete Eugene Sandow with detailed instructions for simple exercises, one paragraph of instructions each for 'the sides', 'the shoulders and chest', 'the biceps and triceps', 'the back, arms and abdomen', and 'for forearms and wrists'.

Physical culture discourses and a variety of live shows addressed the Indian public sphere in the broadest sense of the term. From articles in expensive journals to wrestling bouts in villages, all classes were exposed. Physical cultural education according to secular, modern, and, one should add, Fordist principles, was not the only type around. Also very prominent in the 1920s and 1930s was a genre of publications, cheap yoga books, which advocated a type of education that incorporated nineteenth century notions of Houdini-style culturism only to re-inscribe them, with varying degrees of explicitness, into aristocratic and religious models of the status-body based on lineage, purity, and 'atma'. Examples of this type of text are worth quoting at some length because they reveal the extent to which in 1920s India notions of strength, physical energy, and value were, in some circles, still conceived as being entirely dependent on spiritual value and social (caste) status. Even if by now these texts had, as should be expected, become infused with more secular notions of the body, unlike in positivist conceptualizations of the body here physical strength remained an effect of purity, that is to say, ultimately, of one's position within a hierarchical allocation of social status:

The secret of human power and health resides in the nervous system. It is the nervous system that transmits energy to the tissues and organs of the body. It is not the actual muscle which makes a man strong so much as the vital energy behind it. Exercise not only improves the general health, but directly stimulates the nerve centres. (Bhavanrao 1931: 4)

Health vs Strength: it has been a common belief, possibly inscribed through many ill-conceived notions of acrobatism and athletics which employed rigorous gymnastics for display and military exigencies, that the need for physical exercise is confined to the building of a strong body only. Worse still, much has been added progressively to this false evaluation by the pseudoscientific advocates of non-yogic systems of physical culture, of strength, of sports, of games and even beauty, seeking to achieve their respective objectives through the development of strong bulging muscles. Consequently, except in the case of yoga, until recently no great importance seems to have been attached to the acquisition of pure good health through systematic physical education. At most, modern physical culture may yet be regarded as more a scheme of muscle and body training rather than one of exclusive neuromuscular education for simultaneous development, harmony and health of the internal organs. It is [w]rong to suppose that strength necessarily imparts health. For it is significant to note, in this respect, that many acrobats, athletes and wrestlers, both in the East and West, often suffer from acute or chronic diseases of many kinds. Fortunately, for the future generations, the old misguided notions are yielding place to new scientific evaluations. Dio Lewis, the homopathist [sic], denounced the mania for monstrous muscles and chest which he believes misled the real purpose of physical education. Massey has gone so far enough to state that 'Socrates with a headache is always preferable to a brainless Hercules. The cult of muscle is merely another view of the narrowness that fostered the cult of mind or the cult of the spirit'. [Y]oga realised this and more, when ages ago, it insisted on the necessity of daily physical education for internal purification ('malas[sh]uddhi')—virtually for the health of the nervous system and therefore, of the mind. The acquisition of such good health comes [sic] even more imperative in view of the basic yoga objective of concentration for the health of the subconscious, ultimately leading to the highest spiritual altitude. [E]xercise has many points of contact with education, it is intricately related to mental, moral and social training, each of which alone is partial and incomplete. (Yogendra 1956: 66–9)

On 2 October of 1926, the *Bombay Chronicle* thus featured a photo of Ramamurty, an Indian athlete and physical culturist called 'the Indian

Hercules'. He had disbanded his circus troupe 'to devote his life to improving the physique and health of the nation' and had renamed himself 'the Modern Bhima'. The article, entitled 'Regenerating National Physique', reported that

Professor Ramamurti said that the ancient Indian system of physical culture which is still practiced by many people in this country is based on scientific principles and is intended to cure diseases and strengthen the internal organs, giving sound health and energy, at the same time developing the muscular strength of the body. The system at present followed in the West, on the other hand, mainly develops the muscles, leaving the internal organs unacceted [*sic*] and their benefit disappears when the exercises are given up. 'Pranayam' which is really a part of the Indian system of physical culture is acculated [*sic*] to strengthen the lungs and purify the blood. It thereby helps concentration and meditation which give peace to the 'atma' (soul) and increase physical and mental vitality and promotes longevity. Anyone can acquire such physical strength by merely cultivating his mind. [He claimed that] the Japanese Ju-Jitsu was adapted from our 'bak-kusti', and the European boxing from our 'mushti-judh', which is a more severe feat, being performed with iron gloves. The ancient kings of India themselves used to practice such [*sic*] dangerous games, and that gave them the strength and prowess for which they were so renowned.

The article closed by stating that Professor Ramamurty, 'born in Madras Prefecture in a small village in 1883 as a sickly youth suffering from asthma', also advocated a vegetarian diet.

In the pages of Indian dailies, these notions of the ascetic, yogic, aristocratic, or noble body coexisted with advertisements for types of practices that implied altogether more secular and positivist notions of human nature, including basic proofs of strength, wrestling, and boxing, as advertised in the *Modern Review* (2.1, 2.2, and 2.3), while on 22 September 1928, the *Bombay Chronicle* announced a 'double attraction programme' at the Capitol cinema: the American comedy *Stop that Man* (Nat Ross 1928) was screened along with a 'film of the return fight for World's Heavyweight Championship Gene Tunney versus Jack Dempsey, showing all ten rounds from start to finish'.

Wrestling has been a very popular sport in South Asia since the middle ages and remains so today. Most probably imported into South Asia from Greece and Persia via Alexander the Great and synchretized into indigenous forms under the Lodi and Mughal rulers during the Mughal period, wrestling was practised at court for the benefit of the ruler who selected and had at his disposal a variety of other types of entertainers. Over the centuries, wrestling came to be practised across the subcontinent

1.1: French athlete Louis Seidinger lifting 2400 pounds of flour (*Modern Review*, April 1922, p. 474).

Mr. B.S. Nayampally, one of the favourites of the Indian cinema fans, who has started the National Athletic League in Bombay, which will be opened to-day (Friday). Mr. Nayampally's latest success was in the role of Jehangir in "Nur Jehan."

1.2: B.S. Nayampally, founder of Bombay's National Athletic League (*Bombay Chronicle*, January 1932, p. 16).

in rural villages as much as in the cities. Wrestlers or '*pehelwans*' would be trained under the guidance of a '*guru*' or master, in '*akharas*' or gyms especially devoted to this purpose and, today at least, organized along communal lines. There, wrestlers would abide by strict dietary and religious rules. From the first decades of the twentieth century large industrialists such as the Birla, owners of many of Bombay's mills, and, after 1947, the Indian state, would sponsor wrestling gyms and/or provide within companies the training facilities for wrestling competitions.[16] As in the case of wrestling, where, by the early twentieth century, modern methods of physical training came to be combined with religious observance, notions of 'purity', a strict hierarchical pupilage system, and

1.3: Wrestler Babu J.C. Goho swinging clubs weighing 100 pounds each (*Modern Review*, November 1913, pp. 519–20).

patronage (Alter 1992), each of these practices fused within themselves multiple conceptualizations of the body and spanned ambiguously across the secular-religious divide.

By the 1920s, the language used to advertise these events borrowed as much from cinema as cinema did from these events. For instance, a profile of 'Stunt King' Navinchandra, appearing in *Film World* on 8 September 1933 (p. 19), claimed that the actor had changed 'from a village boy, chided and made fun of for his fragile and girl-like appearance by his village school chums, to a well-built, strong, young athlete, admired by so many for his hair-raising stunts and physical strength', while the National Physical Culture Institute celebrated its fourth anniversary with a 'Grand Physical Culture Exhibition' at the Empire Theatre that promised 'sensational and thrilling feats of strength and dexterity' (*Bombay Chronicle*, 14 April 1928). Figures like Fakir Mohamed, the owner of a Mysore body-building club significantly called Valentino Club, wrote regularly on film-related issues and the physique of actors (Bhaumik 2001: 111). As one of his articles on 'virtue' and 'acting', appeared in the *Variety Weekly* of 21 October 1933 (p. 9), reveals, expectations about film performance incorporated wholesale pre-industrial notions of lineage and status. As Bhaumik has also observed, 'One of the [p]resumptions of the critics regarding good cinema was the convergence [b]etween physical features, acting style of performers and the moral qualities ascribed to a role in the narrative' (ibid.: 159). So, when J.B.H. Wadia's first mythological, *Vaman Avatar/Vishnu's Incarnation as Vaman* (1934), was released in Delhi and UP,

the editor of a Hindu newspaper [s]tarted a virulent campaign against the film. One of his quixotic arguments was that Vaman was an avatar of Shree Vishnu and that, as such, the role should not have been played by a Parsi boy. Much worse; in his estimate it should have been enacted not merely by a Hindu but by a Brahmin boy. (Wadia 1978: 'Vaman Avatar: a Case of Frivolous Objection')

Disgusted, the director decided never to produce a mythological again. When he eventually did, his staunchly secular approach was, as he put it, to make 'my characters appear as normal human beings and my gods and goddesses as the noblest creations of man' (ibid.).

These contrasting pulls between secular and religious notions of the body and, more generally, of identity, continued to be at work well into the next decades and are also an element of contemporary Hindi cinema.[17] The crucial point here is that advertisements for Sharda Films, which began to appear in the early part of 1926, reveal that the films and the construction of action film star Vithal as a means to sell them absorbed some elements from these practices and ideologies and not others. It is important to trace this process of selection and adaptation of existing discourses on the body for the construction of a film star—that is to say which of the available discourses were mobilized and how they were made to work—because it registered and expressed the complex fabric of economic and social pressures out of which Sharda emerged, as well as the trajectories and possibilities this film company, as a sector of the Indian economy, envisaged for the future.

SHARDA FILM COMPANY AND MASTER VITHAL

When advertisements of Sharda's films began to appear in the pages especially devoted to cinema and other types of goods, the *Bombay Chronicle*'s advertising rate was 'Rs 2 per inch per insertion in single column'. In this period, film advertisements tended to be verbose and very few Indian exhibitors used photographs or drawings, unless they were advertising foreign films. The language of these advertisements is worth examining in some depth because, the films themselves not having survived, advertisements are pretty much all we have left.[18] Today as much as in the 1920s, an advertisement can say very little indeed that is of any value about the film it advertises. Rather, the advertisements constitute valuable objects of analysis in themselves, first, because they quite literally articulate fantasies that, to the extent that these are as much about the film industry in India as about other areas of Indian life, must necessarily have been at work in the films also. This is a period in Indian cinema when division of labour had only just set in and when different sectors of the industry were still emerging as discrete entities. The fact that most advertisements at this time are exhibitors' advertisements should not distract us from the principle that in historical analysis it is the relations between the parts that matter, not the ascription of powers of determination (of agency) to any single part. It is from its position within the relations of production that any single player within the film industry acquired its role and historically specific nature. Film advertisements of the 1920s can offer an x-ray of those relations as much as the films would have. The difference lies in the decoding work demanded from the historian.

Second, film advertisements of the 1920s constitute a valuable object of analysis because the horizons and possibilities they articulate are remarkably different in kind. I have already mentioned how, in July 1928, Hindustan promoted Phalke's *Bhakta Damaji,* a 'brand new historical and mythological film', as an 'immortal episode in Maratha history on screen', incorporating into an industrial medium the divinely revealed character ascribed to scriptures and myths and exploiting it as a marketing device. Hindustan also used Hindu mythology in order to address an audience which Phalke imagined as a model of the Indian nation. Unlike *Raja Harishchandra*, the advertisement for *Bhakta Damaji* addressed a nation conceived in terms that were simultaneously 'mythological' and 'historical', religious and secular. Less than a month later, on 18 August 1928, Kohinoor Film advertised the re-release of their own remake of Phalke's classic, *Raja Harishchandra*, by D.D. Dabke (1924) as 'an Interesting Religious and Moral Picture for the Hindoo Community'. These opposite pulls of secular and religious notions of Indianness continued throughout the 1920s and, some would rightly argue, last to this day. Unlike in the following decades, however, in the 1920s in many areas of life little or no gap separated the extreme poles of a secularizing trajectory. The four instalments of Madan Theatres' serial *Ramayan* (Eugenio de Liguoro 1922) were thus screened at the Globe cinema where the Houdini serial *The Grim Game*, Enrico Guazzoni's *Messalina/The Fall of an Empress* (1924), *Spartacus*, and Sansonia's *The Bridge of Sighs* were also shown—a programming which did not prevent the management of the Globe from staging a Hanuman '*jayanti*' (religious celebration of Hanuman's birth) along with the screening of *Ramayan* (*Bombay Chronicle*, 24 April 1926).

In the 1920s, within this medley of religious and secular discourses, advertisements for mythologicals began to highlight elements of the advertised films according to a logic that was no longer primarily dictated by the religious priorities of, and the order pre-established by or within, the filmed myth or scripture. So, whereas the advertisement for United Picture Syndicate's mythological *Sairandhri*, 'a Glorious Chapter from the popular epic Mahabharata' urged the public to 'see how Bhima kills Kichaka and many other wonderful scenes', that is to say scenes that had been passed down as central to the myth by centuries of folk and brahminic (religious) culture, the advertisement for Hindustan's *Hanuman Janma/The Birth of Hanuman* (D. Phalke 1927) in the *Bombay Chronicle* of 18 April 1927 (p. 3) made a special case for 'adventures and warlike scenes':

> This Mythological is full of adventures and warlike scenes
> especially Bal Hanuman's Fierceful fight with Black demons
> Rahu and Ketu in Dark Sky.
> Worth showing to your family and children. Certainly they will be delighted.

In announcing the opening of its 'Grand Mythological Production' *Prithvi-Putra/Prithvi's Son* (G.S. Devare 1926) in the *Bombay Chronicle* of 25 September 1926, Kohinoor Films went a step further and, urging the public to

Please note—It is a thrilling Story of an avaricious Demon King and the plot is mingled with Love Affairs, Tragedy and Stunts.

... reduced divine 'fierceful fights' to the more mundane (and secular) notion of the stunt. Whereas in the case of well-known episodes from the myth, categories that had developed over centuries could easily be adapted to promote the filmed version, in the case of historical films, the task of lifting out elements for special attention often produced long and verbose descriptions, as if the advertisers were not quite sure as to which moments or aspects of a historical (as opposed to a mythical) event would constitute that event as 'interesting'. The advertisement for Krishna's *Jay Somnath* (Harshadrai Metha 1929), for instance, in the *Bombay Chronicle* of 16 March 1929, seems not to know whether to go for 'the charming panorama' or 'the horrors of real war'

A mighty historical drama depicting the glory of Gujarat [f]ilmed amidst the
charming Panorama of Jaipur,
includes a cast of 1500 warriors with a true regalia in genuine historical colours.
Portraying horrors of real war amidst the blaze of cities,
smashing armies battering guns and exploding piles—created artistically
for destruction.

while Krishna's *Mardna Gha/The Master-Stroke* (Kanjibhai Rathod 1927) is advertised in the *Bombay Chronicle* of 16 July 1927 as an

Excellent historical screening, with the aid of His Highness Gaikwar
of Baroda State.
The Master-Stroke or *The Triumphant Warrior and the Glorious Union*
An excellent historical film, the story of which is taken from the history
of Saurashtra.
Marvellous production in which Elephants, Horses and amazing engines
of war are seen,
full of sensation, intrigues, and battle.
By seeing this film, one finds oneself as if actually in the old days of
Saurashtrian Kings.

This secularization of film narratives, at the cost of 'Rs 2 per inch per insertion in single column', went hand-in-hand with a militarization of Indian history along the lines of Rajput kingdoms that fed the gathering of nationalist momentum and, in the 1930s, mobilization.[19] In cinema as in other cultural spheres, secularization and the conceptualization of India as a modern, independent nation in historical rather than mythological terms opened a gap between reality and its representation. By the 1920s this process had been taking place for a while, but Indian historicals did not always follow this recipe to the letter. While acknowledging that the Indian public inhabited a secular and modern world, the advertisement for *Mardna Gha* urged the same public to submit to a new medium (the cinema) that, while fully industrial, is presented in the advertisement as having the power to abolish representational distance. Krishna's 'marvellous production' promised to reclose again the gap modernity had opened up between the agent of enunciation or monstration, that is to say the cinema apparatus, and the enunciated or screened object, between the present and the past. It promised, in other words, to function just as a revealed story or a myth. In the process, the advertisement for *Mardna Gha* re-inscribed the public into a religiously sanctioned, hierarchical system, the feudal 'old days of Saurashtrian Kings'.

Sharda's productions are unlikely to have been much different from any of the other films that circulated at the time and, judging by the titles and the advertisements, Sharda too bought into the 1920s craze for Rajput Ruritanian tales.[20] Many of the films made by the company throughout its short life appealed to a sense of nationalism that drew its momentum also from ideas of India as a warrior nation ready to fight for freedom. Yet, when Sharda advertised its *Shiraz-ud-daula/By Sheer Valour* (Dhanjibhai K. Desai 1927) in the *Bombay Chronicle* of 12 February 1927 (p. 3), it kept its historical object firmly in the past, at a distance, and sought to capitalize precisely on that:

> A page from Indian History, a remarkable Golden Instance, Full of
> interesting incidents.
> A Story of Valour and of Pure Love.
> See to-day, tonight and during this week, A Gorgeous Historical Picture
> By Sheer Valour
> Chief Characters: Miss Dwarki, Miss Tara, Miss Kumudini, Miss Asha,
> Mr Vithal, Mr Gangaram, Mr Janibabu
> A Historical event during the time of the great Nawab Sivaj-ud-daulla
> [*sic*] of Bengal.

At this stage in the company's life, Vithal's name appears in the advertisements, but not always and, initially at least, simply as a member of the cast or, as in the advertisement above, as one of the film's 'chief characters'. To begin with, the company's main concern was to capitalize on the fact that historicals and, gradually, socials sold if they were made and promoted to appeal to a broadening and primarily middle class sense of nationalism. It is not a surprise then that one year before Krishna released *Mardna Gha*, Sharda had also released a film (its first or second) about the glory of a Saurashtrian king. However, when the company advertised its 'Historical Masterpiece Picture' in the *Bombay Chronicle* of 9 January 1926 (p. 3), it promoted Nanubhai Desai's film (1925) as '*Saurashtra Veer*[/*Saurashtra the Hero*]—With a Novelty in the film in the American Style'.

Sharda's next film, *Ratan Manjari* (Manilal Joshi 1926), one of the first with Vithal in the cast, was presented as 'Sharda's Marvelous Production, [f]ull of Trick Scenes, Attractive Story, Beautiful Stunts. [A] Romance full of Love, Mystery and Daring Deeds' (*Bombay Chronicle* 22 May 1926: 3)—in short, a bit of everything—but no mention was made in the advertisements of the actors, including Vithal. A week later, however, as the film was unusually programmed for a second consecutive week, most likely because the Krishna cinema had not found a replacement, *Ratan Manjari* was re-proposed with greater urgency with the following advertisement (*Bombay Chronicle*, 29 May 1926: 4):

> Owing to the request of our patrons, tonight one week more this week
> Sharda's marvellous picture *Ratna* [*sic*] *Manjari*
> Co-starring: Mr Vithal—(Indian Douglas Fair Bank [*sic*])
> Miss Mary the Heroine
> Also a Beautiful Dance on the Stage by Miss Shantakumari.

I return to the live dance shows that accompanied Sharda's and other companies' films in the next chapter. For the moment it is important to note that Sharda, like other companies of the period, made an average of ten films a year. Initially, it is the company's name that Sharda sought to promote, emphasizing it in the advertisements. Well into the first half of 1927, Vithal's name appeared only sporadically in the promotional material. At best, he is one name in a list of 'actors', 'chief characters', or 'well-known cinema stars', as in the following advertisement for *Veer Garjana*/*Rewards of Blind Passion* (A.P. Kapur 1927) in the *Bombay Chronicle* 2 April 1927 (p. 3):

> For the protection of Woman's Honour! Heroism, Nobility, Self-Sacrifice.
> Every man and woman of every community should see
> Sharda's Film Company's Master production,
> tonight and during this week *Rewards of Blind Passion*
> on chivalrous youth and a woman's honour.

Starring well-known cinema stars Mr Vithal and Mr Prabhashanker
with other notable cast.
Drama in nine reels full of Love—Emotional and Sensational deeds.

In spite of the claimed 'mastery' of Sharda's production, little must have distinguished their films from others released in the second half of the 1920s. Like the products of other companies, Sharda's films appealed explicitly to notions of nationalism and self-rule. A closer look at subsequent advertisements, however, reveals that, from 1927, Sharda simultaneously began to distil a new dimension from nationalist historical narratives. In a situation characterized by the lack of generic differentiation, Sharda gradually dispensed with lengthy descriptions of 'charming panoramas', 'true regalia', 'smashing armies', and 'exploding piles', the better to condense the appeal of its productions around a few key concepts. As the advertisements for, respectively, *Asuri Lalsa / Passion* (Nanubhai Desai 1927) in the *Bombay Chronicle* of 17 August 1927 and *Kala Pahad / Masked Terror* (Nanubhai Desai 1927) in the *Bombay Chronicle* of 31 August 1927 put it: 'love, intrigue and dreadful action of high-speed', 'mystery, thunder, action of high speed'. While Krishna and other competitors continued to repeat a by now familiar discourse of Rajput glory, Sharda's advertisement for *Swadesh Seva / My Country! My Country!* (director unknown 1927) in the *Bombay Chronicle* of 14 May 1927 (p. 4) fused the appeal to nationalism with the promised 'novelty on the American style' in this way:

Hello Swarajists or Non-Swarajists, Conservatives or Liberals,
If you wish to attain swarajya see tonight or during this week
Sharda's Historical New Production *My Country! My Country!*
Full of patriotism and self-sacrifice, Prodigious deeds
and clever strategic movements.
In which Mr Vithal (Indian Douglas Fairbanks) plays a heroic part.
Also stage dance with music and sweet song by Miss Sita—
a well known Sharda Actress and Dancer

This unusually large advertisement was accompanied by a photograph showing, from a certain distance, swashbuckling Vithal and his rival. In princely costume, Vithal can be seen leaning against the inner wall of a palace as if holding himself up, displaying agility, and pointing a sword at his rival, forcing the latter down, his face against the wall. From the second half of 1927, Sharda's advertisements further stressed the already emphatic mentions of 'actions of high speed' and 'clever strategic movements' by linking Vithal's name to these ingredients through the association with Douglas Fairbanks. *Swadesh Seva* was released only one month after Douglas Fairbanks had appeared in *The Mark of Zorro* (Fred Niblo 1920) at the Globe cinema, but so had other foreign stars. Besides, Douglas Fairbanks' films had been circulating in Bombay cinemas for some years, and no association had been made till now with any Indian actor. Mr Vithal continued to be dubbed 'the one and only Indian Douglas Fairbanks' for some more months. By June 1928, however, on the occasion of Vithal's first dual role, 'Master'—a term that had previously been used by Sharda only to qualify its productions and itself as a company—was attached instead to the name of the actor whom Sharda had taken care to associate, via the reference to Fairbanks, with the one ingredient, stunts, the company had distilled from historical stories in order to gain a competitive advantage. *Prisoners of Love* was thus promoted in the *Bombay Chronicle* of 6 June 1928 (p. 3) as

> Starring Master Vithal in a dual role for the picture is full of
> love quakes, romance quakes, emotion quakes, villainy quakes,
> loyalty quakes.

The term 'Master' gradually replaced 'the Indian Douglas Fairbanks'. In September 1928 Sharda left the Krishna cinema to lease its own, the West End on Lamington Road, where in the past only foreign films had been shown. The reopening of Krishna cinema the following year under a new banner promising to show only Indian films was marked by the release of Sharda's *Ranghelo Rajput/Warrior* (A.P. Kapur 1929). In the advertisement pre-announcing the film's opening (*Bombay Chronicle* 22 September 1928), the management announced that

> The Sharda Film Company has spent thousands of rupees to make this
> picture a perfection.
> Gorgeous settings, ruins of ancient forts, military equipments of Olden [*sic*]
> times and bravery of Rajputs
> are the main attractions of this Thrilling motion picture.
> Epoch-making incident of the Indian Cinema World.
> It is sufficient to note that
> Master Vithal
> plays the chief role.

This formula was subsequently used as a shorthand for many of the films that followed and, significantly, for their re-release when Sharda began to decline.

In the absence of generic differentiation, mention of Master Vithal, 'the stunt king of the Indian screen', as the *Indian Cinematograph Year Book* called him (1938: 697) six years after Sharda's closure, came to function as a brand name, the guarantee that the audience would get the special 'pep' they had paid for. Film stars were not a new phenomenon in 1920s India, but, unlike American stars, who tended to be studio properties, the likes of Sulochana were not tied to a single producer. Zubeida, for instance, the daughter of Fatma Begum and the Nawab of Sachin, may have been popular with the public but was not liked by producers because she was in the habit of asking for large advances (*ICC* 1928: I, 183). She accepted roles in Kohinoor, Laxmi, Excelsior, Ranjit, and Sagar productions, depending on which company was willing to meet her demands. Unlike these women, Sharda's star was created from scratch from within the company and made films exclusively with Sharda until well after the company's failed attempt at floatation. At which point, still at the peak of his popularity, Master Vithal switched to other companies.

But two further important considerations, both of which follow from the sequence of advertisements discussed above, must be borne in mind while looking at the construction of this male star. Born in 1906 in a village in the Indian state of Kolhapur and, unlike many contemporary film stars, distinctively Indian in appearance, Raghunath Vithal began his film career as 'Mr Vithal, the Indian Douglas Fairbanks'; within one year he became Master Vithal. The reference to America is as crucial as is the switch from Mr to Master. The advertisements suggest that, far from being an indicator of Hollywood influence, the reference to America pointed to a particular dimension of the films: Douglas Fairbanks, rather than, say, Bartolomeo Pagano or Harold Lloyd, was selected as a privileged reference because in the Indian imaginary of the 1920s and after, 'America' marked a utopian dimension, a horizon that stood in stark opposition to British colonial notions of modernization. Ideas about social freedom, political independence, and economic progress were all wrapped up in a particular 'American' imaginary characterized by the kind of physical prowess and exuberance, the apparently unbounded energy and anti-aristocratic heroism iconicized by Douglas Fairbanks, not by anything the British or, for that matter, Rajput culture, had to offer. Sharda's operation suggests that in an India which, after centuries of religiously sanctioned aristocratic rule, had been further subjected to the barely reconstructed feudalism of colonial economic policies, this conception of 'America' was mobilized for a domestic purpose: a particular version, or fantasy, of Indian modernization along industrial lines.

In cultural production as in other areas of life, economic modernization brought about significant degree of commodification. Although a national market was not quite in place in 1920s India and although the majority of the population was tuned into an agricultural economy of (bare) subsistence, more or less feudal social relations, and a rural lifestyle, it is at this point that the industrial labour force begins to make its entry, even if only in the few large urban centres (Sarkar 1983). It is also in this period that a mass popular press took off, including a number of film and women's magazines (Orsini 2002). In cinema, commodification manifested itself not simply in the appearance of the medium, in the opening of cinemas around the city's industrial areas, or in the rise of a sizeable production sector after World War I, but also in the status and appellation of the most prominent members of its workforce. In the case of other actors and actresses eventually promoted to become stars, the shift in status simply involved dropping the Mr or Miss, as for the likes of Sulochana and Zubeida. Alternatively, as for the circus strongman, actor, producer, and director Raja Sandow, or for Nandaram Pehelwan, a regular of Krishna's productions, the professional qualification pehelwan or a name associated with it—'sandow' meaning strongman in south India, after Eugene—was adopted as stage name. Like many other actors of the period, at the beginning of his career Vithal was billed as 'Mr', a term already used in nineteenth-century urban theatre, in the UK as much as in India. To the extent that it associated the name of Vithal with specific narrative ingredients and, within the range of available modes of action, with agility and swordplay, rather than, say, sheer muscular strength, the subsequent appellation of 'Indian Douglas Fairbanks' worked somewhat like a professional qualification, but not quite. As Vithal began to acquire the fully fledged marketing power his name was capable of mobilizing by the end of his career with Sharda, he became not Vithal, or Vithal Fairbanks, but Master Vithal, a term that, in origin carrying connotations of religious status, lineage, and operatic performance, once adopted for the cinema was used first to qualify the company's fast-paced productions and then the type of human energy required to realize them. This is not to say that Vithal, like Maciste or Fairbanks, was a fully fledged commodity, a fantasy about cheap, inexhaustible labour power. Rather, the epithet he acquired stuck and worked because it retained also all of its pre-industrial connotations. It expressed the greater degree of commodification of the performer than on the stage, the fast turnover operation of the producing company, its quick mode of exhibition, and, at the same time, the extent to which sectors of Indian cinema with which Sharda also had to work, including limited and often rural exhibition networks, operated within modes of productions that were anything but industrial.

This tension between not simply different conceptualizations of the actor's function and his work, or of his body, but also between modes of cultural production and circulation that, within Indian cinema of the 1920s, were practised simultaneously, as well as between the different temporalities and socio-economic forces underpinning both, was written into every aspect of Sharda-Vithal productions. This is because the films were shaped by economic pressures which they refracted back, in a distorted fashion, in their address to a public which they constituted while constituting themselves as products of Indian industry. Vithal's films registered the structural conditions and contradictions that characterized 1920s India, that is to say a centre beginning to pull towards industrialization but confronted with a large, rural territory neither equipped to function as a real or potential market for industrial goods nor to provide the workforce needed to produce them. For the most, then, Vithal's performances for Sharda came wrapped up in historical or pseudo-historical (ruritania) narratives that re-staged all the paraphernalia of lineage and other forms of feudal bonds, and that cast him as a heroic figure within or according to those categories. At the same time, precisely because they emerged as industrial products within a nationalist frame that encompassed projects ranging from the neo-feudal to the radically commercial and the progressive, and because they sought to address this frame and capitalize on as much of it as could be reached, Vithal's films re-staged feudal relations also to distil from them a new dimension: agility as a means to loosen up hierarchical bonds and, from them, to disentangle physical energy as a new source of value, as through the device of a masked, that is to say, anonymous and caste-less, hero, or by means of a dual role.

Vithal was not the only figure to function in this way. Significantly, one month after Fairbanks's *Robin Hood* (Allan Dwan 1922) had opened in Bombay, Sharda released *Bahadur Baharvatiyo/Terror of the Hill* (Dhirubhai Desai 1929), advertised in the *Bombay Chronicle* of 23 November 1929 as 'the story of an outlaw full of thrills and stunts' with Mr Navinchandra in the lead. Secularization could be seen to be at work in the popularity of historicals, as opposed to mythologicals, as a means to address the nation, but the narrative frame of Rajput-inspired historicals did little to open up lineage-based notions of social relations. When, from within that frame, Vithal's films began to highlight 'stunts' as a selling point and, in the process, distil from historical narratives featuring noble and aristocratic heroes notions of physical energy, social relations as staged in the films began to appear as unstable. New perspectives opened from which a story could be told, and their simultaneous availability within the one film produced heroes in double roles, law enforcer and law breaker, 'hero' and 'counterfoil'. For this reason, while regularly being cast in heroic roles, Vithal also remained available for films that, judging by the advertisements, pulled unambiguously towards notions of urbanization, social mobility, and individuation, like *Saundarya Sura/Wine of Youth* (Harshadrai Mehta 1928), which, somewhat unusually but significantly, was aggressively marketed through advertisements that appeared in the *Bombay Chronicle* every other day of that week (21, 23, and 28 of January 1928):

> Shri Sharda Film Co. presents a picture of Momentous Moment
> *The Wine of Youth*—featuring the one and only Indian Douglas Fairbanks
> Mr Vithal
> Adapted from the Sensational Story by Mr Narayan Thakur, a famous
> Gujarati Novelist
> Life! Love! Suspense! Follies! Pathos! Thrills!
> Packed full of gripping scenes which surge up to a tremendous climax.
> Replete with stunts, thrills, romance and bubbling humour.
> A picture aglow with the Wine of Life, aflame with the Spirit of Youth.

> *The Wine of Youth*—featuring the one and only Douglas Fairbanks Mr Vithal
> A Record Picture. Early Life's liveliest times with Love's Laughter lost.
> Powerful and Peppy. Alive and Living.
> Life, Frivolity, Youth, Folly, Love, Pathos, Thrills, Stunts,
> Nothing like it before.

> *The Wine of Youth*—Powerful and Peppy. Alive and Living. A Dash of Fun.
> Dramatic consequences.
> The battle of a Strong Man for redeeming his pledge.

But Vithal was not a 'Strong Man'. One week after Sharda released *Saundarya Sura*, Bombay audiences were able to see *The Black Pirate* (Alan Parker 1926), which was highlighted in the *Bombay Chronicle* of 8 February 1928 with a photograph of Douglas Fairbanks in profile as he holds his rival down to the ground, foregrounding the actor's rippling muscles and lending a slightly frontal tone to his pose, even as his face looks down and right at the rival. The reference to Fairbanks notwithstanding, the photograph of Master Vithal in the advertisement of *Swadesh Seva* mentioned earlier bore no resemblance to the image of the American actor in *The Black Pirate* or in any other of Fairbanks's films, nor did Vithal's swordsmanship carry the (colonial) connotations that characterize Fairbanks and other American and British swashbuckling heroes. Unlike Nandaram, who looked like a pehelwan, the circus strongman Raja Sandow, who borrowed his name and whose body shape was similar to that of the athletic Eugene, or the sportsman Ganpat Bakre, who, as a film actor in Surya's historicals and mythologicals, displayed well-delineated muscles (2.5a), the young Vithal had essentially a noble body, more adept at elegant swordplay than at lifting heavy weights and other demonstrations of sheer muscular strength. He was cast in scenes that required agility and, judging by contemporary descriptions, he was capable of displaying it, but he was also often shown in aristocratic-looking garments that constrained his movements and that lent stiffness to his appearance, no matter how agile he was deemed to be (2.4a and 2.4b).

Master Vithal looked and acted the way he did because that was the imaginary at work within the film industry in the second half of the 1920s. The limits within which Sharda and other companies worked at the time, along with other sectors of Indian industry, did not require human physical energy to appear figuratively as sheer muscular strength, as it did, for instance, in Italian films of the same period with Bartolomeo Pagano. One of the few surviving films in which Vithal plays the lead role, *Swarajyacha Shiledar* (Master Vithal 1951, in Marathi) has him engaged in fights using a range of pre-industrial weapons (swords, lances, and small shields), wearing a royal Pathan costume comprising a turban, a tight belted shirt and 'churidars'. One scene shows him washing at a river, bare chested, wearing only a dhoti to cover the lower part of his body and revealing a rather chubby body. The film was made when Vithal was somewhat older and fatter than in his days of glory at Sharda. Nevertheless, *Swarajyacha Shiledar* is an important film as far as Vithal and the 1920s are concerned because it reveals the extent to which, contrary to many American swashbuckling productions of the same period and after, in Indian films fights with swords and similar weapons called for a great deal of mannerism, such as swivelling the sword around several times in emphatic and time-consuming gestures before hitting the target. In these moments, the etiquette of status—the display of elegance, equilibrium, valour—takes the upper-hand over the display of agility and swiftness. Having subsumed this pre-modern code into his earlier films, Vithal was able to continue acting in action roles also as an older and fatter man. Moreover, as if to follow the dictates of (pre-)medieval traditions

1.4a: Master Vithal in *Burkhewala/White Devil* (*Mauj Majah*, 30 October 1932, p. 73).

1.4b: Master Vithal in *Bhedi Rajkumar/Mysterious Prince* (*Filmland Pictorial News*, p. 211, NFAI Collection).

1.5a: Ganpatrao Bakre (*Cinema Vision*, 1(1); Original source unknown).

1.5b: Still from *Love Immortal/Rani Rupmati/Baaz Bahadur* (Bhalji Pendharkar 1931), NFAI Collection, actor unknown.

of martial arts, which considered it somewhat 'impure' (Zarilli 1995 and 1998), *Swarajyacha Shiledar* has no room for body contact.

In *Swarajyacha Shiledar* as much as in the earlier *Ramshastri* (Gajanan Jagirdar 1944), in which Vithal also plays a central role, it is as if the camera, taking its cue from that injunction, confines itself to long frontal shots, not unlike the scene from the mythological *Maharathi Karna/ Karna the True Battler* (V. Damle and S. Fattelal 1928) [2.6], where special effects enable Karna to kill and, at the same time, avoid any form of physical labour. In *Swarajyacha Shiledar*, only during the final

1.6: Still from *Maharathi Karna* (*Cinema Vision*).

confrontation does an initially distant, frontal and static camera break into the scene of action with a short, shot-reverse-shot sequence of medium shots. This mise en scène allows a closer look not at Vithal's movements, but at the weapons (spike and sword) as they are aimed in the direction of the camera. Similarly, in the main fight sequence of *Ramshastri*, Vithal is shown swivelling his sword and Pathani shield through static, high-angled medium shots that are designed to keep Vithal in full view, the distance enabling the spectator to appreciate the actor's elegant handling of himself and his weapons.

Never is subjective enunciation used in Vithal's late films. In *Swarajyacha Shiledar* as much as in *Ramshastri*, whether Vithal is posing or wrestling, the camera never takes up his or his rival's point of view, keeping instead a distance the function of which is the ascription of value not to the physical energy displayed through Vithal's figure or his movements, but to his elegant, stately, or noble appearance. That was the asset Sharda worked with because its mode of operation was such that it sought to address, on the one hand, a rural population which, at best, had only just moved to Bombay to work in the city's mills and, on the other, a middle class that was also of recent formation and which, for all its nationalism, looked upon such newly acquired mobility, the individuating, and the industrial potential it implied with a great deal of concern, if not sheer horror. Vithal's films went both ways, but only in so far as the disruption of the feudal bonds they staged could be seen to go hand in hand with their glorious re-instauration in not too radical a shape. In the name of nationalism and for commercial purposes, Sharda Films made available to a larger social base than was previously the case practices such as the cinema and, with it, visions of self-determination through individual action. Most of the time, however, those possibilities came dressed in noble garb, ultimately suggesting that the future was not in the loosening up of hierarchical bonds to free from them physical energy as an individual source of value, but in re-inscribing oneself into (a higher position within) existing hierarchical categories.

CONCLUSION

It is inevitable that, as a commercial enterprise harbours fantasies of capital accumulation, it should, on the one hand, stage secondary elaborations of labour-power creation through the dismantling of hierarchical feudal bonds and, on the other, that is in one single movement, figure the means to contain and freeze that much-needed energy. In the Indian cinema of the 1920s, as Sharda Films stifled physical energy under layers of Pathan costumes, that energy surfaced in a different guise, most notably in the films of Ganpatrao Bakre for Surya Films. It was not an entirely new phenomenon. A number of mythologicals, including Phalke's *Lanka Dahan*, had featured monkey kings and other demi-gods, like Bhima, who displayed the potential strength of a Bartolomeo Pagano and its reduction to subhuman form, as the brute force of animals and demons. Unlike Vithal, Bakre was a professional wrestler who, as photograph 2.5a shows, did display the potential for sheer muscular energy, but he neither became a demon nor was he reduced, like Ganpat Shinde, to performing in godly-animal roles. In the late 1920s it was a little too late for so sharp a polarization as that.

Ganpatrao Bakre began his film career in the 1920s under the banner of Maharashtra Film, a contemporary of Phalke's Hindustan, and under the direction of Damle and Fattelal. In 1929, when Maharashtra's founder, Baburao Painter, left to start Prabhat studios, Bakre joined Surya Films, a company that, set up by the former manager of Laxmi, Haribhai Desai, sought to replicate Sharda's mode of operation in Bangalore. By the time Surya's films began to be advertised by, and shown in, Bombay cinemas, Bakre, who initially featured in the advertisements as Mr Bakre, was quickly promoted to become Master Bakre or, alternatively, as in one of the advertisements I discuss later, as Stunt-King Master Ganpatrao Bakre. With the shift from Maharashtra to Surya, where he was paid 'the princely salary of one thousand rupees' (*Cinema Vision* 1980: 46), Bakre also began to be cast regularly in lead roles. Within two years with Surya, even as he played Rajput royals, he had become 'devil may care fellow Master Bakre'.

At Surya, just as he had at Maharashtra Film, Bakre acted in a large number of mythologicals, like *Daivi Khadga/Divine Sabre* (G.P. Pawar 1930), which was advertised in the *Bombay Chronicle* on 10 April of 1930 as

A story ancient in its days, but original in execution, woven around the sword as the emblem of the 'Divine Shakti' working her Mighty Will-Right, triumphing by Might, Love Supreme, fast moving action and a great climax.

Half a year later, Bakre reappeared in an exotic romance entitled *Kalika No Kop/Royal Savage* (Sundarrao Nadkarni 1930), which was advertised in the *Bombay Chronicle* of 29 November 1930 (p. 15) in this way:

If you want to experience Jungle thrills, mad unprevented Romance,
and the Ringing atmosphere of tropics
you must see Surya Film Co. Lotus Production *Royal Savage* featuring
Master Bakre & Miss Laxmi.
When the Savage Women first see the Modern Youth
and cupid slings the arrows
and the love chase goes on and on amidst wilderness,
this whole picture carries the audience.
You will Thrill, you will Laugh, you will Cry.

Surya earned quite a name for itself and, according to the *Indian Cinematograph Year Book* of 1938, its films had a reputation for featuring a variety of animals, 'such as horses, dogs, leopards and monkeys' (p. 119). Unlike mythologicals, the various Hanumans and Bhimas of which were looked upon with a great deal of devotion and respect (they had the aura of familiar gods), Surya used animals as a commercial attraction, objects that were exotic because Surya's films addressed and targeted an audience that was more urbanized than Phalke's audience. Appropriately, as in the photograph 2.5a, Bakre donned leopard-skin loincloths while simultaneously projecting the image of an urban 'beau'. *Bahirji Naik* (Bhalji Pendharkar 1943, Marathi), for instance, although a late Bakre film, opens with a scene in which the actor, here cast in the role of a man of noble lineage, stands in front of a mirror in his room, his back to the camera. He is dressing up, admiring his own curly blond hair, attended by a flirtatious woman from whose point of view we also occasionally look at him. When Bakre finally turns, the camera dwells on his profile. However, unlike Bartolomeo Pagano-Maciste or for that matter, unlike interpreters of American and European Tarzan films, who also wore loincloths, Bakre's loincloth carried animal, not colonial, connotations. The son of a leading Kolhapur cloth merchant and a professional wrestler sponsored by the Maharaja of Kolhapur, Bakre could be simultaneously a 'royal' and, accommodating around the one figure a notion of physical, muscular energy that royals (like Karna) should not have to deploy, a 'savage'. The qualities that mythologicals condensed around the two figures of Rama and Hanuman or, better, Bhima, each at the opposite ends of a system that regarded physical labour as impure, did not quite fuse in Bakre either, but came much closer, while the perspective from which audiences were invited to look at both had changed. The following month, Bakre thus featured in a historical, *Chauhani Talwar/Fighting Cavalier* (Baburao 1930, alternative film title *Rangila Nawab*), that showed at the West End for two weeks and was advertised in the *Bombay Chronicle* of 20 and 27 December (p. 15). In the film Bakre played a fierce Rajput chieftain, with a modern twist: haughty royals could now fall in love and women go for savages.

> It is a fight to the Finish When a Rajput of Royal Chauhan Blood
> takes into his head to begin once.
> [W]ithout any sword by your side your heart will throb with heroism.
> [F]eaturing Stunt-King Master Ganpatrao Bakre and Miss Sena.
> Into the Jaws of Death, Into the Mouth of Hell Rode one Dare-devil Rajput
> With sword in his hand he sought his fortune.
> He allowed his heart to be wounded by Cupid's arrow,
> but he knew how to woo, how to love,
> and he got his heaven—a lovely romping woman.
> [F]eaturing the devil may care fellow Master Bakre and beautiful Miss Jenna (*sic*).

These advertisements suggest that a process had begun to set in which, first registered by Sharda's films as an increased sense of (physical and social) mobility, in Bakre' films took a two-pronged direction. On the one hand, the energy freed surfaced sufficiently to be registered and, elaborated from a feudal, commercial, urban perspective, was condensed around a few knots: animals, the wilderness, the savages, the leopard loin-cloth revealing the bare muscles not of a servile semi-divine monkey, but of a common man. On the other hand, the social categories that in the past had channelled physical energy into pre-industrial modes of production had become unstable and, moreover, were revealing themselves to be not quite up to the job of employing it effectively (the wilderness), for now industrial production was beginning to demand new skills. It is at this point that women came prominently to the foreground, marking the newfound mobility of social relations, individuation, in short, the possibilities opened up by modernity. In the next chapter I examine the way in which the representation of women emerged as an important element of action films in the 1920s and 1930s—as a contested terrain which, when deployed in conjunction with notions of physical energy, also helped to set the new terms by which industrializing India was to sustain social reproduction.

NOTES

1. For a detailed account of the effects of colonial economic policy in this period, see Davis (2001).

2. The influenza epidemic of 1918 is estimated to have killed more than 15 million people. These epidemics were quite severe in Bombay Presidency and caused a decline in population (Visaria and Visaria 2005: 493).

3. For the emergence of an Indian industrial labour force in this and the following decades, see also Chandavarkar (1994), Joshi (2003), and Breman (2004).

4. For an account of these events, see Abel (1999) and Bowser (1990).

5. Hughes (2003) is among the few film historians to argue, in my opinion correctly, that exhibition, not production, should be taken as the point of entry into a history of cinema in India. See also Vitali (2006).

6. References to J.B.H. Wadia's unpublished autobiography *Those Were the Days* are given by chapters because the original document does not have page numbers. Chapters 1 to 45 relate to the handwritten manuscript, which ends at the time of the Wadias' last silent film. References for the sound period give the chapter's number as it is given in Riyad Wadia's electronic transcript, kindly provided by Vinci Wadia. Alternatively, when a chapter number was not allocated in the electronic transcript, I have given the title of the section in which the quoted extract appears.

7. See Musser (1990) for this aspect of early cinema in North America.

8. As Dwyer (2005: 23, 43) observes, films based on the actions of Hanuman continued to be among the most popular mythologicals well into the late 1980s. Phalke returned to Hanuman in 1927, with *Hanuman Janma*; Homi Wadia's

Basant Pictures (see Chapter 2 in this volume) produced two films centred around the monkey god, *Hanuman Pataal Vijay/Hanuman's Victory over Earth* (Homi Wadia 1951), with Meena Kumari, and *Hanuman Chalisa/Hanuman's Forty Names* (1969, director unknown), while Wadia Movietone and Basant Pictures' former special effects man, Babubhai Mistri, directed the Tamil and Hindi *Hanuman Pataal Vijayan* (1960) and *Hanuman Vijay* (1974). Although he starred in a variety of roles from the early 1960s, Dara Singh (see Chapter 4) is remembered today nearly exclusively for his performance as Hanuman in the television serial *Ramayan* (Ramanand Sagar 1986–8), for which Mistri, as the director of many mythological films, worked as consultant (Dwyer 2005: 44). Interestingly, Dara Singh's Hanuman in the 1980s television serial seems also to have erased memories of his Bhima (see further discussion in this chapter) in Mistri's *Mahabharata* (1965). As I suggest in what follows, one important factor in the continuing popularity of Hanuman in the twentieth century was industrialization and, with it, the socio-economic pressure to re-imagine ideal forms of physical energy and its uses. In principle, as Rama's right arm, Hanuman is pre-eminently suitable as a discursive terrain for the negotiation of positions against modernization—that is to say for attitudes resisting the reconceptualization of social relations along secular and democratic lines—since in the figure of Hanuman, physical energy remains the attribute of a subhuman species, a monkey whose energy is entirely channelled into the service of his divine master. As I hope will become apparent from my discussion in this and the next chapters, in practice, representations of Hanuman, as of any other figure featuring in the films of this and the following decades, were and remain a more complex affair, encompassing profoundly contradictory discourses, some modern, other less so. It should thus not come as a surprise that, in the 1910s as much as in the 1980s, scenes featuring Hanuman have been a favourite for special effects among Indian directors and producers of mythologicals (see Dwyer 2005: 44). In this respect, Hanuman films can be seen to simultaneously stage fantasies about industrialization as a desirable process.

9. For mythological and devotional films in Indian cinema, see Das (1980), Kothari (1980), Rajadhyaksha (1986) and (1987), Kapur (1987) and (1993), Dasgupta (1989), Prasad (1998), Lutgendorf (2003), and Dwyer (2005). For representations of gods in theatre and photography, see Kapur (1993), Guha-Thakurta (1988) and (1992), and Pinney (2004).

10. Bhima: character in the Mahabharata. One of the five Pandavas, Bhima acquired his strength when, poisoned by a jealous cousin, he descended to the realm of the Nagas (serpent demons) who gave him a liquid that gave him 'the strength of ten thousand Nagas. From that moment he became a second Hercules'. Unlike his brother Hanuman, the 'perfect and measureless' monkey king whose powers are entirely devoted to the service of Rama, Bhima represents 'a type of brute strength; he is of gigantic stature, impetuous, irascible, somewhat vindictive,

and cruel even to the verge of ferocity. [H]is great strength had to be maintained by plentiful supplies of food, as his name Vrikodara, "wolf-stomached", indicates.' (Wilkins 1975: 415–16).

11. Unless otherwise stated, the following account of Bombay's exhibition and production sectors is based on information obtained from the evidence given to the ICC.

12. In 1926 Britain produced twenty-six films (Balcon et al. 1947: 14–15, quoted in Barnouw and Krishnaswamy 1980: 42).

13. Especially in the south of India, see Hughes (1996a).

14. As Dwyer (2005: 14–15) also observes, in this context, the use of film generic terminology is more problematic than it is generally the case. On the one hand, existing filmographies (Chabria 1994, Rajadhyaksha and Willemen 1999, and Verma 2000) differ in their generic classification of individual films. On the other hand, contemporary advertisements rarely use generic labels as we know them today. For instance, the 1931 and 1932 issues of *Cinema* carry advertisements of films of the following categories: Special Exclusive, Social, Jungle, Oriental, Romantic, Semi-Oriental, Stunt, and Fighting. Mythological and devotional films alike were often referred to as Brahminical, Pouranic, or Semi-Pouranic, as they were in *Filmland* in 1934 (quoted in Bandhyopadyay 1993: 30). My classification here is based on an individual film's synopsis as found either in existing filmographies or in contemporary advertisements. In the remaining part of this chapter, where I discuss the emergence of the stunt or action genre, I have relied exclusively on contemporary advertisements and on the film's synopsis as presented in the advertisements. My reasons for doing so have to do with problems relating to the conceptualization of film genre that remain to be resolved within film theory. I have raised some of these issues in the Introduction and return to them in Chapter 5. Here it is enough to say that filmographies' allocation of generic labels to films tends to be a retrospective affair, with little respect for contemporary terminology. Yet, as I hope to demonstrate in this chapter, contemporary marketing terminology is, in itself, a crucial dimension, an expression, of the industrial pressures that constitute clusters of films as a genre. If we are to understand film genres and the narrative strategies that characterize them as structural categories with historically specific socio-economic functions, then close attention must be paid to the articulations of those industrial pressures, whether they manifest themselves in the films as textual-narrative elements, or in the ways marketing strategies instruct spectators to watch the films.

15. For a parallel argument in relation to the uses of European literary forms in Japan, see Fujii (1993). Buck-Morss' discussion of Walter Benjamin's notion of 'wish images' (1989: 110–58) is also pertinent here.

16. Alter (1992) offers a comprehensive history of wrestling in India. See also Zarrilli (1995) and (1998), for martial arts in south India, Awasthi (1983: 76–90) and (2001: 64–72), and De Mellow (1987).

17. Manmohan Desai's films are a good example of the persistence of religious belief in contemporary narratives. In Rajhans (1992), Desai, a self-confessed 'communist', is quoted as stating that miracles do happen.

18. My research for this and the following chapters is partly based on advertisements and articles that appeared in the *Bombay Chronicle* and in *The Times of India* from the mid-1910s to the early 1930s, as well as in all the surviving Gujarati, Hindi, and English-language magazines covering cinema, including *Mouj Majah, Citrapat, Cinema Samsar, Cinema, Kiran, Filmland, Ranjit Bulletin, Variety Weekly, Film World*, and *Talk-A-Tone*. To my knowledge, the oldest surviving issue of these magazines is dated May 1931. Moreover, the preserved collections of any single magazine are discontinuous. Only the two English-language dailies offered the continuity required for the identification of the patterns that characterized the growth of film production in Bombay in the 1920s and, within it, the emergence of an indigenous action film genre. Of the two dailies, I have chosen to focus on the *Bombay Chronicle* because it covered indigenous film production far more extensively than *The Times of India*.

19. Secularization of narrative is meant here to involve rational explanation of events, and therefore an understanding and/or representation of the past in historical, as opposed to mythological, terms. For elaborations on this line of argument, see Todorov (1973), Thapar (1988), Dirks (1990) and, in the context of Indian nationalism, Mukherjee (1984), and Chatterjee (1986).

20. For accounts of the prominence of historical and costume films and, within this genre, the popularity of Rajput Ruritania stories, see Bhaumik (2001) and Mukhopadhyay (2004).

2

Women in Action Films in the 1920s and 1930s

IN EARLY-TWENTIETH-CENTURY INDIA, THE PRESENCE OF WOMEN IN THE PUBLIC sphere was a contentious issue, closely connected to prospects of economic and social modernization, which, within Indian nationalism, found supporters and opponents. Up to the turn of the century, a powerful taboo more or less banned the presence of Indian women on the stage. Public performances by women were dictated by the religious and hierarchical terms of medieval Indian society. *Devadasis* (religious dancers) were raised in Hindu temples and *tawaifs* (courtesans) employed at the courts of maharajas to perform erotic dances, rituals of salutation in which the woman paid her respects to gods, priests, and aristocrats much as a servant would signal his or her subordination to a master. None of these performers were considered normal human beings in the modern sense of the term, nor would ordinary people be admitted to the show.[1] On the nineteenth-century theatre stage, female roles were played by young men, and it was only with the rise of reformist movements, which promoted the theatre as a means to 'reform' prostitutes through 'lawful employment', that we see theatre actresses gaining a measure of social acceptance (Adarkar 1991). But even for figures like the popular Binodini Dasi, the stigma remained firmly in place (Bhattacharya 1998).

Silent Indian cinema incorporated the taboo. In fact, the industrial nature of the medium exacerbated these attitudes because cinema made available to an Indian working class still in the making a sight previously accessible only to the upper layers of society. In 1913, when Phalke made his first *Raja Harishchandra* with non-professional actors, he cast men in the female roles, in spite of his initial intentions to the contrary, because no woman came forward. But even in the 1930s working as a 'film artiste' carried, for women, definite sexual connotations, as if the accessibility of the cinema to the masses rubbed off on the women who worked in it. Writing to a newspaper in 1931, a 'lady artiste' thus claimed that

The world is not aware as regards the inner life of the studios. [I]t is a vain idea to expect society girls with education and culture to come forward to join the films until the present film producing companies set their house in order. [P]roducing companies are formed with threefold motives. First to satisfy their lust and passion, second to enjoy life and make money, and third to misuse public money. [T]he actresses that are usually found to support a film career come from houses of ill-fame who have already thrown their morals to the airs and who find the filmland as a proper scope for their enjoyment. It is but horrible for any society girl to work in such disreputable surroundings. These actresses are naturally very free in their behaviour and are easily accessible for corruption. (Bandyopadhyay 1993: 108–9)

One strategy Indian filmmakers used to circumvent and simultaneously to capitalize on the taboo was to cast women perceived as 'foreign'. Many of the film stars of the 1920s and 1930s, from Sulochana to Fearless Nadia, were what used be referred to at the time as Anglo-Indians. Thought to be outside caste and other types of hierarchical categories, their perceived alienness enabled these actresses to act out roles that broke religiously and morally sanctioned norms of 'decency' while remaining within the bounds of acceptability. As nationalist mobilization gained momentum, however, Indian women began to be ascribed a new kind of visibility. It was not a novel phenomenon: women had been a bone of contention between colonial officials and Indians since the nineteenth century (Mani 1989). Debates about sati and other issues regarding women had functioned as a terrain for Britain to legitimize its colonial operation as the 'modernization' of an indigenous people whom imperial, orientalist discourses constructed as 'backward'. These discourses had since been incorporated and remobilized, first by Indian reformists— for example the possibility of a widow's remarriage—and, from the early twentieth century, by Indian nationalists of various persuasions. Within the broad platform that was Indian nationalism, regressive attitudes about women were sometimes advanced in order to reject British rule in India as a modernizing operation in the name of traditional, that is pre-modern, Indian culture; at other times, more progressive attitudes were embraced in order to call into question the legitimacy of British rule as an insufficiently modern, that is retrograde and essentially neo-feudal, colonial operation. Within this push-and-pull, what was and was not independent India also came to be debated on the basis of what an Indian woman could and could not do (Chatterjee 1993; Chandra 1992). While this meant that Indian nationalism, in its mobilization against a colonial power that presented itself as 'modern', had to open up a little to notions of civil rights for women, in practice it did not go very far, and even that, not for long. As Geraldine Forbes has written, nationalist women

did little to generate a feminist consciousness. They marched and picketed in sex-segregated groups, usually wearing distinctive orange or white saris to emphasize their purity and sacrifice. Their directives came from the Congress Committees. [M]ale guardianship prevailed. [W]omen could come out because the house was on fire. The expectation was that once the fire was out, women would go back inside the house. (1998: 156)

Women's associations and other platforms for debate were formed that had very diverse agendas. Progressive women's magazines offering a public space to the writing of women from all walks of life, including prostitutes (Orsini 1999; 2002), existed alongside figures like Desh Sevika Sangha's founding member and Congress leader Dadabhai Naoroji, who insisted that members should have impeccable credentials because women of high status would elicit respect from the public. For Naoroji, nationalist women were to perform only actions that preserved their dignity and 'innate modesty', and this precluded marching side by side with women of 'undesirable' character (Forbes 1998: 133). Similarly, in 1928, Mahila Rashtriya Sangha's founder and writer Latika Ghosh instructed militant women to think back to the battles between the devis and the asuras: just as the goddesses were losing, the fearsome goddess Durga appeared as shakti and the demons were defeated. Women were the 'shaktis' of the nation, she said and, simultaneously addressing the militant women as so many Sitas,[2] issued this directive: 'Everyone of you must be like a spark which will burn down all selfishness, all petty dreams—purified by fire, only the bright, golden love of the Motherland will remain' (quoted in Forbes 1998: 136).

Latika Ghosh also reminded her readers of the example set by Rajput queens, who first sent their husbands and sons into battle and then prepared for their own death. Not surprisingly, in the 1920s, Indian film actresses could be found performing a measure of stunts in historicals, many of which were indeed based on idealized notions of Rajput history, and in mythologicals. As the advertisement for *Veerangana* (Homi Master 1928),[3] appearing in the *Bombay Chronicle* of 17 March 1928 (p. 3), indicates, in these historical narratives, the presence of Indian women and the actions they were asked to perform—from the accidental exposing of a naked ankle to the slaying of a man—were framed within the legitimating bounds of nationalist ideology:

The story depicts a faithful portrayal of Indian Culture.
Womanhood! A picture every mother, daughter, wife should see.
Huge! Colossal! Fantastic! Thrills piled upon Thrills!
Cavalry! Thousands of Riders! Battles with life! Defying Death!

The extent to which the nationalist ideology that pervaded these genres made some room for, and simultaneously contained, the presence and actions of women in cinema is evident in the early career of Durga Khote. The daughter of a well-to-do family whose husband went bankrupt soon after their marriage, Durga Khote began working for the cinema to make ends meet. She was invited to play her first film role by J.B.H. Wadia in *Farebi Jaal/A Vicious Trap* (1931), the first sound production of Mohan Bhavnani, who had directed the Imperial action hit *The Wildcat of Bombay/Mumbai Ni Biladi/Uthavgir Abala* (1927) starring the Anglo-Indian star Sulochana. But *Farebi Jaal* flopped. It was just not the kind of film a respectable Indian woman would be seen watching, let alone play in. Durga only featured in a short scene of the film where her main task was to sing, but even so, in Durga's own words, written more than fifty years after her debut, *Farebi Jaal* and Durga's participation in it brought her whole family into disrepute (Khote 2006). It was only after director V. Shantaram guaranteed that his films (unlike the Wadias') were going to be 'quality' productions, and that Durga would have a chaperone on set with her at all times, that her father allowed Durga to work for V. Shantaram's studio, Prabhat Film Company. Durga Khote's next film was *Ayodhyecha Raja/The King of Ayodhya* (V. Shantaram 1932), a big-budget mythological about an episode in the life of Raja Harishchandra, while in the following one, *Maya Macchindra/Magical Macchindra* (V. Shantaram 1933), Durga played the queen of a kingdom of men-hating women (3.1). In the end, as this mythological tale went, her kingdom turned out to be an effect of maya. Durga went on to become one of India's biggest and longest-lasting stars.

In 1932 the Rialto cinema pre-announced its reopening as Rialto Talkies with an advertisement that promised 'perfect performances by amateur artists belonging to respectable families' (*Bombay Chronicle*, 11 February: 11). But taboos work both ways. While *Maya Macchindra* was screened in Bombay on the week of 10 December 1932, marking the reopening of Krishna cinema after it was equipped with Western Electric's sound system, when the real possibility of expansion presented itself—as it had some years before *Maya Macchindra*'s release with the influx of immigrants into Bombay—Indian filmmakers and exhibitors

2.1: Durga Khote in *Maya Macchindra* (*Filmland*, March 1933, p. 30).

were quick to exploit the monetizing potential offered by the promise of transgressing the injunction against public performances by women. As the advertisements for Imperial's *Karmayili Kali/Tainted Virtue* (R.S. Choudhury 1927) and Sharda's *Amrit ki Zaher/Wine and Women* (A. P. Kapur 1928), appearing in the *Bombay Chronicle* of, respectively, 12 November 1927 and 4 August 1928, clearly suggest, the industry could have it both ways: pay lip service to reformist ideas and capitalize on the persistence of well entrenched codes of 'decency':

> Prostitution must be abolished because it is the worst plague of the city. What are the pitfalls? For all this, come and see this week *Tainted Virtue* Featuring Miss Armiline [sic] the well-known star

> *Wine and Women*
> Featuring Zeb-un-Nisa and Miss Mani.
> Depicting the Evils of Drink and Dancing Girls.

The appearance of women in Indian action films in the mid-1920s became an industrially significant feature at the end of the silent period and continued well into the first decade of the talkies. These films appeared in spite of the taboo on women in the public sphere and along with foreign productions of the same genre. Many of these were American serials, but films such as *Plunder* (1923), distributed by Pathé and starring Pearl White, followed a long stream of earlier, and apparently less prudish, French productions, like the popular *Protéa* series (1913–17) by Éclair, featuring Josette Andriot in the role of thief or spy, often in black tights.[4] Unlike these foreign films, Indian films were always accompanied by a live dance. As the display advertisement for Sharda's *Ratan Manjari* already cited in Chapter 1 put it,

> Co-starring: Mr Vithal—(Indian Douglas Fair Bank [*sic*])
> —Miss Mary the heroine
> Also a beautiful dance on the stage by Miss Shantakumari.

A woman, in this case a Miss Mary, was also always cast alongside the male star. The very popular Zebunissa often co-starred alongside Vithal. None of the Sharda Films have survived and the advertisements often give little indication as to whether Zebu, as she was often billed, performed stunts along with Vithal. The advertisement reproduced here (3.2a), from the *Bombay Chronicle* of 18 April 1931 (p. 15), shows her in *Bahadur Beti/ She* (A.P. Kapur 1931), a Sharda production in which she was cast in an action role not with Vithal, but with Jairaj.

2.2a: Advertisement of Sharda Fim's *Bahadur Beti / She*, starring Zebunissa (*Bombay Chronicle*, 11 April 1931, p. 15).

What is certain is that when she left Sharda, Zebunissa joined Surya, the south India based producer for whom Ganpat Bakre also worked and which specialized in historical and mythological films containing a great number of stunts. Sharda itself appears to have made very few films with women in the lead role, one of them being *Vasant Bala / Spring Girl* (1926), a 'historical masterpiece, full of love and fighting stunts' (*Bombay Chronicle*, 26 Feb. 1926: 3), in which not Zebunissa, but a Miss Jones played the lead role. Zebunissa, however, 'particularly excelled in vampish roles' (*ICY* 1938: 699), just like Ermeline (ibid.: 598–9) who, as demonstrated by a series of advertisements in the *Bombay Chronicle* at the end of the decade and in magazines of the early 1930s, was regularly cast in lead action roles:

Veer Keshari [/ *Victorious Keshari*] starring Miss Ermeline and Miss Gulab—
Stage dance by Miss Laila
Dare devil stunts and exciting deeds of Miss Ermeline and Miss Gohar.
(*Bombay Chronicle*, 5 May 1928)

Lady of the Lake [aka *Sarovar ki Sundari*] with Miss Ermeline (Emilee)
and Mr Madunrao Vakil
Dare devil stunts from start to finish
Riding of Miss [E]rmeline and most expressive and emotional acting
of Miss Jilloo
are very impressive.
(*Bombay Chronicle*, 11 and 21 January 1928: 12)

2.2b: Advertisement of *Azad Abla/Daring Damsel* (Saqi 1933) (*Mauj Majah*, 20 April 1933, p. 41).

> Imperial Film Co's Super Stunt Picture *Vasant Bengali* [aka *Bengali Bomb*]
> Featuring Miss Ermeline
> Supported by Mr Jal Merchant and Miss Jilloo
> Written and directed by Mr Karani
> It is a superb thrilling picture featuring screen model Miss Ermeline.
> (*Bombay Chronicle*, 23 and 30 August 1930: 15)

According to a short profile in the *Bombay Chronicle* of 8 August 1931 (p. 15), Ermeline was 'good as a horse-rider. She always does manly actions. She is a good sword-woman. She is quick in action. She needs perfection in her face.' But Ermeline was not the only actress to have performed fights and other stunts for the camera:

> Commencing today! When the bells of wedding might turn into
> the death-knell
> and when a woman loses her lover before she knows him properly
> then what role a woman will play to take her vengeance?

> She would fare [*sic*] any trouble, she would be a fighting tigress.
> Then the fangs of a serpent would be less poisonous.
> Such is the fire of girl, who shows the whole world what a woman can do for
> attaining any achievement!
> *A Woman's Vengeance* [aka *Hridaya Jwala/Blazing Heart*]—Sharda Film Co's
> Super Production
> Featuring Mr Khalil and Miss Hira
> (*Bombay Chronicle*, 25 October 1930)

Although none of the films survive, advertisements like these and the billing of a live dance along with the film tell us that the casting of a woman was not exclusively instrumental to a discourse of the nation. Women in films were, first and foremost, a powerful marketing device. In an industry that was struggling to emerge, the presence of women, combined with narrative ingredients such as action, enabled Indian producers to compete against the French, Italian, and American films Indian exhibitors had, until the early 1920s, found more profitable to screen. Advertisements like this one, from the *Bombay Chronicle* of 16 January 1926 (p. 3), leave little doubt in this respect:

> Playing with Death. A brave girl, well-known actress Miss Jilloo,
> with a Bengal tiger.
> See today Royal Art Studio's Picture *Naharsingh Dakoo* [/*Naharsingh the Dacoit*]
> at Majestic.
> American style daring riding.

While it is difficult to judge from an advertisement, like that for *Hridaya Jwala/Blazing Heart* (Vaidya 1930), the type of performance that had been required of Miss Hira, the presence of Ermeline on the bill (and mention of her in the advertisement) guaranteed that the film was indeed a stunt film in which a woman performed the action. Thus in the mid-1920s a particular type of woman, or rather, a particular type of female performance, emerged in Indian cinema as a means of generic differentiation. In the mid-1930s, for reasons that I discuss later, this requirement became more urgent and women in action films acquired a more prominent role. For the moment, it is important to emphasize that the images of women in these early action films had first and foremost a commercial dimension. They met an industrial pressure which we need to take seriously because it forces the film historian to read images of women as commodities. This is not to dismiss or condemn these images simplistically, as objectifications of women or fetishes. 'With its price tag the commodity enters the market. If its substantive quality and individuality create the incentive to buy, for the social evaluation of its worth this is totally unimportant' (Marx, quoted in Buck-Morss 1989: 181). As Susan Buck-Morss has observed in her discussion of Walter Benjamin's re-evaluation of commodified cultural production, 'If the social value (hence the meaning) of commodities is their price, this does not prevent them from being appropriated by consumers as wish images within the emblem books of their private dreamworld' (1989: 181). It is precisely this type of industrial-commercial pressure that enables us today to look differently at cinematic aspects of images of women in action and other films, such as the sensationalism, the sexy elements, or even the gestures deemed capable of explaining the added interest (value) of certain films. In the mid-1920s, more so than for productions starring 'the Indian Douglas Fairbanks' or Ganpat Bakre, films with actresses in action roles carried within them a strong modernizing dimension which, I argue, was not incompatible with the mobilization of images of women for commercial, genre-defining, and marketing purposes. On the contrary, it is only with the greater degree of commodification involved in cinema's deployment of women that the actresses' performance gained a measure of visibility in a public sphere in the making. Such commodification was required and made possible by the opening of new cinemas catering for Bombay's 'mill-hand' inhabitants and the relative expansion of that market. As a cultural-industrial process, the cinema's deployment of women, the commodification of their images, constituted a public sphere in the true sense of the term—a sphere, that is, in which not only aristocrats and priests, but also white- and blue-collar workers were included.

The utopian, modernizing dimension of these early women action films is perhaps most evident in a figure like Miss Padma (3.3a and b), an actress cast alongside 'dare-devil' Boman Shroff in a stream of successful stunt films directed and produced by J.B.H. Wadia.[5]

In his unpublished autobiography, J.B.H. Wadia wrote:

I made my last silent thriller *The Amazon* or *Dilruba Daku* [w]ith Padma in the stellar role. The [s]tory was the reverse of *Thunderbolt*, with Padma as the masked woman and saviour of the people. Of course, I had to avail of a duplicate in female garb to enact her stunts. Even so, Padma had become an adept in fight sequences and her youth and beauty added glamour to the film. It was the box office success of *The Amazon* which had induced me to sign Fearless Nadia in my talkies to come, with whom I was to make that super-stunt film *Hunterwali* and take the Indian film world by storm. (Wadia 1978: ch. 43)[6]

2.3a: Miss Padma in *The Amazon/Dilruba Daku* (J.B.H. Wadia 1932) (courtesy of Vinci Wadia, *Screen*, 7 June 1985, p. 17).

2.3b: Miss Padma in an action role in *Chalak Chor/Black Bandit* (Raja Shadow 1936, Hindi) (*Ranjit Bulletin*, 26 October 1935, p. 44).

Given the trouble of coaching Padma to act in fight scenes, what was at stake in making sure that she would perform at least part of the stunts was the fact that, unwittingly or not on the part of the director-producer, a new dimension would insinuate itself into the final image: nearly undetectable fragments of movement that were recorded by J.B.H. (or Homi) Wadia's camera because it registered the presence of a specific, historical woman engaging in body gestures that were capable of constituting a spectacle worth paying for.

Compare the picture of Miss Padma in *The Amazon* with Durga Khote's as queen Kilotala in *Maya Macchindra*. Durga's image, evoking also images of 'veeranganas', foregrounds a dimension which was social and political: the modernity and valour of the woman in the film was a measure of the modernity and the greatness of the nation. Images such as these were constitutive of a political process, nationalism, which mobilized discourses of social modernization as understood by a coalition of forces that, at its best, was preoccupied with questions of social reproduction. This too is a dimension of the films that we should take seriously because it encourages us to read these images mimetically, as symptoms of specific social relations, to filter the image of the woman's performance through the lenses of the particular ideology that provides the skeletal backbone and structure for that performance, and, ultimately, to confuse the signs of a woman's subjective experience for the frame that is mobilized to control it. There is an important difference between Durga's image in *Maya Macchindra* and images that exploited the commercial potential of the woman's 'youth and beauty' more directly. The live stage dances performed before or after Sharda's films displayed women's bodies in movement, but they did so encased in the legitimation (or rationalization) devised by pre-modern court and village rituals, just as the historicals and mythologicals in which Durga acted anchored and reduced her actions to discourses of military valour, family honour, and other feudal concepts remobilized by nationalism. Even so, the coded forms of dance and of performance in general contained within them, as a covertly present but essential component, the libidinal charge that could be derived—and monetized—from seeing women deployed in gestural registers that exceeded the prevailing norms of socially prescribed modesty. Cinema and, with it, films like *The Amazon* gave the kind of display of women's bodies in movement that could be found in dances and other such performances new, industrialized rationales by absorbing it into the narrative by way of 'action'. To begin with, then, stunt film advertisements, such as the ones quoted earlier, emphasized the extraordinary, the impressive, or the exciting because the possibility of seeing a woman doing things she would not normally be seen doing was what the films offered for a small price affordable to a section of the population to whom live dances, let alone more impromptu types of performances revealing aspects of a real woman's way of moving, had not been accessible in the past. So, although the terms used in these advertisements are common enough and the tone certainly similar to advertisements the world over, in a place and time where a well-entrenched taboo obtained against the presence of real women in the public sphere, films such as *The Amazon* were truly out of the ordinary.

Second, the way that women were (and are) inscribed into action cinema as lead performers of action or stunts highlighted a dimension of the performance that emerged in the necessary discrepancy between, on the one hand, the coded and directed enactment of a role and, on the other, the specificity of a particular actress's indexically registered presence. A space opened up between role and presence in which a particular actress may inscribe her sense of agency in the way that she enacted the scripted and directed (or conventionally coded, as in a dance) role. This space in which physical action conveyed a subjective presence, or, rather, the presence of subjectivity, is also the space that action cinema sought to monetize by exploiting it as a competitive advantage against other genres, like historicals and mythologicals, that were (are) more geared towards the reproduction or regulation of socially desirable registers of (female) behaviour. Casting women in roles that enabled them to adopt gestures and perform movements that exceeded or, at least, significantly diverged from the prevailing codes of modesty thus simultaneously gave the producer a competitive advantage, something valuable to sell, while providing the actress with an opportunity to affirm her subjectivity in the way that she moved her body.

Whether such marks of subjective agency remained merely at the level of marks, as serial affirmations of mere subjective presence, or whether they were elaborated (over a space of a film or even many films) into a veritable discourse of subjectivity, would have to be established by way of an analytical-critical reading of a particular actress' enactment of prescribed roles and functions. Unfortunately, for all the success of *The Amazon*, a figure like Padma, whom J.B.H. Wadia used to refer to as 'a beautiful creature from Bengal', did not materialize again on the Indian screen of the 1920s and 1930s, nor have any of these silent action films survived. Her subjectivity and that of the other women who, like Padma, acted in these films, can today only be imagined as a double absence—

of the woman and of the film as a reproducible item that, ironically, is no more. J.B.H. Wadia, however, continued to make women 'stunt films' after the introduction of sound, even if his new star was a solid Australian, and a blue-eyed blonde at that. This enables us to further explore these questions in relation to the films featuring that peculiar combination of commercial and nationalist discourses which was Mary Evans, known in the 1930s as the action film star Fearless Nadia.

In an essay in which she used Negt and Kluge's critique of Jürgen Habermas's conceptualization of the public sphere to discuss early American cinema's utopian potential, Miriam Hansen wrote:

[E]ven as the public spheres of production reproduce the ideological, exclusionary mechanisms of the bourgeois prototype [industrial-commercial interests] also aim, for economic reasons, at a maximum of inclusion. Lacking [legitimation and] substance of their own, they voraciously absorb [c]ontexts of living that are hitherto bracketed from representation—if only to appropriate, assimilate, abstract, and commodify vital areas of social experience and if only to render them obsolete once exhausted and thus again insignificant. It is in their potentially indiscriminating, inclusive grasp [t]hat the public spheres of production make visible, at certain junctures, a different function of the public, namely that of a social horizon of experience. Negt and Kluge refer to this emphatically inclusive horizon by the self-consciously anachronistic term 'proletarian public sphere,' which they see [n]ot [as] an empirical category [b]ut [as] a category of negation in both a critical and a utopian sense. Negt and Kluge locate the utopian possibility in the very process of (alienated) production, in the 'historical organization of labor power'. For while constituted in the process of separation, [l]abor power contains and reproduces capacities and energies that exceed its realization in/ as a commodity: resistance to separation, *Eigensinn* (stubbornness, self-will), self-regulation, fantasy, memory, curiosity, cooperation, feelings, and skills in excess of capitalist valorization. Whether and how those energies can become effective depends on the organization of the public sphere. (Hansen 1995: 141–3)

Films featuring stunt woman Fearless Nadia involved the greater visibility of images of real women in the public sphere over a larger share of the national territory—an intensification of the indexical marks of the woman's presence *and* the commercial exploitation of those marks. The double nature of this movement is important because the inclusion of elements previously excluded from, and the broadening of the registers of experience deemed suitable for, representation went hand-in-hand with a drive to commodify some of those experiential marks but not others. This commercial drive ultimately rendered some of the newly assimilated and commodified marks once again insignificant, but never to return to the status-quo-ante. The range of things that came to be seen as suitable for cinematic representation in the 1930s overlapped, to some extent, with the range deemed representable in the past and more were added. But as new elements were included, others were left behind. This selection process was not symptomatic of a forward linear trajectory of progress towards modernity. For one thing, from the mid-1930s, even as the registers of body movement shown on the Indian screen became more permissive, Indian women in action roles more or less vanished, to be replaced by the safer image of a white woman. The point of retracing the terms of these inclusions and exclusions is that, over the growing number of films produced in India in these decades by a variety of producers, such terms can themselves be read as marks, symptoms of a generalized, unconscious, but very specific sense of a direction or horizon for 1930s India. To ascribe such choices to individual figures like directors, for instance, says very little about the social function of the films they made. In the first part of this chapter I have argued that it was commercial pressures that led to the broadening of the field of representation and, with it, to the inclusion into films of images of real women. Such images emerged in the 1920s and continued to characterize the cinema of the following decade because they had a social function. Had they not, they would have become obsolete. To understand what made Fearless Nadia films possible or even necessary, we must thus first examine the economic conditions and pressures that led, in the 1930s, to the intensification and re-modulation of those commercial pressures. Among other things, this will entail addressing in some detail two knotty questions of Indian cinema historiography: the introduction of synchronized sound and the emergence of distribution.

Nadia's films played out the conditions of their possibility at many levels. After outlining these conditions, I will return to the films to examine how Nadia 'moved' within the limits set by the economic pressures that underpinned her films. Nadia is understood here not as a biographical entity, but as a cinematic figure which, precisely as cinematic, bears the indexical traces of a specific historical subjectivity. A subjectivity is not an abstract concept. It is the unstable and very real effect of discursive strategies to which attach specific temporalities, and the historical layers and socio-economic blocs that constitute them. Through an analysis of the films' strategies of narration, I will discuss the ways in which Nadia's films staged specific horizons, possibilities deemed open to 1930s India, and how, from within those possibilities, some (and not others) are presented in the films as preferable. But the ways in which these forms function—the forms' operation as strategies of narration and address—are rooted in, and were ultimately orchestrated by forces 'outside' the texts that must be closely reviewed. If, as I contend here, narrative forms draw their function and meaning from specific historical forces and their movement, then the economic-historical fabric in which the cinematic figures do their 'figuring' must be drawn into the textual analysis. Its conceptualization becomes part and parcel of the analysis and thus of the understanding of the films as affects and functions of the public sphere, of the social relations constitutive of that fabric.

THE 1930s

In the early 1930s, economic pressures intervened that crucially refashioned the Indian public sphere and, with it, the Indian cinema that addressed and shaped it. Although somewhat weakened by the World War I, the pattern of colonial exploitation of India had remained fundamentally unchanged until 1929. With the Depression, it underwent a qualitative shift. From 1929, as manufacture in Britain and in every other country in the industrialized world more or less collapsed, Britain developed a new kind of imperialist interest in certain types of dependent industrialization, in India and in other parts of its empire. From the early 1930s, moves towards indirect economic control through collaboration with Indian business groups began to include the setting up of subsidiary manufacturing units behind tariff walls by foreign companies (Lever Brothers and Metal Box in 1933, Dunlop and Imperial Chemicals by 1936–7) as well as the device of foreign-controlled 'India Limited' groups. Significantly, by 1935–6, items like electrical goods, sugar machinery, telecommunications, and wireless apparatus had almost caught up in value with textiles in British exports to India.

From the point of view of the Indian bourgeoisie, the Depression did create a number of problems. Agricultural prices had started declining from 1926, but from 1930 the collapse was catastrophic. However, the slackening of the old forms of colonial economic ties also presented opportunities for major advances on other fronts. Commercial and rural depression led to a transfer of capital from trade, usury, and land purchase to industry. Apart from market protection, provided by the Lancashire crisis and government tariffs, Indian industry actually benefited from the fact that agricultural prices declined much more sharply than industrial prices. Throughout the 1930s, when the world's largest economies were experiencing sharp falls in industrial activity, India's manufacturing output grew at roughly twice the rate of that of the US, the UK, and Germany. Indian mill production of piece goods went up from 2356.5 million yards in 1929–30 to 2982.7 million in 1932–3 and 3905.3 million in 1938–39. Sugar, cement, and paper industries also developed rapidly in this period, while Tata Steel became strong enough to do without protection from 1934 (Sarkar 1983: 257–60).

The most important feature of the 1930s expansion of India's large-scale manufacturing was sectoral diversification. While the share of the country's two main traditional industries, cotton and jute, began to decline, other industries, like sugar, cement, paper, and matches developed, bringing about a spread of industrial processes and factory organization into sectors of the economy that had previously been served only by handicraft or by imports. For our purposes, industrial expansion and diversification impacted on the social make-up of the country in one fundamental way. Contrary to cotton and jute, which were situated in or around Bombay and Calcutta, the new industries were located away from these cities. Sugar plants, for instance, were concentrated in the Punjab, Bihar, and Orissa. Simultaneously, existing industries also began to decentralize, most notably textiles. The technology of textile production was such that a region with a large unskilled labour force and limited capital had advantages, especially when the demand for cotton products shifted from yarn to cloth as it did in the 1930s. Many mills thus opened across the country, most notably in the south, while the number of mills in Bombay city decreased proportionally (Morris 2005: 607–42).

India's population increased rapidly during this period—by 10.6 per cent in 1931 and 15 per cent in 1941—adding 61 million people to the country over a period of ten years (resulting in a total of 389 million in 1941, against 338 million in 1931). By 1931, Bombay had grown into the British empire's fourth largest city and its population rose sharply during the decade. But with the crisis of its cotton mills, which now competed with mills outside Bombay Presidency as well as with Japan, the migratory influx to the city slowed down (Kosambi 1986: 54–7). At the same time, censuses for this period indicate that urbanization across the country increased at an unprecedented rate: whereas in 1921 and 1931 the urban population represented respectively 31.1 and 37.5 per cent of India's total population, in 1941 49.7 per cent of Indians lived in cities. Most of this urban growth was concentrated in the north, around Delhi, the Punjab, and Uttar Pradesh, and in the south, in Madras, Bangalore, Travancore, and Cochin (Morris 2005: 648–51). Figures show that it was directly connected to the increment of employment in factories in these areas.[7]

By contrast, whereas in 1911 employment in the textile industry and in public administration represented respectively 33 and 2 per cent of the Bombay's working population, in 1931 public administration employees had grown to 6 per cent, while cotton mill workers had dropped to 31 per cent of city's working population (Kosambi 1986: 59). Finally, whether in Bombay or elsewhere in the country, in factories or in the service sector, real wages, which had been falling from 1907 until immediately after World War 1, increased fairly significantly in the inter-war period (Morris 2005: 647).

In 1927 India had a total of 309 permanent cinemas, seventy-five of which were in Bombay Presidency, with twenty-one of these in Bombay city itself. The following year, the number of permanent venues dropped to 241, but by 1938 it had risen by 393 per cent to 1213 permanent units and an additional 444 touring cinemas (Dharap 1978: E-3). If the figures reported in *Cinema*'s annual for 1933, which gives the number of cinemas in that year as 1200 (Bhaumik 2001: 116), are anything to go by, this expansion of the exhibition sector took place during the first half of the 1930s. Be that as it may, four points need to be made. The first is that, in spite of their exponential increase, in 1938 India still had a comparatively low number of cinemas (one cinema for every 320,692 people), a situation that has not radically changed to this day. Second, however low the density of cinemas across the country continued to be, the sharp increase in the number of venues in these years took place at a time when, due to the arrival of synchronized film sound, the costs incurred by exhibitors also rose sharply and suddenly. According to an advertisement in *The Times of India* of 21 April 1931 (p. 18) addressed to the managers of 'small cinemas', Western Electric's sound projection equipment cost Rs 16,625 'excluding custom duty, landing charges, port dues and freight from port of entry to theatre'—and this only a few years after the average cost for one film had ranged between Rs 10,000 and Rs 25,000. Third, the expansion of the exhibition sector in the 1930s did not go hand in hand with a comparative expansion of production, that is if we take the number of films made as reference. These increased by 189 per cent, from 91 films in 1927 to 172 in 1938 (Rajadhyaksha and Willemen 1999: 30–2), by far the largest proportion of which were in Hindi. If, on the other hand, we take capital as a point of reference, the picture changes somewhat. For the moment it is enough to observe that average production costs did increase sharply: from the second half of the 1930s, figures reported in the *Indian Cinematograph Year Book* indicate that a film could cost anything between Rs 60,000 and Rs 113,000 to make (1938: 87–98). J.B.H Wadia's accounts corroborate this.

During this decade, Bombay's cinemas doubled in number, from twenty-one in 1927 to forty in 1938. Of these, twenty-two showed only Indian films, ten only foreign films, and eight a mixture of both. Of the city's nine cinemas with 1000 seats or more, seven were exclusively devoted to Indian films. But finally, and most importantly, Bombay figures show that by far the majority of the 904 new cinemas that had opened across the country between 1927 and 1938 were located outside India's main urban centres. A new and smaller city like Bangalore, for instance, that was growing under the impetus of a textile sector that had begun competing with Bombay in this period (Nair 1998 and 2005), in 1938 had no fewer than thirteen cinemas. But smaller towns also accounted for the sharp rise in venues. The number of copies made per film for distribution increased: while in 1927 no more than six copies were made, in 1938 the number of copies for a Hindi film ranged between twenty and twenty-six; by contrast, a film in Bengali required an average of eight copies (*ICY* 1938: 87–98). Crucially, a comparison between Sharda's revenues from a single film (as projected in the company's floatation prospectus) and those of the big-budget Wadia Movietone production *Jai Bharat/Victorious India* (Homi Wadia 1936) (as reported in the *ICY* of 1938), reveals that while in 1929 65 per cent of Sharda's revenues came from the Bombay market and 35 from the combined sales in Bangalore, Lahore and Calcutta, in 1936 the situation had reversed: the Bombay circuit, including Sind, represented no more than 33 per cent of *Jai Bharat's* total revenues, while the combined revenues from the Central Provinces, Delhi, the United Provinces, Lahore, the Punjab, the North Western Frontier Provinces, Bengal, and Madras were responsible for the remaining 67 per cent.[8]

Given the sharp rise in the number of cinemas across the country and the increasing weight of a market outside India's main urban centres, the rise in the number of copies made per film is, however, not as significant as may at first appear. It suggests that in the 1930s films did begin to circulate over a larger and more dispersed territory than in the 1920s, and that the polarization which characterized the 1920s was clearly no longer so sharp a feature of the Indian cinema-scape, but films also circulated at a much slower pace than was the case at the time of Sharda. Whereas in 1927 a film in a small cinema in a non-urban area would not stay on the bill for more than two days, revenue figures and the number of copies made, on average, per film indicate that in the early 1930s a film would not only reach parts of the country it did not reach before, but also that, once there, it stayed longer on the bill than had been the case five to eight years earlier. This means that available audiences had grown in size. As a result, production costs increased fourfold (if not more) at a time when the rupee was kept at a high rate in order to sustain the value of the British currency within the gold standard. Films became longer. Much of the rise in costs must be accounted for by the larger number of copies made, the higher cost of (sound) stock, and the longer shooting time required by sound production—anything between two and seven months in the mid-1930s, while Sharda and other companies of the 1920s released an average of ten films per year. Production costs also increased because, with a larger available market, now a film could afford to be more expensive to make. Accordingly, publicity costs also became an important item of a producer's budget: big-budget productions like *Jai Bharat* and *Zambo/Sher-e-Jungle* (M. Bhavnani 1937) which cost a total of Rs 110,000 and Rs 112,500, respectively, each devoted Rs 25,000 and Rs 21,000 to publicity (*ICY* 1938: 85).

Finally there was transport. Interestingly, as the following extract from an article by I. B. Patel in the *Indian Cinematograph Year Book* clearly states, as late as 1938 transport costs were shouldered by exhibitors:

[T]he exhibitors get no concession in the freight from the railway companies though they pay roughly Rs 35 lacs [*sic*] [Rs 3,500,000] annually to the railways for circulating the films from one part of the country to the other. Now, if the Railway Companies gave some relief in freights, the turnover of films will increase and the cinema will be enabled to penetrate into the interior. This expansion of rural cinemas will ultimately benefit the railways. (ibid.: 323)

I.B. Patel's complaint raises a number of important questions. To begin with, given the number of cinemas now operating across the country, Rs 3,500,000 'annually for circulating the films from one part of the country to the other'—equivalent to an yearly sum of Rs 2885 or a weekly Rs 55 per cinema—was not a large figure, not even in 1930s India. I.B. Patel's attitude towards this figure is a good indication that while in the 1930s the demand for films outside India's main cities had indeed grown, a network was not in place for circulating films. Hence the sectoral position on behalf of which I.B. Patel advanced his complaint: 'exhibitors'.

However reliable the information contained in the *Indian Cinematograph Year Book* may actually be, its importance as a document about, and by, the Indian film industry lies in the fact that it represents one of the early manifestations of a new group of operators, distributors. Film advertisements of the 1920s, which were placed in the newspapers and paid for by exhibitors, mentioned the name and the location of the cinema in large letters, but did not carry information as to how the advertised film could be booked. Moreover, as I have mentioned in Chapter 1, in spite of the large numbers of films produced in that decade and the shortage of cinemas outside the cities, whether a booking agent had helped to finance the films of one or more producers, he remained tied exclusively to a single producer. Everything in the *Indian Cinematograph Year Book* of 1938—from articles such as I.B. Patel's to personality profiles, films' revenue figures, numbers of cinemas per city, and advertisements for industry-related products and services (which included carbons, lamps, and arcs for projection, as well as film distribution services)—suggests that while in 1938 this was no longer the case, distribution was still only just beginning to emerge as a distinct sector, dependent on but separate from producers and exhibitors. The *Indian Cinematograph Year Book*, edited by the Bombay exhibitor Bejan Dadiba Bharucha, was the first of its kind: it constituted the emerging sector's showcase and simultaneously provided precisely the kind of information a (would-be or already operating) distributor was likely to need.

In the early 1930s cinema was not the only sector of cultural production to operate in the face of the absence of a national circulation network, but the answers to two of the knottiest questions of Indian film historiography—when and how exactly did distribution and sound projection emerge?—lie in the manner in which, at a time when sound projection came on the horizon both as an inevitable and considerable cost for exhibitors, and as a means for producers and exhibitors better to exploit cinema's expanding (non-urban) market, distribution developed as the solution to the problem of how to find the capital to realize sound cinema's commercial potential. The Indian newspaper industry provides an important comparison and useful reference point for the development of both film sound and distribution. Indian-owned newspapers arrived on the scene in the second decade of the nineteenth century. In the beginning, whether British or Indian owned, all newspapers in India circulated quite strictly on a regional basis, but the introduction of new means of transport and communication in the middle of the nineteenth century—the railway and the telegraph—opened up the possibility for newspapers to be spread over wider geographical areas. In the second half of the century, a number of English-language newspapers, both British and Indian owned, became recognized as 'national' papers and were read in different parts of the country, but they remained rooted in a region around an urban centre (Calcutta, Madras, Bombay, or, in the north, Allahabad). The Indian-language press developed slowly, and was fairly strong only in Bengal and in Bombay until the latter part of the century. It was not until the second decade of the twentieth century that Hindi dailies with significant circulation began to appear, and the impetus came, again, from Calcutta. By the first decades of the twentieth century, the British-owned press had grown into a homogeneous English-language elite press with a 'national' journalistic profile. The Indian-owned newspapers provided a striking contrast: they were highly heterogeneous and segmented on many levels. There were newspapers in English as well as in a multitude of vernacular languages, produced within a range of different technical and financial conditions, and circulated with varying degrees of professional competence exclusively on a regional basis. This situation did not change until the widespread use of computers and digital printing in the last twenty years or so (Stahlberg 2002: 49–55; Jeffrey 2000).

In most cases, Indian newspapers neglected the commercial side; they were idealistic enterprises concentrating on developing and distributing ideas within a relatively localized area, and the nature of the enterprise enabled them to do so. Many never felt the commercial need to address, and thus never perceived the absence of, an integrated national market. The contrary was rather the case: most newspapers survived precisely because no competitor reached their territory. Indian cinema could not afford to do so. As Sharda's operation showed, even if costs were kept to a minimum, films were expensive to make and, from a purely commercial point of view, were worth making only in so far as a market large enough to recover the initial investment and generate a surplus was in place. Whereas Sharda's films were designed to meet the limits of a market that comprised little more than India's few urban centres, the growth, diversification, and expansion of Indian industry in the 1930s opened up new possibilities for cinema. Large parts of a previously untapped territory became available and the possibility of making films in Indian languages did give Indian producers a competitive advantage against foreign distributors, something to attract also the small exhibitors in the less urbanized areas who, perhaps with a recently opened cinema and a limited potential audience, might instead have preferred cheap copies of old foreign films. But the possibility of showing films in India's many vernacular languages (or at least in Hindustani) was not, in itself, enough. Film historians have retrospectively, ascribed an instrumental role to that possibility, buying more or less wholesale into the nationalist underpinnings of much of cultural historiography (and film historiography in particular).[9] But from a purely economic–commercial point of view, the making of sound films in the many Indian languages did not quite make sense. Divested of the nationalist, instrumental credentials that have retrospectively been ascribed to it, the desire to make films in Indian languages appears as no more than one of the ways in which the more fundamental drive to exploit an expanding national market manifested itself. As such, the impetus for films in Indian languages was not triggered by nationalist feelings, but the other way around: purely commercial–industrial interests made it possible, which were then wrapped up in nation-building discourses.

Like the transport of films up and down the country, indeed more so than transport, sound film equipment required large investments on the part of exhibitors. By far the majority of exhibitors were small entrepreneurs who, like producers, had been plagued from the outset by the lack of revolving credit. Sound was thus introduced very gradually and comparatively slowly. Even in Bombay, where at this point sufficiently large audiences, and thus the guarantee of a return on the investment that sound projection represented, had been in place for some time, the city's forty cinemas converted to sound over a period of three to four years. Compared to the time taken by European and American cinemas, this was long. The first Bombay cinemas to make the move were the Capitol, the Empress, the Globe, the Pathé, the Rialto, and the Wellington, all of which showed sound films in 1931. A year later they were joined by the Excelsior, the Empire, and the Alexandra, which showed English-language films, and by the Imperial, the Krishna, the West End, and the Majestic, which showed Indian talkies. In 1933, the Carlton, the Palace, and the Roxy also came on board. By then, the *Bombay Chronicle* had stopped carrying the programme of cinemas showing only silent films, which included the Super, the Vishnu, the Edward, and the Crown cinemas.

Silent films continued to be shown well into the 1930s and Indian silent films continued to be made until 1934. In 1932 nearly twice as many silent films (forty-three) were made than sound films (twenty-eight). The following year sound productions overtook silent films, but marginally (eighty-four as against sixty-seven). The tables were finally turned in 1934, when only eight silent films were made, against 103 sound features (Rajadhyaksha and Willemen 1999: 30–2). Once again, the impetus for this development was provided by the potential of a non-urban market that was emerging due to the expansion, diversification, and decentralization of Indian manufacturing. Unlike other industrial sectors, however, whatever film production there had been in India, the modalities of provision and the cost of equipment caused it, at least until the 1940s, to be primarily centred around Calcutta first and then Bombay. In 1931 the Calcutta-based Madan Theatres still controlled more than 120 of India's cinemas. Madan was among the first companies to venture into sound film production: it released eight sound films in 1931 and sixteen in 1932 (Barnouw and Krishnaswamy 1980: 67). But, unlike other companies, this monopoly also faced the problem of equipping its large chain of cinemas with sound film projection. Confronted with the reality of the enormous cost this would have involved, in that same year Madan began to sell its theatres. In less than two years only one Madan theatre remained, the Regal in Calcutta. While in the 1920s the bulk of Indian films had increasingly been made in Bombay and Bombay Presidency, from the years of the Depression onwards Calcutta production was practically phased out. The so-called 'studios' that opened in the 1930s, like Prabhat and Bombay Talkies, were mostly based around Bombay.[10] What was needed to exploit the non-urban market that began to take shape in the early 1930s was thus not so much film sound or Indian-language films, as, first, a network that would allow films to reach that non-urban exhibition market, second, the financial structure that would enable Indian cinemas to invest in sound projection equipment, and, third, the mechanism that would pump the revenues generated from this larger, non-urban market back into sound film production. From this cycle the capital could be drawn to equip more non-urban cinemas for sound. Banks having historically refused to invest in cinema, a new sector emerged to fulfil these multiple functions.

FROM ARTISTIC PICTURES CORPORATION TO WADIA MOVIETONE

In the early 1930s booking agents were neither heavily capitalized entities nor did they constitute a cohesive, well-organized network. On the contrary, even the ones who were able to invest in film productions could not, as a rule, put up sufficiently large capital for a producer to rely on a single agent. Until the late 1920s, booking agents were tied to producers or to large exhibitors like Madan because there was simply not a developed enough exhibition market across the country for them to do otherwise, in spite of the greater number of films produced in that decade. In 1927, witnesses to the ICC reported that a booking agent's task was to 'receive enquiries for the booking of the films, [d]istribute these films upcountry, collect the hire, get back the picture, and pay the income to the producer each week after deducting [the agent's] dues' (*ICC* 1928: 577). The Indian distributor developed as an entity in his or her own right in the 1930s out of the exhibitors' and producers' drive to exploit a then only just emerging and expanding national market. However, this market remained mainly a horizon with many obstacles in the way of its materialization and exploitation. Indian distributors developed as a distinct sector by inhabiting, coping with, and finally exploiting those difficulties.

Very little material from the 1930s survives today to offer a fully fledged overview of the instrumental interconnections between early distribution and early sound projection and production. According to Barnouw and Krishnaswamy, by 1941 no less than 887 distributors operated across India (1980: 145). This patchwork of small operators suggests, first and foremost, that their role and function were (are) clearly not comparable to those of Hollywood or, for that matter, European distributors at any time. The first advertisements carrying details as to how and from whom the advertised film could be obtained began to appear around 1933. As the advertisement for *The Wife/Ghar ki Lakshmi* (Kanjibhai Rathod 1931) appearing in the *Bombay Chronicle* of 23 May 1931 (p. 15) stated, films could be booked by 'writing to' the producer, or to an agent; at best a telephone number was provided. An important characteristic of Indian distributions at this early stage then, and, by implication, of Indian sound films' mode of circulation, was its slow pace. Equipping a cinema for sound projection also involved considerable time and delays. Western Electric's advertisement, quoted in part earlier, suggests not only that sound projection equipment was comparatively expensive, but also that equipment had to be ordered several months in advance and that supply was limited. Moreover, its cost could be 'spread over one or two years'. Scarcity of material notwithstanding and however anecdotal this approach may appear at first sight, a closer look at the relations between director-producer J.B.H. Wadia, the Super cinema at Charni Road Junction, Bombay, and Manchersha B. Bilimoria, offers a glimpse of how this time–delay factor lies at the root of both Indian distribution and film sound.

What follows is a detailed account of the three steps outlined at the end of the previous section as they materialized in the relationship between these three figures, beginning from J.B.H Wadia's silent cinema production, to Wadia Brothers' transition to sound production in near simultaneity with the Super cinema's equipping for sound projection, and, from there, to Wadias production's in a growing, sound-equipped cinema exhibition market which, although not quite a fully-fledged integrated market, had begun its transformation into as near to a national market as India was ever to see. The chapter closes with an analysis of Wadia Movietone's best-known stunt films that seeks to delineate which aspects of these films were instrumental in making that transition to a national sound cinema market seem possible—how, in other words, the horizon contemplated by a producer, an exhibitor, and a distributor took material form not only in their business transactions, but also in the films' forms and their orchestration. The question underpinning the analysis is this: how did the films' narrative strategies position spectators within social relations that, in so far as they were cinematic, imagined viewers as subjectivities ideal for a dream of industrialization? Elements of this dream governed the making of these 1930s films, as products as much as texts. As we will see in the following chapters, this horizon did not materialize as the constellation inhabited by the Indian film industry until several decades later, at which point it took an altogether different form.

The older son of a Bombay Parsi family that had acquired its wealth through ship-building from the time of the East Indian Company, and a lawyer by profession, J.B.H. Wadia made his first silent film, *Vasant Leela/ Sons of the Rich* in 1928. Released that year at the Majestic cinema in Bombay under the banner of Artistic Pictures Corporation, *Vasant Leela* was made on a minuscule budget of Rs 4000: Rs 2000 from its scriptwriter, J.B.H. himself, and Rs 2000 from its director, G.S. Devare. Devare was then working as cinematographer-director for Kohinoor and *Vasant Leela* actually saw the light of day because the two had full and free access to Kohinoor's equipment and facilities. Defined by J.B.H. Wadia as a 'B class success', *Vasant Leela* generated sufficient revenues for the partners to recover their initial investment, but Devare decided not to continue this precarious operation in film production. Instead he opened a film-processing, - printing, and - editing laboratory on Kohinoor's premises which enabled him and J.B.H. Wadia to make ends meet. Soon after, Wadia also opened Wadia Film Exchange, procuring Indian and foreign films for cinemas. His next venture into silent film production was as scriptwriter and associate director for a more robustly financed Kohinoor production, *Pratigya Bandhan/Bondage* (1929), directed by Devare. The film was shot in just over a month. In order to 'enhance its box office appeal for the masses' (Wadia 1978: ch. 29), *Pratigya Bandhan* was released with the alternative title of *Aflatun Abla*, which can be loosely translated as 'An Amazing Woman'.

Encouraged by the success of *Pratigya Bandhan*, J.B.H. Wadia resolved to make his own film. Writing in his autobiography that the idea for *Pratigya Bandhan*'s story came from 'a successful American serial called *The Broken Coin* [Francis Ford 1915], [starring] Francis Ford, [G]race Cunard and Eddie Polo', J.B.H. also

thrust in the ubiquitous character of a Masked Man, who materialised in the nick of time to rescue the heroine. Its prototype was, of course, Douglas Fairbank's *The Mark of Zorro*. [I] wanted to make a cheap stunt film based on *The Mark of Zorro*, the phenomenal film of Douglas Fairbanks the permutations and combinations of which still sustain a sizeable part of [the] Indian film production sector. I for one must have indulged in returning to the theme or making a partial use of it many a time in my screenplays. (Wadia 1978: ch. 29–30)

J.B.H. Wadia pumped some of the profits generated by his film distribution and processing activities into the silent production *Diler Daku/Thunderbolt* (1931). This too was a very cheap production. J.B.H. shot it with an old Pathé camera 'that was lying around at Kohinoor' and which he bought second hand for Rs 500 (and paid for it in five monthly instalments of Rs 100). In order to avoid incurring the cost of renting a studio and not being able to afford the necessary raw stock, J.B.H. and his brother Homi resorted to shooting *Diler Daku* entirely on positive stock found at 'the fag end of films', in outdoor locations only and in ten shifts. As his lead actor, he cast Yeshwant Dave, who 'had never faced the camera before but was a good gymnast', good at 'somersaults and long jumps' (Wadia 1978: ch. 31). The script was 'derived from *The Mark of Zorro* [with] a few elements from Robin Hood'. He then advertised his new production widely as 'a genuine stunt sensation': the story of 'a masked saviour of the poor, known as Thunderbolt' (*Screen*, 3 May 1985: 14). Very little else is known about the film apart from the fact that it was released under the banner of Young United Players and released, in Bombay in 1931, first at Super cinema. Although, as J.B.H. Wadia himself put it, it was 'a C grade' film, it was, in this category, a great success. After its short run at the Super, *Diler Daku* was thus passed down to the Venus cinema in Parel, which 'was hardly better than a tin shed' (Wadia 1978: ch. 32).

It is at the time of *Diler Daku* that J.B.H. Wadia first met Manchersha B. Bilimoria. Knowing him as 'a successful businessman', the director-producer entrusted Bilimoria with the distribution of the film on a commission basis. A graduate in accountancy from St Xavier's in Bombay, in the first years of the 1920s, while at college, M.B. Bilimoria was working as secretary for New Oil Mills Ltd. In 1923 he began operating as a booking agent dealing in foreign films (American serials and old Italian sword-and-sandals features) and as a small dealer of cinema-related machinery. In 1931 he was acting as Surya's 'distributing agent' for Bombay Presidency while continuing to deal also in cheaply acquired foreign films. In the late 1920s, when J.B.H. Wadia met him, M.B. Bilimoria did all this from a small office on the premises of the Edward cinema. By 1937, four years after the dismantling of Madan Theatres' exhibition chain, M.B. Bilimoria had established a number of business relations outside Bombay 'for the purpose of exploiting and exhibiting pictures controlled by him'. A year later, when the *Indian Cinematograph Year Book* was published, M.B. Bilimoria was 'contemplating expanding the distribution side by opening offices in Nagpur, Calcutta, Delhi, Lahore, Karachi and Africa in the near future' (*ICY* 1938: 37–8). Moreover, as the advertisement on the back cover of the *Indian Cinematograph Year Book* states, in 1938 M.B. Bilimoria was still dealing in 'cine-films machines, spares and carbons for arcs', the latter (used for projection) being his 'specialty'.

In 1928, Edward cinema was still controlled by Madan Theatres. The cinema was either already leased to Bejan Dadiba Bharucha at the time, as an agent for Madan Theatres, or it finally passed under B.D. Bharucha's control in 1932, when the exhibitor joined forces with M.B. Bilimoria. In 1938 D.B. Bharucha figured as the editor of the *Indian Cinematograph Year Book*, but ten years earlier, he was working for Kemp & Co. as head cashier and inspector of the company's shops. In 1928 he leased the Apollo-Surya and Venus cinemas in Dadar-Parel, with partner Tehmuras J. Anklesaria. After joining forces with M.B. Bilimoria, D.B. Bharucha took control not only of the Edward Theatre, but also acquired the Palace, the Surya, the Lamington Talkies, and the Gaiety at Trichinopoli. Not, however, the Super cinema, where *Diler Daku* was initially released. When *Diler Daku* was released in 1931, the Super was a new, recently opened cinema that, however, had been built and equipped exclusively for the projection of silent films. Its opening was pre-announced in the *Bombay Chronicle* on 16 August 1930 (p. 10) with the following advertisement:

> Picture Palace Super Cinema—stylish and stupendous
> [w]ill show only superb silent pictures,
> pictures you will love to see, over and over again.
> Watch for opening date.

But the 800-seats Super did have one advantage. As J.B.H. Wadia's reminisces in his biography,

[The] surprising fact was that there were even Parsi families among its patrons, when the community, by and large, had not been attracted toward the Indian cinema. It was also, perhaps, the only first run theatre then to which batches of Chinese men and women of the Red Light District at Playhouse and its unique white lane also came beamingly week after week. (Wadia 1978: ch. 31)

Whereas the Venus, where *Diler Daku* was soon passed down, was at the time controlled by D.B. Bharucha and T.J. Anklesaria, the Super was in the hands of Parsi brothers Rushtomji and Ruttonshaw Dorabji, who also had the Wellington and perhaps the West End in Bombay. Unlike D.B. Bharucha, who at the time appears not to have had venues outside Bombay Presidency, the Dorabjis also controlled two of Madras's largest cinemas, the New Elphinstone and the Wellington. By 1937 the Venus—'a tin shed' that, however, had 900 'seats', or at least places— had passed under the Dorabjis' control. Four years earlier, in 1933, the latter also converted their more upmarket Super into a sound film venue. The film screened for its reopening was J.B.H. Wadias' first sound production, *Lal-e-Yaman/Sons of the Soil* (Homi Wadia 1933). In the meantime, D.B. Bharucha had 'toured India in quest of fresh avenues of business'. In 1938 he became the 'managing director of All India Theatres Syndicate Ltd, controlling a chain of theatres in Gujarat' (*ICY* 1938: 36).

One obvious way of mapping the relations between these figures and their activities, their consolidation and expansion just as other industrial sectors were also emerging, expanding, and decentralizing, would be to follow the money trail. But in Indian, even more so than in other cinemas, this is not a route fully available for inquiry, at least not to the extent that it would provide consistent and unchallengeable evidence. All we know is that *Diler Daku* generated reasonable profits (Rs 20,000) which J.B.H. Wadia deposited with M.B. Bilimoria 'as reserve fund in his [Bilimoria's] books of accounts towards [J.B.H.'s] next film' (Wadia 1978: ch. 33). J.B.H. also decided to close Wadia Film Exchange and to concentrate his efforts on a new production. The result was *Toofan Mail/Storm Train* (J.B.H. Wadia 1932), a silent film produced under the banner of 'Young United Players (for Wadia Brothers)' and again, released at the Super. Yeshwant Dave was cast in the role of hero and a newcomer, Miss Padma, as the heroine. A trained dog was also cast. The film was again shot on locations, partly to save studio rental costs and partly because its scriptwriter, producer, and director intended the film to evoke the atmosphere of early American serials starring Helen Holmes.

The story of 'a dashing young signal cabin man [Dave] and his lady love [Padma], the daughter of a retired station master, and how they single-handedly outwit a gang of railroad robbers' (*Screen*, 3 May 1985: 14), *Toofan Mail* unabashedly borrowed from Kalem's American serials while simultaneously reshaping elements of the same so that the film would resonate with the changes Indian society was experiencing in the early 1930s.

This film too no longer survives, but we will be able to examine more closely how those elements played in that context when I discuss Wadia Movietone's *Miss Frontier Mail* (Homi Wadia 1936), a Fearless Nadia vehicle that, in some respects, was the sound remake of *Toofan Mail*. For the moment, it is important to note that the title of J.B.H. Wadia's third silent feature referred quite directly to India's fastest mail train. It had, as its producer put it, 'inbuilt publicity'. In addition, unlike in the earlier film, in *Toofan Mail* Padma was cast, the stunts of a woman adding to the film's competitive edge and modernizing appeal. As I have already mentioned, by 1932 the *Bombay Chronicle* no longer carried the advertisements of cinemas showing silent films.[11] So, instead of an advertisement, on 9 April 1932 a picture appeared in the *Bombay Chronicle*, with a title as for a short news item—'A Scene from *Toofan Mail*'—and a caption reporting that 'Miss Padma and Mr Adi Patel play the principal roles in *Toofan Mail* a railway stunt picture produced by Wadia Brothers, to be recently released in Bombay'. Yet not a word was said about the film's dashing male hero. Significantly, the publicity for the film (3.4a) mentions quite visibly the film's distributor but not the cinema where the film was to be shown because it was addressed to exhibitors, not viewers.

It is impossible to say whether all this was the work of Wadia or of Bilimoria. The fact remains, however, that for *Toofan Mail*, a late silent film, a new advertising strategy was adopted. Inspired by the practices of American distributors, J.B.H. Wadia mounted a campaign addressed directly to exhibitors, providing them with 'four-page leaflets offering suggestions for publicity and advertisement, duly supplemented by appropriate slogans, catch-points and blocks of my two poster designs, in reduced size' (Wadia 1978: ch. 33) [3.5]. In this way, the producer-director effectively bypassed newspapers that anyway circulated on a regional basis, reaching, or seeking to reach, a market that, as the advertising strategy indicates, he conceived as 'national' and expanding.

It is at about this time that the *Bombay Chronicle* introduced a new unsigned column, entitled 'Shown on the Screen'. On 3 July 1932 (p. 3) it reported:

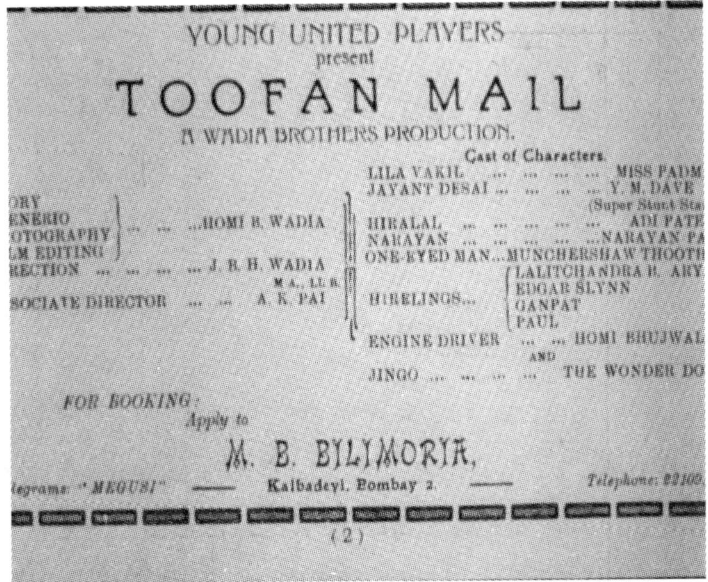

2.4a: Advertisement for *Toofan Mail* from the documentary *Fearless: The Hunterwali Story* (Riyad Wadia 1993), courtesy of Vinci Wadia. Original source unknown.

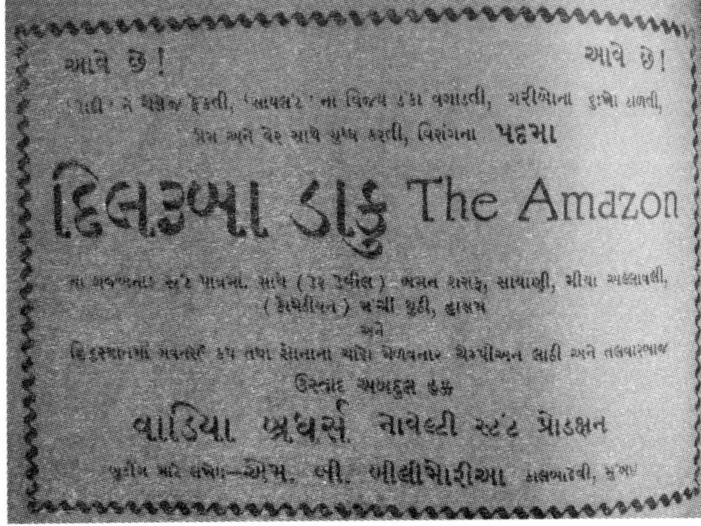

2.4b: Advertisement for *Dilruba Daku/The Amazon* (*Mauj Majah*, 23 April 1933, p. 21).

2.5: Poster of *Toofan Mail* from the documentary *Fearless: The Hunterwali Story* (Riyad Wadia, 1993), courtesy of Vinci Wadia. Original source unknown.

A stunt picture at the Super: Wadia Borthers, whose efforts have resulted in *Toofan Mail*, have changed stunt technique and ideas. Hitherto nothing but meaningless sword fighting and hand fighting against impossible odds have dominated the silent films. They have introduced realistic, original stunts. The picture features Y.M. Dave supported by Mr Adi Patel and Miss Padma. This stunt picture of Wadia Brothers is a Railroad thriller. *Toofan Mail* is, perhaps, the first great railroad drama produced on the Indian screen.

Toofan Mail was indeed heavily marketed as India's first railroad film. Carrying over into the new decade many of the elements that stunt films of the 1920s had made their business to foreground, from physical agility and animals to social mobility and women performing in unconventional ways, *Toofan Mail* pushed the same sales points in a new direction, quite directly incorporating aspects of, and preoccupations triggered by, India's industrialization at every level of the film—from advertising and stratified mode of exhibition to its source of capital and narrative strategies. *Toofan Mail* was a symptomatic instance of this process. Unlike earlier stunt films, *Toofan Mail* presented modernization along an industrial path explicitly and as a desirable horizon. As the extract from J.B.H. Wadia's autobiography quoted at the end of this paragraph indicates, this fantasy was sustained by performative and textual elements that ranged from notions of technology and its unreliability (or destruction) to the mobility required of the actor's body to deal with, adapt to, and use industrial technology. Moreover, just as Yeshwant Dave's stunts were conceived as focusing around that synecdoche of industrialization that is the railway, so the film's mode of production was deemed to demand more sophisticated technology—often in the actual absence of state-of-the-art equipment. Location shooting and the chosen subject matter called for greater mobility of the camera. A fantasy being the all too real perception of a desire, the unavailability of equipment led the Wadias' crew to devise in-house items, like a 'specially manufactured camera dolly for moving shots'—in reality 'a wooden chassis on four second-hand pneumatic tyres and tubes', or a camera crane—'it was rather heavily built and required ten handymen to move it to and fro and up and down' (Wadia 1978: ch. 41, 43). Nor were agility and other acrobatic skills involving industrial technology deployed exclusively by the performing bodies:

Once, after having taken a jump from the footbridge on a slowly moving train, [Dave] was required to run up to the engine and shout to the engine driver to stop the train as it neared a bridge which was half blown up by the villain and his men with dynamite. It was a crude 'trick shot'. For my purpose I required the camera to be placed in the engine with myself, Homi and Yeshwant. ... I [also] wanted to make a thrilling shot of a train going over the camera at top speed. For this purpose, Homi and I hid ourselves in a railway 'nala' (a small ditch) with our second hand Eyemo camera. At the right moment Homi edged it out on a railway sleeper and took the shot of the train going over our heads till the last compartment. To give the effect of high speed the shot was taken with 8 frames per second instead of the normal 16 frames. Then we came out and attended to some more shooting with our artistes on the rail tracks. (Wadia 1978: ch. 34)

As industrialization insinuated itself into the Wadias' silent films as a positive drive, as a cluster of choices that ranged from narrative elements to modes of operation on set and advertising strategies, the type of movements required of the performing bodies in the films changed, visibly and within a relatively short period of time. *Toofan Mail* featured, on the one hand, the agile gymnast Yeshwant Dave in the role of a cabin man

2.6: Poster of *Sinh Garjana/Lion Man* (*Cinema Vision* 1(1)). Original source unknown.

and, on the other, a trained dog. J.B.H. Wadia's next film, *Sinh Garjana/ Lion Man* (1932), released under the banner of 'Young United Players (for Wadia Brothers)' within five months from *Toofan Mail*, sought to fuse the animal and male stunt components while dispersing other narrative elements of earlier stunt films elsewhere in the text. The film tells the story of a man (Boman Shroff) who dons a lion's mask to fight injustice. As the film's poster also shows (3.6), the divinely endorsed physical qualities of the various Hanumans and Bhimas that earlier stunt films had begun releasing, however gradually and reluctantly, from religiously sanctioned, lineage-based hierarchical bonds, in *Sinh Garjana* were carried through, but were entirely divested both of the supernatural character they had in mythological films and of the hierarchical features they retained in a figure like Ganpat Bakre. Similarly, *Toofan Mail* required Dave to display a great deal of agility, like Vithal, but differently so because Dave's role did not carry the latter's aristocratic connotations. This is not to say that this newly acquired mobility brought about vague notions of 'freedom' of movement. Rather, the actors' body movements were now simultaneously remodulated to adapt to industrial needs. *Sinh Garjana*, for one, required Shroff to wear a constricting costume made of a lion's skin and head that severely inhibited his sensory perception.[12] Here is J.B.H. Wadia on the subject:

I purchased a lion's head and skin for my use. Boman used to don it cheerfully and looked a sight and a fright in the bizarre costume. He never complained even when he perspired profusely inside the skin dress, nor when he could not breathe freely in the mask. [I] wanted Boman to take an unusual stunt [s]liding from one side of the hilltop to another with the help of a pulley specially prepared for the purpose attached to the rope. There was a yawning gap of 30 to 40 feet in between. [I] selected the hills on Tardeo Road. [T]he underdeveloped area was still a lush jungle. [A]ny rehearsal was out of question and my dare-devil of a hero volunteered to take the stunt without any thought of the risk involved. He held the pulley firmly in his hands with the fantastic lion mask on his head and as Homi handled the Eyemo camera, he merrily slid over the chasm from one end to the other. When Boman reached his destination he collided against the rocky terrain with such force that the thud sounded like that of a canon-ball. We all clapped in appreciation. Then I shouted to Boman to get up. But he remained motionless. We feared that he had been badly hurt. We all shouted to him in a chorus twice or thrice but he remained dead as [a] dodo. At last he got up slowly and looked in our direction with the mask still on and all of us heaved a sigh of relief. Later on I asked him: 'But why did you not get up at once when we all asked you to do so?'

'What do you mean? I never heard you at all. [I] thought the camera was still on'.

The lion mask had stuck so closely to his ears that he had failed to hear our voices. (1978, ch. 41)

Describing the shooting of a scene in which Shroff had to fight a large group of people and finally be beaten unconscious by them, J.B.H. Wadia concludes:

Boman was somewhat lanky but his bones seemed to have been made of metal. [I]f ever there was a film hero who deserved to be called 'the man of steel', it was [B]oman Shroff. [I] have not come across a more daring stunt-puller than Boman in my experience of fifty years. He never said no to any stunt, however risky it was. I publicised him as 'dare-devil Boman Shroff'. He retired as an artiste many years ago but has continued with Wadia Brothers and has been the production secretary of Basant Pictures, my brother's concern, for the last fifteen years. (ibid.: ch. 39)

The bodies of actors playing action scenes in 1920s mythologicals and historicals could be rather bulky, like Karna in *Maharathi Karna,* because sheer bulk and volume was an expression of the characters' high status. Operating within an Indian profession that retained strong hierarchical and religious categories, wrestlers like Babu J.C. Goho also proudly displayed their bulk, which was simultaneously a sign of their social position and of their physical might. As J.B.H. Wadia's description clearly suggests, the figure of Boman Shroff retained that sense of physical might; by now, however, it was divested of hierarchical status. Accordingly, Shroff was 'lanky'; his physical tolerance or capacity to resist external blows resided not in voluminous flesh or muscles, but in his 'bones of metal'.

In *Sinh Garjana* Boman Shroff wore a constricting costume, all the while displaying the agility of a monkey, the professional skills of a circus acrobat, and the capacity to take a beating. It is in this variety of modalities that one can grasp the extent to which these films staged a fantasy, rather than specific trajectories for, industrialized modernity. Moreover, just as Dave and Shroff's way of being agile demanded not fast swordplay, but strength, 'somersaults and long jumps', so did the strategies for shooting and conveying different types of physical skills change. Whereas Vithal's masterly, ritualized swordplay was filmed from a distance by a static camera that retained the whole body of the actor always in full view, the better to convey (and exploit) the elegance of his characters' aristocratic status, it is clear from the passage quoted above that in *Toofan Mail* the space of the action and the body that moved in it were beginning to be broken up into a series of separate camera shots that highlighted parts of the actor's body and movements from a broader range of points of view than was the case in Vithal's films. I return to this point at a later stage, when I examine the *mise en scène* of Fearless Nadia's films. To anticipate my argument somewhat, it is this sense of a synthetic space that provides the clearest manifestation, at a formal level, of the fantasy of industrialization that films like *Toofan Mail* and, later, *Miss Frontier Mail*, also staged at the level of story content.

Industrial modernity as a positively desirable horizon became central to Wadia Movietone's (sound) stunt films, but trains and the male actor's performance were not its sole diegetic manifestations. The woman and her performance became an essential function for staging that desire, although by no means the only one. Not much is known about J.B.H. Wadia's next feature, *Vantolio/Whirlwind* (1933), apart from the fact that it was marketed as a 'marvelous stunt sensation' under the banner of 'Wadia Brothers', and that, like its predecessor, it starred Boman Shroff and Padma.[13] In the following Wadia Brothers production, *Dilruba Daku/The Amazon* (Ahmed H. Essa 1933), Padma was given the lead. Performing with Shroff and national lathi and sword champion Ustad Abdul Haq, Padma played the role of 'a masked woman calling herself "Rakshita or the Amazon" who donned [that] disguise to fight the evil machinations of a tyrannical minister'. The film's subplot centred on the love between a prince and 'a pretty commoner' (*Screen*, 3 May 1985: 14). I have discussed Padma and the women in silent stunt films who preceded her at the beginning of this chapter. I return to the points raised there shortly, as I discuss in greater detail how the elements that characterized the Wadias' silent stunt films resurfaced and were recodified into Fearless Nadia productions. Here it is necessary to return to the economics of the films and examine the mechanisms and interests that enabled those elements to be carried over into sound cinema.

It is not altogether clear where the money for J.B.H. Wadia's silent films came from. The most likely hypothesis is that the films were cheap enough for the box-office revenues of one film to cover its production cost and generate the capital for the following film. At no time in their silent period did the Wadias have more than one film in production. A revolving production schedule with more than one film on the go kicked in only with the company's shift to sound. As it was, in 1933, after producing five successful silent 'stunt sensations', J.B.H. Wadia found himself with the same capital he had started off with: Rs 20,000, which, again, he left with M.B. Bilimoria as 'reserve' for his next film (Wadia 1978: ch. 46).

In the meantime, as the following extract from the column 'Shown on Screen' in the *Bombay Chronicle* of 30 July 1932 (p. 3) clearly suggests, M.B. Bilimoria had also tried his hand at, or at least had begun directly investing in, film production, all the while continuing distribution for the Wadias (and, most likely, for other producers) as well as the sale of cinematographic equipment and spare parts:

Sweet Angel [aka *Mastikhor Mashuq* (G.P. Pawar 1932)] at Super: Mr M.B. Bilimoria's stunts picture *The Sweet Angel* featuring Miss Amboo and Bulbule, the two popular stars, is to be released from today at the Super. This picture is full of interesting accidents with a sensational plot behind it. The story is of the adventures of an innocent young girl brought up in the jungles, and her companion, who was [*sic*] providentially united. The feats of young Miss Amboo in this picture deserve commendation. The scenes and the photography are up to the mark. This fine stunts picture should not be missed by the public at the Super during this week. The acting of the young Kumar and of the villain are praiseworthy.

After *Dilruba Daku*, J.B.H. determined to produce a bigger picture, a 'quality' film with sound, but he lacked the capital. It appears that so far his dealings with M.B. Bilimoria had been confined to a formal distribution agreement on a commission basis and an informal surplus deposit and book-keeping service. The decision to finally venture into sound production led J.B.H. Wadia to ask his booking agent to invest Rs 20,000 of his own towards J.B.H.'s next feature. Instead, M.B. Bilimoria proposed a more committing and far-reaching deal. Dated 7 August 1933, the contract between, on the one side, J.B.H. and Homi Wadia or 'the producers' and, on the other, M.B. Bilimoria, Nadirshaw Tata, and Burjorji Tata or 'the financiers', stipulated that the Wadias were to make a 'Cinema Talkie Film called *Lale Yaman*'. The financiers were to pay to the producers a maximum of Rs 35,000 to cover 'all out-of-pocket charges and expenses' for the completion of the film, plus a lump sum of Rs 2000 for the producers' labour. In return, the Wadias were to 'transfer to the financiers all rights of exhibition [i]ncluding all necessary publicity matter and one positive print of the film'. M.B. Bilimoria was solely responsible for exhibiting the film 'throughout the world' and for this he would receive a commission of 17 per cent 'on the bookings'. What was left of the revenues after the exhibitor's share and Bilimoria's commission had been subtracted, and the financiers' money paid back, was to be divided between 'the financiers' and 'the producers' on an equal basis of 50 per cent. Finally, and most importantly, the contract committed the two parties to produce and finance two more 'talkie films, successively one after the other'. On completion of the third film, the financiers had the option to 'continue the same business upon the same terms for a period of three years', on condition, however, that 'a studio be erected at their own cost' comprising a 're-producing set of a known make'.[14]

The company thus proceeded to make *Lal-e-Yaman* (J.B.H. Wadia 1933), an oriental fantasy released under the banner of Wadia Movietone.[15] J.B.H. Wadia wrote on the shooting of his first talkie:

Lal-e-Yaman was far from being a perfect film. In fact, as a pioneering effort on my part, it simply could not be. [W]hen shooting was more than half-way through, Homi and I decided to show the rush print to Bawaji [Rushtomji Dorabji of Super cinema] and MBB [Bilimoria]. As a seasoned exhibitor Bawaji kept his reactions to himself. Soon afterwards MBB called me at his office and informed me that Bawaji had liked the rush print. He wanted to convert his cinema into a talkie theatre immediately, provided I agreed to give *Lal-e-Yaman* as its opening attraction. This was like Manna from heaven for me. Why in Dickens should I refuse when other exhibitors had not shown any interest in my film? Accordingly the release was fixed at the renovated Super Talkies on 29 September 1933. [W]e were working at fast speed. But now the tempo became feverish and we finished our shooting schedule working around the clock, going outdoors during the day and shooting our indoors in night shifts. (Wadia 1978: ch. 48)

Two points can be made on the basis of this series of events. First, the partnership set up under the new contract changed the nature of the Wadias' mode of production. Although simultaneous multiple production did not quite set in from the start, the agreement with, and the capital of, M.B. Bilimoria and the Tatas forced the producers into the type of schedule and mode of operation that are constitutive of revolving production. Whereas from the 1930s American studios had financed yearly production schedules by means of a revolving credit system that granted them the freedom to allocate the credit made available by the banks on a year-by-year basis as they saw fit, with no involvement on the part of the banks in the studios' day-to-day operation, it is evident from J.B.H. Wadia's biographic account that this was not the case at Wadia Movietone. Second, from 1933 until the dissolution of the partnership in 1941, all expenditure incurred in the course of production, no matter how small, had to be passed via M.B. Bilimoria for his approval. The only exception being the

sum of Rupees 500 per month [allotted] to [Burjorji] Tata Seth [in charge of the company's recording and camera department] to expend them as he saw fit and he was never asked to render account. The amount may appear to be small today but it was a handsome figure in the early Thirties. [T]ata Seth enjoyed complete autonomy. [N]ot only were our equipment repaired and renovated in the workshop, we also manufactured small spare parts and built a few gadgets. (Wadia 1978: ch. 46)

Whether these were the 'gadgets' that M.B. Bilimoria sold or items like the home-made crane and dolly used on the set of *Toofan Mail* is not clear. What is more important is that as he committed the producers to (a measure of) revolving production—a production the financial management of which he personally and directly handled—Bilimoria simultaneously played an instrumental role in the conversion of Super cinema to sound. The Wadias' previous features, although silent, had proved to be good box office. Whether the money for the Super Cinema's sound projection equipment came (as a loan or otherwise) from Bilimoria, or whether it had simply been Bilimoria's offer of exclusive exhibition rights for a sound film that was likely to be good at the box office to convince the Dorabjis to put up with the cost of sound projection, the fact remains that M.B. Bilimoria emerged as a distributor in the fully-fledged sense of the term as a result not of his production-financing capacities, but of the specific nature of his intermediary role between producer and exhibitor. Caught between two sectors of the film industry that, although older and more developed than his line of business, did not have the capital to take the one step (sound conversion) that had by now become the condition sine qua non for their survival and growth, M.B. Bilimoria functioned as a factor towards the solution of a problem which, that very year, caused the collapse of Madan Theatres.

M.B. Bilimoria was not the solution, but a 'factor' towards it because he too did not have the kind of capital required for sound conversion. Since 1931 he had been acting as Surya's representative for Bombay Presidency, but in 1933 Surya closed down, perhaps cutting off its booking agent from his existing south India connections. According to its producer and director, *Lal-e-Yaman* cost some Rs 60,000 to make. Publicity, fifty trailers, and no less than twenty-five prints involved additional costs that may well have represented anything between Rs 20,000 and Rs 40,000. The film played at the Super for a record of fourteen consecutive weeks (Wadia 1978: 'The Story behind the Making of *Lal-e-Yaman*'). The company's extant account statements[16] show that, after the exhibitor's share and the distributor's commission were subtracted, *Lal-e-Yaman* revenues from the Bombay Presidency area amounted to Rs 68,131, equivalent to 47 per cent of the film's total net realizations from the domestic market (Rs 145,139). The remaining 53 per cent came from the

Central Provinces, Lahore, Calcutta, Madras, the Punjab, and Delhi areas, with the latter generating by far the largest income outside of Bombay Presidency (Rs 34,396). Estimating (generously) the total cost of the film to have been Rs 100,000 and assuming (from the high number of copies made) that the film was released more or less simultaneously in each of these areas (where, however, it is unlikely to have played for as long as it did in Bombay), a little mathematics suggests that *Lal-e-Yaman* must have recovered its cost of production comfortably within the fourteen weeks it played in Bombay. In his autobiography, J.B.H. Wadia states that 'the investment was recouped in less than six months' (Wadia 1978: ch. 48).

Some more mathematics show that from all this M.B. Bilimoria was left with a gross income of Rs 40,093. By far the largest share of it came from his commission (about Rs 31,295), which was calculated as a percentage (17 per cent) of the gross revenues as they were (most likely) after the exhibitor's share of 40 per cent had been subtracted and (certainly) before subtracting production costs. By contrast, M.B. Bilimoria's own net share of the box office amounted to no more than Rs 8798. On the basis of an initial investment of Rs 11,660, the distributor of the Wadias' first talkie thus made a net profit of Rs 28,433, equivalent to a 243 per cent rate of earning. But the crucial significance of these figures is not so much the speed at which M.B. Bilimoria made his investment work, but the extent to which the distributor's (by far) biggest interest lay not in the size of the surplus generated by any one film he invested in (his net share of the box office), but in the sheer volume of its circulation. Bilimoria's main source of profit was the commission on distribution, and this was calculated on a film's gross revenues. Although the various contracts between the Wadias and the financiers set a high interest on any money borrowed above the capital initially agreed with the financiers, everything suggests that, initially at least, as a small financier, M.B. Bilimoria would himself have had to borrow the money. Charging interest over the bank rate would have generated some profit for him, but it would not have been a significantly high gain. At the same time neither would Bilimoria have had any true interest in keeping the cost of the film down. The only thing that really made a difference from his perspective was a film's gross income, from which he drew the largest share of his profits.

As to what came on top of M.B. Bilimoria's commission, that is to say his share from the box office after the exhibitor had drawn his due and production costs paid back, it was a sufficiently small percentage of the distributor's overall earnings to allow him to hold it back. And M.B.

Bilimoria did just that, not only with his share, but with everybody else's. Indian newspapers having traditionally circulated exclusively on a regional basis, a producer based in Bombay had no real means to know when and for how long any one of his or her films played outside Bombay and a few other cities. M.B. Bilimoria exploited to its full potential the horizon (the fantasy) of a national market for cinema, by capitalizing on the time gap between, on the one hand, the moment an exhibitor handed over to him the 60 per cent share of the box office due to financiers and producers and, on the other, the moment of delivery of that share to them—exploiting, in other words, the delay between a national market as aspiration, horizon, or fantasy and its commercial realization. As Vinci Wadia, J.B.H.'s son, also observed, M.B. Bilimoria 'made J.B.H. wait'.[17] Instead of returning it, M.B. Bilimoria made that money work in a way that was likely to enhance the gross box-office revenues of the films he would distribute next. Whether this type of operation involved direct investment in a cinema's conversion to sound or more indirect facilitations is not the point. A late agreement, dated 27 January 1941, between M.B. Bilimoria and Super cinema stipulated a number of safety clauses to the exhibitor's immediate advantage. For instance, if in any week during the exhibition period allocated to a film the box office fell below the floor at which it was profitable for the exhibitor to run the film, the distributor would 'make good of the deficit'. While, at one level, this provided a safeguard for exhibitors—a safeguard which ultimately sustained the expansion of the exhibition sector in semi- and non-urban areas, at another level it also provided a buffer for producers, keeping a film running and exploiting its shelf life to the utmost. This is to say that in the early 1930s, when the expansion, diversification, and decentralization of other industrial sectors created new possibilities—a larger potential and primarily semi- and non-urban market for Indian cinema—sound film projection and production emerged as, simultaneously, the way to realize that potential and the obstacle to its realization. The Indian distributor developed by functioning as the 'egg-timer' that presented to exhibitors the creation of the dispersed lumps of capital needed for their cinema's conversion to sound as a possibility and, in one single move, made possible the production of the kind of film that would make that horizon become real and good.

To put it another way, it is not suggested here that distribution emerged in India as a result of account fiddling. There was much more at stake than small-time gambling. M.B. Bilimoria's operation acquired its shape from the lack of an integrated national market. It required the

1920s booking agent to find himself caught in a new set of economic and social contingencies that, far from being unique to the cinema, were brought about by, and shaped every other sector, of the Indian economy and public sphere: unprecedented degrees of nationwide industrialization and, with it, the emergence of a national market for film, larger, more widespread chunks of the population beginning to be transformed into an industrial labour force endowed with some disposable income and leisure time. The 1920s booking agent became a distributor by finding himself at the receiving end of, and thus finding the means to exploit, the difficulties involved in adjusting to the new situation. The one essential factor in the generation of the capital required to overcome these obstacles was timing. And the likes of M.B. Bilimoria, 'a successful businessman', used it to the utmost, in the process enabling the slow expansion and consolidation of an exhibition sector equipped with sound projection cinemas. Whereas Madan Theatres was a large, centrally managed operation, M.B. Bilimoria acted as an intermediary between small producers and even smaller, for the most non-urban, exhibitors. The smallness of the agencies and of the amounts involved lent M.B. Bilimoria a great deal of flexibility within a time factor that he could expand and contract as he saw fit. And it was that factor which was ultimately instrumental in the introduction of sound cinema in India, over a large territory, in the absence of large capital and of an already integrated national market (as was the case in the US). By the same token, the dispersed clusters of contacts across different sectors of the industry—with individual exhibitors, producers, and cinema equipment dealers—that made M.B. Bilimoria's flexibility possible and functional meant that while, at one level, the 1930s did bring about greater division of labour within the film industry, in effect, when Indian distribution developed in the same decade it did not grow into a cohesive, horizontally integrated sector, but into a multitude of small operators, each fending off his or her own vertical line of business deals.

By 1937, M.B. Bilimoria was 'contemplating expanding the distribution side by opening offices in Nagpur, Calcutta, Delhi, Lahore, Karachi, and Africa in the near future' (*ICY* 1938: 37–8). A look at Wadia Movietone films' net realizations over a few years shows that whereas in 1933, 47 per cent of *Lal-e-Yaman*'s income came from Bombay and 53 per cent from the rest of the country, from Wadia Movietone's second sound feature, *Baag-e-Misar/The Garden of Egypt* (J.B.H. Wadia 1934), onwards, 60 per cent or more of a film's income came from areas other than Bombay while Bombay Presidency itself never again generated more than 40 per cent.

Significantly, Wadia Movietone's largest share of income did come from the 'Delhi, Lahore [and] Calcutta' markets.[18] The sources of this were all sound productions, but not all were, to begin with, stunt films. In 1934, soon after *Lal-e-Yaman* and in quick succession, Wadia Movietone made four films in a variety of genres, including a mythological: *Veer Bharat/ Heroic India*, *Baag-e-Misar* (J.B.H. Wadia), *Kala Gulab/The Black Rose* (J.B.H Wadia), and *Vaman Avatar* (J.B.H. Wadia). Of these, only *Veer Bharat* was a stunt film, an inexpensive 'stop-gap' production with Boman Shroff. This type of schedule, based on spreading the risks over a cluster of different, well-tested selling points, was carried through into the following year. It was in 1935 that Mary Evans was brought to the attention of M.B. Bilimoria and Wadia Movietone's producer. What J.B.H. Wadia saw when she walked into his office was 'a blonde young woman, milky white skin, pearl white teeth and a flaunting torso. She carried a sexy figure which even then was rather on the plump side'. Having made *Dilruba Daku* with Padma and having realized the commercial potential of a stunt film with a woman in the lead, when J.B.H. learned that this woman 'had been in a circus as a young girl, [w]as now a dancer-cum-acrobat on the stage in North India, and [was] a hot favourite with her audience' (Wadia 1978: 'The Fascinating Story Behind the Making of *Hunterwali*'), he saw that she could become one of the means by which Wadia Movietone expanded its market. Mary, or rather Nadia as she was soon to be known as,[19] was thus put on the payroll with plans to cast her in the company's stop-gap stunt productions as well as in their other films.

FEARLESS NADIA'S STUNT FILMS

In J.B.H. Wadia's own words, Padma was a 'beautiful creature from Bengal'; 'petite' and 'doll-like', her beauty was 'eye-filling'. Nadia could not have been more different. In addition, Nadia's Hindi 'was nothing to write home about'. Nadia was thus coached and her commercial potential tested. She was given the second role opposite Sardar Mansoor in *Noor-e-Yaman/Light of the Land* (J.B.H. Wadia 1935) and a part in *Desh Deepak/ Light of the Nation* (aka *Josh-e-Watan*, J.B.H. Wadia 1935), a tale of succession infused with nationalism the script of which (by Joseph David of *Alam Ara* fame) was apparently inspired by the history of 'ancient Iran' (Wadia 1978: '*Josh-e-Watan: An Experiment that Went A-Wry*'). In the film, Nadia played the role of a slave girl. She was given a song and dance number and, in a scene in which her character was being sold at the slave market, J.B.H. had '[t]he slave dealer drag her on the dais dressed in scanty clothes revealing her limbs in no uncertain terms. He describes her beauty limb by limb and I took close-ups of her legs, her buxom torso, her pearly teeth, her sparkling eyes etc. Vasant Jagtap was my cameraman' (ibid.: 'The Fascinating Story behind the Making of *Hunterwali*').

Although clearly not the petite beauty that Padma was, the producer recognized that Nadia's female traits could be better exploited because, unlike Padma, Nadia was white. But there was another aspect to Nadia's presence. When the time came to test her stunt skills, she was cast in *Hunterwali/The Lady with the Whip* (Homi Wadia 1935). The following extract describes a moment in the shooting of this film:

She was supposed to swing from one end [of the hall] to another by holding a chandelier as her enemies were pursuing her. I was present and I suggested that since the stunt was hazardous we should use a duplicate. But Nadia refused and insisted on taking the stunt herself. [W]e took a rehearsal keeping our men ready to catch her in case she slipped but nothing untoward occurred. So Homi gave the signal for the shot. [B]ut as luck would have it the rope broke and she slipped down. [N]ow where stunts were concerned, I was always most cautious and I suggested that we should not take the swing with her. [S]he again insisted to take the stunt herself after a new rope was tightly fixed to the chandelier. She gave the shot convincingly. (ibid.: 'The Fascinating Story behind the Making of *Hunterwali*')

Did the rope break under Nadia's weight? Whether it did or not, the fact is that in spite of their initial skepticism—about Nadia's skills as much as about her 'plump' appearance—in the end the filmmakers deemed that Nadia 'gave the shot convincingly'. In the textual analysis that follows I discuss the factors that made Nadia's performance appear 'convincing'. Here it is enough to say that *Hunterwali* was premiered in Bombay at Super cinema, like every other Wadia production before it. Its cost of production is not known, but given that *Hunterwali* was intended as a stop-gap production, it is unlikely to have cost more than other Wadia Movietone productions of that type. Its 'convincing' stunts, however, meant, for one thing, that *Hunterwali* brought in roughly twice as much in box-office revenues as any of the company's previous films, Rs 256,148 to be precise (after exhibitors' share and the distributor's commission were subtracted). So far, *Lal-e-Yaman* had held the Wadia Movietone's record, and that had brought in Rs 152,793. Significantly, *Hunterwali* played particularly well in the north, the largest share of its revenues coming from the Delhi, Lahore, and Calcutta circuits, as well as, of course, from Bombay Presidency.

Little differentiated *Hunterwali* from the many films that, since the 1920s, had sought to distil the stunt ingredient from their given narrative format—except Nadia's performance. *Hunterwali* was a costume drama. It opened with a prologue setting the scene for a disruption of royal succession. The 'wicked prime minister Ramanlal' has killed the ruler and throws his sister and her infant son Jaswant out of the palace. Twenty years later, the adult Jaswant (Boman Shroff) is hit by a royal car and given a bag of gold in compensation, which he refuses, in the process earning the admiration of Princess Madhuri (Nadia). When Ramanlal imprisons Madhuri's father and tries to force her to marry him, Madhuri becomes the masked Hunterwali, 'protector of the poor and punisher of evildoers'. But Jeswant surprises Hunterwali as she bathes in the nude. After a long duel, he captures her and hands her over to Ramanlal, claiming the bounty the minister had put on her capture. Hunterwali manages to escape. Less predictably, she joins forces with Jeswant and, jointly, they defeat the minister. (Rajashyaksha and Willemen 1999: 263). *Hunterwali* was a Ruritania tale or costume drama that proposed an interesting compromise: the alliance between lineage succession and more or less judicious commercial enterprise. We have, to begin with, the incorporation of royal blood (Princess Madhuri and Jeswant) into an economy in which power is no longer unproblematically administered through lineage and in which monetary concerns loom large. However, within that compromise formation, there is the refusal of monetary compensation from a fancy royal car, signalling the rejection of an economy oriented towards the production of luxury industrial goods and those who can afford them. The option preferred instead is the bounty or ransom, which Jeswant can rightfully claim because he chances upon a different idea of modernity, symbolized by the naked, white Hunterwali, and because his fighting skills are such that they enable him to gain control over her.

Nadia's commercial potential as initially spotted by J.B.H. Wadia lay in creating situations that showed her doing untoward things for a woman. Bathing in the nude was one of those, but *Hunterwali* did much more than that. As Hunterwali, Nadia was scantily dressed and shown engaging in strenuous physical activity, wearing shorts that revealed large parts of her white and abundant flesh as she moved. Unlike Padma or, for that matter, Yeshwant Dave and Boman Shroff, but rather in a way reminiscent of many a male hero of 1920s mythological and historical films, Nadia fought several soldiers at once or jumped over high walls all the while carrying around the physical bulk deemed appropriate to the royal status of a Princess. A prominent scene in *Hunterwali* in which Nadia runs after and jumps onto a cart in motion seems to have been designed to show precisely that. Nadia's actions in this scene are marked primarily by her weight. Her costume (tight shorts and knee boots) emphasizes the bulk of her behind, which she drags, finally, onto the cart with very visible difficulties. Moreover, it is as if the scene—consisting of a long shot either through a frontal camera at more or less 90 degrees from the line of action, or otherwise placed behind the cart—had been put in especially to display Nadia's body in all the splendid fullness of its (partly naked) bulk.

Hunterwali's novelty lay not in its Ruritania format, nor in the casting of a woman performing stunts. Like 1920s stunt films featuring women in the lead, *Hunterwali* worked on the commercial and modernizing potential of showing a woman doing things she would not normally be seen doing. But this is not to say that the indexical mark of her physical presence was the same as that of an Ermeline or a Padma. As far as Nadia is concerned, even a passing glance at the films tells us that her appeal lay in the combination of sheer bulk with mobility and strength. The royal heroes of 1920s historicals and mythologicals could be bulky, but they hardly moved. While Nadia's combination of bulk and mobility may strike us, today, as awkward, what was 'convincing' about her performance as she gave it to the camera was this yoking of physical movement in a style already pioneered by Dave and Shroff with (her) voluminous flesh. *Hunterwali* paired the modernizing connotations of images of women doing unconventional things with notion of status, or at least with the sheer physical volume associated with hierarchical status, as in the body of a Karna or in traditional wrestling. By attaching it to the body of a modern, white woman, volume-as-status was inscribed as a factor of modernity. Dave and Shroff's films too evoked notions of modernity, and their bodies were indeed agile, but in their films the body endowed with agility and similar physical skills had lost most hierarchical connotations. Nadia brought these connotations back through the back door and, what is more, presented volume-as-status as available for, or adaptable to, a variety of uses which were marked, in the films, as modern and desirable.

Nadia could run, jump, ride a horse, swing from a rope, lift weights and men, throw punches, wield a sword, shoot a gun, swim, ride a bicycle, and even drive a car. She could also dance, but women had done that for the stage and for cinema for some time. Some of her skills, like dancing, swinging from a trapeze, or riding a horse, she was likely to have learned during her circus and travelling live-performer experience. But for the rest she was trained at Wadia Movietone, which had a gymnasium and very efficient and bold extras on the staff whom I dubbed 'The Fighting Squad of Wadia Movietone'. Every morning they were ready for practice with Nadia, and later on John Cawas. There was a trapeze, a double bar, also a rope attached to a tree for practicing acrobatic swings and also weightlifting equipment. The contingent used to devise novel stunts and fights. The floor was fully covered with sand and they fell on it cheerfully and bounced up again, like football. It was here that Nadia practiced holding a man overhead in her hands and John Cawas holding two of them each in one hand. The artistes would climb up the tree holding the rope and reach the top up to 15 to 20 feet high. (Wadia 1978: 'The Fascinating Story Behind the Making of *Hunterwali*')

No matter how much coaching and training she would be put through, images of Nadia's body in movement were marked indexically by her weight. That lent her performance a special appeal, because Nadia's heaviness provided the Wadias with a point of departure for the distilling of a (visual) sense of movement out of the full, actual presence of a human figure in motion. Nadia's actions, in *Hunterwali* as in her other stunt films, consisted of gestures that were designed to display agility, yet nothing in Nadia's body suggested lightness and ease of movement. Training gave Nadia the capacity to perform the gestures evocative of agility and strength—to implant into the diegesis the ideas or concepts of agility and strength. Her female sexual appeal connoted those ideal skills or gestures as positive and desirable, but her weight did little to give a visual dimension to those concepts. Other elements were thus added in the diegesis to anchor the impression of physical effectiveness. Unlike contemporary Indian action films, the soundtrack of which is designed to convey the effect of strong physical impact, in *Hunterwali* and other Fearless Nadia films a soundtrack was added to each and every action scene that was designed to compensate for Nadia's plump appearance. Consisting of high-pitched shouts by several voices, including a female one, possibly Nadia's own, this sound track added lightness and rhythm to the action scenes.

But a different indexical mark than the one left by Nadia's female, heavy presence was added to the mise en scène primarily through the casting and performance of Boman Shroff and, later, of John Cawas. Unlike Shroff, whose athletic and agile performance I have discussed earlier in this chapter, John Cawas was a physical culturist and weightlifter. Winner of the 1930 All-India Bodybuilding Championship, Cawas had acquired a reputation for his muscular strength (3.7), which he displayed in feats like carrying a Chevrolet containing four passengers on his bare back. While Shroff's performance lent agility to Nadia's action scenes in *Hunterwali*, Cawas's helped to distil from Nadia's bulky presence a sense of muscular power.[20] From *Miss Frontier Mail* onwards, Cawas was regularly cast as Nadia's partner in action, while Shroff contributed to the choreography of scenes as 'assistant director'. Moreover, for scenes requiring a great deal of swinging and other mid-air acrobatic skills, the Wadias resorted to doubling Nadia with Raja Sandow, the leaner and more athletic old-timer of 1920s stunt films. All of this enabled the status-as-volume associated with Nadia's heavy appearance to feature as a point of departure, the object of a transformation in the action scenes, by giving substance to the concepts or ideas (of agility and strength) evoked by Nadia's gestures. The bodies and performance of these men connoted more precisely the nature or type of physical efficacy such gestures symbolically (in Peirce's sense of the term) evoked. This orchestration of performance, image, and sound suggests that Fearless Nadia's films, from *Hunterwali* onwards, played out a fantasy that, far from simply involving the remobilization of volume as status, consisted, rather, in subsuming volume-as-status into a narrative economy evocative of notions

2.7: John Cawas, from *Fearless: The Hunterwali Story* (Riyad Wadia, 1993), courtesy of Vinci Wadia. Original source unknown.

of modernization in order to reformat or reshape the status body into a body type (or types) more suitable for industrialization. The films' narratives and, above all, Nadia's presence quite literally presented modernity as desirable by attaching the signs of modernity onto a female body. But that desirability was more specifically played out as a fantasy of physical transformation—the refiguration of a (female and modern) body that became all the more appealing, 'convincing' or desirable in its cinematic transformation, as it was made to appear mobile and strong.

Made in the aftermath of *Hunterwali*'s unexpected success and as its follow-up, *Miss Frontier Mail* (Homi Wadia 1936) was based on a narrative format that his scriptwriter, J.B.H. Wadia, had already pioneered with his silent feature *Toofan Mail*. In the film Nadia plays not a princess, but the amateur hunter Savita, while her younger brother Jayant (Jaidev) is an amateur filmmaker. Savita and Jayant's father is unjustly arrested for the murder of the railway's station master. As a result of this, Savita meets Sundar (Sardar Mansur), the son of the railways' president who works as a cabin man, and the two fall in love. The true culprit responsible for the murder turns out to be Savita's uncle, Shyamlal (Sayani), who has financial interests in an airlines and who, in his alter-ego of Signal X, wants to cause a train crash in order to promote his air services. A related sub-plot concerns John Cawas, who comes to the rescue of Sundar in his battle against Signal X's gangsters and Gulab, the gansters' boss and Shyamlal's lover. Gulab falls in love with Cawas, whom her gangsters have captured, and leaves Shyamlal for him. Shyamlal does succeed in causing the train crash but in the end, after Jayant catches the gangsters on camera, Signal X is shot down as he tries to get away in an aeroplane.

Whereas the notion of modernity at work in *Hunterwali* remained relatively vague, carried as it was primarily by Nadia's transformation, in *Miss Frontier Mail* modernity is clearly connoted as industrialized. The film's title sequence shows a train passing at great speed and, from the beginning, industrialized modernity, symbolized by Sundar among other elements, is presented as a desirable horizon. Images of the railways as a symbol of that horizon abound. Shots of trains travelling at great speed, crossing the frame, at times shot from the ground, function in the film like a refrain. Often such images are used to mark the transition from one scene to the next, pushing the narrative forward. Moreover, other industrial machinery is prominent throughout: not only trains, but also railways' exchange mechanisms and bridges, cars, aeroplanes, cinematic equipment, special weapons, explosives, high tension electricity lines, and more or less elaborate telecommunication systems. A great deal of attention is paid to explaining how some of the machinery works. Given the importance ascribed to these images and objects from the very opening, one would expect what follows to negotiate the limits and nature of ideas of industrialization. And indeed some of the technology so carefully and ostentatiously displayed is positively connoted, while other equipment is not. Cinema is good and so are the telegraph and trains. These objects are presented as being within ordinary people's, and the heroes', reach. They delineate a horizon that is marked as positive in the sense of possible or achievable. By contrast, the one aeroplane featuring in the film is marked 'Western', while Shyamlal's futuristic wireless (3.8) is secretive and, like his special poisonous gas gun, used for mischievous and selfish ends only. The latter set of equipment thus delineates a type or degree of industrialization that is presented as negative, in the sense of premature and, as a result, as 'harmful'. But beyond these broadly defined and, on the whole, rather abstract boundaries, there is very little in the film that suggests how the desired degree or type of industrialization is to be achieved. Industrialization remains here a horizon, something to aspire to, not a real situation that, in as far as it is already in place, has to be delineated cinematically. To begin with, the limits set to industrialization by the narrative—trains and telegraph versus Shyamlal's futuristic operation—do not seem to work, strictly speaking, as limits. Their function appears simply to be the positive marking of industrialization, as if we were being told that there is nothing to fear about going down the industrializing path. The possibility of industrialization's negative effects, like Shyamlal, belong to the world of science fiction and even when they threaten to materialize, they are, in the end, brought back under control.

Second, in spite of the attention paid to industrial technology, including cinema, and given that its usage is presented in the story as the prime

2.8: Still from *Miss Frontier Mail*, Shyamlal's futuristic communication technology (courtesy of Vinci Wadia).

trigger for the events, *Miss Frontier Mail* is characterized by a remarkable lack of spatial continuity. A crucial sequence in which John Cawas comes to the rescue of Sundar is a typical instance. Shyamlal's gangsters are trying to prevent Sundar from manipulating the railway interchange, so that a train crash can take place. They pursue Sundar out of his control cabin and fight against him, on or along the railway tracks. Cawas witnesses the scene from his house and intervenes, taking on the gangsters himself and enabling Sundar to return to the cabin to resume his work. Throughout, the fight is also witnessed by Shyamlal's lover and the gangsters' boss Gulab. At moments close-ups of Gulab's face inscribe her as the onlooker, as at one time Cawas is, through a medium- to close-up shot. And yet never does the camera actually take up their point of view, presenting instead the scene from either one or the other side of the tracks, irrespective of which character is inscribed as the onlooker.

As Ashish Rajadhyaksha, among others, has argued, the biggest quandary faced by very early cinema, including Phalke's, was how to find ways to tell a story or present a scene only part of which would fit into the camera frame or onto comparatively short rolls of celluloid. Although made in the mid-1930s, at first sight it appears that *Miss Frontier Mail* is characterized by a similar uncertainty. Human figures move to the right and left of the screen with little or no regard for the direction of their movement in the preceding shot—a lack of continuity that contrasts sharply with the immediate sense of direction offered by frequent shots of trains crossing the landscape and the screen towards the camera, at what seem only a few metres from it. In reality, however, that is no contradiction. Seen from the historical perspective of early cinema, the task at hand in *Miss Frontier Mail* was not to stitch separate parts or shots of space or motion back together, but to break continuous space up and, through synthetic space, to convey a sense of movement in the first place. Recurring images of a train moving across the landscape and the frame or towards the camera at great speed do precisely that, indicating that the film's focus was not the carving out of preferred options from a range of available ways of arranging space synthetically. Lack of spatial continuity and of continuity of action is *Miss Frontier Mail*'s very logic—discontinuity itself as a highly desirable objective. And it is this tendency to cut space and motion up as freely as it could be done given the technology and the material at hand that betrays most clearly *Miss Frontier Mail*'s central preoccupation: to be an ode to, and a fantasy of, industrialization, intended as a broad range of possibilities, a horizon the substance and means of realization of which were yet to be visualized (3.9).

2.9: A recurring shot in *Miss Frontier Mail*, courtesy of Vinci Wadia.

While a measure of that substance was given to be seen in the bodies of Boman Shroff and John Cawas as the agile and muscled body respectively, none of their interactions with the star are orchestrated in the films in such a way as to convey a continuous sense of space or coherent clusters of related movements. Most of the action scenes in Nadia's films are conceived as separate vignettes, each displaying two or, more often, a group of people fighting. When Nadia fights her rivals with an ally and co-star, as with John Cawas, the camera tends to be positioned in such a way as to offer the stars' best view, sometimes frontally at a distance and eye level, other times from a higher angle. Occasionally a body part is seen in a medium shot or close-up, but never from the star's point of view, because every one of Nadia's and Cawas's gestures is performed for the camera. The idea of shooting instead the scene in such a way as to convey a visual sense of, say, a fist's physical impact is entirely absent. At best, to use C.S. Peirce's terminology, physical impact is signalled symbolically: a shot of the star performing the scripted action gesture is followed by a shot showing the hit rival, for instance, falling on the floor. The bodies and performance of Nadia's male co-stars do connote more precisely the nature or type of physical efficacy Nadia's gestures evoke, but, for all this, the symbolic dimension of representation dominates in each action sequence of Nadia's stunt films, as also in the performances of her male partners. Significantly, in *Diamond Queen* (Homi Wadia 1940), where Cawas and, with him, stunts evocative of muscular power are given greater room than in other Nadia films, muscular power tends to be conveyed by showing Cawas and Nadia lifting one or two men on their heads. At one point in *Miss Frontier Mail*, the bodybuilder is seen holding two men by their necks, one for each of his biceps, and the camera does dwell slightly longer on this frontally shot image than is the case in other moments of the film where other exploits are performed. But here too the camera remains at a long distance, entirely dispersing the indexical impression of muscular strength that could have been conveyed had the camera cut in on to a closer shot of Cawas's biceps. In this, as in other Nadia's films, physical exploits are given frontally to the camera, not from a point of view rendering the movements in a coherent space of action, as a set of physical interrelations between the diegetic figures.

This is not to say that Fearless Nadia films fail to exemplify moments of the fantasy they so enthusiastically stage at a diegetic level. For all their spatial discontinuities, Fearless Nadia's films remain instances of an incipient industrialization. But the terrain over which they fought that battle was not over the bodies and movements of the film's male heroes. Shroff and Cawas simply anchored Nadia's gestures, the better to make her body available for a range of potentially unlimited figurations of movement. Nadia alone provided the fantasy terrain for notions of industrialization, the incipit of that process, as the idealized figuration of Indian modernity. Heaviness was not the only indexical mark of Nadia's presence. As we have seen, other dimensions of her physical presence on screen were picked up by J.B.H. Wadia from the moment when she walked into his office. But neither can the way in which Nadia gave herself to the camera be reduced to 'blond hair, milky white skin, pearl white teeth and a flaunting torso'. At one level, Nadia was given to move in a space that was, to begin with, diegetically incoherent, discontinuous. Moreover,

[f]or Nadia, [l]ove scenes represented a certain problem, as her way of moving, of dancing and singing didn't correspond to what the public normally expected of a woman. [T]he singing and dancing was often left to the supporting actress. At the same time, Nadia's popularity was also notable for her special sex appeal. (Wenner 2005: 93–4)

Nadia's whole way of moving added to the spatial discontinuities of the diegesis, for it infused the cinematic figuration of movement with a gaucheness that was entirely Nadia's own. Nadia's films abound with instances of bodily awkwardness. A gym sequence in *Miss Frontier Mail* that was quite clearly devised to monetize images of Nadia's naked body parts is a case in point. Nadia's performance in this scene is very controlled: she can be seen carrying out her exercises as if from a fitness manual, and even adding gestures from the generic menu of American serial heroines à la Helen Holmes, such as light little jumps.[21] Controlled except for one moment, when, in the effort of lifting her body from the floor, Nadia bent her knees, lost her balance and threw all codes of female beauty and decorum out of the window (3.10).

It was precisely this gaucheness that made Nadia's 'special' sex appeal, that was constitutive of Nadia's function as a fantasy of modernization.

2.10a–l: Gym sequence: Stills from *Miss Frontier Mail*, courtesy of Vinci Wadia.

Her style attracted the public precisely because it 'didn't correspond to what [they] normally expected of a woman.' There was a dimension in the way in which the actress duly performed the scripted stunts that exposed a kind of desperate spontaneity as Nadia gave herself to the camera. It brought into the public sphere aspects of a woman's and, more generally, of a person's way of being that had not been part of the cinematic repertoire before because they were unmarked, outside existing codes of womanhood as defined by social mores as well as by the market. Ultimately, this also made her 'convincing' material to convey the visual sense of a body in movement and its unbound possibilities—the refiguration of movement not according to the codes of lineage, nobility, and honour, but as an intrinsic, even a defining, quality of the real human body as caught by the industrial apparatus of the cinema.

Another time, perhaps a little at a loss after a stunt and facing a camera still running, Nadia found nothing else to do to recover her wits than to raise her hand in the air and shout 'Hey!'. It was a gesture that she borrowed from the Russian and gypsy dances she had learned before joining the cinema, but which she adopted for the first time in a film scene entirely on her own initiative. The camera recorded the action and the editor did not cut it out. After witnessing the audience's reaction at this very moment in the film, the Wadias were quick to scoop up both gesture and shout and to incorporate them into their next Nadia film, and the next, until a gesture that had been generated as a spontaneous reaction became part of a new market code: a symbol, the films' signature, an ingredient of every Nadia film trailer and poster and, finally, a generic form of 1930s Indian action films.

The 'spontaneous gaucheness' factor in Nadia's performance and the filmmakers' exploitation of its monetizing potential make Fearless Nadia's films an exemplary instance of the way in which the Bombay cinema began to envision a new horizon for itself as a national industry. The films generated added value for Wadia Movietone by appropriating, assimilating, and abstracting vital areas of social experience previously excluded or bracketed from representation. Aspects of that experience (like Nadia's fist gesture and shout) were commodified, abstracted over a series of films, and codified into a genre. Others aspects (like the bending of one's knees) were not, appearing, perhaps over and over again, unwittingly, in Nadia's films without ever being scooped up for commercial exploitation. Written into this more or less unconscious process of selection was a programme: for the first time since its inception, Indian cinema looked at areas outside the country's main urban centres as a national, potentially integrated market for industrialized cultural production. And the films staged just that possibility, breaking space up and, being instances of an industrializing economy, simultaneously positioning and imagining the viewer as an ideal entity for that economy, spatially and physically mobile. In this sense, Nadia's films mediated new terms of social reproduction: this time around, unlike in Vithal's films, the social relations reproduced were such that they were conceived as functional to an economy that was industrial, for that was Wadia Movietone's ideal horizon. As J.B.H. Wadia saw it,

I had planned [*Hunterwali*] as another stopgap film between my melodramatic subjects. But *Hunterwali* clicked at [the] box office like nobody's business. [Its] fantastic success changed the image of Wadia Movietone radically: [it] was metamorphosed into a film company that specialized in stunt films. In result I bade goodbye to my idea of making socials and melodramatic films.

Hunterwali's success changed the company's 'image' and its production schedule. *Hunterwali* told the company's financiers one thing. Here is J.B.H. Wadia, again, describing the situation five years after the partnership was launched:

I convened an urgent meeting of the partners of Wadia Movietone in the studio sometime in 1938. I told M.B. B[ilimoria] that the time had come for Wadia Movietone to go in for social films. M.B. B[ilimoria] said he needed some time to think [it] over. After a fortnight or so he called me at his office. [A]stute businessman that he was, he spread out sheets of paper before me. They were the statistics of the box office returns of some major film companies like New Theatres, Bombay Talkies, Sagar Movietone, Prabhat Film Co., juxtaposed against those of our films. The figures showed that the earnings of Wadia Movietone films in the Bombay Circuit were unquestionably more than those of other companies. They revealed that Wadia films were decidedly more popular in rural cinemas and second run cinema houses. [T]hen M.B. B[ilimoria] smiled, patted me on the back and said: 'Jamshed, we have to run Wadia Movietone as a business concern. We can't afford to kill the goose that lays golden eggs for us. Don't you think so?' I had no answer because it was M.B. B[ilimoria] who always brought in monies for production and I had never felt stranded for want of cash, not even once. In result I produced four more Nadia vehicles: *Diamond Queen* [Homi Wadia 1940], *Bombaiwali* [/*Bombay Girl*, Homi Wadia 1941], *Jungle Princess* [Homi Wadia 1942] and *Muqabala* [/*The Contest*, Nanabhai Bhatt, Babubhai Mistri 1942] between 1939 and 1942. (Wadia 1978: 'N.M. Roy and the Second World War'.)

Over a period of ten years the assimilation, into the existing templates of the historical and mythological film, of modes of human physical action that were marked by traces of a real woman's way of moving enabled J.B.H. Wadia's films to demarcate themselves against those templates.

This incorporation into the text of the film of registers of experience previously excluded from the representable gave the films a competitive advantage. In the trajectory from Padma to Nadia, these new registers—the indexical marks of the woman's actual presence—underwent a kind of mainstreaming. Spontaneous features were scooped up and reproduced over a series of films, abstracted from their existential basis and commodified for commercial exploitation. They became a generic feature. Enabling the people who exploited them to break into the industry and gradually occupy a central, defining ground in and of its stream, these registers of experience and their commodification into generic features can still be read today as symptoms of the direction taken or aspired to not only by a sector of Indian cinema, but of some Indian cinema as a sector of the Indian economy at the time. If these films came, for a time, to exemplify the commercial-industrial template dominant in a specific (the Bombay, the second run, and the rural) market, their narrative strategies helped put in place the social relations necessary to realize that economic horizon. The mainstreaming of newly assimilated registers of behaviour led to the development of narrative strategies designed to sustain and reproduce the social relations of production that would enable India to carry out an unprecedented degree of industrialization and industrial diversification over a larger area than had been the case in the previous decades. In other words, M.B. Bilimoria did not relent.

In 1941 J.B.H. Wadia's determination to return to a more varied generic schedule led to the dismantling of his partnership with M.B. Bilimoria. Homi, Nanabhai Desai, Babubhai Mistri, Nadia, and Bilimoria left to pursue the same line of work under a new banner, while J.H.B. produced *Raj Nartaki/The Court Dancer* (Modhu Bose 1941). Basant Pictures, Homi's new company, continued to exploit roughly the same range of gestures for a few more years. By the early 1940s, however, World War II had begun to change things. Not long after the War, India started the constitutional process that led to its independence. Concrete steps were taken at constitutional level to implement a programme of industrialization. But Indian cinema was not included in Nehru's programme, nor was the Congress capable of implementing too radical a degree of industrialization on a national scale. The likes of Basant Pictures thus found themselves confronted with a situation of uneven development, producing films in an industrial mode without being able to release them in a uniformly integrated or similarly industrialized market. At that point, Nadia's performance became too modern for Indian cinema and, simultaneously, no longer sufficient as a fantasy of industrialization for those sections of the cinema which pulled in that direction. Moreover, other selling points were added, marking the industry's new central ground or stream: animals, songs, new types of bodies, myths, and romance. Ironically, with his customary foresight, J.B.H. Wadia had anticipated the required degree of diversification. But the War prevented his *Raj Nartaki* from breaking into the industry's emerging stream—the feudal melodrama. J.B.H Wadia was thus able to rejoin his brother's operation in the full sense of the term only when Basant Pictures caught up with him and with the industry's emerging melodramatic trend, after experimenting for several years with a variety of narrative ingredients others than Nadia's stunts.

Finally, incipient industrialization in parts of the country and resistance to it in other parts led to the consolidation of a particular generic format: ingredients which were less glaringly or radically exploitable and films, the narrative strategies of which lent themselves more readily as terrains for the regulation of socially desirable registers of (female) behaviour. These films mediated social relations deemed suitable for independent India as it was envisioned by a coalition that emerged as the ruling one in 1948. Its vision did not call for sweeping industrialization, as for instance was the case, in Italy in the 1950s. While the main ingredient of the Indian stunt film, action, became a constituent of the all-encompassing feudal family melodrama, action and stunt alone were no longer deemed capable of sustaining a market on their own. It is to this ingredient alone that I turn to in the next chapter, where, after a brief incursion into the Bombay cinema of the 1950s, I discuss its slow re-emergence as a generic feature of an entirely different constellation, the 1960s.

NOTES

1. On devadasis see Srinavasan (1984) and (1985), Parasher and Naik (1986), Anandi (1991), Nair (1994) and Meduri (1996). On tawaifs see Oldenburgh (1990), Kesavan (1994), Nevile (1996), and Feldman and Gordon (2006). Hunt (1993) traces a parallel dynamics of high status access and, with industrialization, of the greater availability of female performance in eighteenth-century France. Her account clarifies the connection between the visibility of women and the formation of the French public sphere.

2. According to Hindu mythology, Sita, the wife of Rama, had to prove her 'purity' or chastity by passing the test of fire.

3. The prototype of the 'veerangana' draws from Indian folk theatre, songs, and calendar art. It refers to a female figure of aristocratic rank who 'takes over

the throne when a kinsman dies, leads her people into battle dressed as a man, displays astonishing military skills and dies defending her kingdom against invaders' (Thomas 2005: 52). The figure of the 'veerangana' was remobilized by Indian nationalism along with other elements of pre-colonial south Asian culture. For 'veeranganas' in late-eighteenth- and early-nineteenth-century Indian cultural production, see Kathryn Hansen (1992).

4. For more information on Éclair's *Protéa* series, see Bousquet and Mannoni (1992) and Abel (2004).

5. Born in Calcutta in 1913 as Nileemadevi Bannerji, Miss Padma or Padmadevi made her debut in *Prithviraj Sanyogita* (N.D. Sarpotdar 1929) (*ICY* 1938: 651). After working for the Wadias in the silent stunt productions *Toofan Mail, Vantolio/Whirlwind*, and *The Amazon*, in 1933 she joined Baburao Patel's company, Gandharva Cinetone, where her image was radically restyled to conform to more traditional female roles, as in the mythological *Sati Mahananda/Song of Celestial* (Baburao Patel 1933, Hindi). In the 1930s, she became popular as 'Bulbul of Bengal'. Significantly, a promotional biography appearing in *Cinema*'s annual issue of 1933 (p. 57) makes no mention of her earlier action roles. The actress is instead presented as 'fond of music', 'the wealth of her voice' reminiscent of a 'forlon [*sic*] nightingale', while in her private life she is said to be 'an affectionate mother, fond of her home and hearth', and 'an attentive hostess'.

6. For the folk-theatre antecedents of the cinematic 'daku' (dacoit or bandit), see Hansen (1983).

7. For these developments, see also Chandavarkar (1994), Joshi (2003), and Breman (2004).

8. For clarity of argument, here I have not taken into account the revenues from foreign markets. Figures from Sharda's prospectus and from the *ICY* suggest that by the mid-1930s foreign sales had also increased.

9. Barnouw and Krishnaswamy's seminal historiography of Indian cinema, *Indian Film* (1980), is a case in point. The authors invoke the cost of sound projection as the cause for the collapse of Madan Theatres (of its exhibition chain first and then of the company as a whole). However, when it comes to explaining the fact that sound was introduced in cinemas nationwide within years of Madan's collapse, the authors elude questions of cost completely. *Indian Film* thus ascribes the 'popularity' (read: the possibility) of sound cinema in India to the country's ostensibly innate love for (Indian) music, in effect invoking pre-industrial practices as instrumental factors in one of the biggest steps Indian cinema had to take towards greater industrialization.

10. All except New Theatres, which was based in Calcutta.

11. The Wadias' silent stunt films were, however, advertised in the Gujarati magazine *Mauj Mahaj: Sinh Garjana* on 30 October 1932 (p. 4), *Whirlwind* on 12 March 1933 (p. 23), and *Dilruba Daku* on 23 and 30 April 1933 (p. 21 and p. 4 respectively) (3.4b).

12. For the relationship between industrialization and anaesthesia, see Buck-Morss (1992).

13. In his autobiography, J.B.H. Wadia wrote that he deposited a copy of *Vantolio* at the National Film Archive of India (NFAI). It appears, however, that the NFAI has only the film's trailer.

14. Two-and-a-half years later, on 22 December 1935, a new contract stipulated that Bilimoria and the two Tatas would each 'advance a loan' to the Wadias of up to Rs 50,000 (for a total of Rs 150,000). By 1938 the company had accumulated profits amounting to about Rs 68,800. However, the Tata brothers having failed on their commitment and M.B. Bilimoria having advanced most of the money himself, on 5 June 1939 a new contract was drawn up stipulating that while the 'Wadia Movietone partnership' was to continue with a capital of Rs 153,000, Bilimoria was to bring Rs 107,100 ('seven parts') and the two Tatas Rs 15,300 each ('one part each'). Such 'loan' was interest-free, but any additional investment on the part of the financiers above their agreed commitment would be advanced on an interest of 6 per cent 'over Bank rate' (and never below 9 per cent). Whether the remaining Rs 15,300 towards the agreed capital of Rs 153,000 came from the Wadias or from Wadia Movietone's existing capital is not clear, but the share of each partner in the company's profits, losses, and assets was agreed to be 3.5 annas in the rupee each for the Wadias, 7 annas in the rupee for Bilimoria, and 1 anna in the rupee each for the two Tatas. In addition, J.B.H. Wadia, Homi Wadia, and Burjorji Tata would receive a monthly salary of Rs 450, Rs 350, and Rs 350 respectively. M.B. Bilimoria's rate of commission and the exclusive basis of his rights over the films did not change.

15. *Lal-e-Yaman* featured Karimja in the role of prince Parviz, the heir to the Yemeni throne married to Lalarukh (Kamala). Parviz is imprisoned by his stepmother (Mohini), who claims power, but a mystic sufi fakir gives him a magic dagger that makes him invisible. Lalarukh, disguised as a man, rescues her husband who, with his magic dagger, sets out to free his people, killing the Apeman (Shroff) and the genii (B. Khan), rescuing the captive princess (Padma), and finally defeating the soldiers who had been sent after him. In the end the king (Jal Khambatta) learns of the plot and repents, while Lalarukh sacrifices her life so that Parviz can marry the princess (Rajadhyaksha and Willemen 1999: 257).

16. Access to these and any other document mentioned here pertaining to Wadia Movietone, including the contracts relating to the partnership, was kindly provided by Vinci Wadia, J.B.H. Wadia's son. I would like to thank him for his help and for the constancy with which he preserved these invaluable sources of information about a crucial moment in the history of Indian cinema.

17. During a conversation between Vinci Wadia and the writer that took place in Bombay in March 2006.

18. Notwithstanding its melodramatic tone, the following extract (from the text of a speech J.B.H. Wadia gave at the preview of *Raj Nartaki* at the Taj Mahal Hotel in Bombay on 2 October 1942) corroborates my argument about the expansion of the non-urban market: 'Sometime in 1938 or 1939 M.B. B[ilimoria] rang me up at the studio and asked me to come urgently to his office in the premises of Edward Theatres. [W]hen I reached, M.B.B. introduced me to some

five or six exhibitors who had come from North India (from Peshawar, Lahore, etc.) flourishing imposing pathani caps with decorative plumes. They were just eager to have the "darshan" of the producer whose films were their bread and butter. They embraced me in turn and overwhelmed me with their blessings in chaste Urdu. There were tears of joy not only in their eyes but mine also. How I wished I had asked M.B.B. to give me their names and addresses!' (Wadia 1978: 'The Team of Wadia Brothers').

19. Born in Perth, Australia, in 1908, Mary Evans worked with Zacko's Russian circus before touring the Asian subcontinent with Madame Astrova's ballet group, doing live shows in between silent films for British and Indian troops. As India's most popular female action star of the 1930s, she became known as Fearless Nadia (Rajadhyaksha and Willemen 1999: 155). For more information on Nadia, see Wenner (2005). It is worth noting here that *Plunder*, shown at the Novelty cinema on Sandhurst Road, was advertised in *The Times of India* of 7 January 1924 (p. 5) as starring the 'World's Greatest Serial Star, the Peerless Fearless Pearl White'.

20. A letter appearing in *Variety Weekly* of 16 December 1933 (pp. 15–16) states that at the time John Cawas was the 'Chief Instructor of the Hercules Gymnasium' in Pune. Signed by the secretary of the gymnasium, R. Babu, the letter announces that John Cawas was planning to join the film industry, that he was looking for producers interested in employing him, and that he was already training for the role: 'Here are a few of the items he will be performing: supporting a broken bridge on a cliff so that a handful of men, their horse, etc. may safely cross over to escape from the enemy's hands; once more building a wooden footbridge with his hands for the same reason; scaling walls etc.; crossing from roof to roof with the help of a rope, carrying with him the rescued princess at the same time; throwing men clean off as did Elmo and Eddie Polo of those days, together with the work of stunt kings like Richard Talmadge and others; jumping into the river from a great height. [I]t may be added that all Mr Kavas [*sic*] work is going to be real—no camera tricks.'

21. As, for instance, in *The Hazards of Helen: Episode 26* (Kalem 1915).

3

Interlude: The 1950s

THE BOMBAY FILM INDUSTRY DURING
NEHRU'S ADMINISTRATION

FROM THE LATE 1940s, ACTION FILMS MORE OR LESS DISAPPEARED AS A DISTINCT genre. Soon after independence and partition, the Congress officially launched a programme of industrialization, but that particular horizon does not feature in the Bombay cinema of the period in any prominent way. The action ingredient was incorporated into Hindi cinema as an element in the development of socially conflictual narratives within the frame of a consensual nation-building project, but throughout the 1950s it was not used by film companies as the principle means to gain competitive advantage, as it had been by Sharda in the mid-1920s and by the Wadias ten years later. No longer deemed capable of sustaining a market in its own right, in the 1950s action and stunts seem to have lost their function, as if the social ground that cinema was called upon to sustain in those years had grown less preoccupied with notions of physical energy and its uses. The structural conditions underpinning the social fabric had changed and, in spite of the Indian state's programme of industrialization, whole sections of the Indian economy were not as inclined towards industrialization as the state's ideological brief would have them be. As Madhava Prasad (1998b) has argued, Hindi cinema was one of those areas of operation that eluded government influence, but the Bombay film industry was not an isolated sector. The films it produced and their generic features met economic and social considerations that were broader than cinema, let alone Hindi cinema. A closer look at those conditions will enable us better to trace the disappearance of action films in that decade as well as their re-emergence in the early 1960s as a marginalized but important stream of Hindi cinema.

In the first half of the twentieth century, the population of India had risen by 60 per cent, but its agricultural output had hardly risen at all.

The availability of foodgrains had declined and, over a period of fifty years, while urban areas acquired new industrial and commercial advantages, rural poverty increased. Economic historian Meghnad Desai has argued that the Congress's policy de facto slowed down India's growth along capitalist, industrial lines. India had built up a textile industry that was able for a while to compete internationally, and a steel industry, but it lacked machinery and consumer durables. Soon after independence and partition Nehru determined on a policy of industrialization, but not to build on the industries India had established in the previous decades. The Congress rejected the path of growth through exploitation of comparative advantage—exports of agricultural and light industrial goods (especially textiles). Pessimism about the terms of trade, as well as about the prospect of finding western markets for its products, led India into a strategy of import substitution. The country was to build up its own machine-goods industries, restrict imports of 'non-essential' goods and regulate its larger private firms to avoid the formation of monopolies. Throughout Nehru's tenure, this policy of import substitution, with the public sector playing a leading role, dominated social-political strategy. The state mobilized savings in environments with fragile capital markets, but domestic savings proved unequal to the task of ambitious industrialization. As prospects of private foreign capital flows were limited, there was soon a demand for foreign aid. Thanks to the Cold War, aid flowed from both camps, each giving as much for political purposes as for economic assistance. In this climate, exchange rates were regulated or fixed (Desai 2002: 237–8).

Two forces were at play in the years after independence: an industrial 'big bourgeoisie' which, internationalist in intent but not sufficiently strong to compete in the global market, relied on the state and its policy of contained expansion in chosen sectors; and a politically influential, localized, and predominantly landed 'small bourgeoisie'. Congress legitimacy in democratic India depended on the latter. The fundamental contradiction of emerging capitalism in India stemmed, for Desai, from the uneasy cohabitation of these two bourgeois blocks, with the landed small bourgeoisie as the dominant faction (Desai 1975). While Nehru was committed to industrialization and social modernization, the imbrication of this class in pre-capitalist structures led Nehru's Congress to face the paradox of being formally wedded to a programme of industrial development and social progress without having the power to implement the most radical elements of this path (Kaviraj 1997: 58–9).

The (Gramscian) notion of passive revolution has been used by Indian historians to describe this relation of force within the ruling coalition. However, given that, as I have argued in Chapters 1 and 2, the ups and downs of action and stunts as ingredients of the Indian cinema are a discursive expression of the material considerations that confront Bombay cinema as an industry at any given time, a more precise picture of the structural constraints that effectively led the Congress to slow down the putting in place of a capitalist economy (in spite of its ideological commitment to industrialization) is required in order to fully understand why, for the duration of Nehru's administration, action cinema was marginalized. According to Vivek Chibber, the weakness of the Indian policy apparatus has its origin in the refusal of the bourgeoisie to countenance being subject to state discipline. In the 1950s and after, vertical links that would have connected firms to state agencies and state agencies to the Planning Commission were virtually absent, and horizontal flows of information between state agencies were tenuous. The result was that the implementation of industrial policies was left to a bureaucracy that devised its own ad hoc rules of thumb. This created imbalances in the system. Not having an interest in being disciplined, firms fought off attempts to build a state suited to the task. Once the state policy apparatus was in place, the biggest firms were also able to bend its policies to their own needs (Chibber 2004: 199–207). In this situation, the position of the film industry was simultaneously symptomatic and anomalous, not least because, far from being a united bloc, the Bombay cinema of the 1950s comprised sectors and companies that were affected by, and which, as a result, responded differently to, the state's economic policy. It is in the nature of those responses that we can identify the factors that led action cinema more or less to disappear in this decade.

Although in the run-up to independence a section of the film industry expected the Government of India to recognize the potential of cinema, both as a medium and as an industry, the Congress did not do for the film industry what it was committed to doing for other sectors. Nehru himself had remarked that cinema was not a priority for the new nation, causing considerable anxiety in industry circles (Prasad 1998b: 32–3). Significantly, he introduced a ban on the construction of new cinemas which lasted until the late 1960s. In the 1940s and 1950s director Mehboob Khan came forward as a representative of the film industry's demands for state support, but, as is evident from the ICC documents, Mehboob's demands were far from new. Government support—both financial and nominal in nature—had been seen, and sought, as crucial to the development and growth of Indian cinema since the late 1920s. Over the years, prominent industry figures tried to convince the British and Indian governments that such aid would grant filmmakers access to corporate finance and bank loans, freeing producers from exorbitant rates of interest charged by shark lenders and, in the longer term, perhaps promote if not greater integration within the industry, at least more balanced relations between exhibitors, producers, and distributors. But nothing was done until 1969.

While demanding state support throughout the 1950s and after, in line with other industrial sectors, the Indian film industry rejected, bent, and, to some extent, evaded the forms of regulation and disciplining that the state sought to impose upon it. Complaints against duty on imports of equipment and spare parts as well as on raw stock were made repeatedly by producers since 1948, as they had been before to the colonial administration. While these were never successfully bypassed, calls to the government for reductions of entertainment tax were made by exhibitors and by other sectors of the industry since the tax was first introduced in 1922. Over the years, as government steadfastly refused to lift the tax, ways were found of (partly) evading it. In 1969, when the state attempted to introduce a margin of support in the form of the Film Finance Corporation (FFC), powerful sections of the industry did all they could to contain what they interpreted as a threat of state intervention. As I argue in Chapter 5, the threat was real enough but, again, was promptly and typically counteracted. First conceived in the wake of the 1951 Film Enquiry Committee and its report, but implemented only in 1969 as part of a policy package that sought to regulate the movement of finance within the country, the FFC failed to break through exhibition networks and their locally entrenched financial circuits because, since the 1950s, cinema, along with other sectors of the economy, had developed ways of operating that were oblivious to official policy, even though not unaffected by it.

If this way of operating made the Bombay film industry of the 1950s symptomatic of India's broader economic fabric, according to Prasad, an ongoing struggle between two broadly defined tendencies actually characterized Indian cinema in those years:

[o]ne committed to an ideological mission in keeping with the goals of the postcolonial state's controlled capitalist development and aspiring to the achievement of a homogenized national culture; the other moored in a pre-capitalist culture employing a patchwork of consumerist and pre-capitalist ideologies and determined to maintain its hold over the production process from the outside. (1998b: 32–3)

In practice, these two factions coexisted quite peacefully in the 1950s. As Prasad has argued, this coexistence resulted in a generic format that, emerging as the dominant format during Nehru's rule, resolved the 'conflict by staging the complicity of modernizing bourgeois ideology with pre-modern enclaves of power and authority' (1994: 49). While there is little doubt that a compromise of sorts between these temporalities and forces was indeed the preoccupation of 1950s Hindi cinema, for our purposes, the economic fabric that underpinned the feudal family romance must be more precisely delineated than Prasad's seminal book allows. The strategies by which the Hindi melodrama of the 1950s sustained that compromise marginalized cinematic presentations of a fundamental aspect of modernity: the commodification of an individual's physical energy, or labour power. Elements that the cinema of the previous decade had mobilized to gain competitive advantage—stunt and action, but also a woman's way of moving, the visibility of which preeminently testified to social modernization—also vanished with the feudal family romance. In their place, in the late 1940s and 1950s narrative ingredients that seemed designed especially to contain or hold back the commercial exploitation of the most radical aspects of the cinema of the earlier decades began to be accorded priority. Finally, there is the fact that the action ingredient did not entirely disappear. This last consideration suggests that tendencies must have been at work throughout the 1950s that, although not strong enough to commercially exploit this and other ingredients to their full and radical extent, were nevertheless part of the Bombay cinema of the 1950s—recessive elements which remained on standby, as it were, ready to remobilize both action and women at a later stage. This happened when structural conditions began to change in the 1960s. These were anomalies, asynchronic tendencies within Bombay cinema of Nehru's period, but nevertheless constitutive of it. It follows that, over and above the general characteristics of the compromise mediated by the Hindi feudal family romance, the question for our purposes is this: which notion or aspects of modernization must have been at work in the 1950s for the compromise to turn out that way? What kept individual producers from continuing to rely on sales points that had proved effective since the mid-1920s?

Immediately after the arrival of sound, Madan Theatres collapsed, and exhibition was restructured along more localized lines. With the exception of Bombay Talkies, the Bombay film producers that emerged from the mid-1930s were mainly family concerns. In 1947 Bombay Talkies declared bankruptcy. Four years earlier, a breakaway group of the company established Filmistan (1943)—a Bombay-based company that thrived on mid-budget productions selling on their star and music value. Producers who could make more than one hit started their own companies—Mehboob Khan (Mehboob Productions), Raj Kapoor (RK Films), Dev Anand (Navketan), and, of course, Homi Wadia (Basant Pictures)—but even for these relatively big and stable companies, finances were precarious. Films were financed with loans taken by producers from moneylenders who charged high interest rates. Producers pre-sold their films to distributors, who in turn 'sold' them to exhibitors. The producer became the primary risk taker and his or her need to liquidate the debt gave the distributor and the exhibitor considerable bargaining power. As Wadia Movietone's overnight transformation into a stunt-films-only producer indicates, J.B.H. Wadia was already subject to these pressures. But the Wadias, at least, could afford to harbour the hope of an expanding and more integrated national market. By contrast, restrictions on new cinema building, enforced by Nehru in 1947 and in place until the mid- to late 1960s (depending on state governments' individual policies), meant a chronic shortage of cinemas that, in the 1950s, in a situation of expanding film production and growing production costs, gave exhibitors the upper hand, in spite of this sector's actual lack of cohesion and integration across the national territory.[1]

This is not to say that the whole of the Bombay film industry was in line with the Indian economy as shaped by the state's insufficient and structurally weak policies of planned development. While the 1940s were marked by the rise of companies like Raj Kapoor's and other family-run production houses, as well as by the institutionalization of that particular brand of social realism commended by the 1951 *Report of the Film Enquiry Committee*, Mehboob Khan, for one, had clear industrial and global ambitions. On his first trip to Hollywood in May 1947, Mehboob screened and won critical acclaim for *Humayun* (1945). Speaking to the press, Mehboob's distributor, J.P. Jhalani, declared:

If a reciprocal agreement can be made with some large American company to help us build our [the Indian filmmakers'] studios and equipment with the best American facilities, it undoubtedly would be of material benefit to both our countries. When India achieves its independence in 1948 the opportunities in its film industry can be greatly achieved [*sic*]. (*Citizen News*, 24 May 1947, in Reuben 1999: 126)

After the technical innovations of *Andaaz/A Matter of Style* (1949) and in spite of the fact that no facilities existed for the processing of (35mm) colour film in India at the time, Mehboob Khan decided to make

Aan/Savage Princess (1952), a massive colour venture, and the film was screened in the US and Europe. Its production went hand in hand with the building of India's largest studio facilities at the time, Mehboob's own in Bandra. As the ostentatious sets of *Aan* indicate, spectacle and magnificence were to be a reflection of the potential and grandeur of an industry that Mehboob envisaged as having global prestige and scope. And while *Aan*'s epic proportions were to represent the modernity of independent India in the international arena, in India itself Mehboob's film operation stood out as an industrial venture driven by production, relying on comparatively large capitals, equipped with modern technology, and, in spite of Mehboob's lip-service to communism, fully commercial in intent and capitalist in nature.

The true struggle within the film industry was between, on the one hand, this type of radically capitalist operation—film companies like Mehboob Productions that made big-budget film production their primary concern and sought to expand it—and, on the other, fragmented production and distribution sectors entirely dependant for their finances and schedules on the terms and conditions imposed by locally entrenched exhibition networks. In this situation, the likes of Mehboob Productions were far from typical of the 1950s. By far the majority of Hindi films of this and the following decades were produced by small production units relying on precarious finance, competing for the limited exhibition space, and struggling to meet the generic dictates of an exhibition sector whose power to command had increased steadily from the 1940s, practically by default. Industrialization was not a consideration for this and other dominant sectors of the Indian economy, nor was centralization and, through it, faster circulation of films over a territory larger than the patch immediately controlled by any individual exhibitor. From the 1930s a film industry had developed consisting of three separate operators that proceeded to exploit a growing market. While in other parts of the world, most notably in the US, this drive led to greater and state-sponsored industrial integration, in India it triggered the proliferation of a patchwork of inter-sectoral, even clientelist, business deals because this was the agenda within the ruling coalition, the unwritten programme of the power-blocs upon which Nehru's legitimacy in a democracy rested. The cinema that resulted sustained that balance within the compromise: not modernity and industrialization, but their containment.

From the mid-1940s onwards companies like Filmistan, R.K. Films, and Mehboob Productions, elaborated and crystallized the narrative conventions that came to constitute the feudal family romance. Madhava

Prasad has argued that the rise and consolidation of this genre in the 1950s was a result of the fact that by far the majority of films were conceived as single units put together by an impromptu combination:

[T]he producer was at best a small-scale [e]ntrepreneur who could depend on the availability of low-wage casual labor and freelance acting talent with enormous price differences between the stars, the 'character actors' and the extras, and could rent all the requisite technical services and equipment. [T]he sources of finance dictated the logic of film-making and led to the star, the music, the dialogue and other component values taking on an independent existence of their own and entering into combinations for the space of production, outside of which they remained in a 'free' state. (Prasad 1994: 59–60)

This mode of operation was well removed from Wadia Movietone's, where all staff, from star to technicians, scriptwriter, and extras, was on contract because J.B.H. Wadia's ideal template was the factory model of the Hollywood studio. From their inception after World War I, individual Hollywood studios gradually specialized in a limited range of genres. In that context, characterized by a powerful production sector directly or indirectly controlling distribution and exhibition, one of the functions of genres was marketing, that is the branding and differentiation of a specific studio's product. Unlike in Hollywood, in Bombay, from the late 1940s, the Hindi feudal family romance emerged as the expression of a highly fragmented production sector under direct or indirect pressure from exhibitors. In this situation, a broad range of ingredients was relied upon, all the better to break into a stream the discursive terms of which were defined by a patchwork of locally entrenched and culturally diverse operators. As a result, the central stream of Hindi cinema produced a generic frame that was capable of subordinating other generic categories, 'incorporating [d]isparate ingredients' and relegating 'films with a distinctly different generic identity [t]o the more provincial [e]xhibition outlets' (Prasad 1994: 88). 'Disparate', perhaps, but, on the whole, more conducive to sustaining ideas of family, (Hindu) religion, caste, and the regulation of socially acceptable female behaviour, than to disrupting these categories for commercial exploitation.

The Hindi feudal family romance's generic conventions were sustained by, and symptomatic of, the films' function as a means to circulate capital which was generated in an economic landscape shaped by a modernizing centre's failure to enforce its planning policies on a reluctant and powerful bourgeoisie still very much entrenched in localized, regional, and essentially pre-industrial networks. Production centres in the south, like Madras, made a steady stream of socials and other genres that were not, as a rule, seen in the first-run houses across the rest of the country, even if by the late 1950s Madras had grown to boast the best production facilities available to the entire Indian film industry. By contrast, a Hindi film would have some exposure in each of the five exhibition circuits, but it would not, as a rule, be exhibited intensely across the national territory. Melodramas of the 1950s and 1960s, in Hindi and in other national languages, were thus expensive, glossy productions, at times with extremely long turnover times, so that producers, depending on local exhibition networks, remained more or less confined within the allocated linguistic and financial district belt. The cinema produced under these conditions registered precisely that, ignoring action—both as one of the strategies by which greater product circulation could be achieved, and as a cinematic expression of a fantasy of industrialization that was simply not within the horizon of the people who enabled that cinema to circulate.

POST-INDEPENDENCE EUPHORIA AND THE
MARGINALIZATION OF ACTION

In 1977, J.B.H. Wadia wrote:

My early 'stunt films' [w]ere derided by clever film critics and discerning cinegoers. But it is an irony that for the last twenty years, if not more, this trick of the trade has been availed of ad infinitum in our highly rated 'social' films and enacted ad nauseum by our beloved top stars, male and female, of course, with the unsung help of their 'doubles'. [A]fter all, there is little difference between the honest-to-goodness early stunt films and their follow-ups in the social genre. (Wadia 1978: ch. 26)

For once, this veteran of the industry was not quite right. Although by no means devoid of it, the Hindi social of the 1940s and 1950s was not built around action, whether we understand action as a narrative ingredient or as a selling point. Resulting from that particular combination of industrial and pre-capitalist economic relations that dominated in the film industry and which characterized the Indian government's failure to impose its economic policies for capitalist growth, the Hindi melodrama rehearsed the modalities by which India was to become a 'modern nation'. The social, economic, and political issues that were constitutive of post-independence nationalist mobilization—issues of social mobility, industrialization, urbanization, individuation, and so forth—were celebrated in all cultural domains. In cinema they came dressed in different guises, from Ruritania tales of broken and/or re-established lineage to contemporary urban melodramas of romance across castes. A broad range of horizons was imagined for India through these narratives, but the aspirational populism and nationalist euphoria that characterized the first decade of Nehru's rule marginalized entirely, in films as much as in economic planning, the question of *how* social mobility and economic growth were to be achieved. Representations of physical energy, its release from hierarchical bonds, and its commodification were displaced by a more urgent though related sets of preoccupations. Independent India being nominally wedded to a programme of modernization and older systems of social regulation being disrupted, the Hindi melodrama helped negotiate the new terms of socially acceptable behaviour, the relations that were to create India as a nation: the nation-building sets of discourses dominated all others. It was the urgent question of what kind of nation was to be built—to whose benefit?—that absorbed and marginalized other concerns. These other preoccupations (such as individuation and urban labour power) henceforth needed to be couched in explicitly nation-building discourses and conflictual narrative protocols. In that situation, the more radical sectors of capitalism were contained, in the discourse industry as much as in other industries, by the reigning compromise formation or power bloc set on frustrating most of the development state's planning thrust.

Mehboob Khan had dreamed of a fully-fledged industrial operation. Relations of power between the cinema's three sectors, however, determined that, in order to occupy the middle ground in the industry's geography, Mehboob Productions too had to abide by the conventions that had emerged as dominant in the 1950s. This meant producing films that, among other things, more or less banned representations focused on physical energy while squarely castigating notions of individuation. In Mehboob Khan's *Andaaz*, for instance, Dilip Kumar plays Dilip, a young man whose enterprising spirit and personal maturity earn him the trust of Neena (Nargis), the orphaned daughter of a rich man from whom she has inherited a large business. Neeta is married to Rajan (Raj Kapoor), an immature man of her own social class, but appoints Dilip as manager of her company. In spite of this line of events, Dilip, as the ordinary man of modest origins who rises to become company manager, remains a paper-thin figure. Were it not for Neeta's decision—one that will cost her a life sentence in prison, and Dilip his sanity—the film gives little or no indication as to the factors that render Dilip socially mobile, that is to say, if we exclude individuation, which is presented in the film as, precisely, madness. The true problem—bourgeois Dilip's lack of aristocratic status—is never squarely articulated in the film (except in that he drives a flash car while Neeta rides a horse), but displaced instead by a barely disguised issue of lineage: Rajan suspects Neeta and Dilip of adultery. And while the spectator is not encouraged to side with Rajan, it is only by investing the character and persona of Dilip Kumar with signs of aristocratic status (his innate ability to run a company, his posture, and his piano-playing skills) that the film manages to pull us to his and Neeta's side.

By staging oedipal fantasies similarly infused with notions of lineage and offering extremely idealized, childlike representations of the less well-off, Raj Kapoor's films, especially the still extremely popular *Awara/ The Tramp* (1951) and *Shri 420/Mr 420* (1955), made a mockery of the whole issue of how to implement the measures to achieve economic comfort and basic human rights. *Awara* centres on Raj (Raj Kapoor), the son of a strict judge who is forced to move to the city with his mother when, the latter having been kidnapped by low-life Jagga, is repudiated by her husband and thrown out of the family home. The story, which dwells on Raj's struggle to survive in the city's slums, where hunger and the need to support his ill mother pushes him into Jagga's world of smuggling and crime, is told, partly, as a flashback of the judge's memory. Called in to judge the hero, whom he does not recognize as his own son, the judge and father is instead invited to the witness box by Raj's defence lawyer and sweetheart Rita (Nargis). The judge's testimony, prompted by Rita, unwittingly reveals that petty crook Raj is, in reality, the judge's son. The other side of *Awara*'s story is revealed through the criminal, Jagga, who interrupts the trial sequences to address the spectator directly from his shelter in the city's slums: a petty crook because from a deprived background, Jagga had been a victim of the judge's unforgiving law. In revenge, Jagga kidnapped the judge's wife to make him believe, wrongly, that he has raped her and that the judge's wife will thus give birth to a criminal son. When the destitute Raj arrives in the city, Jagga proceeds to disprove the judge's system of belief by turning Raj, the judge's own son, into a small-time crook.

The question of the status of Indian state law as a means to fulfil policy objectives looms large in *Awara*. For the moment, however, the nationalist ground is recovered through a splitting of the law into the two characters of the judge and his adopted daughter Rita: lineage and continuity provide at once the problem and the solution. *Awara*'s story was designed to touch the sensibilities of a nominally reformist middle-class public whose benevolence towards the 'outlaw underdog' was little more than a strategy for containing social unrest. The film confronts the latter possibility as a threat, the potential proliferation of evil crooks like Jagga. As we shall see in Chapter 5, by the mid-1970s, the palliative of reformism is not abandoned, but the state and its legal institutions are no longer thought capable of embodying it. The perspective of the outlaw from the slums—Jagga's end of the tale—acquires, from then on, a new dimension.

Characters like *Awara*'s Raju have often been compared to Chaplin's tramp, but whereas Chaplin's films tended to advance a critique of the system, however humanistic, films like *Awara* made ample room for complacent attitudes vis-à-vis Nehruvian India's social and economic malfunctionings. In *Andaaz* as much as in *Awara*, social mobility is, at worst, presented as an achieved state, rather than as a process. Alternatively, when, under the coating of humour and/or melodramatic tragedy, the factors that may make mobility possible are allowed to surface, the process of achieving it is presented unproblematically in pre-capitalist terms, that is as the achievement of status as patina. We thus have the seeming paradox of an industrial commodity, film, foregrounding in its narratives combinations of lineage and tame social reform that translated as benevolent patronage on the part of an idealized 'better off'.

It was not until the late 1950s, with the financial crisis of 1957, that the first symptoms of disillusion vis-à-vis the accomplishments of the independent state began to emerge in the Hindi melodrama. Firmly rooted in that dominant genre, Guru Dutt's *Pyaasa/Eternal Thirst* (1957), released ten years after independence and partition, was the first in a series of films critically addressing the state of the nation by grafting the personal, emotive layers of the story onto the social, economic, and cultural dimensions of nationalist modernization. The film tells the story of Vijay (Guru Dutt), an unsuccessful poet whose work is sold by his brothers as waste paper. Vijay's desire for recognition as an individual and a writer is matched by his love for Meena (Mala Sinha), his college sweetheart. Meena, however, is married to a publisher who, refusing to publish Vijay's work, offers him temporary employment as a waiter. From a very modest background and reduced to unemployment, Vijay is forced to live on the streets, where he meets Gulab (Waheeda Rehman), a young prostitute who falls in love with him and his poetry. When a beggar wearing Vijay's coat is found dead, Gulab, thinking Vijay dead, uses her savings to have Vijay's poetry published. The book becomes an instant success, but while the publisher and Vijay's brothers reap the benefits, Vijay lies destitute in an asylum. The end of the film has Vijay disrupting a large gathering called by the publisher to pay tribute to, that is to market, the poet's work. Failing to be recognized as the author and forcibly removed from the gathering, Vijay leaves the scene with Gulab.

The modernity of *Pyaasa*'s critique of the ruling coalition, and of the latter's failure to meet the promises of social improvement advanced only ten years earlier, does not lie so much in the fact that Vijay finally fulfils his desire for love and romance with a low-class prostitute, rather than with the upper-class Meena. What makes *Pyaasa* a truly remarkable film is Dutt's determination to directly confront the contradictions of nationalist modernization against a then still-pervasive, condescending sense of accomplishment, within a medium and an industry, Hindi cinema, which was crucially implicated in those tensions. Like *Awara* and *Shri 420*, *Pyaasa* is populated by those masses who had been, and, in 1957 continued to be, excluded by social reforms, and both directors address themselves to the class that was responsible for the exclusion. But whereas Raj Kapoor's films rested on a notion of incompleteness, suggesting that India's social problems could be solved with more of the same reforms, *Pyaasa* located the problem squarely in the fabric of Indian capitalism, that is to say in the middle-class's imbrication in pre-industrial relations. So in *Awara*, Rita and the notion of state law that she embodies are, on the one hand, presented as if dissociated from the lineage-based ideology of Raj's father and, to that extent, proposed as a solution; on the other hand, precisely as the adopted daughter of the judge, Rita is herself a symbol of continuity and lineage. Far from disqualifying her, this fact buttresses her capacity to function as the solution to Raj's problem with the law. By contrast, in *Pyaasa* the ostensibly modernizing economic forces sustained by the Indian state (the publisher and his clique) are seen to have incorporated caste-based attitudes, and, to that extent, to be an obstacle to the achievement of basic universal human rights like freedom of speech and economic welfare.

As he walks away with Gulab, leaving the publisher, Meena, and the public behind, Vijay nevertheless leaves the possibility open, however dimly, for a cultural practice capable of taking on board the voices of a larger sphere than the Hindi melodrama of the 1950s was able to sustain. As Partha Chatterjee has written, in India the market for cinema and other industrial commodities

[i]s spread all over India but it does not incorporate the whole demographic mass of the country. It only skims off a thin top layer of consumers from all the regions, and constitutes itself as an 'all-India' market. This layer, thin as it is in comparison to the whole population, nevertheless includes not only the bourgeoisie, but also most of the middle classes, the richer landed classes and even a section of the relatively better-paid working class. The big bourgeoisie does indeed seek to build homogenous cultural patterns within this market— in the print medium, principally by the adoption of the English language as the practical language for 'all-India' communication, but more effectively in the audiovisual media (radio, cinema, and now television), through the propagation of a peculiarly neutral, aseptic and non-literary brand of Hindi. [B]ut the important feature of this 'all-India' market is that it does not even attempt to include within it the whole of the Indian people. Consumerism in India, which is the 'growth sector' on which Indian monopoly capital banks for continuing its process of accumulation, is a phenomenon restricted only to something like the top 10 or 15 per cent of the total population of the country. The rest are outside the pale of the 'all-India' market, and can never be incorporated into it unless the full historical process of a bourgeois-democratic revolution can be completed. (Chatterjee 1997: 152–3)

In many respects, *Pyaasa* was a limit text that collapsed under the pressure to identify in its very strategies of narration the terms by which to push forward, within the industrial medium of cinema, the progressive aspects of that process. In the 1960s, Hindi cinema split into the broadly defined categories of avant-garde, parallel, and popular cinemas, creating more clearly differentiated genres. Some of these genres did tap into a broader market, others did not, precisely because, while being constitutive of an industry, they sought to push cinema against the exploitative nature of capital accumulation. What follows in the next two chapters is an account of the factors that, over a period of fifteen years, led to a return of the stunt and action films, first at the periphery of the industry and then, by the mid-1970s, as part of the of Hindi cinema's defining ground. The question I raise in relation to the films examined in the next chapter is: how did fundamental aspects of a process of bourgeois 'revolution' and, within it, concerns about value creation, manifest themselves in Hindi action cinema of the 1960s?

NOTES

1. Figures for touring cinemas (Dharap 1978: E-3; Pendakur 2003: 20–1) do not essentially challenge this picture. While since 1938 their number has increased proportionally with permanent cinemas, over the years, touring cinemas have become an almost exclusively south Indian phenomenon. Touring exhibitors operate locally, at best regionally, and have been present in large numbers in the states of Andhra Pradesh, Karnataka, Kerala, and Tamil Nadu. In 1983, they outnumbered permanent cinemas only in the states of Kerala and Karnataka. Elsewhere they have been gradually phased out, either by permanent cinemas or by video parlours. In 1983, twenty-five out of thirty-one Indian states had less than one hundred touring cinemas; fifteen states had none. Since the 1930s, touring cinemas have also tended to rely on a different cluster of films than that screened at permanent venues.

4

The 1960s

THE BOMBAY FILM INDUSTRY IN THE 1960s

THE EARLY 1960s SAW THE EMERGENCE OF A PARTICULAR KIND OF HINDI ACTION film, wrestling movies starring the wrestler Dara Singh. These films were not the only type of Hindi production to contain the action ingredient. However, unlike other films of the 1950s and 1960s, Dara Singh's movies were built nearly exclusively around that ingredient. Their star became extremely popular and remained so well into the early 1980s. Unlike the action films of the 1970s, most notably Amitabh Bachchan's, Dara Singh's wrestling films never demarcated the film industry's central generic ground.[1] In the next few pages I examine the factors within Hindi cinema that contributed to relegating Dara Singh's wrestling films to the margins of the industry.

In the early 1960s box-office revenues increased by 25 per cent. However, under pressure from escalating inflation and from 1966, of currency devaluation, the two main production centres, Bombay and Madras, also saw a sharp rise in production costs. Combined with constant increases in entertainment tax, the rise in production costs led to a significant polarization of the production sector. Whereas in 1963, 13 per cent of all Indian films were made by 'studio-owner producers', 41 per cent by 'regular producers', and 46 per cent by 'other than regular' or ad hoc producers, by 1965, 'regular producers' were responsible for no more than 23 per cent of all Indian films, with 'studio-owners' and ad hoc producers accounting for 19 and 58 per cent respectively of all cinema production.[2]

The insistent calls, made by the trade press of the period to producers and films stars, to help to reduce production costs even as box-office revenues were increasing are a good indication of the Bombay film industry's mode of functioning in this decade. On the one hand, rising production costs forced distributors, the sector which advanced the money for production, to demand a higher share of the box office from exhibitors; on the other, exhibitors, who were simultaneously paying higher entertainment tax, also demanded from distributors a larger share of the revenues, in the process effectively eating into the capital available for production. In India in the 1960s, the power relations between the three sectors were such that these pressures, while resulting in higher exhibition costs, also further strengthened exhibitors. As independent producer J. Om Prakash stated at the time in an article entitled 'The Invisible Sieve',[3]

Of the many problems facing the industry today, the most pressing that calls for immediate consideration is the problem of equitable sharing of revenue of our pictures. Statistics of the box-office collections in all territories show that there has been an increase of about 25 per cent. But simultaneously the share of the distributor has gone down by about one third. These two aspects of the film business reveal the fact that exhibition of films in our country is not based on fair terms. Mostly the distributors have to submit to the dictates of the exhibitors, for whose exclusive benefit pictures are apparently screened (*Filmfare*, 16 December 1960: 42).

India's chronic shortage of cinemas gave exhibitors the capacity to enforce their terms and priorities on distributors and, indirectly, on producers. By the mid-1960s, this led to a situation where less 'regular producers' could afford to make a sufficient number of films to deserve that name: while some joined the category of 'studio-owners', the majority was forced into reducing production to an ad hoc basis. And as a smaller number of producers could also afford exhibition, at least in large central cinemas, the number of films produced and released dropped, reaching, from 1962, record lows not touched since the first half of the 1940s, during World War II. Tamil film production also decreased in the same period.[4]

By the second half of the 1960s, the stand of exhibitors had not changed. Rising production and exhibition costs and higher box-office revenues led to increasing competition among producer-distributors, a situation which further strengthened exhibitors. As producer-distributor Tarachand Barjatya complained in an article entitled 'Producers Must Obtain Fair Terms from Exhibitors',

It appears that there is no limit to the increase in the rentals demanded by exhibitors, and producers and distributors are left with no choice but to submit to their dictates. In fact, producers and distributors themselves go and offer them higher rentals in order to get an early release date for their films. *Sangam/ The Confluence* was screened at a cinema in Bombay on a rental of Rs 17,500 per week and *Oonche Log [/Elite]* was subsequentially [*sic*] screened on Rs 18,500. But because *Pyar Mohabbat [/Love]* was not getting a release date its producers and distributor themselves offered to pay a rental of Rs 21,500 to the theatre. Thanks to this booking other big budget pictures like *Mehrban [/Benevolent]* and *Ram aur Shyam [/Ram and Shyam]* had also to agree to the same rental for booking the theatre. Even at other centres, a number of exhibitors make a combine or pool and start dictating terms—from a percentage plus a hold-over to a high theatre protection or fixed rental. And in every case the producers and distributors now have to pay as rental or protection a bigger amount than what they were paying earlier as hold-over (*Screen*, 14 July 1967: 6).

The writer went on to suggest that the remedy to this situation was for all 'Indian producers to unite and stand up to exhibitors', with whom new terms of exhibition should be agreed upon and applied in centres across the country. But exhibitors, strengthened by the shortage of cinemas, had become too strong and comparatively cohesive a lobby to concede to new and, from their perspective, disadvantageous terms. When, in 1966, a few producers looked for an alternative by marketing films through, and granting broadcasting rights for the songs to, Radio Ceylon, thereby hoping to pressure exhibitors into accepting terms of exhibition more advantageous to the producers, the executive committee of the Central Circuit Cine Association (CCCA), the Indian Motion Picture Producers Association (IMPPA), and the Film Producers' Guild of India issued a statement declaring that 'we will not acquire the films of those producers who violate the [IMPPA and Guild's] decision and if the films of such producers have already been acquired, they shall not be taken delivery of by the respective distributors of the circuit' (*Screen*, 6 June 1966: 1). Still confronted with distribution and production sectors that effectively complied with the terms of, because under direct and indirect pressure from, exhibitors, two years later eleven Bombay producers headed by J. Om Prakash decided to distribute their own films in the East Punjab, Delhi, Uttar Pradesh, and CPCI (Central Provinces and Central India)[5] circuits. This time around the small group of producers found support in the sector's representative bodies, the IMPPA and the Guild, which suspended the release of all new productions in the central circuit (*Screen* 19 January 1968: 1). With a freeze on new Hindi releases and the IMPPA and Guild's threat to stop production completely, in February 1968 Delhi cinemas were reduced to showing foreign films only. A month later, when Bombay producers organized a huge rally 'against exhibitor's high rentals' (*Screen*, 22 March 1968: 1), the Theatre Owners Association retaliated by stopping exhibition in Bombay for 'an indefinite period' (*Screen*, 12 April 1968: 1).

The following week, exhibitors announced the founding of Pradarshak Sahakar Chitra, 'a newly floated concern for motion picture production by exhibitors and theatre-owners in Bombay with an initial investment of Rs 1 crore [10 million] to go into production immediately'. Typically, they invited producers to 'cooperate', including J. Om Prakash, who, four months later, was elected president of the Guild (*Screen*, 19 April 1968: 1).

At one level, this series of events and its outcome was a symptom of the stronghold exhibitors had acquired on the industry over the years, practically by default—as the expansion of production and the emergence of a distribution sector from the mid- to late 1930s had not been paired with an equivalent expansion of exhibition and the formation of a nationally integrated market for films. This imbalance was an effect of a situation of uneven development which, as I will discuss shortly, was in no way unique to cinema. Here it is enough to say that it was symptomatic of a broader state of affairs in which a few urban and industrializing centres produced for a territory otherwise tuned into a rural economy. Nehru's policies in the 1950s had been unable to change that in any radical way. The policies adopted by the Congress from the early 1960s further escalated the divide by eroding the legitimacy of central economic planning. Within the cinema, in spite of the lack of true sectoral cohesion, in the 1950s and early 1960s exhibitors had grown into a powerful bloc. Their leverage was reflected in the distribution of capital across the film industry's three sectors. In 1968, out of a total investment in cinema of Rs 41 crore (Rs 410 million), Rs 26 crore (Rs 260 million) or 63 per cent was invested by exhibitors, while small and large producers were responsible for no more than Rs 6 crore (Rs 60 million, 15 per cent) (*Screen*, 5 July 1968: p. 13).

In November 1968, the state of Maharashtra relaxed existing regulations for cinemas and granted licences for semi-permanent cinemas in areas where the proportion of venues was lower than one per 10,000 inhabitants (*Screen*, 22 November 1968: 1, 12). Significantly, the only opposition to these measures came from exhibitors. At another level, however, producers' attempts to put pressure on exhibitors clearly indicate that in a situation of rising production costs and demand, that is in a situation of industrial growth, the exhibitors' reluctance to expand was beginning to be perceived, in the 1960s, as unsustainable. Exhibitors' reluctance to expand was rooted, partly, in the fact that a shortage of venues was instrumental in maintaining exhibitors' power over the other two sectors. The other factor was the essentially rentier nature of the economy that sustained the Indian exhibition sector. This is to say that exhibitors, perhaps more so than the other two sectors, operated within two temporalities and relative modes of production: on the one hand they played the game as set by rules of market demand, pushing the price up by maintaining scarcity; on the other, they simply resisted the drive for growth that characterizes a capitalist enterprise, enjoying instead the value of their land assets. Throughout the 1950s and most of the following decade the latter tendency dominated. Towards the end of the 1960s, however, in conjunction with the gradual lifting of state governments' sanctions against the construction of new cinemas, Bombay witnessed the opening of a new type of venue: the suburban upmarket cinema hall. The announcement for the opening of the new 'Shreyas' in Ghatkopar is worth quoting at some length, because it points to a crucial aspect of the change that began to take place at the time:

I am not a man from the film industry. Before I built this theatre my only 'association' with films was confined to seeing them. [A]s I have been staying at Ghatkopar, I have felt for a long time that in this fast growing suburb we must have a good cinema house where we could see pictures under ideal conditions, and that it should not be necessary for us, residents of Ghatkopar, to go all the way to the city to see pictures in a good theatre. It so happened that [my uncle] possessed land—a sizable plot—on the main Bombay–Agra Road. Fifteen years ago [an] engineer friend of my uncle [t]old him that it was an ideal site for a cinema-house and that he should apply for a license to build one. [A]n application was made, but the government, which was not in favour of the construction of new cinemas, turned the application down. It was only in 1960, when I established myself in the business of readymade garments, real estate and finance, that I became interested in the project. [S]oon after my association [with my uncle] the license was granted. At first, as a dealer in real estate, I thought of disposing of the lease of the land with the license to a regular exhibitor, or else a regular builder of cinema-houses. But as days passed, I felt that instead of giving the land to others, I myself should undertake the construction project. And as I had friends who were prepared to join me in this venture and undertake financial as well as other responsibilities, we decided to construct the theatre in 1962 on our own. But my original plan was quite modest. We had seen other suburban cinemas and we thought we should build a small theatre with accommodation for 600 to 700 spectators. [B]ut then came the Chinese aggression [a]nd my plan was put into cold storage. [I]n 1964 the plan was revived. I formed a new partnership concern along with a few friends. But this time I had made up my mind that, after all the annoying delays, the proposed cinema-house should not be second-rate but first-rate, as good as the best anywhere in the city of Bombay. [I]t has taken almost two and a half years to build the theatre and fit it with the latest equipment. Considering all the factors, [I] think the time taken to build the theatre is not very long. [T]he design is the original construction of a young and enterprising architect. [N]ormally, the architect is obliged to devise space economy measures. But in the case of our cinema space was no problem. [T]hanks to the huge size of the foyer and lobbies, which are wide enough to hold the full contingent of two shows, picture-goers will never have any difficulties in entering or going out.' (*Screen*, 19 May 1967: 9)

The advertisement for the new Shreyas shows the extent to which the exhibition sector, which had historically been rooted in a rentier economy (Prasad 1998b), was, in the late 1960s, still tightly connected to land speculation. But rentier and real estate economies are not quite the same, nor do land and real-estate speculation fully explain the upmarket character of the new Shreyas. As Madhava Prasad has observed, in the past the economic logic of exhibition had made it so that while exhibitors controlled the largest share of capital invested in the film industry, very little of that capital was actually reinvested in cinema, whether in exhibition—as in improvement and enlargement of existing venues, or in the opening of new venues—or in production. From this point of view, the share of box office claimed by the exhibitor represented a kind of interest on the land occupied by the cinema. By contrast, the advertisement for the Shreyas reveals that while land continued to be a factor in the exhibitor's operation, a new speculative logic was now also at work whereby box-office revenues—how many people and how much they were prepared to pay for their ticket—had become a more central consideration in the exhibitor's profit-making operation.[6] From this second perspective, the amount invested in the construction of the cinema was not rent on land, but 'capital', understood in the fully capitalist sense of the term, as money invested for accumulation through the production and circulation of commodities.

Unlike existing suburban cinemas, the 1071-seat Shreyas was equipped with state-of the-art sound and projection technology, air conditioning, and a large car park. It was the first in a series of new cinema halls catering for a growing suburban (middle and working) class. In the next section I examine the broader economic factors that, from the 1960s, led this section of the population of Greater Bombay to emerge and increase steadily in areas like Ghatkopar that, situated to the north-east of Kurla along the eastern railway, emerged to house the white and blue-collar workforce needed by new industries. Over a period of ten years, these settlements and the perceptibly higher disposable income available to their inhabitants provided the impetus for the opening up and expansion of the exhibition sector with upmarket suburban cinemas. In 1968, figures for Indian film production showed a significant recovery. By then

Madras had overtaken Bombay as India's largest production centre, in spite of Madras' lower allocation of raw stock: out of the 351 films made in India that year, only eighty-nine were produced in Bombay, while Madras made 227, fourteen of which were in Hindi (*Screen*, 10 January 1969: 1, 11). A year later, for reasons that I discuss in the next chapter, the situation reversed itself: Bombay production jumped by 223 per cent to 199 films, while Madras fell to 208. While the type of action film that emerged in the next decade and the conditions that generated it will be the subject of the next chapter, in this chapter I discuss the kind of action cinema that began to be produced from the early 1960s, under conditions of intense competition within a fragmented production sector before the (relative) expansion of exhibition that characterized the mid-1970s.

The dynamics underpinning the relations of force between film production and exhibition were not unique to cinema. Other sectors of the Indian and the Bombay economies underwent parallel developments because they were triggered by the same structural conditions.[7] In order to understand the action cinema that was produced and circulated in those years—in order to see how that action cinema met functions that, while immediately identifiable in commercial terms, were simultaneously sustaining the putting in place and reproduction of the social relations needed to fulfil those commercial objectives—a review of the structural changes that characterized the 1960s is in order.

THE ECONOMY IN 1960s INDIA

The specific strategies by which 1960s action films met and buttressed the socio-economic dynamics constitutive of 1960s India were characteristic of India's cinema, but the socio-economic pressures that generated those dynamics were not. Like any other industrial cultural product, the Hindi action cinema of the 1960s responded to economic pressures that were rooted in international developments but which, in India, triggered specific reactions. From a comparative perspective, it is important to take these transnational factors into account. Among other things, they led to the emergence of other types of action cinema elsewhere—to mention but a few examples from the late 1950s and early 1960s: Italian peplums (sword-and-sandals films), Mexican wrestling movies, Japanese *yakuza* films and, in Hong Kong, Shaw Brother's '*wuxia*' productions. Some of these other action films circulated in 1960s India, others did not. But whether they did or not, the differences between these films and Indian action films of the period are rooted in the diverse and historically specific responses of these individual (Indian, Italian, Mexican, Japanese, and Chinese) national or regional economies as they were increasingly forced to move according to the terms set by globally expanding capitalism and its centres. Italian peplums were among the films that fed the imagination of the most prominent among the Indian action films of the 1960s, Dara Singh's wrestling movies, and there are material reasons why Italian peplums and not, say, Mexican wrestling films, reached India. But the manner in which Dara Singh's films incorporated and adapted the conventions of the Italian peplum, and the reasons for those incorporations and differentiations, can only be fully grasped by drawing into film analysis the national and transnational factors that made this cinematic encounter possible, even necessary, in the first place.

As a consequence of the reduction of trade barriers at the end of the 1950s, from the early 1960s the growth of global trade accelerated spectacularly and unexpectedly. After years of anti-colonial struggle, countries in Africa, Latin America, and Asia became independent. With the end of the Marshall plan and of the Korean War, the World Bank intensified funding to these new economies as it sought to harness them to the American side of the Cold War. As a result, in the 1960s all Third World regions increased their degree of industrialization and urbanization to a far greater extent than they improved their GDP per capita (Arrighi 1991). In India, between 1951 and 1969 there was a 300 per cent increase in the index of industrial production, including a 70 per cent rise in the consumer goods industry (Vanaik 1990: 28–9; Vaidyanathan 2005: 961). Film production was part of that. From the mid-1960s, as the country experienced an industrial downturn, Bombay became the only area that was experiencing industrial growth.

But the late 1950s in India also brought a massive foreign-exchange crisis that marked the point at which some of the critical shortcomings of the Indian development model became apparent to state managers as well as to the public. The immediate result was a drastic scaling down of planned development's targets. One of the problems highlighted by the crisis was that if the pace of development was to be maintained, exports would have to be increased. But, their level of productivity having been shaped by the luxury of local monopolies, Indian firms did not have the capacity to expand into export markets on their own. Efforts to provide special assistance to firms in this direction began immediately, but instead of a centralized and carefully coordinated system for administering the schemes, the method that was actually adopted was similar to the other aspects of industrial policy—they were handed over to the bureaucracy, which, lacking effective means of coordination, established myriad schemes that were overlapping, discontinuous, and administratively cumbersome and, in practice, reduced the legitimacy of the measures. As Vivek Chibber (2004) put it, 'The dynamic result of the planning process was to delegitimize the idea of disciplinary planning, while at the same time weakening its main agent,' the Planning Commission. This left the field open for large business houses to turn the policies to their own advantage and use them to secure safe monopolies over product lines with high immediate returns while barring other firms from entering their markets.

Although film exhibition was far from a cohesive or, for that matter, a corporate entity, the relations of force I have outlined earlier between exhibition and an increasingly fragmented production sector reveal that a mechanism similar to the one described by Chibber was also at work in the film industry. Exhibitors were in no way corporate entities, but the broader economic and political conditions were such that they were capable of acting as a block, preventing new producers from breaking through into the market even when the government relaxed the rules on the opening of new cinemas and took steps to expand that market. The action cinema that was made in the 1960s was designed to meet this situation.

Following the defeat in the 1962 border war with China and the indecisive clash with Pakistan in 1965, the Indian government greatly stepped up its military spending. In both 1965–6 and 1966–7 there were famines that impelled the government to import large quantities of wheat from the US. Inflation accelerated and the balance of payments plumetted into deficit. Under international pressure the rupee was devalued in 1966 (Desai 1975: 11). Planned development through state capitalism was virtually abandoned from 1966, but state expenditure did not diminish. Figures from the Reserve Bank of India show that between 1960 and 1970 the overall expenditure on education and general administration increased at a much faster rate than in the previous decades (Chatterjee 1997: 54–5).

Migration from rural areas into cities like Bombay provided the workforce needed for industrial production. According to the 1961 census, nearly 15 per cent of the manufacturing labour force was then in cotton textiles, which were situated in the city centre. But, from the 1960s, India's cotton industry began to lose ground in world markets, (to China for example). In spite of this, the years of the Third Five-Year Plan and the Annual Plan registered a high growth of employment which was due to the growth of other, newer branches of manufacturing, like chemicals and pharmaceuticals (Joshi and Joshi 1976: 64–5).[8] Unlike the mills, the new factories were located in the extended suburbs east of the island—small-scale engineering, chemicals, and pharmaceuticals on the eastern railway route along the Bandra-Kurla road and large-scale public-sector units in the fertilizer and oil industries around Trombay, to the south-east (Ramasubban and Crook 1995: 158–9). Whereas in 1961 only one-third of the population of Bombay lived in the suburbs, by the 1990s the suburbs had grown to house as much as two-thirds of Greater Mumbai's inhabitants (D'Monte 2002: 20). Moreover, in sharp contrast to the average wage of a mill worker (Rs 7120 a year), a chemical worker would earn an yearly average of Rs 14,367 (ibid.: 84). Salaries overall rose much faster in this decade. By increasing the share of 'unproductive' labour, employment was created and the purchasing power of a small but significant number of people increased. Finally, employment in factories meant not simply higher disposable income, but also a certain regularization of 'productive' and 'unproductive' labour time. Unlike the small farmer, the factory employee possesses what is generally referred to as 'leisure time'. Factories and higher salaries created a sensibly larger market for industrial goods, including films.

In the 1960s, Bombay's industrial sector expanded well above the national rate, but in this decade as in the past, industry and commerce continued to grow along two parallel tracks: the first comprised large, government-run companies providing public services and a handful of private corporations; the second consisted of more fragmented production, a multitude of small-scale industrial units. The share of the small-scale sector in India's total industrial production had risen steadily since the mid-1950s and continued to do so in the following decades. There is a tendency for small units to substitute capital (machinery and plant) with labour and to use labour more intensively (Vanaik 1990: 32–3). In a context where manual labour has historically been cheap, this made profitability higher in the small unit sector than in large (and better unionized) corporations. But that workforce needed to be formed. The sectoral restructuring and growth of Bombay's industry in this decade involved not only a sensible expansion of the consumer market. Higher disposable incomes and commodities consumption also required different modes of value creation than had been at work in the preceding decades and a fundamental reformatting of the workforce that was to produce (and consume) those industrial goods.

It is my contention that such formatting also took place through action cinema, for it too was caught in the economic dynamics just described.

These socio-economic pressures surfaced in this type of cinema as a concern about the presentation of physical energy and its optimal uses that was not at work in other clusters of contemporary Hindi films. As a fantasy and a preoccupation, the foregrounding of the action ingredient in these 1960s action films took a different form than in earlier stunt or action cinema, for now the nature of the socio-economic demands constitutive of these films as products was not the same as in the previous decades. Small film producers wanting to profit from the emergence of a suburban public sought to break through the market block imposed by an exhibition sector that was reluctant to expand. The prime ingredient they mobilized to achieve this objective was action, or the figuration of physical energy. As we have seen in the previous chapters, action had been available in other forms before. In the 1960s new cinematic forms of it began to circulate. The ideal conditions for the realization of that objective as imagined by small producers are not to be found in the recovery of action per se. It is in the specific selection among the modes of cinematic action available to the films, and in the manner in which these were changed, adapted, and re-presented in the Indian action films of the 1960s, that we can read the modalities of a horizon that, while immediately ascribable to small film producers, in reality touched larger, even dominant, sections of the Indian economy at the time.

DARA SINGH AND THE HINDI SMALL-BUDGET FILM

The film analysis that follows shortly will focus exclusively on Dara Singh's films, but the ways in which these films addressed their imagined market drew on a set of conventions that was drawn from other cultural practices—not all of them films or, for that matter, Indian. A look at these practices as well as at the type of film productions that circulated at the time—especially those also containing the action ingredient—will enable us better to clarify the specificity of Dara Singh's films. Through the formal inclusions, exclusions, and remodulations that characterize these films we may catch a glimpse of their socio-economic function. Dara Singh's wrestling films staged the conditions for the transformation of a rural workforce into an industrial labour force: small-units-based industrialization was the horizon of the production sector that made these films. They were not the only ones inscribed into this frame, but the ways in which Dara Singh's films presented the prevailing industrial conditions—through their cinematic presentation of physical energy and its valorization both as a narrative element and as a selling point—

speaks volumes about the historically specific relations of production that required human energy to be formatted in that way. Given that the industrial horizon these films thus staged was necessarily also a dimension of the Indian cinema as a sector of Indian economy as a whole, a clearer understanding of *how* Dara Singh's films imagined that horizon can only be arrived at by way of a preliminary examination of the cultural stock available to the films, its functioning at the time and, finally, its remobilization and transformation into, precisely, 1960s Hindi action films.

One of the problems facing the Indian film industry in the early 1960s (Bombay and Madras alike) was the flooding of the market with American-distributed films. The problem was acute in the city centre, where, as producer-distributor Tarachand Barjatya then wrote,

[F]oreign distributors, who have blocked funds in India, have started acquiring top theatres on lease or booking playing time for long terms in them by advancing them huge amounts. [O]ur producers and distributors cannot compete with them. And thus pictures are screened at infinitely inferior cinemas. The best cinemas are all taken up on lease by foreign distributors. (*Screen*, 14 July 1967: 6)

By 1963, companies represented by the Motion Pictures Export Association of America (henceforth MPEAA) were earning, in India, profits of US\$1 million. Like every other foreign company operating in Indian territory, the majors were restricted to converting (that is to sending back as hard currency profit to the US) only US\$400,000 annually. The remaining accumulated monies in Indian rupees, or 'blocked funds', had grown to US\$6.5 million by 1971. By Hollywood standards, this figure was minimal, but the operation of American distributors in India cannot be understood in strictly financial terms.[9] The MPEAA, which has historically acted as a cartel, was then licensed by its members to distribute their films in western and eastern Europe, in East Asia, and in parts of South and South East Asia. One of the organization's purposes was to secure distribution of its members' films on an exclusive basis in territories where severe currency shortages existed. American foreign distributors met once a year to determine programme prices according to what a market was deemed capable of yielding: the longer a nation's audience had been cultivated to consume their programmes, the higher the prices. Once the market was secure for American films, the MPEAA left distribution to individual member companies. In India, Twentieth Century Fox distributed Paramount, MGM, Disney, Universal, and United Artist Pictures; Warner and Columbia maintained separate distribution networks. The joint venture gave Fox 65 per cent of the pictures released in India, which was a significant market share of the supply of English-language films in that market. To counter it, Warner and Columbia had ties with key theatres that gave them control over screen time in those theatres the whole year around. In some cases, Warner advanced money to build theatres which it did not own (Pendakur 1985).

Outside the urban circuit, in suburbia and in rural areas, the leverage of American distributors affected Indian distributors in a slightly different way. State policy ruled that, in addition to entertainment tax, which is paid to state governments, exhibitors must pay duty on prints to central government proportional to the value of the film. So, complaining about the 'paucity of outlets' in an article that appeared in *Screen* on 21 April 1967 (p. 17) entitled 'More Cinemas Needed', the writer claimed that 'small exhibitors [are] denied certain films as their prints are too costly'— a fact that, he argued, further restricted Hindi cinema's market. Because these measures applied to imported as well as to Indian films, in order to avoid high import duties (paid by foreign companies to central government), American distributors took to the practice of undervaluing all but the most prestigious of their products. This was not unique to American distribution in India: well into the 1980s, American domestic film consumption sufficed to make ample profits and anything added to that was regarded as marginal bonus. Moreover, in the 1960s Hollywood faced an overproduction boom which landed the industry in severe crisis. Studios found themselves with unsold stock and, by 1969, the industry's overall losses amounted to US\$ 600 million (Cook 2000: 11).[10] American capital began to flee the country. While in the American market studios eventually created an artificial product shortage to counteract the leverage that overproduction gave to exhibitors, in foreign markets films with American capital became cheaply available. Whereas in Europe large amounts of American capital found profitable investment in co-productions, in India, along with blocked funds, American money was primarily employed to secure exhibition and to 'cultivate' the market.

Not unlike in the 1920s, in this decade American-produced films distributed in the Indian market would thus fall within two broadly defined categories: new and costly Hollywood productions, which were reserved for city centre cinemas where they would run for several weeks, and cheaply produced, cheaply imported films, many US-European co-productions, which were circulated faster than prestigious Hollywood films. In 1966, for instance, *La Vendetta di Spartaco/The Revenge of Spartacus* (Michele Lupo 1964) was released in Bombay at the end of May for one week; *Maciste contro i mongoli/Hercules against the Mongols* (Domenico

Paolella 1963) with Mark Forest, was released at the Excelsior and Alexandra on 9 July for a week and, from the following week, at the Alexandra and the Kismat cinemas. *La Rivolta dei sette/The Spartan Gladiators* (Alberto De Martino 1964) was on the bill at the Metro on 19 August also for a week. Significantly, Mario Bava's *Ercole al centro della terra/Hercules at the Centre of the Earth* (1961), with Reg Park, was distributed first in Bengal and Uttar Pradesh from 7 July 1967 by Eagle Films, before reaching the Maratha Mandir in Bombay three weeks later via the distributors Bimal Roy Films. There, it was soon followed by *Maciste nelle miniere di re Salomone/Maciste in King Solomon's Mines* (Piero Regnoli 1963), also with Reg Park. In Madras, the situation was very much the same.[11]

In the early 1960s peplums produced in Italy with American money represented a significant share of American imports, although they were by no means the only genre. In addition to prestigious Hollywood productions, Bombay cinemas were flooded with American and/or US-European co-productions like the historical epic *Esther and the King* (Raul Walsh 1960), modern and Italian Westerns such as *The Magnificent Seven* (John Sturges 1960) and *Per un pugno di dollari/A Fistful of Dollars* (Sergio Leone 1964), early James Bond features, horror films, and Hammer productions, like *The House of Wax* (André de Toth 1953) and *The Kiss of the Vampire* (Don Sharp 1963), as well as with other types of exploitation films, from motorcycle movies like *The Wild Angels* (Roger Corman 1966) to cheap thriller comedies and soft-core, such as *Le Spie vengono dal semifreddo/Dr Goldfoot and the Girl Bombs* (Mario Bava 1966), *Le Saint prend l'afflût/The Saint against Agent 001* (Christian-Jaque 1966), and *Il Pelo nel mondo/Go Go Go World* (Antonio Margheriti 1964). Japanese soft-core or yakuza productions were also available, like Nikkatsu's *Ore ni sawaru to abunaize/Black Tights Killers: Panic in Tokyo* (Yasuharu Hasebe 1966).

In the Indian and in other markets, Italian peplums preceded Italian Westerns, James Bond, Hammer, and other exploitation imports by several years.[12] More importantly, unlike, for instance, Leone's Westerns, which in India were billed for 'adults only', peplums were granted a universal certificate and were heavily advertised, accordingly, in family magazines like *Mother India* (formerly *Film India*) and the less glossy *Picture Post*. These were films set in ancient Rome and featuring popular muscle men like Steve Reeves, Reg Park, Mark Forest, and Alan Steel. They were cast in the roles of (western) mythological heroes like Hercules and Samson, or of Maciste—the slave strongman popularized by Pastrone's *Cabiria* in 1914 and, throughout the 1920s, interpreted by former dock worker Bartolomeo Pagano in a series of ancient Roman and contemporary urban tales of mystery and wrongs undone. Produced on a shoestring budget in Italy with capital fleeing an American industry in crisis, the selling point of the peplums was the American bodybuilding star. Indeed the films are caught in a fetishization of their heroes' oiled and muscled bodies that, stylistically, led not only to synthetic space and fragmentation of the body, but also—and here lies the peplums' uniqueness—to emphatic shots, sometimes close-ups, of the actors' tense muscles, the camera dwelling on them for undue lengths of time to emphasize the human effort. In these moments the narrative is interrupted as if to lift out for special contemplation the eroticized but nearly abstract image of physical energy. Like other cheap American imports, Italian peplums would stay on the bill of city centre cinemas for a week, only to be moved immediately afterwards to peripheral venues for which they represented a more affordable alternative to the latest Hindi big-budget production. For their part, small Indian producers and distributors struggling to find an outlet for their films found themselves competing with these types of American imports often produced in Europe.

In 1964, two years after his breakthrough film *King Kong* (Babubhai Mistri 1962), Dara Singh starred in two productions, one entitled *Samson* (Nanabhai Bhatt 1964) and the other *Hercules* (Shriram 1964). While the names of Babubhai Mistri and Nanabhai Bhatt point to a straight line between the 1930s and the 1960s, that is to say from Dara Singh back to Wadia Movietone, for which both Nanabhai Desai and Babubhai Mistri worked, these titles are indicative of the extent to which Dara Singh's films borrowed from Italian peplums, rather than from other imported action films, and not only for their titles. Italian peplums were not Dara Singh's only source of inspiration, but even when he was cast in other types of narratives, requiring different performances—for instance, as Sikandar (Alexander or emperor), as a *daku* (bandit), or a *rustom* (champion), and, in the 1970s, as a more urban hero like Agent Q in *The Killers* (Maruti 1969)—the type of exploits required of the hero were clearly defined by the selling point of peplums and their muscular heroes. I return to this point in my analysis of the films. For now it is enough to observe that the films' advertising booklets give a good indication of the extent to which peplums provided the competitive template for Dara Singh's films (5.1). But the ways in which similar stories or actions were staged and refilmed for the Indian market in the 1960s are rooted in the conditions that Dara Singh's films encountered there. Again, these

4.1: Booklet of *Faulad* (M. Hussein 1963), courtesy of NFAI.

were structural conditions that were in no way limited to the cinema. Even so, the importance in the Indian economy of that period of small-units-based industrial production relying on intensive labour, in the cinema took specific forms.

From 1962 escalating inflation and, in 1966, devaluation led to a sharp increase in the cost of raw stock, machinery, and essential spare parts. Producers and their financiers, many of them distributors, found themselves confronted with two options. The first was to reduce costs, including casting, but, in so doing, also to reduce the film's competitiveness in the eyes of the exhibitor. The second option was to increase turnover, by selling a higher number of tickets, by charging more per ticket, or both. Barring higher ticket prices, foreclosed by the exhibitor, film production overall decreased. Production also fragmented still more and was further polarized as the number of ad hoc producers increased sharply. Costs were reduced at all levels of production and exhibition—by bypassing central exhibition networks and circulating the films instead, or primarily, in suburbia and rural areas. Exhibition in these years did not expand but, significantly between 1961 and 1962, for the first time since the inception of cinema in India, the average rate of increase in the number of permanent venues was accompanied by a significant drop in the number of travelling cinemas (Dharap 1978: E-3). In this context, the small-budget, quickly produced film boomed. As film director and former stuntman Kamran explained in an article entitled 'Faith in Small Budgets', within this network films and the money invested in them circulated at a much faster pace:

Small budget [films] [e]ntertain the public even in small stations [towns]. [They] are numerically more than big-budget-pictures [and] keep [a] lot of people alive by giving them work. [W]hile big ones take $2^1/_2$ to 3 years or even 5 years for completion it is possible to complete six small budgets within the time of making one big-budget picture. While big-budget consume about 70 lakhs [7 million] per picture not less than ten small budgets could be made within the cost of one big-budget picture. [T]he chances of failure of small budgets are always negligible, the distributors are all happy having not only covered their investment but having made a decent profit. The producers are also happy in making a small profit. [I]t is very difficult for a small-budget picture to make a jubilee. If they run to eight weeks is [sic] itself a jubilee and a feat. They are generally within 7 to $7^1/_2$ lakhs [700,000 to 750,000] and their modest run in all places is enough to make them commercially successful (*Picture Post*, December 1968: 119–21).

In August 1962 *Filmfare*, a glossy English film magazine devoted to the promotion of respectable big-budget Hindi and American films, uncharacteristically reviewed a Hindi film called *King Kong* (Babubhai Mistri 1962):

> If a critic were to evaluate *King Kong* in terms of cinema, he would probably not have a good word to say about it. Set in the pattern of an Arabian Nights fantasy, *King Kong* [h]as the acrobatics of *Sinbad the Sailor*, of Tarzan killing a crocodile and of Samson's devilry. Even the hero is a crude copy of Hercules as portrayed in spectacular American and Italian films. Fast, funny and primitive in cinematic art, *King Kong* may amuse the groundlings. It is a film in which performances do not matter at all. However, King Kong and Dara Singh, who have successfully performed to the delight of thousands at the wrestling carnivals in Bombay, do display a conscious effort to act their roles. Kum Kum looks quite fetching, and even impresses with a couple of provocative dances. [S]umming up, *King Kong* is a crude entertainer. (*Filmfare*, 10 August 1962: 25)

King Kong was not the only Indian film containing action and stunts at this time. Premnath, for instance, had featured in a number of films in the late 1950s that contained feats of strength, such as the historical adventure *Qatil/The Killer* (M. Hussain 1959). Films containing action were also made featuring well-known actors like Mahipal, Azad, and Ranjan, who were cast in the jungle production *Zimbo* (H. Wadia 1958) and in the adventure *Matwala/The Opportunist* (M.A. Thirumgam 1958). Sivaji Ganesan was also a regular in Hindi versions of Tamil nationalist historicals containing battle scenes, such as *Veerapandiya Kattaboman/ Amar Shaheed/Our Martyr* (B.R. Panthalu 1959), as was M.G. Ramachandran, who starred in the swashbuckler *Hamen Bhi Jeene Do/ Let Us Also Live* (M.G. Ramachandran 1960). Films featuring women in dynamic roles were also around. Kum Kum, to whom I return later, played the title role in *Wild Cat* (Zahur Ahmed 1960), a remake of the 1927 hit *The Wildcat of Bombay* and its 1936 remake *Bambai Ki Billi* (Nandlal Jaswantlal), while Ragini played a turbaned woman with a whip in *Naag Rani/Cobra Girl* (Nanabhai Bhatt 1963). Leaving aside Shivaji Ganesan's and MGR's productions, which were caught in a separate dynamics of Tamil nationalist politics centred on the film star, among all of these other action films *King Kong* was deemed to deserve a review in *Filmfare* because, in spite of its low production value, its peripheral circulation, 'crude' performances and script, *King Kong* was based on a calculation about the cinematic market viability of the extra-cinematic popularity of its wrestling star.

As I have mentioned in Chapter 1, wrestling has been popular in South Asia since the middle ages in courts as well as in villages. Either way, it was practised under the religious (spiritual and physical) guidance of a guru. By the 1920s some professional wrestlers moved outside the hierarchically organized sphere of traditional wrestling and found employment in cinema, like Nandaram who made films with Krishna Film Company. But after the arrival of Nadia in the 1930s and then with the temporary demise of the stunt film and the emergence of the feudal family romance, wrestlers would find work in cinema at best as stuntmen.

Since World War II, in India, as in the US, Canada, Europe, Latin America, Japan, and parts of Africa, professional wrestling has become a major industry with close ties to the media, from advertising to television. The bouts have incorporated the media's requirements of spectacularity and, in India as much as elsewhere, professional wrestling bouts are more or less pre-planned shows in their own right, with one wrestler playing the 'good guy' and the challenging champion 'the bad guy'. In India, there is a fledgeing circuit in Bombay and Calcutta, owned (in the 1970s and 1980s) by B.J. Mulla's Sterling Promoters, with a monopoly on the most popular wrestlers. Indian professional wrestling today abides by the conventions of the World Wide Wrestling Federation, but Sterling Promoters, like most national wrestling operators, has in its stables its own 'world champions' (Rajadhyaksha 1980: 6–7).

Born in 1928 in Dharmuchak, a village in Punjab, where he took part in local wrestling contests, Dara Singh became a professional wrestler after migrating for a few years to Singapore in search of work as a labourer.[13] Having learned a variety of techniques, very few of them orthodox within traditional South Asian wrestling, he returned to India to become, with his brother Randhawa, India's first free-style wrestler. By the late 1970s Dara Singh and his brother ranked as the highest paid Indian wrestlers, with Dara as 'world champion'. Then, on average, an Indian wrestler would get Rs 2500 to Rs 3000; by contrast, Dara Singh and Randhawa would get a share of the total gate money, and this could top 1 lakh (Rs 100,000) (Ibid.: 9).

Prior to *King Kong*, Dara Singh had worked in a few films as a stuntsman,[14] but Babubhai Mistri's decision to cast the Indian wrestler in his first lead role was less original than it may appear at first. By the 1950s, the former Wadia Movietone's special effects master had become a prolific director of mythologicals, but in the 1960s he was no longer a mainstream name, either as a director or as a producer. To this day, well-established distributors operating in the main circuit guarantee exhibition space and time for the films they have financed by granting the exhibitor a significant share of the box office. Casting a well-known star is believed to, and often does, generate high box office revenues. A popular director can have the same effect, that is if his or her name is taken as a sign of high production value. By contrast, in the small-budget sector, production value is low and directors count as next to nothing when it comes to accessing exhibition venues. Nor can small producers and distributors afford well-established stars. As a result, in low-budget productions, 'star construction' plays a crucial role. But actors and other pro-filmic elements can be ascribed value in many different ways. By examining which aspects of Dara Singh's performances were prioritized and how these were conveyed by the camera we can identify elements of the fantasy of industrial exploitation that generated the films as objects. As commodities, Dara Singh's films sold well. This is to say that the figurations of physical energy that these films present can also be read as symptomatic of the wider socio-economic pressures in which cinema, as a sector of the Indian economy, was inevitably caught. Given that modes of address are the dimension of texts or films where notions of subjectivity are most clearly and directly inscribed, the way in which value is ascribed to Dara Singh's performance in these films simultaneously tells us about the modalities of the ideal subjectivities deemed necessary to sustain that economic horizon. It tells us, in other words, how large sections of the Indian population were addressed, cinematically, in such a way that would ideally make them functional to some of the economic changes that India underwent in the 1960s and, more importantly, that were endemic to the film industry.

Although not yet the highly paid Indian 'world champion' that he became in the 1970s, not long before being approached by Babubhai Mistri, Dara Singh had won the 'King Kong' title, a dubious world wrestling award, against the bulky Hungarian wrestler Emile Czaja. As Mohamed Hussain, the director of many subsequent Dara Singh films, made clear in 1965, the outcome was that

there is a craze with the people to see [Dara Singh]. [T]o see him in action in the ring side is costly. Each ticket would be not less than Rs 10 which poor people cannot afford and so cinema has provided an alternative source where the common man could see him at a cheaper rate. (*Picture Post*, November 1965: 27)

Babubhai Mistri's *King Kong* was built primarily, if not entirely, around that wrestling event. Whereas wrestling matches of that calibre were only to be seen in cities, the films could be taken elsewhere. Most of Dara Singh's films did not have access to the main exhibition circuit, where, as we have seen, exorbitant rates applied, but were distributed in peripheral areas, sometimes directly by the actor and the producer themselves.[15] In this context, billing the wrestling star gave the films a strong advantage against similarly cheap products competing for the limited exhibition venues. Throughout the 1960s, when Indian films were regularly produced in 35 mm, Dara Singh's films would invariably be copied onto 16 mm, thereby adapting to the low-cost projection equipment of small cinemas in rural parts of the country. From 1962 to the end of the decade, films featuring Dara Singh would be advertised and reviewed regularly in the trade press for the benefit of distributors and exhibitors. As to magazines targeting film-goers, such as *Filmfare*, *Mother India*, and *Picture Post*, only the latter, the cheapest of the three, covered the films and their star in each and every one of its issues—not in the form of reviews, but through interviews with Dara Singh, his directors and producers, straight advertisements, stills and plot synopses accompanied by photographic extracts.

While these marketing strategies sustained Dara Singh's stardom after the success of *King Kong*, the films themselves—their title, script, and, above all, their mise en scène—were designed, from the beginning, to build the Indian professional wrestler into a film star and to capitalize on the investment. The tensions that the fulfilment of this task produced at the level of narration are worth considering in detail, not least because an understanding of such tensions requires opening up the interface of culture and economics in such a way that it becomes possible to examine the contradictory narrative layers at work in *King Kong* and other Dara Singh films as ideal preconditions for, as well as as effects of, the economic circumstances that generated the films as commodities in the first place. To repeat the point made earlier, these circumstances were themselves symptomatic of the dynamics constitutive of the Indian economy in the 1960s. My analysis of the films will endeavour to demonstrate that, situated within that socio-economic context, Dara Singh's films, in their figurations of physical energy, projected the ideal relations that made the films profitable and, through them, the conditions to sustain that 1960s Indian socio-economic context.

DARA SINGH'S WRESTLING FILMS

King Kong, like most of Dara Singh films of the 1960s, is set in an undefined countryside. Unlike the idyllic rural India of 1950s melodrama,[16] produced by an urban imaginary of an 'elsewhere', this is a fable-like rural wasteland which knows no outside. The story of *King Kong* takes place in the kingdom of King Hingoo, where it is a tradition for the king to bestow on the strongest man the title of King Kong. When the king summons the title bearer (Emile Czaja) to kill a wild animal that is creating havoc in his realm, he is surprised to find that the animal has been killed by a young man (Dara Singh) just as it was about to attack the princess (Pravin Choudhury). As the young man claims for himself the name of King Kong, a contest is arranged between the two contenders. The young man wins and the king confers on him the title of King Kong. Invited for the occasion to the royal palace, the new King Kong is revealed to be none other than the son of the former ruler, who had been unjustly deposed and murdered by Hingoo. The new King Kong is imprisoned, but, partly with the help of the princess's maid (Kum Kum) and her sinuous dances, he manages to break out, defeats the whole palace, and forces Hingoo to recognize him as the rightful heir to the throne.

This was, at the time and until not long ago, a very common storyline in Hindi and other Indian cinemas.[17] Before the arrival of cinema in India and, in cinema, since the 1920s, it has functioned as a terrain to stage ideas of modernity and resistance to it because it dwells on one problem: the conceptualization of social identity. *King Kong* and his hero straddle two temporalities: on the one hand, the film narrates a story of interrupted lineage within which the hero may owe his strength to his royal blood; on the other, the film is also a tale of social (class) mobility in which the hero's strength is not just his own, but also that which enables him to simultaneously claim for himself the title of King Kong and have that claim officially sanctioned. There is very little in the film that allows us to pigeonhole it as firmly inhabiting either one or the other temporality because one of the issues the film negotiates is, precisely, the loosening (or not) of hierarchical social relations and the formation (or not) of a socially mobile individual. The sets are either country wasteland or the court, and no city is anywhere to be seen, and yet different elements at all levels of the film pull us first one way and then the other. *King Kong's* storyline, as that of many other Indian films, does resolve in favour of a reassertion of the importance of hierarchical social relations: the young man turns out to be of royal blood. But to reduce each and every element of the film to this conclusion would require that we ascribe greater importance to the script or story than to every other filmic element. We are allowed to watch a large part of the film without knowing that the young man is of royal blood, and, more importantly, there are long sections and many aspects of the story and of the mise en scène that work against a hierarchically oriented resolution, ascribing physical strength and power to the hero as an autonomous individual. What follows is an attempt to disentangle some of these knots, the contradictory discourses concurring in *King Kong* and constituting it as a complex, layered fabric. My objective, as I examine the narrative strategies at work in specific scenes, is to open up the connections and explore the determinations within this discursive texture, their changing rendition of 'action' as the film's prioritized narrative ingredient and selling point, and the pressures constitutive of the economic context of which the film was part and which it necessarily addressed.

King Kong opens with a long shot over a country road: we see the royal King Kong riding a horse-drawn cart at great speed, moving towards and then past the camera. Although the scene is reminiscent of the opening of many Italian peplums, the contrast between Czaja's very fat body and that, say, of a Steve Reeves, is striking. The following shot cuts to the royal palace, where King Hingoo tells King Kong that his assistance is needed to kill a wild animal. As King Kong promises to do it, royal guards walk in to announce that the princess has gone to the forest. The party leaves for the hunt of the animal and to the rescue of the princess. Throughout this scene the camera is static, offering a frontal, theatrical view of the palace's room where King Kong, king, and soldiers confer. We cut to a medium shot of the princess against a country landscape, screaming in horror as she comes face to face with the gigantic dragon-like beast. Cut to a long shot: she runs and takes refuge in a large hole in the ground, but the animal puts its paw in it and grabs her. The camera is in the hole with the princess. As she is about to be dug out of her refuge by the gigantic paw (an image that evokes the American *King Kong*), we cut back to the wasteland. A young man wearing a leopard-skin loincloth and sheepskin boots chases the beast away. A fight ensues between the beast and the man—the latter so small in comparison that he can be seen (in a long shot) to fit, standing, in the beast's mouth. With his mighty biceps, the man holds the beast's mouth open. For the first time since the beginning of the film, the camera cuts in and out—in to close-ups of the man's muscles as he holds the animal's fangs wide open, and out, partly to highlight the minuteness of the man against the beast.

Hit several times in the back of its throat by the young man's lance, the animal finally collapses. The man runs to the princess's refuge, jumps in, and awakens the princess, who has fainted. The camera is, and remains, inside the hole: a medium shot designed to dwell on the man's straining muscles as he lifts the woman out of the hole. Cut to the royal party as it reaches the scene and sees the animal lying on the ground. The shot is frontal, the men walk towards the camera. As the king orders King Kong to go and kill the animal, and as King Kong gestures towards it, a cut shows us the young man appearing from behind the dead beast and approaching the party. Follows a brief but meaningful exchange between the king, the royal wrestler, and the young man, mostly in long shots, with the characters standing in profile for the benefit of the camera. 'Who killed the beast?' asks the king. 'I did' answers the young man. The king: 'And who *are* you?' The young man: 'I am King Kong'. The king: 'Is that so? Who gave you that name?' The young man: 'My mother'.

In the young man's suitably ambiguous answer lies a great deal of Dara Singh films. 'Mother' can be inscribed as the symbol of reproduction across two temporalities simultaneously: as the carrier of lineage and as the bearer of any man. To that extent, the young man's answer allows the film to postpone the question as to whether or not he owes his strength to lineage. The mother in *King Kong*, and in the majority of Dara Singh's films, occupies a special position: she is the source, and often the motivator for the deployment of the hero's strength. One way of looking at this is to say that she holds the moral ground which enables Dara Singh's heroes to deploy physical strength for 'justice', even when in *King Kong*, as in most of Dara Singh's films, physical strength can take forms that are objectively very brutal. Another way of understanding this special relationship between 'mother' and 'physical strength'—one that also runs through the Hindi action films of the following decades, from Amitabh Bachchan's to Sunny Deol's—would be to say that 'mother' inscribes the hero's action into a discourse of (re)production, leaving the question open as to what is being (re)produced.

The young man's answer calls for an explanation: there is a royally-appointed King Kong, but since the young man appears to be very strong, a contest is called for, supervised, and legitimated by the king himself. This first wrestling match, between the bulky Emile Czaja and the leaner, agile and muscled Dara Singh, sets in motion the circular structure of *King Kong*. Most of Dara Singh films of the 1960s are built around a circular structure: two wrestling bouts, book-ending the film, appear to echo each other. On closer inspection, however, the closing bout tend to display a far more synthetic sense of space and fragmented body than the opening bout. To anticipate my argument somewhat, and in spite of the story's superficial reassertion of hierarchical status, I suggest that what is at stake in these changes in narrative strategies within the one film is the possibility and the difficulties of inscribing physical energy into a new economy—one that is no longer as firmly and solely regulated by hierarchical social relations as was the economic system symbolized by king Hingoo.

Wrestling films from all over the world share a standard stock of shooting strategies. A static camera, alternating long shots of the wrestling ring with shots of the public watching the contest, are common across the board. Rarely in wrestling films does the camera step into the ring so as to produce a synthetic figuration of space and bodies in action.[18] The reasons for this are twofold. First, wrestling films are often made on the back of actual wrestling matches, where the camera is not allowed in the ring. Second, for the punter, these films represent cheaper substitutes of the far more expensive wrestling event. Frontal long shots offer the film spectator a view of the bout that reproduces the vision of the public in the arena. The Mexican films featuring Santo, aka 'el Enmascarado de Plata' (Silver Mask), are a good example of this mode of narration.

Dara Singh's films break with the stylistic conventions of the wrestling film, not so much because, as in *King Kong*, the bouts they feature were especially shot for the film, but because there are clear indications in the choreography and in the mise en scène that different formal solutions are sought for the shooting of fights. *King Kong*'s first wrestling bout starts with a frontal long shot showing the royal wrestler in the foreground, in profile to the left and facing the young man to the right, while, in between the two, in the background, stand the king and his soldiers, ready to watch the bout. As soon as the two start fighting, the camera cuts in towards them, in a medium shot, then back to the king, also in medium shot, and then again back to the two fighters. Cut to a long, frontal shot designed to allow the full spectacle of classic wrestling moves, which is followed by a medium shot of the king looking, and then back to the fighters, also in medium shot. The camera alternates between these two types of shots, long and medium. Sometimes it allocates the look to the king, who, with his visual expressions, seems to provide a kind of commentary on the fight. Since his face lightens up every time his wrestler gets the upper hand over the hero and vice-versa, part of the pleasure for the spectator is to see his/her own satisfaction at Dara Singh's winning moves confirmed, in reverse as it were, in the king's displeasure. At other times, the camera retains the position of an objective narrator, mostly from a distance with long shots and, once, a bird's-eye view of the fight, but, occasionally, also with rare close-ups on the wrestler's body parts.

This scene is characterized by the lack of clear orchestration between subjective and objective modes of narration. Spatial discontinuities are the rule, as if the collation of one shot to the next and the ordering of the interrelations between different points-of-view presented a problem.

Nor is there a single subjective shot conveying the point of view of the wrestlers. However, three distinct levels can be identified. The medium shots convey, or try to convey, the look of the king, who also functions as a diegetic manifestation of the narrator, as if the narrator, not trusting the ground on which he stands to tell the story, felt the need to evoke the hierarchically defined authority of the king to legitimate his account. At the same time, the long shots reproduce a view of the bout as seen in a professional wrestling arena, at a greater distance than the king, as if outside or above the ring. Third, the rare close-ups break the conventions of wrestling films by, as it were, cutting into the ring and lifting out for special attention selected elements of the wrestling performance. To use Roman Jakobson's terminology (1988),[19] the king's point of view bolsters the conative function of the enunciation (of the mise en scène): the medium shots of the king as he observes the bout inscribe the spectator as the addressee of an injunction to look, and to look closer, but not too close, counteracting the distance established by the objective long shots and acting as a middle point between the latter and the occasional close-ups.

In an illuminating account of the effects of the availability of printing technology on modes of literacy in early modern Spain, Wlad Godzich argued that it is necessary to distinguish between 'oral' and 'auditive' cultures. By definition, for the construction of its narratives, an 'oral' culture relies upon a shared thesaurus of formulae and motifs, a collective memory that, as Walter Benjamin (1999b) also wrote, is open to the experiential dimension of the everyday life of all its participants. By contrast, although also orally delivered, an 'auditive' culture does not establish a dialogical relation with its audience. Characterized by a high level of rhetorical fabrication, auditive modes of address seek to conquer the audience. The audience does not participate: neither does a recited text or a speech internalize their lived experience, nor does the audience internalize the text or speech's arguments. The audience is subjugated, seduced, or persuaded by the flow of the rhetorical theatricality (Godzich and Spadaccini 1994: 79). Such is an epic, although epics are only one among the range of practices falling under the category of auditive culture. Further, in an earlier work, Godzich emphasized that epics and any mode of narration relying on verse imply a performative dimension that is crucial to the decoding of meaning. Written versions of early medieval European epics, for instance, did not have quotation marks, that is to say, the texts did not clearly distinguish when the words pertain to the dialogue of one fictional speaker as opposed to another, or to the storyteller. This is because, when performed or recited, the shift from one fictional speaker to the other would be signalled by the storyteller non-verbally, for instance by a different inflection of the voice, or with a gesture. Mimicry, music, dance, stance, voice levels, gaze, and so forth formed the range of semiotic means available to the storyteller to achieve distinctive modalities without sacrificing the coherence of the whole. Early written or printed versions of the same stories deprived the reader of the non-verbal organizing dimension performed by the storyteller (Godzich and Kittay 1987: 16–17).[20]

The lack of clear coordination between different narrative layers in the wrestling scene described above appears to stem from a similar problem. There is, on the one hand, the story in the form of a script or—scripts being rarely used in Indian cinemas—more likely, of a prose outline. From that the director selected salient moments, highlights of the story to be translated visually. On the other hand, there are the events and actions staged for the camera. What characterizes this and other scenes in Dara Singh's films is a tension between these two layers and an indecision as to how to coordinate them, as if an epic mode of narration, or at any rate a mode of narration reliant on the coordinating role of a storyteller, was expected to be at work and yet came to lack, or was disrupted by, other intervening considerations. These considerations— which in this scene take the form of long- and high-angle shots of the bout as if from the stalls of an arena, or of non-subjective close-ups on parts of the wrestling bodies—stem directly from the pressure to ascribe value and give full play to the performance of the actors as professional wrestlers. That is to say, they are effects of the material conditions imposed, in the 1960s, on small producers by an exhibition sector that blocked their products out of the market's defining circuits.

Film stars are a marketing device the world over and, to that extent, star construction is always a manifestation of the conditions characterizing exhibition at any given time and place. The important point here is that in the 1960s, in this sector of the Bombay film industry, exhibition pressures resulted in modes of address that, firstly, incorporated into cinema at least two broadly defined regimes available within the cultural domain inhabited by *King Kong*: traditional wrestling, with all its hierarchical and religious paraphernalia, and the far more commercially oriented professional wrestling championships. Transformed by the industrial medium of cinema and combined in, or rather as, the filmic text, these two levels are rendered in this scene as the king's and the objective narrator's look respectively. In this first bout, these two regimes are orchestrated in such a way as to result in what I hesitatantly call an epic voice. This epic, or rather pseudo-epic, voice describes the events emphatically, keeping the pro-filmic (the actions of the actor-wrestlers) at a distance that is as much spatial as it is temporal. We seem to be in the 'once upon a time there was …' mode of narration. In C.S. Peirce's classification, this regime of enunciation relies primarily on the symbolic dimension of the image. For instance, in the previous scene, when long shots show us the young man as he stands in the mouth of the beast holding its fangs open and hitting its throat with a lance, the hero's strength, as a concept, is signified rather than performed. In this first bout, as also in the fight against the beast, the indexical and iconic dimensions of the images are also necessarily at work: in both instances these are images of real actors standing in front of the camera and performing actual movements. But the long and medium shots of the wrestlers rely primarily on the symbolic dimension of the enunciation, by highlighting, for instance, the expression on the king's face and the bulk of the hero's opponent.

Second, in this first bout, considerations stemming from the terms dictated, however indirectly, by Indian exhibitors translate, in the filmic text, as close-ups of the wrestlers' body parts. Unlike in truly auditive narrative regimes, here degrees of the experiential, of the immediate material conditions that made *King Kong* possible as a film, are allowed to surface and to interfere with the modes of address obtaining also in traditional and professional wrestling. That is to say, what distinguishes this scene of *King Kong* as a specific moment of the Hindi film industry are these close-ups of the wrestlers' body parts, for that is the form the importance ascribed to the wrestlers' performance as the film's one selling point takes at this specific historical conjunction. The pseudo-epic mode of narration does not exhaust the mise en scène of this first bout, for it does not explain the non-subjective close-ups of the wrestlers' body parts. Like the medium shots conveying the point of view of the king, the close-ups form an injunction to look, and to that extent they have a conative function. But as non-subjective shots, they also reveal something about the source of that injunction, the filmic narrator, and of the value 'it' ascribes to these images of the wrestlers' body parts. In Jakobson's terms, these close-ups have an expressive function: they are the diegetic manifestations of the way the 'speaker' of the narrative experiences the economic conditions inhabited by the film and, to that extent, the historically specific filmic effects of the pressures that the Indian exhibition sector was able to exercise on Bombay's low-budget film production.

I shall return to this point at other stages of my analysis. For the moment it is important to note that in the final bout, which echoes this one in the film's circular structure, the relationship between the pro-filmic and the camera is negotiated differently: the close-ups on the bodies are allocated to the wrestlers as subjective shots. Unlike the first, the second bout is shot on colour stock. We are in a desert-like wasteland, scattered with a few rocks. The young man and the princess's maid have flown the royal palace, bringing with them the princess who now lies on the ground, unconscious (again). High on the top of a rocky hill appears the royal wrestler, who throws a rock in their direction but misses them. The self-appointed King Kong (Dara Singh) moves towards the royally appointed namesake and the fight begins. A medium shot of the royal wrestler's upper body from Dara Singh's point of view is followed by a long shot of the two wrestlers in profile facing each other. After a few wrestling moves from this angle, we cut to a medium shot of Dara Singh as seen by his rival, followed by a shot-counter-shot sequence that shows each fighter from the other's point of view, nearer and nearer every time. When Dara Singh throws himself at the royal wrestler, the camera does not move, framing, for a short moment but in extreme close-up, the left biceps of the hero as he jumps just to the left of, above and beyond the camera. Cut to a long shot of the fight, and then to a series of medium shots of the fighters' upper bodies as they interact. As Dara Singh is pushed against a rock, in the background, next to the rock, we see the (revived) princess and her maid looking at him with anxiety. Cut to a medium shot of the rival as seen from Dara Singh's point of view, a counter-shot of Dara Singh approaching, or rather, charging the royal wrestler, and a long shot of the two fighting.

During the rest of the bout, the mise en scène alternates between the wrestlers' subjective shot-counter-shot sequences, and long shot sequences. Subjective shot-counter-shot sequences lend the scene a degree of spatial continuity. The wrestlers' movements are presented in such a way as to invest them with an integral sense of reality, with verisimilitude. In contrast to the long shots, where the position of the camera activates awareness of the narrator's position, in subjective sequences the camera's position changes according to the position and the movements of the actors. These images convey a sense of the wrestlers' physical strength not as an abstract attribute, but as a process into which the spectator is also inscribed. They rely primarily on the indexical dimension of the image, because the physical relation between the camera and the actors' bodies is crucial for the spectator's decoding of the image as meaning 'human physical strength'. Furthermore, whereas in the first bout, the long shots were carried by an objective narrator, here the distant look reproducing the view of the bout as from the stalls of a wrestling arena is allocated to the princess and her maid, or to the princess's brother, who is hiding behind a rock (even if in practice the eye lines do not always quite match). Alternatively, as a third mode, we see both wrestlers fighting in medium shots that are too close to be ascribed to the diegetic spectators, nor, for obvious reasons, can they be allocated to the fighters themselves. This third mode, an objective narrator revealing in detail the wrestlers' moves and crucial body parts, was already at work in the first bout—in the rare close-ups. Here it clearly inscribes the film spectator as a privileged (non-diegetic) observer—and emphatically so, since, like the close-ups in the earlier bout, these medium shots too rub against the spatial relations established by the mise en scène so far. They carry an injunction, not a polite invitation, to look. But now, neither the injunction nor the look is carried by a narrator whose legitimacy rests on the authority of a king. Instead, at the very moment the wrestlers are allocated a subjective perspective and, with it, the spectator granted a subjective view of the action, so is the narrator allowed, as it were, to break into the ring. The narrator here produces an objective, closer look at the action that, precisely as objective or neutral, lends legitimacy to the characters' and the spectator's subjective look. The value of this double address or look as a commodity—as one of the film's sales points—is detailed, subjectively and objectively legitimated visual access to the deployment of human physical energy.

None of the action films discussed in the previous chapters addressed the viewer in this way, stitching him or her into the film text as the imaginary (subjective) 'appreciator' of physical energy and, simultaneously, as the (objective) agent entitled to invest it with value. Early action films did fetishize physical energy, but they did so by relying on legitimating categories that often pre-dated industrialized culture, like notions of honour or lineage. Wadia Movietone's films went a little further, but there the presentation of physical energy rested primarily on the symbolic dimension of the images. While Boman Shroff and John Cawas's actions lent a degree of substance to Nadia's symbolic evocations (gestures) of agility and strength, neither did the mise en scène foreground their (as opposed to Nadia's) performance, nor did it suture the viewer into an identificatory relation to it. In those films, figurations of physical energy were given to the camera in such a way that the experiential dimension of the actor's performance was kept at a distance, all the better to present the human deployment of energy as desirable. By contrast, Dara Singh's films sought to monetize the visual impression of the effort required to accumulate and expend physical energy.

When discussing his film career, Dara Singh draws a very clear distinction between the films in which he 'only wrestled' and those in which he 'acted' as 'an artiste'. The distinction seems to be based on whether the film simply contained some action scenes that required his wrestling skills or whether the films was made 'around' him, focusing on the actor as a wrestler or an actor in his own right. Whereas *Pehli Jhalak/First Sight* (M.V. Raman 1954) falls within the first category, *King Kong* was a crucial turning point because, as Dara Singh put it, he was 'approached by a producer who wanted to make a film with me in the lead role'. According to the rules and regulations of the Indian fight composers' association, in the 1960s at least, 'fight composers [were] not to accept parts as fighters' (*Screen*, 17 June 1966: 2). In spite of this, from 1962 onwards, that is from *King Kong* onwards, Dara Singh has insisted on choreographing for the camera his own action scenes because, he claims, action scenes as filmed in Hindi productions featuring contemporary stunt actors like Azad, Mahipal, and Ranjan 'did not look real. There is a lot of acrobatics, but no sense of strength'.[21] Dara Singh could do his own action choreography early on, irrespective of the regulations of the fight composers' association, because of his commodity value. It is not a question of the leverage or not of Dara Singh over producer and director. Rather, in this sector of the film industry where 'star construction' offered the single most important chance of access to cinemas against fierce competition, at the level of film production such exhibition-determined considerations led to a division of labour that valued the operation of the lead actor, however unknown in cinema, as that of a film star. *King Kong* negotiated such attribution of value in its very narrative strategies, first and foremost by allowing greater play to the physical performance of the actor-wrestler than narrative strategies aimed at stressing the hero's value symbolically would allow. This is as much the case in *King Kong* as in the many bouts in other films—for instance in *Rustom-e-Rome/Rome's Hero* (Radhakant 1964), which I discuss below, or in *Dara Singh Iron Man* (Kedar Kapoor 1964)— where Dara Singh can be seen wrestling undisturbed for considerable lengths of time, the camera standing still and at a certain distance from the action, as if to respect the spatial and temporal continuity of the pro-filmic action and allow optimal view of his skills. In such scenes the camera often produces a frontal view, as if from the stalls of the arena, but bird's-eye views of the fight are also frequent.

Second, *King Kong* attributes value to the wrestler by allocating to him and to his challenger a subjective point of view during the fight, as well as (to Dara Singh's character at least) a personal dimension. The extent to which this obtains across Dara Singh's early body of work can also be seen in *Rustom-e-Rome*. The film is set in Western antiquity: Rome and Babylon are at war, and the kingdom of Jhama is caught in the war and attacked. The queen of Jhama flees the palace with her two sons, but they are separated: the elder son is brought up by the commander of the enemy king, Suhel, a usurper who wants for himself the kingdom of Jodhia and its riches, while the younger son is adopted by a gang of dacoits. Distraught at the loss of her sons, the mother is helped by a priest and resigns herself to raising his adopted child, a girl. During a wrestling contest organized by Suhel, the two brothers (Dara Singh and Azad) challenge each other in a sword fight, but, with equal muscle power and a common enemy, they become friends and eventually recognize each other. In the end, with the help of the priest, the two brothers manage to recover Jodhia's treasure. The priest's child turns out to be the queen of Jodhia and the elder brother, Firdaus (Dara Singh), wins her love.

Like *King Kong*, *Rustom-e-Rome* features two main (opening and closing) wrestling sequences. Both are set in a Roman-style arena bordered with several classical Roman or Greek statues. At the centre of the arena stands a wrestling ring, fenced off by ropes and elevated from the floor. During the first bout (between Firdaus and Suhel's bulky wrestler) the arena's stalls are filled with the shouting crowd. The camera is mobile but never enters the wrestling ring, inscribing, in turn, King Suhel, his queen, the priest and his daughter in the royal stalls as bearers of the camera's look. Only at the end of the contest, when the two wrestlers trample open the ropes of the ring and conclude the fight in the arena itself, with swords and lances, does the camera move closer. The first subjective shot for the fighters takes place here: from Firdaus's point-of-view we see, in close-up, the torso of his rival as he receives the final blow from Firdaus. Follows a sword fight between the two brothers, in the same arena and primarily outside the ring. At this point, extreme subjective close-ups on the brothers' faces, superimposed with images relating to their past, emphasize both the strain of the fight and the personal drama of sibling recognition.

Whether or not this alludes directly to the fact that Randhawa, Dara Singh's brother in real life, was also a well-known professional wrestler is impossible to say. The point is that two years after *King Kong*, when Dara Singh could claim a greater star and commodity value in the film industry than was previously the case, the terms obtaining in the exhibition sector were still such that his films continued to draw on the marketability of the actor as a real-life professional wrestler. Hence the setting—which reproduces a wrestling ring all the while placing that ring in the kind of Roman circus that would be seen in Italian peplums, one type of film Dara Singh's films would be competing against for access to exhibition venues. Hence, also, the mode of fighting, wrestling, which, however, is combined with the fighting style and the weaponry available to heroes of Indian and foreign swashbuckling and sword-and-sandals films. Above all, the drive to break into an exhibition network reluctant to expand in spite of rising box office revenues, explains *Rustom-e-Rome*'s emphasis on the hero's private life—extreme close-ups on the actor's face conveying feelings and the visual evocation of the character's past as memory individuate the wrestler as the real-life person Dara Singh, as opposed to other wrestlers.

Third, Dara Singh's films invest the wrestler's body with special value by quite literally fetishizing the parts of the body that are seen to produce physical energy. *Rustom-e-Rome*'s closing action sequence combines three types of fighting. There is, to begin with, a wrestling bout (between Firdaus and Suhel's wrestler), which is followed by a fight (between Firdaus and Suhel), both of which, this time, take place in the Roman arena now empty. In addition, the actual bout is inter-cut with images of the younger brother at court, fist-fighting against Suhel's son. Most of the bout is shot at a distance from outside the ring. Occasionally Suhel, the only witness to the match, is inscribed as looking, although the camera is always positioned on the opposite side of the ring. Whereas in the fist-fight at court between Firdaus's younger brother and Suhel's son, the camera remains at a distance, in this second bout, unlike in the opening one, the camera occasionally cuts into the ring to dwell on a close-up of Firdaus' tense biceps as he holds the rival by the throat. This type of shot, which relies primarily on the symbolic dimension of the image (biceps equal muscular power) is repeated with greater emphasis in the ensuing fight outside the ring: having knocked out Suhel's wrestler, Firdaus now goes for Suhel himself. As Firdaus strangles Suhel, the camera moves in and behind the latter to produce a shot-counter-shot sequence: medium shots of Firdaus's tense upper body as he holds Suhel's throat alternate with emphatic close-ups of Firdaus's strained face, neck and shoulders as seen from Suhel's point of view. Whereas Suhel is allocated a subjective perspective, the need to invest the hero's body parts with special value here effectively deprives him of a subjective look. The camera is positioned on his side of things, but remains at a distance, all the better to display Dara Singh's strain as exuding from the image of the upper part of his body.

In these moments the actor's body is fragmented, just as it is in subjective shot-counter-shot sequences of the bouts. The difference is that in subjective shots the fragmentation of the body answers a sense of spatial continuity and subjective perspective. This is not the case in these symbolic, fetishistic moments: the part of the body that is seen to produce strength and energy is ascribed a value that is independent of the spatial relations as established by the actor's movements. Independent to the point that these images of muscles and strained body parts begin to function as free-floating narrative elements, standing in for the character and effectively rendering his other traits irrelevant. In these moments Dara Singh's films can be seen to complete a process the first symptoms of which became manifest in 1920s Sharda stunts films: the loosening of pre-industrial social relations to distil from images of the human body a visual sense of physical energy so as to make human energy available and functional for exploitation in a different, more industrial, economy. In other words, these representations present, over a period of a few decades, the transformation of physical energy into labour power.

This is not to say that Dara Singh's films registered the full commodification of physical energy. While the films did address a context in which industrialization intensified, as we have seen earlier in this chapter, this was not the case for the whole of the Indian economy. Nor were the films free from the pressures of an exhibition sector that boldly refused to go that way—pressures that forced film production increasingly to fragment into a growing number of small operators. As a result, Dara Singh's films relied simultaneously on narrative strategies that reinscribed pre-industrial categories and conceptions of both physical energy and social relations. Generic facets of cultural forms take root because they respond to structural conditions that are economically and socially pertinent in and to the time and place that mobilizes them. These forms are borrowed from existing practices and are restyled by new ones, like cinema, because they are deemed capable of conveying important meanings about the particularities of the situation encountered by the practices that borrowed them. By considering which productions Dara

Singh's films sought to compete against, and the modifications the narrative strategies of the latter underwent as they were incorporated, the better to allow Dara Singh's productions to generate a surplus, a picture of the temporalities and economic forces seeking to ascribe value to Dara Singh's performance comes into view that explains the social function of his films: the pertinence of their conceptualization of energy in 1960s India thus becomes 'readable'.

Dara Singh's films borrowed a great deal from the Indian and foreign films that also circulated in the 1960s. It would indeed be surprising if they had not. There are, however, aspects of Dara Singh's films that point to definite inclusions and exclusions. For instance, James Bond films also circulated, as did Indian films inspired by them, such as *CID 909* (Mohammed Hussein 1967) starring Feroz Khan. But, at least until the early 1970s, Dara Singh's films paid no attention to James Bond productions. Technology, a central aspect of James Bond films, was simply not a preoccupation or a factor in Dara Singh's films, whether at the level of production or of narration, not even in the urban thrillers Dara Singh began to make at the end of the 1960s. I return to these later productions briefly in the next chapter. For the moment it is enough to say that Dara Singh's films addressed the Indian industrializing context which generated them through a different window: the physical energy required by industrial or industrializing modes of production. That concern did not feature so prominently elsewhere in the Hindi cinema of the 1950s and 1960s. Nor was it a defining factor in much contemporary foreign cinema. Of the national industries that produced films centred on the action ingredient in this decade—most notably Mexico, Hong Kong, Japan, and Italy—only Italian peplums reached India, and only peplums ascribed value to sheer physical strength. *Rustom-e-Rome* is one of the many Dara Singh films that were designed to evoke the Italian peplums circulating in India at the time. The actor-wrestler knew these films well and, by his own admission, admired their stars because, as he put it, 'strength' in these films, 'looked real'.[22]

At one level, besides the fact that the arrival of the peplum in India was facilitated by American money, part of the appeal of these films was that their stories centred on heroes who present a peculiar combination: both demi-gods (like Hercules) and professional fighters, that is gladiators (like Maciste and Spartacus). Although singularly Italian, this combination of religious and industrial connotations resonated at several levels in a historical context caught between traditional Indian wrestling, international wrestling championships, and an industry and economy still imbricated in pre-industrial, localized structures. More importantly, Dara Singh's films incorporated wholesale the stock of gestures available to the strongmen of the Italian peplum. In addition to featuring standard wrestling moves, the films straightforwardly adopted all the peplum's tropes: the breaking of chains, the lifting of rocks, the bending of iron, the pulling down of Roman columns, and so forth. In Italian peplums, these tasks were conceived to display nearly static bodies with strained muscles and to allow the camera to dwell on them for as long as necessary for the spectator to register the value on display. The laws of verisimilitude demanded that even for a Hercules such shots would last long enough to interrupt the narrative flow, effectively producing images of the strongmen's tense muscles which required the indexical presence of actors with the well-defined musculature of bodybuilders. Not so in Dara Singh's films. In *Rustom-e-Rome*, King Suhel keeps the old priest in a dark and cavernous prison. Firdaus manages to break in and frees the old man. This operation involves, first, breaking the chains tying the old man to a rock and, second, raising a heavy steel door. Dara Singh performs all this very convincingly, and the camera does move closer to the action, but never close enough for his musculature to become the focal point of the image. Nor is the time devoted to the image long enough to convey indexically a visual sense of physical effort. The result is that the actor's movements come across as a series of gestures iconically evoking peplum films, but the performative dimension of the actor's actions is kept at some distance. A pseudo-epic narrative voice thus appears to be at work in these moments, which interrupts the display of the actor's straining body, even if highlighting physical strain was very much the reason to stage the scene in the first place. The narrator is, as it were, called back to narration and, what is more, called back to narrative conventions that ascribe star value to the actor by prioritizing the symbolic and iconic dimensions of the image.

What surface in such scenes are contradictory pressures which, on the one hand, at the level of the pro-filmic (of the choreography), led to the incorporation of what were deemed to be the selling points of the Italian peplum, and, on the other, at the level of the mise en scène, result in a rendering of these selling points, these gestures, in ways that go against their purpose as intended in the Italian peplums. The explanation for this discrepancy is that in Dara Singh's films such gestures and their filmic rendition are not underpinned by the same economic dynamics as those at work in Italy in the late 1950s and 1960s. As filmed in Dara Singh's movies, gestures borrowed from Italian peplums evoke the actions of the heroes against which Dara Singh found himself competing on the Indian market, and to that extent are quite directly symptomatic of the pressures Indian exhibitors exerted on Bombay film production in the 1960s. It is these pressures, as outlined in the first part of this chapter, which enable Dara Singh's films to break with the conventions of wrestling bouts and of other wrestling films, but not in a uniform and consistent manner, precisely because the pressures came from a sector, exhibition, that in the 1960s was still very much defined by localized, often pre-industrial, at times family-based networks of wealth creation. From these determinations the films derived some of their generic stock—including notions of lineage and valour, or pseudo-epic modes of address. The incorporation of some elements—the fetishization of physical energy or individuation—was made necessary by the pressures shaping a production sector that, while driving for growth and expansion, was simultaneously increasingly fragmented and, like the majority of Indian industrial operations at the time, forced into small units of production.

Dara Singh's films rely on subjective narration, spatial continuity, and notions of individuation just as easily as they resort to other well-established conventions. Some of these, like traditional wrestling, are very old, hierarchically determined, and essentially at loggerheads with notions of individuation. Others, like professional wrestling championships, are less old but equally well established and functional when it comes to ascribing value to the image of the wrestler. Yet others, such as the conventions of Italian peplums, derive from the immediate film-generic-industrial context inhabited by the films. In all the films of Dara Singh, these different temporalities are marked by different cultural practices and their generic conventions, along with the notions of identity they imply. These markers are directly and specifically associated with the modes of production, and their concomitant conceptions of physical energy, that underpin both the films' textures and the industry within and for which the films were designed. This coexistence manifests itself as tensions and discontinuities at the level of mise en scène, the effect of which is that, at times, physical energy as an attribute of the star, as a commodity is emphasized instead at other times his moral integrity or courage, while at yet other times his lineage and honour. A point of interest from this multilayered perspective is the films' cinematic handling of desire and, more crucially, of images of women as, simultaneously, narrative strategies to ascribe individuation to the hero and sales points in the competitive market.

According to their star, Dara Singh's films were conceived with 'no sex content' and in such a way as to emphasize the strength of the hero, 'so that parents would be able to take their children to see the films and encourage them to be like the hero'.[23] Accordingly, all films starring Dara Singh were awarded a 'Universal' or 'U' certificate. But the fact remains that for all their marketability among family and young audiences, the films sold on two main ingredients: the display of Dara Singh's physical strength and its social counterpart, sexuality. Sinuous dances, suggestions of nudity and romance never take the form of explicit sex, but function nevertheless as a way to signal the desirability of the hero's attributes and to expand the films' potential market.

Often, but not always, the hero's desirability is rendered through a woman's look. This is because the sexual elements of the films can function also as a symptom of the fact that, rather than an effect of noble lineage, the hero's value can be autonomous, belonging to him as a free individual irrespective of his social status. In *King Kong,* for instance, the final showdown between Emile Czaja and Dara Singh is preceded by the only other colour sequence of the film, a dance. Revealed to be the son of the displaced king, the young man is imprisoned. The princess's maid (Kum Kum) is called upon by the king to dance in front of the court and, with her dancing, to postpone the sentence pending on Dara Singh, who is chained to a large wooden pole at the margins of the dance floor. There are countless examples in Indian cinema of very much the same kind of dance—for example in *Sholay* (R. Sippy 1975) Basanti (Hema Malini) performs a dance to save Veeru (Dharmendra). As a rule, as in *Sholay,* both prisoner and dancer are part of a show the function of which is to display the power and authority of the one who orchestrates the event (see Chapter 5). But this is not quite how it all turns out in *King Kong.*

After a frontal shot showing the king sitting on his throne in front of the dancing floor, we cut to a close up of Dara Singh's torso and head, chained to the pole. Enters the maid, to the left: she starts dancing around the chained hero. From this point onwards, no attention is paid to the king any more. He vanishes in the background as if no different from any other element of the rudimentary set. With a cut, the camera pulls out so as to follow the maid's body moving sinuously away from the hero, dancing and even rolling on the floor. All the while, she addresses her dance to the camera. We look at her from a point of view that initially appears to be objective, not least because, according to the spatial relations established so far, she is moving away from the chained hero. Eventually, however, as the maid raises herself from the floor and approaches the camera, this turns out to be positioned behind the pole, over the hero's right shoulder: slowly it pulls out to frame, in the foreground and in an extreme close-up, the hero's right biceps and, in the background but moving towards it as if to kiss it, the dancing maid. Now facing him, she kneels down, her face right in front of his thigh, in a medium shot that cuts off the hero's upper body. As she rises and starts dancing around him again, the camera moves out so as to frame the whole dancing floor. Cut to a close-up of the hero's face, still in chains, followed by a close-up of her ankle. The camera follows her right leg, arm and body, up to her face, presumably from Dara Singh's point of view. Indeed, by the time she approaches the hero once more, the camera is behind him. In the frame, we see once again, in the foreground and in extreme close-up, the hero's biceps and, in front of it (towards the background), the woman, singing (5.2).[24]

Here as elsewhere in *King Kong* and other Dara Singh films, the wrestler is allocated a subjective point of view and his character invested with a personal dimension. As this scene indicates, a corollary of individuation is the attribution of desire: the hero chained to the pole looks at the maid dancing and even focuses on particularly appealing parts of her body. As the look of desire flows between the two, an abrupt spatial discontinuity is allowed to take place, the purpose of which is to combine the need to allocate to the hero a subjective look and, simultaneously, to inscribe him into the narrative as the object of a fetishistic look. To begin with, with this narrative movement or leap, the desirability of the hero as an individuated being himself capable of desire, and the ascription of value to his biceps become one and the same thing. Moreover, the discontinuity allows the visual impression of muscular power and its desirability to be reinforced: the woman's sinuous dance, addressed, simultaneously, to the hero and the viewer, serves as a device to convey the full productive potential of the hero's musculature.

Women play an important role in Dara Singh's films. This was also the case in action films made in the 1920s and 1930s, and continues to be so in the Hindi action cinema that was made after Dara Singh. Dara Singh's films contain memorable performances by, among other actresses, Kum Kum (in *King Kong*), Mumtaz, and Helen (in *Ek Tha Alibaba/Once There Was Alibaba* [Harbans 1963], *Hercules, Aya Toofan/A Storm Came* [Mohammed Hussein and Kedar Kapoor 1964], *Rustom-e-Rome, Tarzan Comes to Delhi* [Kedar Kapoor 1965], *Sikandar-e-Azam/Alexander the Great* [Kedar Kapoor 1965], *Rustom-e-Hind/India's Hero* [Kedar Kapoor

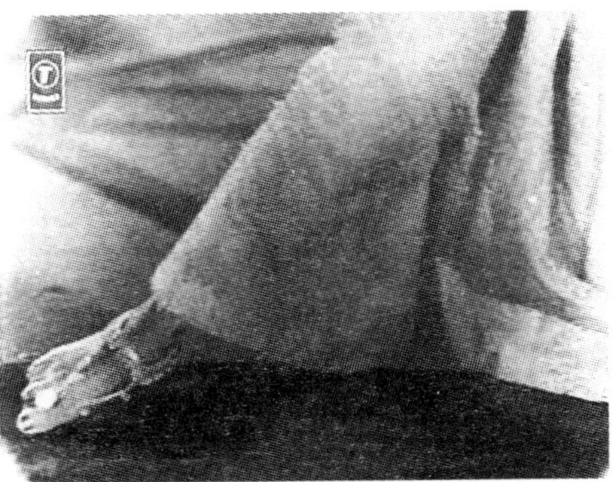

4.2a–c: Stills from *King Kong*: Dance sequence.

1965], *Toofan/The Storm* [Radhakant 1969], *The Killers*, and many more). Many of these female performances are remarkable for their glaring sexual explicitness and their exploitative, commercial dimension. As in earlier action films, here too representations of women are, on the one hand, symptoms of the relations of production constitutive, in the 1960s, of Bombay cinema—marketing strategies devised to help the films to break through in a competitive and restricted exhibition market—and, on the other, the narrative, cinematic dimension whereby the social relations needed to sustain ideal modes of production are staged, mediated, and (cinematically) reproduced. We have seen that *King Kong* opens with a problem about the identity of the hero that leaves open the question of 'what' is being reproduced. Asked who gave him the name of King Kong, the young man's (Dara Singh's) answer—'my mother'—is suitably ambiguous. A mother being both the carrier of lineage and the bearer of any man, that answer places the hero within two (pre- and modern) temporalities at the same time. The dance scene just described pushes the hero into a modern economy, suggesting that the values that are being reproduced are, simultaneously, individuation and muscular power—social relations conducive to individuation as the pre-condition for, and the effect of the productive exploitation of the hero's muscular power.

To put this another way, as soon as the hero is allocated individuated subjectivity and a modern identity, the attributes of his value, now released from hierarchical conventions, are simultaneously re-channeled into a regime of social reproduction that fetishizises not his lineage or his courage, but his strength, his physical energy, and his equally physical desirability. Nowhere is the requirement to re-channel a potentially free-floating energy more evident than in *Ek Tha Alibaba*. Made in the aftermath of *King Kong's* success and released soon after Arthur Lubin's *Thief of Baghdad* (Italy, US, and France 1961) starring Steve Reeves, *Ek Tha Alibaba* is important because, designed to capitalize on Dara Singh's breakthrough with *King Kong*, the film went to extreme lengths to monetize its ingredients—Dara Singh himself and sexualized representations of women. These had proved to be selling points in the previous film and are here promoted more directly for their profit-making potential.

The film opens with a close-up shot of a woman's legs, walking around a swimming pool. The camera moves out slowly to reveal the lower part of a woman's body wrapped in a towel and walking towards, or rather at, the camera. The cut comes only when she is close enough for the camera's eye to be filled with her pelvis (still wrapped in the towel).

This is Milli (Helen), the king's daughter, getting ready to go bathing in a pond at the edge of the forest. Once in the pond, an alligator approaches and Milli starts shouting for help. We cut to a low-angle shot of a man in a loincloth and armless sheepskin jacket standing high on a cliff, as seen from Milli's point of view. The camera moves in slightly. He takes off his jacket and—as Tarzan did numerous times—he jumps into the water with a knife in his hand, and fights with the alligator. Although inter-cut with two underwater shots, the fight is shot primarily from a distance. We look at the hero battling against the alligator from Milli's point of view. Close-ups of her face inscribe Milli, now outside the pond, as the sole spectator. From this distance, we see the hero's muscled arms surfacing from underwater and holding the beast by its neck and fangs. There is, so far, little or no abstract fetishization of physical strength as a free-floating attribute. That burden is carried by Milli, for that is precisely what her look admires and keeps at a distance. However, at the very end of the sequence, when the hero, having killed the alligator, gets out of the water, he approaches Milli and they talk. At this point, the camera moves closer, into a medium shot that frames the hero (to the left) and Milli (to the right) looking at each other, their profiles to the camera. After a short exchange, she exits the frame (to the right), leaving the camera to dwell on Dara Singh's mid-torso for too long to dismiss the delay as an editing 'mistake'.

Taking her cue from Christian Metz (1974) and his conceptualization of the subject in cinema, Laura Mulvey (1975) distinguished three looks: the look of the camera at the pro-filmic, the look of the spectator at the image, and the intra-diegetic look between the characters. Cinema, or rather films advancing claims of verisimilitude, tend to suppress all marks of the enunciating subject, of the look of the camera, by subordinating it to the logic of the intra-diegetic looks. An important function of Milli's (intra-diegetic) look at the hero here is (to use Jakobson's terminology again) a conative one: Milli's look at Dara Singh enjoins the spectator to do the same. After she has exited the frame, the resulting image, Dara Singh's torso, keeps on carrying Milli's desire, enjoining the spectator to continue looking. But the camera's look at this point is not, strictly speaking, subordinated to Milli's intra-diegetic look. Milli's exit leaves us with a frontal medium shot that, unlike the one conveying Milli's subjective point of view, is characterized by a visible gap between the camera and the characters' looks. The function of Milli's presence in the frame is to re-route the look of the camera at the hero onto and via a female character. Milli's exit essentially disrupts the logic of the intra-diegetic looks between the characters. The postponement of the cut leaves the enunciating subject naked, as it were. Its marks, no longer displaced onto the woman, are exposed. As the interpellation of the spectator and the injunction to continue looking take on an emphatic tone, the emphasis brings to the surface the source of the injunction, revealing a narrator with an invested interest in the attribution of value to the image of the wrestler's torso and, through or as the narrator, the economic pressures that led the filmmaker to attribute (commercial) value (and film time) to that image. From this perspective, the dominant function of this image is expressive, in the sense that it registers and expresses the material pressures experienced by the filmmaker and underpinning the film as a commodity. Here, to reduce the matter to a construction of masculinity would be to miss the point. The look at the hero is allocated to a female character by the narrator, that is, by the mise en scène. The delayed cut in this scene separates out the means of representation (addresser and addressee, camera and spectator) from what is being represented. While the ascription of masculinity pertains to the latter (the represented), the delayed cut after Milli's exit shows that, beyond the social categories and positions orchestrated by the mise en scène, a different level is at work, in and as the image, which ultimately presides over narration. I will return to this point shortly.

The sexual dimension that surfaces in *King Kong* in the public frame of the dance is pushed to new limits and integrated into a more private sphere in *Ek Tha Alibaba*, with significant consequences. Soon after their adventure at the pond, Milli and the hero have a late night date in the forest. They are sitting on a rock, talking. Initially we look at this romantic exchange frontally, the actors' upper bodies both in frame and in profile. Soon, however, the exchange breaks into shot-reverse-shots. But while Milli is allocated a subjective point of view, this is not quite the case for the hero. When reversing to his side, the camera keeps at a distance, the better to display his bare chest and arms. Suddenly, as things get going and Milli, playing hard to get, hides behind the rock they were sitting on, a large King Kong-like ape appears from behind, threatening to attack her.

Dara Singh's films are populated with wild animals. Some of them even appear in the credits, listed below the star and the crew. They are, as in earlier stunt films, figurations and displacements of the hero's physicality as seen from an aristocratic, lineage-based perspective for which physical labour is beyond the pale of humanity. On the other hand, within a more modern framework, indeed from the industrial perspective of any cinema, these animals were no more than narrative devices to display the deployment of the actor's strength, to ascribe value to it, and, ultimately, to sell and generate a profit from the films, as they were in some Fearless Nadia films. The least one can say is that in *Ek Tha Alibaba* the giant ape interrupts the sequence, threatening a temporary degeneration of the chaste romance. Once the presentation of physical energy is released from hierarchical social conventions and attached instead to a character who is invested with a subjective dimension, the film is left with the problem of how to channel the hero's energy in a productive way. Accordingly, the appearance of the ape triggers a series of physical exploits, the first of which is to fight and chase the beast away. Significantly, at this point, with a cut, the camera moves out, re-establishing a distance from the pro-filmic that is large enough for the spectator to see no more than two figures in a long shot pursuing each other around a rocky landscape. The performance of the actors—be it Dara Singh or the anonymous stuntman wearing the gorilla suit, the sense of physical energy it must have inevitably required, and its cinematic display for commercial exploitation are disrupted and contained by pseudo-epic narration. Both performers are reduced to fable-like figures, the man against the beast.

The circular structure of Dara Singh's films, the formal changes between opening and final bouts, quite literally mediate the modalities by which, in 1960s India, the deployment of human energy does or does not acquire value. This is less abstract a claim than it may appear. I have argued that the delayed cut after Milli's exit in the scene just described shows that, beyond the social categories orchestrated by the mise en scène, a different dimension is at work in and as the image, presiding over the narration. The linguist and Jakobson's collaborator Louis Hjelmslev (1953) conceptualized any cultural item as consisting of levels of expression (the raw materials) and of content (the semiotic field). He further differentiated the semiotic process constitutive of any cultural item into matter, substance (the broader field of available choices), and form (the choices made, that is the actual text).[25] In this particular instance, the marks of the enunciating subject (the look of the camera) that are brought to the foreground as Milli exits are part of the form of expression and of content of the film. While notions of, say, strength and masculinity, and all the other semiotic and narrative categories at work in the scene— what Roland Barthes called the cultural codes—pertain to the form of content, everything that constitutes the scene as a material object—from the body of the actors and the celluloid their image is printed on to the capital invested to produce that image—falls under the category of form of expression. The postponement of the cut after Milli's exit 'expresses' also the latter level: the investment in Dara Singh's body under the specific relations of production and exhibition as outlined at the beginning of this chapter. The film is not simply 'built around' that investment. As a commodity, the film *is* that investment, while the narrative strategies the film resorts to—the changes from one bout to another—are the workings of that investment, for *they* generate its value.

It would be reductive to stop at this (at the level of form), just as it would be short-sighted to ascribe the narrative tensions at work in the films to the relationship between the wrestling champion and actor Dara Singh, and the director and/or the producer as agents operating in a medium where established conventions were at work that also shaped their films. The Hindi film industry in the 1960s was not a homogenous terrain nor are the action star, the director, and the producer clearly defined categories. Kamran, for instance, who directed many of Dara Singh's films, was a seasoned stuntman, while Dara Singh himself directed and produced several of his films. A better way to understand the narrative tensions at work in the films is to view the films as symptoms of, and mechanisms for sustaining a wider social, cultural, and economic context—in Hjelmslev's terms to relate their form of content and of expression to their substance of content and expression. All this is summed up by a place and a time: 1960s Bombay, understood as a configuration crossed over by coexisting temporalities, few of them synchronous with the films themselves.

The relay of interest groups which constituted that time immediately presided over the production, distribution, and exhibition of these films, as well as over the generic stock and discourses available to their producers, directors, and actors. But the same relay also presided over the ways in which these immediate pressures were orchestrated in the films, as specific stories and their mises en scènes. In the early 1960s, the expansion and restructuring of Bombay industry gave a special resonance to notions of commodification, of human energy as labour power, as of any other commodity, including films, and the value of both. Within the Hindi film industry, growth encountered resistance from the exhibition sector, traditionally, in India as elsewhere, the most impermeable to change. Pressure against their recalcitrance came primarily from producers, who found it increasingly unsustainable to remain within the narrow financial margins imposed, however indirectly, by exhibitors. As a result, Dara Singh's films were screened in rural areas to potential migrants and in the extended suburbs east of Bombay inhabited by the labour force of the city's new factories. In the next chapter, I will discuss the factors that allowed film production finally to grow in the 1970s, when a new Hindi action cinema emerged as defining the Bombay film industry's central stream. Here I have tried to show how, under conditions of industrial growth and growth containment, Hindi film production sought nevertheless to accumulate surplus value. Available for a lower share of the box office than distributors of more prestigious Hindi productions would demand, while at the same time, with the wrestling champion on the bill, offering exhibitors the possibility of high box-office returns relative to the average revenues of rural and suburban cinemas, Dara Singh's films staged that value accumulation potential and the obstacles to its realization in, or rather, *as* their narrative strategies. These reveal that the horizon at work in and as the films was a far more industrialized operation than had been the case in the 1920s and 1930s, and, moreover, differently so. The fantasy Dara Singh's films staged was buttressed by a multitude of small production units which, unlike corporate operations, tended to substitute capital with labour and to use labour more intensively, in industry as much as in cinema. For this reason, unlike, say, 1920s Krishna productions featuring 'pehelwan' Nandaram, Dara Singh's films ascribed value to images of the wrestler by conveying the visual impression of physical energy understood not as an attribute of hierarchical status, volume, agility, or speed, but as muscular power.

Dara Singh's films were the first, in Bombay, to do so—to monetize that particular notion of physical energy—because it was only at that point that, within sections of the Indian economy, a sufficiently intense drive for industrialization had taken root, legitimized on a national scale by a decade or more of development planning. One of these sections was film production, the growth and integration of which, however, was blocked by a national market caught in localized, pre-industrial networks, controlled by exhibitors not ready or willing to expand. This did not prevent Dara Singh's films from projecting, at times, fantasies of muscular power as value, borrowing narratives that gave energy as an attribute of lineage only to distil from them sheer human energy as an abstraction ('muscles' as a symbol of energy), a commodity for commercial exploitation. The films also devised the strategies to channel its productivity, most notably by valuing muscular energy through images of female sexuality, all the while monetizing also those channelling strategies. But Dara Singh's films did all this sporadically—fusing muscle or sheer energy fetishization with other conventions and conceptualizations of a body's value, because pre-industrial social relations and modes of production were constitutive of the horizon of sectors that, within Bombay cinema and in other parts of the Indian economy, were in reality dominant sectors. In the next chapter I discuss the opening up of this force field to new incentives. As we shall see, these new factors did not push cinema in the direction so insistently proposed by Dara Singh's films because the compromise that began to take form in the 1970s saw a combination of pre-industrial forces and finance, not industrial, capital.[26]

NOTES

1. From the second half of the 1980s, Dara Singh's popularity owed primarily to Ramanand Sagar's television epic *Ramayan*, in which Dara Singh played the role of Hanuman. This ninety-one-episode serial marked Doordarshan's first major success and defined one important generic strand of national television. It did not, however, define the film industry's main generic ground. I return to this in Chapter 5.

2. Figures and categories terminology from *Screen* (7 November 1966: 11).

3. The 'sieve' of the title is the cinema screen, because, as the writer claims, that is where most of the profit generated by a film ends up.

4. Telugu, Kannada, and Malayalam film production increased, but their numbers were still much lower than those of Hindi and Tamil films (Rajadhyaksha and Willemen 1999: 30–2).

5. Central Provinces and Berar was a province of British India. It covered much of present-day Madhya Pradesh, Chhattigarh, and Maharashtra. Central India Agency was also a political unit of British India. It covered the northern half of present-day Madhya Pradesh.

6. Significantly, it is also at this juncture that the practice of so-called 'dragging' begins to get a bad press in trade magazines. Throughout the 1950s, the large and slow-moving investments made in glossy social dramas resulted in the marketing strategy of, and race for, 'jubilees' (runs of twenty-five, fifty, etc. weeks). Films would be kept on the bill for several weeks in order to achieve a 'silver' or other jubilee, irrespective of the number of tickets sold. In early 1966 'dragging' began to be perceived as a serious problem by each of the three sectors of the industry. See 'Dragging of films to be ended' in *Screen* (15 April 1966: 1).

7. The cotton industry is a good example. Indian cotton production is habitually associated with large industrial groups. As a whole, however, the production of cotton goods has involved industrial and pre-industrial modes of production. Interestingly, between 1951 and 1969 the cotton industry witnessed not only a high degree of fragmentation: 'available data point to a sustained expansion of small-scale industries. [Throughout the 1950s and 1960s,] net output of non-factory industry more than doubled. The cotton cloth output of

the non-mill sector, consisting mostly of handloom and small-scale power-loom units, increased fourfold. [A]round 80 per cent of the increase in total cloth output was contributed by the decentralized sector' (Vaidyanathan 2005: 961). As Vivek Chibber (2004) has argued (see next section), this was the indirect result of the failure of government policies for planned industrial development. The film industry was not directly targeted by those policies, but it was nevertheless caught in the same economic dynamics.

8. Between 1961 and 1981 the number of factories in Maharashtra doubled from 8233 to 16,594, and employment in the organized sector rose from 8 lakh to 12 lakh (800,000 to 1.2 million) workers (D'Monte 2002: 84).

9. English is one of India's official languages, but the Indian market as a whole has poor purchasing power. The small share of the population that does have adequate purchasing power, comprising many who are also the English speakers, equals a third of the American market, but in the eight years from 1955 to 1962 gross revenues of the MPEAA companies in India grew from under US$2 million to just over US$3.2 million. That is, compared to MPEAA earnings worldwide, as well as in terms of the average Hollywood budget, the Indian market was then insignificant. From 1955 to 1962 the total revenues of the MPEAA members from the Indian market increased, as a percentage of foreign revenues, from 0.65 per cent to 1.08 per cent; compare this to the 80 per cent of foreign revenues represented by the numerically smaller market of Europe (figures from Pendakur 1985).

10. Murphy (1972) believed that this was only the tip of the iceberg and that the true extent of Hollywood's losses in these years would never be known (quoted in Cook 2000: p. 11).

11. In Madras, in 1961, *La Vendetta di Ercole/Goliath and the Dragon* (Vittorio Cottafavi 1960), with Mark Forest, was released at the Odeon in the week of 8 September and again, at the Sarani, in the week of 3 November. *Cartagine in fiamme/Carthage in Flames* (Carmine Gallone 1959) was shown for a week at the end of September, followed by *Gli Ultimi giorni di Pompei/The Last Days of Pompei* (Mario Bonnard and Sergio Leone 1959) in the week of 20 October, by *Davide e Golia/David and Goliath* (R. Pottier and Ferdinando Baldi 1959) on 17 November at the Sahnis, and by *Ercole e la regina di Lidia/Hercules Unchained* (Pietro Francisci 1958, with Steve Reeves) on 22 December at Globe Talkies. In 1966, Anand cinema showed *La Rivolta dei sette* in the week of 18 March and *La Vendetta di Spartaco* in the week of 22 July. In the week of 29 April, the New Elphinstone screened Riccardo Freda's *Maciste all' inferno/Maciste in Hell* (1962).

12. Sergio Leone's *Per un pugno di dollari* (1964) did not reach Bombay screens until 1967, while *La Vendetta di Ercole*, *Cartagine in fiamme*, *Gli Ultimi giorni di Pompei*, *Davide e Golia*, and *Ercole e la regina di Lidia* were shown in 1961.

13. See Dara Singh's autobiography (1993).

14. In *Sangdil/Hard-hearted* (R.C. Talwar 1952), *Pehli Jhalak* (M.V. Raman 1954), and *Jagga Daku/Jagga the Dacoit* (Chandrakant 1959).

15. Conversation with Dara Singh (Juhu, Mumbai, 22 March 2004), according to whom 'the films exhibited all over India, mostly in villages, where wrestling was popular'.

16. See, for instance, the films of Mehboob Khan, and especially *Aan/The Savage Princess* (1952), *Amar* (1954), and *Mother India* (1957).

17. A case in point is the all-time popular *Pakeezah/Pure Heart* (Kamal Amrohi 1971), in which Meena Kumari plays the role of the daughter of a courtesan-dancer, herself a courtesan and a dancer, who falls in love with a high-caste man. The couple is finally allowed romance and marriage by a classic happy ending: Pakeezah turns out to be the daughter of a high-caste man.

18. Ralph Nelson's *Requiem for a Heavyweight* (1962) is an exception, but it is not really a wrestling film: the protagonist, played by Anthony Quinn, is a boxer who, because of corporate corruption in the boxing business, is degraded into becoming a wrestler.

19. For Jakobson, six elements have to be in place for an act of communication: an addresser, an addressee, a context, a code, contact, and a message. A function attaches to each of these elements. During communication, each of the six elements is at work but, at different moments, the orchestration of their operations varies, their functions undergoing remodulations and adjustments. So, at a particular moment priority may be given to establishing contact (phatic function), as for instance when, at the beginning of a phone call, we say 'Hallo', meaning 'Are you listening?' In cinema the equivalent would be the distributor or producer's logo, calling for attention and asking 'Are you ready to watch?' At another moment the emphasis may be on giving a context (referential function), for instance with a title card giving the name of the place and the time in which the story is supposed to take place. At yet another moment the emphasis may be on the addressee (conative function), as when in a horror film or a thriller the music tells the spectator to pay attention because something is about to happen, or the loud volume and the direct address to camera in advertisements, advising viewers to buy so-and-so product. An example of the metalinguistic function, pertaining to the code, is the question 'Do you know what I mean?' during a conversation, while a camera lingering on a woman's body parts when such lingering has no specific narrative functions would be an instance of the expressive function (pertaining to the addresser) in cinema. According to Jakobson's model, during a speech act each of these functions are always cooperative, but at each moment one element or function is dominant, in the sense of being given priority over the others.

20. My use of the term 'epic' here refers not to a specific set of 'texts', but to a mode of narration manifestations of which can be found in all pre-modern cultures. There is a large body of literature on Hindu epics. Within this body of work, Romila Thapar (1987) was among the first (and continues to be one of the few) scholars to have opened up discussions of religious narratives to questions of governance. Along the same line of argument as Godzich, Thapar has observed

that an epic is essentially a literary crystallization of the heroic ideal. She argues that to search for conclusive dates and other factual evidence in epics, in the *Odyssey* as much as in the Mahabharata, is to search for the impossible because the purpose of epic literature was not to produce a chronological sequence of events. In the vision of the bard, the event, which may once have been historical, transcends its historicity and become symbolic (Thapar 2000: 613–14). Here I have preferred Godzich's discussion of epics as one of the many forms of auditive culture primarily because Godzich, as a literary historian, pays greater attention than Thapar does to questions of narration and modes of address. His analysis thus opens up a productive analytical framework to examine the interweaving of discursive practices, socio-economic relations, and modes of governance. Second, I have relied on Godzich, rather than on the large body of work on Indian epics, because my intention in adopting the term 'epic' is resolutely not to advance the claim that narratives circulating in as far back as (perhaps) the fourth millennium BC, such as the Hindu epics, continued to structure in a fundamental way the narrative strategies of films made in the early 1960s. For a critique of that kind of ahistorical (but very common) line of argument in the context of discussion about Hindi cinema, see Vitali (2002).

21. Conversation with Dara Singh, Juhu, Bombay, 22 March 2004.

22. Ibid.

23. Ibid.

24. The same type of dance is shown in *The Criminals/Hum Sab Chor Hain* (Maruti 1973) an urban thriller starring Dara Singh which I discuss briefly in Chapter 5. In *The Criminals* more or less the same dance is part of a dream dreamt by Sheyla just as she makes up her mind to switch sides and leave a gangster for Mohan (Dara Singh). As in *King Kong*, this is one of *The Criminals'* few colour scenes. Dara Singh is chained to a pole and the oniric dance, performed in front of him, stages Sheyla as she is physically (and sexually) threatened by a gang of men.

25. See also Christian Metz's (1974: 208–19) application of Hjelmslev's concepts, and the entry on Hjelmslev in Ducrot and Todorov (1972). For an application of Jakobson and Hjelmslev's concepts to the study of cinema and film narration, see Willemen (2005b). My use of these terms here, as elsewhere in the book, borrows from the latter essay.

26. For a seminal account of the relationship between industrial and finance capital, see Harvey (1999).

5

The 1970s

THE LITERATURE ON THE 'ANGRY YOUNG MAN'

BY AND LARGE, FILM HISTORIANS HAVE TENDED TO PAINT THE HISTORY OF HINDI cinema in two rough brush-strokes: one delineating a period running, roughly, from the 1930s, when synchronized sound was slowly and gradually introduced, to the consolidation of the feudal family romance, or 'social' in the 1950s; the second one indicating, equally roughly, the contemporary era, starting from the fragmentation of the social into more distinctive generic bundles in the early 1970s. In this linear historiographic narrative, the emergence of the action film as a mainstream genre of Hindi cinema in the transition from one to the other has been discussed on the basis of two models.

The first model is represented by a large body of literature that has allowed itself to be caught in a circular discourse: on the one hand, Hindi action cinema, understood as the cluster of films featuring Amitabh Bachchan as the 'angry young man', is seen as the outcome of a script-based production practice that, within the Indian film industry, was new and unique; on the other hand, these films are understood to owe their existence, specificity, and success to their star. The emergence of Amitabh Bachchan as a film star is thus referred back to a change in the practices of film production, while those changes are simultaneously referred back to the emergence of the star's forceful personality. Studies rehearsing this type of argument tend to dedicate little more than a *pro forma* paragraph to the socio-economic context of the Bachchan action films, the rest of the text consisting of descriptions, even eulogies, of the star persona, conflating the actor and the characters he played or reducing the 'context' to biographical notion of personal history.[1] When commentators do attempt a more analytical approach to the generic patterns that characterize these films, the focus remains on the hero and the star, who, compared to earlier heroes and actors, provides the starting point for the identification of 'new' narrative structures.[2]

This circular way of proceeding is by no means unique to historians of Hindi cinema.[3] But the problem is not, as some film historians have put it, that the generic categories available to historians of Indian cinemas derive from European and North American cinemas,[4] but, rather, that in film historiography the nature and existence of a film genre is too often treated as a fait accompli. Books on specific bundles of films tend to define genres retrospectively: having identified a set of shared ingredients or selling points in films that are marketed under a label dictated by some sectors of the film industry, a search is undertaken for similar ingredients in other films—only finally to reproduce in the definition of the genre the marketing strategy that the industry developed to promote a particular group of films at a particular time. Genre definitions conceived in this way project contemporary marketing discourses backwards into film history. A concomitant effect of this (lack of) methodology is that, in the Hindi variant as much as in other cinemas, all memory of antecedents is reformatted and brought into line, retroactively, with contemporary marketing. The 'as never seen before' claim used in the industry to sell the films is thus incorporated and sold to us anew, this time around by the film historian. The paradox is that this is done by way of a backward projection that claims that things have always been like the current marketing priorities require them to have been.

Lending legitimacy to the discourse of the film industry's marketeers—for whom star value sells films and films sell star value—many historians of Hindi cinema tend to project the qualities ascribed to the star-hero onto the particular audience that is deemed to be the films' intended market. The Amitabh Bachchan hero is 'lumpen proletariat' and so, we are told, is the films' most dedicated public. In reality there is no evidence that this was indeed the case; on the contrary, as we shall see in what follows, what evidence there is indicates that what sets Amitabh Bachchan's action films apart from pre- and co-existing films containing or emphasizing the action ingredient is precisely the fact that Bachchan's films were exhibited in first-run venues patronized also by the middle class and previously reserved for the melodramatic fare that defined, until the late 1960s, the industry's central ground.

The invocation of 'the public' as cover for the deployment of specific marketing strategies has allowed critics a further displacement into a dichotomy—the people and the state—that, especially in the context of Indian cinemas, has been rehearsed ad nauseam in discussions of the melodrama. At this point, critical positions polarize between those (the populists) who endow the public with an active, culture-producing, and, more often than not, transgressive role, and those (the orthodox) who see the same public as the passive target of a monolithic notion of state ideology. With criticism caught between the state and the public, the economic-commercial processes most immediately determining the films are simultaneously acknowledged and dismissed: through the short-hand term 'formula film'. As an eminent cultural historian put it, the film industry is 'merely' handling already circulating sentiments and fantasies (Kakar 1989: 28).

This refusal to engage with the most basic processes of cultural production and circulation while simultaneously projecting them onto the circumscribed terrain of the nation is baffling, not least because it hovers around, without addressing, a tension between, on the one hand, geographical, social, and political specificity, and, on the other, economic networks unproblematically assumed to be global. Again, this is not unique to accounts of Hindi or other Indian cinemas. Film historiography has remained caught in an analytical framework that, having developed alongside specific European and American cinematic practices, has tended to emphasize the national dimension of cinema at the expense of the local and transnational interconnectedness of its many forms. Today this historiographic framework is enshrined in a majority of Film Studies departments across the world. But diverse types of action cinema emerged at specific times worldwide, more or less simultaneously. Action cinema is a highly hybrid, transnational category, the national and regional forms of which retain distinctive characteristics. Yet, while there may well be good reason for critics to regard the Indian state as one of the factors determining the shape of (any) Hindi cinema, when it comes to action cinema, as opposed to, say, melodrama, most critics have tended to explain away its emergence in India in terms of global influence, where 'global' is restricted to Hollywood. Incidentally, this is also the line of argument that was adopted in the 1920s by the Indian Cinematograph Committee and, in the 1970s, by Indian film magazines, even if American pressure was not a factor unique to those years. The customary emphasis on Hollywood appears, in turn, to rule out other pressures—such as the competition, in the 1970s Indian domestic market, from Italian Westerns and Hong Kong martial arts films. The impact of these films on the Hindi and other Indian action cinema of this decade is far more evident than that of the American action film.[5]

This market-led approach has produced a fanciful account of the emergence of the action film in Hindi and other Indian cinemas. It is a narrative that, while seemingly incapable of remembering, let alone accounting for, the precedents of the Hindi action films of the 1970s, paradoxically takes its cue from a historicist model of cultural periodization, one generic series succeeding the earlier one, one star the next. Ignoring the modes of production that generated Amitabh Bachchan and his action films and obscuring their (far from linear) mode of circulation, historians have tended instead to transpose onto the star that subliminal quality of final instance that, until the 1960s, film theory ascribed to the film author or director. The director or the star are thus endowed with extraordinary powers of determination, as if s/he were above or outside the very set of tensions in which s/he, along with other elements of production, is caught. This type of approach implies a humanist concept of the individual as independent from the historical conditions that overdetermine subjectivities, and a notion of culture as pertaining to a different realm than the material conditions of which cultural items are the products. Since, as Peter Bürger (1984 and 1992) has argued, the latter notion of culture was historically intertwined with the rise of bourgeois social relations out of a religiously sanctioned status hierarchy, the question worth asking is whether the shift—in critical as well as marketing discourses—from director back to star[6] is a response to a new phase in the development of capitalism and, within it, of the industrialization of culture.

This is the starting point for the second and far more productive approach to the emergence of the action film as a defining genre of Hindi cinema's narrative stock and commercial middle-ground, an approach pioneered by Madhava Prasad in his now seminal *Ideology of the Hindi Film: A Historical Construction* (1998b). Prasad's main preoccupation is not Hindi action cinema or any of the other genres he examines. Located in a broadly defined tradition of Marxist cultural theory, Prasad raises the much larger 'question of the state as a factor in cultural processes', that is, the study of cinema 'as an institution that is part of the continuing struggles *over* the form of the state.' (1998b: 8). Engaging with a long-standing debate on the nature of the state in Indian historiography, Prasad sets out to examine 'at the most general level, the political, economic, historical and cultural determinants of popular Hindi cinema' in order to arrive at 'a historical construction of a conjuncture in recent Indian history, when, in the midst of a major political crisis, the Bombay film industry underwent a significant transformation, affecting its overall structure as well as the formal properties of individual film texts' (1998b: 14).

Prasad's immediate focus is thus, on the one hand, the fragmentation of the narrative frame that had dominated Hindi cinema since the mid-

1940s—the 'all-encompassing' feudal family romance or social—into the distinct action, parallel, and middle-class genres in the 1970s; and, on the other hand, the connections between such generic fragmentation and the socio-political turmoil—a 'disaggregation'—that characterized the first decade of Indira Gandhi's rule. To begin with, Prasad argues that 'three mutually-reinforcing factors served as the conditions of possibility' of the social: '(1) backward capitalist conditions in the film industry; (2) a transitional state-form determined by the interests of the dominant coalition, characterized by the deferral of bourgeois dominance; and (3) the persistence of pre-capitalist ideologies and the continued authority of traditional elites' (1998: 117). The feudal family romance of the 1950s was the symptom of a 'heterogeneous' (as opposed to vertically and horizontally integrated) mode of production—the outcome of industrial and pre-industrial practices—within which 'the star, the music, the dialogue, and other component values [had] an independent existence of their own, [e]ntering into combinations for the space of production, outside of which they remained in a "free" state' (Prasad 1994: 59–60). While this allowed the social to function as an all-encompassing genre effectively incorporating a variety of generic ingredients (including action) and marginalizing others (such as kissing), it simultaneously made limited demands of cohesion and integration on the elements that the films did incorporate. The star image of the Hindi melodrama of the 1950s, Prasad argues, was sustained not by the cinema's industrial conventions, as it was in the US, but by 'the prevailing Hindu codes of iconicity' and the 'innate charm' attributed to the aristocracy, while the actors embodied in their roles and personae 'a certain conception of the heroic' (1998b: 133).

As the feudal family romance staged and sustained the conditions of social reproduction in Nehruvian India, in the 1960s, when 'a period of intense political upheaval [b]rought into crisis the political form of the national consensus (represented by the dominant integrationist role of the Congress Party)' (Prasad 1998b: 117), the social lost its legitimacy: 'the film industry faced a challenge to its established aesthetic conventions and modes of production', a crisis that 'it was able to survive by a strategy of internal [and generic] fragmentation' (ibid.: 118). While the forces unleashed at a political level were contained by Indira Gandhi's authoritarian populist government, according to Prasad the attack on the film industry came in the new role of the Film Finance Corporation (FFC).

The idea of the FFC was originally suggested in the 1951 *Report of the Film Enquiry Committee*, two years after the government appointed

S.K. Patil to examine all aspects of the film industry. The report, however, was ignored until 1960, when the FFC was set up under the Ministry of Finance to give low interest loans to selected projects, mainly within the independent sector, and to assist the industry 'by providing, affording or procuring finance or other facilities for the production of films of good standard' (Rajadhyaksha and Willemen 1999: 162). Transferred four years later to the Ministry of Information and Broadcasting, the FFC soon began to confine itself to supplementing the budgets of mainstream or internationally known filmmakers until 1969, when Indira Gandhi and her information and broadcasting ministers, Nandini Satpathy and I.K. Gujral, announced new guidelines. The FFC's funding would now be devoted to the production of cinema that was realist, narrative centred, developmental, and culturally distinctively Indian.[7]

Claiming that 'the crux of the matter was not the ideological danger of state-sponsored cinema [s]o much as the economic danger of the emergence of a formidable competitor' (Prasad 1998b: 122–3) and of state-sponsored fiction cinema, Prasad argued that

The problem that the industry faced was how to continue to function with the existing mode of production without the readymade narrative framework of the feudal family romance. The FFC project's long term threat was a reorganization of film-production on the basis of the centrality and autonomy of the production sector. This was the factor that prompted a search by established industry figures for compromise solutions involving a workable mix of star and narrative values. Salim–Javed [scriptwriters of the Bachchan formula] also identified themselves with this project for internal reform. But the resolution that imposed itself finally was one which would make this change unnecessary. This resolution was made possible by *the intensification of the value deriving from the star system* through the infusion of political power into the figure of the star on the model of the populist cinema of Tamil Nadu. The star became a mobilizer, demonstrating superhuman qualities and assuming a power that transformed the others who occupied the same terrain into spectators. As the auratic power of the represented social order diminished, there was a compensating increase in the aura of the star as public persona. (ibid.: 134, emphasis added)

A stricter use of the script was crucial to this process of star value accumulation. The Bachchan persona was different from that of earlier stars 'because in it there is a degree of integration of star-value with narrative that [was] unprecedented in the Hindi cinema' (ibid.: 133).[8] This new form of narrative—namely Salim–Javed scripts—placed new demands upon the star.

My objective, as I map the ups and downs of the action film in the Bombay film industry, is to arrive at a structural understanding of the genre—that is to grasp the connections between the economic dynamics that generate the films as industrial products or commodities and the instrumental function of the film texts in mediating the social relations deemed necessary for cultural-industrial production by forces constitutive of the Indian economy at any given time. From this perspective, Prasad's argument is extremely useful: by pointing to the socio-economic ground of the feudal family romance, Prasad also opened up a line of enquiry in the historiography of Hindi cinema not dissimilar to the one I now pursue here. However, from the perspective of a line of inquiry that seeks to understand the functioning of the generic categories constitutive of a cluster of films as structural categories, the concept of a heterogeneous mode of production does not hold. All societies are compromise formations, in the sense that multiple temporalities always coexist within any one society. The question is not whether one industry is integrated or not, but of the different nature of the integration, and the different interests at work in or as the industry and their mode of interaction.[9] For this, the FFC and notions of socio-political disaggregation are both too punctual and too broad.[10]

I return to this point in the next two sections of this chapter, where I discuss at length the economic and commercial considerations that led the Bombay film industry to change the generic structure that, until the late 1960s, had defined its centre. For now, the question that arises in the light of Prasad's argument is this: if, as Prasad argues, Amitabh Bachchan's action films were the outcome of a process whereby 'the value deriving from the star system' was 'intensified' through a process of narrative integration, what was the nature of that value?—not as ascribed, today, by the industry's marketeers, but as seen or ascribed then, by and in the time which knew Amitabh Bachchan?

PRELUDE

In 1972, when *Zanjeer/The Chain* (Prakash Mehra 1973), the film that brought Bachchan to the attention of the public, was being produced, many stunt actors were available at the low end of the market. Dara Singh was still extremely popular. As in the 1960s, however, Dara Singh continued to be cast exclusively in films that were far from central to the industry's main generic ground, including, increasingly, in mythological films. His wrestling movies and thrillers having been an important moment in the process of secularization that had characterized the emergence and consolidation of action cinema in Bombay since the 1920s, Dara Singh eventually ended his acting career playing Hanuman in Doordarshan's *Ramayan*, that is in the same type of role as Ganpat Shinde in Phalke's *Lanka Dahan* some seventy years earlier.[11] More to the centre of the film industry's defining ground than Dara Singh was Pran, who was a favourite for roles involving a measure of action. Amitabh Bachchan belonged to neither (marginal nor central) category. A former stage actor and radio announcer, he was a relatively unknown actor who had been cast in minor roles in a range of films—from war movies to romantic stories about middle-class couples—often alongside NFDC (National Film Development Corporation) acting school graduate and film star Jaya Bhaduri who was later to become his wife. Stars of the period were, on the whole, versatile, and the likes of Dilip Kumar could play romantic characters as well as more active roles involving some action. However, film magazines for the English-educated public, such as *Film World*, regularly policed the boundaries of Hindi cinema's generic and commercial ground by warning established stars against the risk of being 'typecast' whenever a star acted in a film containing some action. The opposite—that is the possibility of being typecast in melodramatic roles—was not perceived as a threat, but as a step forward in the actor's career. Originally, *Zanjeer*'s main role was offered to Dev Anand, but since at the time he was experiencing a revival, Dev Anand rejected it, evidently regarding it as a bad career move. Unlike Dev Anand and other stars, in 1972 Bachchan had very little to lose. Prior to the release of *Zanjeer*, he had been more or less absent from film magazines. The rare mentions of the actor consisted of sniggering one-liners dismissing his performance as 'sleepwalking'.[12] Unlike well-known stars, who were often referred to as 'thespians', Bachchan was deemed a bad actor because he seemed to lack their melodramatic capacity to emote on stage. He did not, in other words, fit the bill of what was then Hindi cinema's defining generic template. Amitabh Bachchan was thus cast in *Zanjeer* because, as an ordinary actor devoid of melodramatic skills, he was a cheap, 'good-looking' male body available within the central to upper end of the market.

Zanjeer was a cheap production with poor sets, no star value, and narrative ingredients that, until then, had been deemed to appeal exclusively to a larger but unofficial market at the lower end of the industry. The only unusual features for a cheap production were, first, the commissioning of, and adherence to, a script (Kabir 1999), then an uncommon practice in the Hindi cinema in general. But when Salim Khan and Javed Akhtar were first approached by the producer, neither of them was a prominent figure in cinema.[13] Nor was the existence of a script for production in any way binding. As Akhtar explained in a long interview (Kabir 1999: 81–2), the script for *Zanjeer* was not written for any particular star, and certainly not with Amitabh Bachchan in mind. The absence of so central a marketing instrument as a star put a particular burden on Javed Akhtar and Salim Khan's work. *Zanjeer*'s script systematized the incorporation into the film of selling points that had proved their effectiveness in the large, lower end of the market, adapting them to some of the generic requirements of the industry's central stream, including the construction of a distinctive star and character persona suitable for future exploitation.

Second, because of the absence of a star in the cast, the release of *Zanjeer* was preceded by a much larger than usual advertising campaign in the trade press, with multiple full or two-page advertisements that sometimes presented the films as scripted by 'Salim–Javed, writers of *Seeta aur Geeta*' (/*Seeta and Geeta*, Ramesh Sippy 1972).[14] This was followed by blanket distribution across the country. *Zanjeer* was advertised in *Screen* on 11 May 1973 and distributed simultaneously in Bombay, Bengal, Delhi and Uttar Pradesh, Punjab, Central India, Mysore, Hyderabad, Tamil Nadu, Andhra Pradesh, and overseas. In central and greater Bombay, the film was distributed directly by Prakash Mehra Production which succeeded in placing it in twenty cinemas, ten of which were in the suburbs.[15] In Calcutta, too, the film was released in several cinemas (thirty-one) more or less simultaneously.

As far as Bombay was concerned, *Zanjeer* did not fetch most of the best venues,[16] but it did have an unexpectedly long run, one of the longest of the year along with *Seeta aur Geeta* and a dozen other films (*Screen*, 11 January 1974: 1, 4). In *Screen*'s annual review it was not included among the films of 'artistic merit', but it did bring Amitabh Bachchan to the attention of crucial exhibitors. As I have shown in the previous chapters, star construction was by no means a novel idea, neither in Hindi nor in other Indian cinemas. Star construction had been an important feature of Tamil cinema and politics for years, but it was also a crucial factor in film production and exhibition in the 1920s with Sharda-produced Master Vithal films, in the 1930s with Wadia Movietone's Fearless Nadia, and in the 1960s with the wrestling films of Dara Singh. *Zanjeer*'s successful run was followed, two years later, by the phenomenal box-office returns of *Sholay/Flames of the Sun* (Ramesh Sippy 1975) and, to a lesser extent, of *Deewar/The Wall* (Yash Chopra 1975).[17] With the success of these three films, the Javed Akhtar–Salim Khan script became a 'formula'—a template that infused star value into Amitabh Bachchan by buttressing his figure with the plots, diegetic figurations, and choreographies that had proved to work, as for Dara Singh's films, in the lower end of the market. The new formula 'mainstream-ized' this existing (1960s) generic format by investing larger sums into its constitutive ingredients. However, this process led to films that were profoundly different from Dara Singh's because they mediated a new, post-1960s juncture of Bombay cinema as a part of the Indian economy. The new pressures that characterized this configuration and the horizons that it envisaged as most conducive to surplus accumulation are themselves inscribed into Amitabh Bachchan's action films, at many levels of the texts. I discuss these films later in the chapter, but in order to trace the connections between the generic choices that constitute these texts and their context—in order, that is, to establish with some historical accuracy the structural functioning of these films—the layered economic fabric that generated them must first be delineated in some detail, for this is what, in 1970s India, ascribed value to Amitabh Bachchan and to the films' many other ingredients.

INDIRA GANDHI'S U-TURN

If the value of the stars who dominated Hindi cinema in the 1940s and 1950s—feudal romance 'thespians' such as Dilip Kumar—was infused with the charm of an aristocracy that embodied pre-modern ideals of subjectivity *because* the film industry was imbricated in pre-industrial relations and/or a landed economy, what then were the economic patterns, the relations of production, and the types of capital that lent value to Bachchan and the narrative that framed his star status? What follows is a revaluation of the changes that characterized the Indian economy shortly after Indira Gandhi came into power, taking into account international pressures and, following from that, a series of considerations about the film industry's place in that changing economy. I will turn to the action films that Amitabh Bachchan made between 1973 and the late 1980s once I have retraced the economic pressures that generated the films as commodities in the first place and which, in so doing, left the marks of their interests in the body of the texts.

Finding that its markets at home and abroad had come under increased pressure from lower cost exports from developing economies, the US, from the 1970s, redirected its economy towards the FIRE (finance, insurance, and real estate) sector. Manufacturing did remain the foundation of the new capitalist order, but it turned global. The crisis of profitability in First World countries left a lot of finance in search of more profitable investment and created an overabundant liquidity which was recycled as loan capital on apparently favourable terms to Third and Second World countries. This new regime enabled the US to run large deficits in its balance of trade while reflating effective demand and investment, which, in turn, created an expanding demand for imports of those industrial products that North American businesses no longer found profitable to produce. Relative to First World countries, in the 1970s as in the 1960s, Third World regions increased their degree of industrialization. Throughout the 1970s, this economic expansion was financed by borrowing on the international money market (Arrighi 1991; Brenner 1998).

During the 1960s the Indian economy had grown significantly but the state's policies of economic planning had begun to lose legitimacy, fuelling calls for internal liberalization both from state managers and from the capitalist class. The problem was that, in an economy with a shortage of foreign exchange, internal liberalization easily translated into a drain of foreign reserves. Announced under the prime ministership of Lal Bahadur Shastri, plans to dismantle the regime of controls and regulations on industrial activity that came with planning were held at bay by memories of the 1957 crisis. In 1965 and 1966, however, India had experienced two of the worst droughts of the post-War era, making the nation almost entirely reliant on food aid from the Johnson administration in the US. Johnson recognized this as an opportunity to force the kind of policy changes that the World Bank had been demanding on the US's behalf. Under Indira Gandhi, India accepted the package of reforms in return for food and promises of continued flows of financial aid. The package included a devaluation of the rupee, a new agricultural strategy reliant on new high-yield seeds and technology provided by Western firms that formed the basis of the Green Revolution, a roll back of the industrial licensing regime, and a loosening of controls on the prices and distribution of several industrial commodities (Chibber 2004: 217–19).

But the package did not stay in place for long. By 1970 it had already been reversed. The turn towards liberalization had depended on the continuation, even acceleration, of the flow of aid from the World Bank and the US. Without such aid, the removal of controls held the danger of causing another foreign exchange crisis. When the promised increase in aid did not materialize, Indira Gandhi immediately reimposed the import, price, and distribution controls that the package had targeted, while the forty-two industries that had been freed from licensing were again placed under the purview of state authorities (Chibber 2004: 221). In August 1972, general insurance was nationalized, followed by the coal-mining industry soon after. The Foreign Exchange Regulation Act (FERA), passed in 1973, placed numerous restrictions on foreign investment and the functioning of foreign companies, while ceilings were imposed on urban landownership (Chandra 2003: 14).

Above all, in 1969 Indira Gandhi had nationalized India's fourteen largest banks more or less overnight. Five years later, in order to reduce national expenditure and thus the budget deficit and to curb consumption and thus check inflation, she introduced a highly unpopular scheme of compulsory deposits amounting to a freeze in wages and salaries: salaried employees were to deposit all wage increases and half of their additional dearness allowance into a compulsory savings deposit with the government. Simultaneously, to placate the disgruntled low-salaried groups, a ceiling was imposed on all dividends paid by private companies, while tax payers whose annual income exceeded Rs 15,000 were asked to put an additional 4 to 8 per cent of their income into compulsory deposits (Chandra 2003: 19). Credit centralization was part of a broad programme of economic and political centralization that responded to the rise of finance capital in the US by sheltering India from its pressures. Indira Gandhi's administration, not the World Bank or the IMF, took full control of the rupee capital flow within the country. So, while by the 1980s India's industrial manufacturing and overall performance was bettered only by China and South Korea, unlike South Korea, whose total long-term debt services rose from 3.1 per cent of GNP in 1970 to 10.2 per cent in 1986, India's total debt services over the same period, like those of China, barely changed (1.1 in 1970 and 1.6 in 1986) (Vanaik 1990: 281).

The centralization of credit had huge repercussions on the shape of the Indian industry and finance that grew under the state's protectionist aegis. Although large sections of the Indian capitalist class were dependent on the government, not only for industrial licences, quotas, and import allocations, but also for investment funds from nationalized banks and other government-controlled industrial and agricultural development programmes, the hostility of this class to the Congress took the form of withholding fresh investment into now state-controlled financial institutions (Chandra 2003: 29–30). Indeed, the sector to grow most as a direct result of the centralization of finance was the so-called 'black' economy (Vanaik 1990: 36). The black economy had first become a significant sector in South Asia during World War II, but in the 1970s, with credit centralization, the underside of state-sponsored private capitalist development expanded faster and further. The large body of work produced by historians on this particular feature of the Indian economy has tended to agree on two points: that the black economy has grown and is growing, and that the boundary between the black and the official or 'white' economy is anything but clear. As Achin Vanaik observed, in India, this black economy is closely integrated with the white economy:

Black savings flow into the capital market and into bank deposits (with few questions asked), thus providing resources for investment. [A] black economy is not unique to India, but its size—conservatively estimated at 40–50 per cent of the recorded economy in 1990 (and growing)—is almost certainly significantly larger than in other industrializing countries, such as Brazil, South Korea and Mexico, if only because of the array of Indian government controls. (ibid.: 36)

As Jan Breman as shown, in this context, also characterized by the closure of more cotton mills, large sections of the industrial labour force were 'expelled' from the formal sector. Alternative employment had to be found in the informal sector. This, in turn, triggered a process of deskilling (2004: 143–90).

THE BOMBAY FILM INDUSTRY IN THE 1970s

> *Mard ka baap to Dara Singh hi ho sakta hai*
> [Who else but Dara Singh could play the role of Mard's
> (Amitabh Bachchan's) father?]
> —Manmohan Desai on casting for *Mard*

From the early 1970s, with the nationalization of banks and more capillary forms of credit centralization, a spiralling share of Indian capital found a parallel and, on the whole, cheaper channel of circulation in the film industry. This, in itself, was not an entirely new development. In the 1930s, with the open support of the Congress, film stars had been offered a sizeable share of their salary in the form of unaccounted money. Part of it would be (colonial) tax free, and its reception was considered a nationalist act (Barnouw and Krishnaswamy 1980: 57). It is a well-known fact that since then, and to a different degree after World War II, the Indian film industry has continued to function as an ancillary circulation belt for undeclared money. Which is why figures for cinema—from box-office returns to companies' financial records—are either not available or downright unreliable. But the point here is not whether or not a share of the capital circulating within the film industry is white or black, but of mapping the type(s) of capital constitutive of a specific cluster of films and its modes of circulation within and without the industry. From this point of view, the 1970s mark an important change in the Bombay film industry's relation to the state as the agency regulating the movement of capital within the nation—important because one of its effects was to alter the balance between the types of interests at work in and as the mainstream of Hindi cinema.

As Prasad (1998b) argued, unlike in Hollywood, in the Bombay film industry industrial capital has never been dominant: merchant capital (the distributor-financier) and landed interests (the rentier class of exhibitors) have tended to rule instead. In the 1950s, this combination of capitalist and pre-capitalist interests infused the dominant narrative formula and the star persona with feudal notions of status. By contrast, the films of Dara Singh resulted from a combination of small merchant and industrial capital that occupied a marginal position in relation to an exhibition circuit controlled by landed interests. Whereas until the end of the 1960s the rentier class of exhibitors strongly resisted what Prasad calls 'the expansionist drive of the logic of the market' (1994: 47), from 1969 onwards credit centralization significantly raised the stake of merchant capital in Bombay cinema.

The creation of the FFC and its failure were symptomatic of this development, although in themselves not the cause. Whatever the film industry's imbrication in the black economy at any point in time, since the inception of cinema in India, the industry's relations with the state have been marked by a great degree of ambivalence and contradictions from both sides. Industry demands for support addressed to both the colonial and independent governments came with varying degrees of resistance (at times effective, at other times less so) to any form of duty and regulation—from entertainment tax to import duty on equipment and raw stock. High taxes, centralized raw stock allocation, and censorship notwithstanding, Nehru's administration more or less ignored cinema as a cultural practice and as an industry, focusing instead on radio and limiting itself to appointing a committee whose industrial and ideological guidelines might just as well have never been issued. This made for a relatively peaceful coexistence marked by a great deal of laissez faire. The creation of the FFC in 1960 and, nine years later, its venturing into fiction film production, were certainly a radical change in policy on the part of Indira Gandhi, but the real objective of that exercise ought to be understood from a broader perspective than Prasad allows. The FFC may well have been intended as an agency for the reorganization of film production on the basis of the centrality of the production sector, but even a passing glance at the *Report of the Film Enquiry Committee* of 1951— a report that correctly ascribed to distribution a directly determining role in film production—would have told the ministers in charge that, in the long term, tackling the problem from the production end of the business was not going to be an effective way to achieve so ambitious an aim. The question here is not of assessing the competence or the immediate intentions of the ministers in charge, but of situating the creation of the FFC and the mode of implementation of its policy within the broader structural constraints which other government planning bodies were also facing. This context allows us better to understand how the film industry saw the FFC's operation and to weigh the industry's (by no means uniform) reaction to it. Given the support for market liberalization at the time, both within the capitalist class and among ministry managers—a support that was in turn drawing on a discourse of government policy inefficiency and incoherence—the film industry could not have seen in the FFC the emergence of a powerful competitor. Rather, as Prasad (1994) also observed, the main fear was that of state interference, even heavy-handed intervention, in the industry's modes of operation. Retrospectively, those sections of the film industry that went so far as to suspect plans of nationalization were not all that far off the mark: they saw the FFC as yet another instance of a larger policy package aimed at financial centralization—something Indira Gandhi was actually undertaking in many other sectors of the Indian economy through, among other things, nationalization, with no room for negotiation.

But the FFC was abortive from the start on both counts. It failed to reorient the industry towards production because it never sought to intervene in 'the nexus between theatre owners and the financier distributors' (Prasad 1998b: 126)—on the one hand, leaving the state-produced films without exhibition outlets and, on the other, effectively continuing Nehru's policy of non-intervention in cinema. The FFC's turn to the production of commercially viable films shows that while Indira Gandhi put a temporary halt to liberalization in other industrial and financial sectors, the film industry itself was allowed to proceed in the free-market way, with distributors and exhibitors left unaffected. At the time, filmmaker Mrinal Sen described Satyajit Ray's support for the

FFC's new found commercial bent as a call for the 'prevention of alleged cruelty to money-backers' (*Filmfare*, 24 March 1972: 51, quoted in Prasad 1998: 126), but this definition could just as well have applied to the FFC from the start. With the rest of the economy under close government scrutiny, the FFC's abortive agenda enabled the film industry to develop its role as a sheltered network for the circulation of money evading government control to a degree that it had never achieved before. At this point, the merchant and landed interests that had been constitutive of the industry since the 1930s and which had dominated in the 1950s, metamorphosed into speculative finance capital. Amitabh Bachchan's action films were both instruments and effects of this transformation.

In the 1960s, Hindi film production had fallen to record low figures not touched since World War II. Figures for Indian film production for 1968 showed a significant recovery, but out of the 351 films made that year, only 89 were produced in Bombay (Madras made 227, 14 of which in Hindi) (*Screen*, 10 January 1969: 1, 11). A year later, the situation reversed itself: Bombay production jumped by 223 per cent to 199 films (while Madras's fell to 208). A number of factors tend to be cited as the cause of this sharp increase in production. One is the gradual lifting of Nehru's ban on the construction of new cinemas. Licensing was somewhat relaxed in Bombay in 1956, but this did not lead to a significant increase in the number of venues nor in films produced. When, in 1968, the state of Maharashtra further relaxed licensing regulations, the only ones to oppose this measure were the exhibitors. Their stand did not change radically in the 1970s. Significantly, between 1969 and 1970, when the sharp and sudden increase in Bombay productions took place, as few as twenty-three new cinemas opened across the country—one of the lowest rates of increase since 1927 (Dharap 1978: E-3). Exhibitors changed their position only when the conditions for this sector to continue to be able to demand a larger and larger share of the box office materialized because the nature of the capital circulating as films had also changed. I return to this point shortly. For now it is important to note that, licensing regulations notwithstanding, exhibition circuits did not expand, at least not until 1974, because shortage of cinemas was in the interest of the stronger, better-organized, and better-financed sector of the industry. Since the 1930s, scarcity of venues had enabled theatre-owners to demand higher and higher shares of the box office. As we have seen in Chapter 4, throughout the 1960s this did not paralyse the production sector, but it certainly polarized it into the few who could count on sufficiently large returns from the box office to guarantee a degree of revolving credit and, with it, regular production, and those who relied on the volatile intermediation of small financier–distributors. As the number of ad hoc producers grew, the number of films produced fell.

Another factor held responsible for the rise in Bombay production in the early 1970s was censorship. Following a series of reforms, the early 1970s saw a massive drop in the number of censored films: from 114 in 1972 to 38 in 1973 and 26 in 1974 (Rajadhyaksha and Willemen 1999). But these reforms, which are all the more remarkable for having being implemented during one of the most oppressive regimes India has ever seen, are more likely to have been an effect, rather than the cause, of the sudden doubling of the number of films produced in 1969. That is to say, the drop in censorship was a government measure that reflected and facilitated a drive to circulate more films (or more capital as films)—a drive that was triggered by the broader economic dynamics I have outlined in the preceding pages: the facilitation of an increased, accelerated turnover of money flows loosened the grip of the censors, not a commitment to ideological modernization.

Finally, the factor most insistently invoked to explain the rise in production in the late 1960s and the consistent growth of this sector thereafter was the pressure of American cinema's. During Indira Gandhi's regime, American companies operating in India could repatriate only a small share of their profits. They used part of the blocked funds to guarantee the exhibition of their product, in the process marginalizing a large section of Indian production, which could not afford to offer as much to the exhibitor. By 1971, film-related American blocked funds had grown to US$6.5 million. By Hollywood standards the figure was minimal; less so by Indian standards. The MPEAA pushed to repatriate them, while the Indian government, short of hard currency, would not allow it. A further bone of contention between the MPEAA and Indira Gandhi's government was the issue of reciprocity. Many film-producing countries had demanded trade reciprocity from the MPEAA on a voluntary basis. Instead, probably because of India's need for hard currency and the existence of a large market abroad for Indian films, the Indian government demanded reciprocity as part of a trade agreement. The MPEAA members' distribution networks would have absorbed the Indian films at no great loss to the majors, but the MPEAA refused because it would have set an undesirable precedent. This situation led to an MPEAA embargo which lasted until 1975 (Pendakur 1985). That year, diplomatic intervention resulted in a new agreement that stipulated a lowering of imported films, from a maximum of 150 to 100. More importantly, the MPEAA was to withdraw and leave all film import and distribution activities to the FFC. Gross revenues earned by the American majors could be spent for operating expenses, for remittances abroad, and for other designated expenditures. Under the latter, allocations were made for production and co-production of films in India, script review, and (not surprisingly in an economy threatened by an impending foreign exchange crisis) interest-free loans to any government-sponsored body, returnable after five years in hard currency.[18]

This series of events did free some exhibition space, but this is not to say that as a result of it, exhibition opened up in any significant way. The biggest increase in the number of cinemas in those years took place between 1973 and 1974, when 517 new cinemas opened, bringing the total number of venues in the country to 5304 (Dharap 1978: E-3). Nor was a significant share of the films produced in 1969 and after made with blocked funds. The priorities of the exhibition sector continued to determine the operation of distributors and producers throughout the 1970s. When exhibition did expand, in 1974, it did so only because the means had become available for exhibitors to grow without altering the terms by which they secured accumulation of surplus and their dominant position in the market. This happened after the squabble between the Indian government and the MPEAA. The single most important factor responsible for this development was the large amount of money that had become available in the film industry following the nationalization of banks when, unlike other sectors of the Indian economy, cinema emerged as one of the industries that had not come under the close scrutiny of the Indian state and the plethora of regulations and red tape that centralized control inevitably involved. Within a few years into this regime, the production sector found ways to make films that met these new economic pressures without, however, fundamentally altering the relations of production that had characterized the film industry for nearly four decades. The landmark films of Amitabh Bachchan's action persona, *Sholay* and *Deewar* were manifestations of, and responses to, this configuration.

Having called for the dismantling of state planning and for liberalization since the late 1950s, two years into Indira Gandhi's rule and just as that horizon was beginning to materialize, most notably under Lal Bahadur Shastri, the Indian capitalist class suddenly saw any prospect of liberalization vanish. Ways had to be found to make money circulate faster than state channels allowed. Historically, producing films had been one way of making capital work, but now two new considerations presented themselves to cinema: the greater amount of money available for production and the speed at which it was to circulate. No glossy Hindi melodrama, targeting primarily the upper end of the market and customarily produced over a period that could extend to years, was likely to be up to the task. These pressures required, on the one hand, a larger market—one that included peripheral theatres as well as central exhibition venues—and, on the other hand, modes of production and exhibition characterized by a high turnover of films, as was already characteristic at the lower end of the market. The films of Dara Singh satisfied the latter two requirements (peripheral venues and fast turnover of films) but not the first: their production budget was too small. The problem was: how to coax large, central exhibition venues dedicated to costly melodramas to show films that, while produced quickly and guaranteed to attract the lower end of the public, were likely to fail at the box office with the one class of people—the middle class—who could afford to regularly patronize the more expensive venues?

For the financier this was simultaneously the problem and the solution, since one of his priorities, maybe even the main one, was to recycle money that was evading taxes. Allowing the exhibitor to claim an exorbitant share of the box office enabled him to do just that. So long as the initial 'black' capital turned 'white', everybody's demands could be accommodated. As Manjunath Pendakur among others has observed, within the Indian film industry the rate of failure was then, and continued to be thereafter, very high: of the 132 films made in Hindi in 1983, only seventeen were reported to have recovered their negative cost, while for every film that recovered its cost in 1985, eight incurred a loss. 'It is widely believed in the industry that more films [were] not recovering their investment [in 1989] than was the case ten years [earlier]' (Pendakur 1989: p. 70). Whether these figures are reliable is not the point. The fact remains that in spite of the apparent unprofitability of filmmaking, from the early 1970s the number of films produced increased significantly and consistently, as if then individual films' profitability became less important. Estimates have it that in the late 1980s, Rs 2500 million was invested annually in production and that, for instance, in 1985, production incurred losses in the range of Rs 1200 million. That this did not lead to a drop in production in the following years shows that the growth of this sector in the 1970s and 1980s took place not in spite, but *because* of the phenomenal increase in declared production losses. For the financier seeking to shelter capital from tax and other forms of government control, these were not, strictly speaking, losses, but a non-industrial type of capital gain: the savings from unpaid taxes and the interests charged to the producer evidently sufficed to justify the operation, including the forgoing of a larger share of the box office to the exhibitor than had previously been the case.

The benefits of this strategy, however, are too short term to fully explain the opening of a new type of suburban cinema, such as the Shreyas in suburban Bombay, from 1969 or, five years later, the relative expansion of exhibition with more than five hundred new cinemas across the country. As Madhava Prasad (1999b) observed, in India the category of the exhibitor is constituted by a rentier class whose source of income is a large share of the box office plus rental fee. The practice of extended 'jubilees'—which involves showing the film for weeks on end even when box-office returns do not justify the exercise—suggests that rental fees represent an important basis of the exhibitors' business, like a rent on land. For this type of exhibitor, the film's success or failure at the box office is not a primary consideration. But as the owner's account of the construction of the Shreyas in Ghatkopar (quoted in Chapter 4) clearly indicates, in the late 1960s box office and the type of clientele did matter to another type of exhibitor. Having opened a large suburban cinema with parking, air conditioning, and state-of-the-art equipment, for this type of exhibitor a higher than average rental fee or share of the box office to screen 'low class' entertainment would not have been sufficient to offset the risk of losing the regular clientele for whom expensive equipment and air-conditioning had been installed in the first place. To make a truly viable proposition for the most powerful sector of the industry, the production sector began to incorporate the long-term priorities of this type of exhibitor. Larger amounts of money were thus wrapped around those narrative ingredients that had proved to sell at the lower end of the market, including and above all action, in order to make such productions saleable to a more affluent section of the population. Over less than four years, the combination of these selling points with the ingredients of melodramas that, infused with nationalism and notions of aristocratic status, had proved saleable in the market which had, until then, defined the industry's generic ground, led to the landmark action films of Amitabh Bachchan.

I return to this point, in detail, in my analysis of Amitabh Bachchan's action films. For the moment it is enough to observe that, as the following extract from an article, appearing in *Screen* on 9 January 1970 (p. 6), shows, the infusion of larger amounts of money into specific narrative ingredients was a consideration that was explicitly aired in the trade press of the time:

Why a Rs one crore [10 million] budget for *Talash* [/*The Search* 1969]: Ralhan explains.

[O.P. Ralhan's] main capital was the reputation of a jubilee hit-maker derived for the success of his *Phool aur Patthar* [/*Flower and Stone* 1966]. With it, the usual practice in film business would have been possible for him—the production of another movie with the same star cast within Rs 50 to 60 lakhs [5 to 6 million]. And he would have sold it for Rs 80 lakhs [8 million] and thus tucked away something near Rs 20 lakhs [2 million]. But the writer-director in Ralhan conceived the *Talash* project differently. He wanted to make it a really big budget movie and fashioned the happenings accordingly. A good deal of action was to take place in the office as well as the house of a multimillionaire tycoon. Again, the hero was to avail of a holiday and stay in a swanky hotel. And Ralhan decided that these sets should look real. [T]hus the things needed to make the production values as he had conceived them went on swallowing money, totaling up to the advertised cost of one crore of rupees [Rs 10 million]. The distributor showed reluctance to pay his price for the rights of his film. [Ralhan] told *Screen* this was the first big movie in India to have been made from a producer's own money plus the money borrowed from a financier and no advance from a single distributor. Had he not taken a big risk by this? Sure, but he had every confidence of success.

From the early 1970s, as larger amounts of money were pumped into production, production costs rose sharply. *Sholay* is the film that exemplified this new configuration most explicitly. As Anupama Chopra has documented, Sippy Films intended *Sholay* to be a very big-budget production from the beginning, and sold it to their habitual distributors, the Rajshris, accordingly, at Rs 220,500 per territory or double the average price (2000: 58). Money was pumped into every level of production. To begin with, Sippy Films decided that *Sholay* would be India's first 70mm film with stereophonic sound, which, given the technology available in India at the time, meant shooting the film on 35mm and then blowing it up for 70mm in London (ibid.: 57). This lengthened shooting time considerably. The sequence in which Gabbar Singh (Amjad Khan) kills Thakur Baldev Singh's (Sanjeev Kumar) family, for instance, took no less than twenty-three days to shoot, while twenty days were needed to shoot the two short sequences showing Radha (Jaya Bhaduri) extinguishing the lamps while Jai (Bachchan) plays the harmonica and watches (ibid.: 73–7). In addition, *Sholay* was shot outside Bangalore, where no infrastructure was in place: 'The entire village had to be constructed, starting with a road leading up to the location. [I]n places the ground had to be leveled. [T]he script also required a temple and a mosque' (ibid.: 45). Whereas the Wadias in the 1930s, as well as most filmmakers, in India and elsewhere in different decades, shot on location to reduce production costs, Sippy Films appears to have made the same choice for the opposite reasons. Needless to say, *Sholay*'s overall cost rose well above the budgeted Rs 10 million (ibid.: 58). And yet, for all the delays and lengthy shooting schedules, the film was shot at a much faster pace than earlier big-budget melodramas. Whatever its exorbitant production cost, ten weeks after its release the initial investment was recovered and the money circulated many times over.

Whereas in 1970 the average Hindi film was produced for under Rs 1 million, a star-studded film for about Rs 5 million and a low-budget film for Rs 150,000, by the late 1980s, the average Hindi film required about Rs 7.5 million, a star studded film would cost between Rs 20 million and Rs 30 million, and a low-budget film would come close to Rs 2.5 million. Costs of all inputs rose: sets, equipment rental, and the salaries of technical personnel. The most significant rise, however, was in stars' salaries, raw stock (all of which was imported), print, and publicity costs. The cost of colour raw film rose due to the devaluation of the Indian currency against the US dollar. A star's salary, on the other hand, increased 400 per cent between 1975 and 1985 (from Rs 1.5 million to Rs 6 million). The salary of a top director rose by 300 per cent (from Rs 1 million to Rs 3 million) and that of a top music director from Rs 400,000 to Rs 800,000 (Pendakur 1990: 231–2).[19] Interestingly, fight composers saw the biggest relative pay increase—from Rs 15,000 in 1975 to Rs 100,000 in 1985— and even though their salaries remained significantly lower than those of stars, their sharp rise during these ten years speaks volumes about the value ascribed to action as a narrative ingredient and a selling point.[20] Advertising costs also increased, but with circulation guaranteed by the distributor–exhibitor nexus and, within that, by star value, the increase was comparatively small: all-India publicity for a big-budget film cost Rs 1.2 million in 1975, rising only to Rs 3 million ten years later (Pendakur 1990: 231–2).[21]

In the 1950s, the value of the star derived largely from the industry's imbrication in a pre-capitalist economy and its attendant ideological currents. In the 1960s, when things began to stir in Bombay's economy, cheap wrestling films imagined value as physical energy because, within the constraints imposed by exhibitors reluctant to align themselves with the city's industrial growth, the economic dynamics that generated the films were a combination of small merchant and industrial capital. From the early 1970s, with financial centralization, an element that had been present in the film industry for decades in small doses—speculative finance capital—entered in a big way and produced a new star by gradually pumping larger amounts of money into narrative ingredients that were already circulating in the large share of the market not covered by central exhibitors. The Bachchan action films were part of a generic restructuring that fit the horizon of this new speculative force—a horizon that, for the sheer financial power behind it, became constitutive of Hindi cinema's base ground, the cluster of generic features defining the terms by which the films competed to occupy that central ground. That horizon can be seen to be at work in the narrative strategies of these films, in the modes by which this new economic configuration imagined its ideal (that is most profit-yielding) addressee.

THE ACTION FILMS OF AMITABH BACHCHAN

The films made with Amitabh Bachchan in the role of action hero in the 1970s and 1980s are organized around a recurring set of preoccupations. Much has been made of the Bachchan action hero's outlaw status, a feature that in the literature has tended to be discussed as a new and radical development. In reality, by the 1970s, the heroes of Hindi cinema had been breaking the law for some time. Popular dacoits had animated the Indian screen since the 1920s and, before cinema, in the many forms of folk theatre such as *nautanki*. The dacoit narrative continued well into the 1970s, not only in cheap productions featuring Dara Singh—as, for instance, in his *Sultana Daku* (M. Hussein 1972), but also in glossy, ground-defining films such as, for instance, *Mother India* (Mehboob Khan 1957) and *Ganga Jumna* (Nitin Bose 1961). Unlike the dacoit, Bachchan's character was an urban hero. However, this role had also already been made familiar, again, but not only, by Dara Singh, who made several cheap urban thrillers, like *Kabhi Dhoop Kabhi Chhaon* (Chandrakant 1971) and *The Criminals/Hum Sub Chor Hain* (Maruti 1973).

The Criminals opens with a long and frenetic title sequence: over the image of a nearly naked woman, dancing wildly to loud rock music with several men, run the titles announcing: 'Starring/Dara Singh and Sheikh Mukhtar/in and as/The Criminals!' In the film, Dara Singh plays an honest mechanic whose brother, a policeman, is killed because he had information on a criminal ring. But the brother leaves behind a notebook containing that information, and much of the film sees Dara Singh trying to recover it so as to bring his brother's murderers to book. In the process, the hero finds himself embroiled in a world of crime and corruption—a world in which the police are either acting on behalf of, or are incapable of dealing effectively with, the criminals. Chased by the police and by the criminals, the hero ends up, unjustly, on the wrong side of the law.

In *Zanjeer*, Bachchan plays not an outlaw, but a policeman who abandons the force because, much like Dara Singh in *The Criminals*, he finds the police, at best, ineffective. The two films, however, differ in their position vis-à-vis notions of the law. Dara Singh's hero must enforce the law by himself because the institution whose task it is to do so, does not; but the Dara Singh hero never turns his back on ideas of legality. He always survives in the end because the validity of the law—understood as a set of norms agreed upon by 'the people' and as the embodiment of the state—is never questioned. The people—be they the nation or a king's subjects—and the state always act in unison, and it is the equivalence of the two that guarantees the hero's legality, honour, and survival. Indeed, in many of Dara Singh's early films, the wrestler's task is precisely to reaffirm the unity of the hero as a representative of the people with (and at times as) the royal head. Similarly, in the urban thriller *Kabhi Dhoop Kabhi Chhaon*, the hero, a wrestler, is trying to prevent a murder when he accidentally kills a man. The hero gives himself up and is put on trial and imprisoned, only to be released soon after so as to take part in an important wrestling competition. The victory in the ring earns the hero acquittal in court.

The hero's problem with the law in most of Bachchan's films are far more serious because they stem from a fundamental and irreversible separation between the people or nation, whose voice is often represented by the hero's mother, and the modern state. In Bachchan's action films, the father figure is not only always symbolically connected to the latter: he is also always absent or seen to be failing in some other way. In *Zanjeer*, Vijay (Amitabh Bachchan) becomes a policeman because of his father's death, which, in turn, was caused by the father's failure. The failure of the patriarch recurs in every action film made by Bachchan until the early 1990s, where it also always leads, if not to the father's death, certainly to the separation of the mother from the failed father. In *Zanjeer*, the father is released from prison only to return home and discover that the brand of (poisoned) pills he smuggled killed his ill daughter. His determination to go straight prompts the boss of his gang to go on a killing spree leaving Vijay orphaned. In *Deewar*, Vijay's father is a trade union leader who, forced to betray the workers' interests, disappears in humiliation, leaving the mother to fend for herself and her sons, and Vijay literally branded as a thief. In *Sholay*, the father figure and law enforcer, the (ex)policeman and benevolent landlord Thakur Baldev Singh, fails to capture the bandits, is maimed as a result, and retires to live as a widowed landlord. In *Muqaddar ka Sikandar/The Emperor of Fate* (Prakash Mehra 1978), Sikandar is a nameless, orphaned boy taken in by the family of a lawyer who unjustly accuses the boy of theft and rejects him. Adopted some time later by the lawyer's maid (who gives him his name), Sikandar and the adoptive mother are expelled again from the lawyer's home. It is only as an adult that Sikandar is finally accepted by the lawyer, who is now so ill that he can no longer practice. By now, however, Sikandar's adoptive mother has died, while the lawyer's daughter, with whom Sikandar had fallen in love as a child, is to be married to Sikandar's best friend, a law graduate. In *Trishul/The Trident* (Yash Chopra 1978), the father, a construction engineer, abandons the mother, pregnant with the hero, in order to marry the daughter of the company boss, forcing hero and mother to survive as labourers on construction sites. In *Shaan/Dignity* (Ramesh Sippy 1980), the father figure, the hero's older brother, is a top cop who, however, is not good enough to beat the villain, who kills him, leaving hero and younger brother to fend for and avenge the older brother's widow.

In the 1950s feudal family romance, representations of the family functioned as a way of negotiating the imbrication of the democratic state with pre-modern notions of lineage (Vitali 2000). Whereas in Dara Singh's early films the mother and father figures are subsumed under notions of lineage and its re-establishment, Dara Singh's urban films mostly do away with the family. By contrast, in Bachchan's action films the family is central, as is its dismemberment, which usually takes place prior to the title sequence. At one level, the prominence of this trope in the Bachchan action films points to the extent to which these narratives resulted from an attempt to adapt the ingredients of cheaply produced action films to the conventions of a genre that, until the 1960s, had defined Hindi cinema's dominant generic ground, the feudal family romance. At another level, it is also evident that the function of the family in Bachchan's film is no longer the same as in the feudal melodrama. Torn asunder, in Bachchan's action films the family functions as the terrain over which the relationship between the nation and the state is mapped and characterized, first and foremost, as a tragic separation.

The pervasiveness of this trope suggests that the problem in these films is not the legality (or not) of the hero, or the law as such, but the perception of the legal system as ineffective and corrupt. The perception, rather than the fact, of inefficiency, because in the films the unity between the nation (which is presented as subject to the law) and the state (which is seen as the entity embodied by the law) is simultaneously given as desirable and ripped open. Historically, the separation between state and law was an effect of the emergence of the public sphere as a civil sphere, separate from the royal court. Which is why in India, as in any other democratic country, the law is, constitutionally, 'the people', not 'the state'. Yet Bachchan's films stage the split between the people and the state as a traumatic event. The realization that the state may not be truly representative of the people comes as a shock rather than as the (welcome) premise of democracy. The films do present the split between the nation and the state firmly from the perspective of the nation, but this is not to say that the question of the representativeness of the law is just as easily resolved. The narrative function of Bachchan's action heroes is to mediate the split between state and nation—a function that, on the one hand, foregrounds, while regularly failing to resolve, the hero's relations with the mother as the upholder of morality, of the greater good, the symbol of the nation and its reproduction. On the other hand, it lands the hero straight into the multiple tensions between two simultaneously inhabited worldviews, two temporalities: a pre-modern one, which lends the protagonist a heroic, tragic character whose role is to uphold the continuation of lineage, reconstituting the family and taking the father's place; and modernity, within which the protagonist is no more than a representative of the ordinary man, responsible for his actions and for their sanctioning, taking the law into his hands as it is the constitutional right of any citizen in a democratic system.

This central contradiction becomes clearer if we reconsider *Awara*. Although in this 1951 film the question of the status of the state looms large, the representativeness of the state is never in itself the problem. The crux of the matter being the legitimation of specific power blocs as 'the state', *Awara* splits the law into the two characters of the judge (and his lineage-based worldview) and his daughter Rita (and her reformist outlook), leaving to Rita's interrogation and the judge's answer the largest share of the narration. By the early 1970s, the other side of *Awara*, Jagga's narrative—the story of a petty crook and his revenge against an unjust judge—takes over. While in *Awara* a virginal Rita is at once the mother figure, the reciprocated love interest, the embodiment of just law, and a symbol of the state, Bachchan's heroes inhabit a gap—a world in which each of these entities occupies a separate sphere. Inhabiting this gap comfortably and unambiguously would enable the hero to make (and, if he so wished, to break or change) the law, have the woman, get along with mother, and being recognized as an exemplary citizen at the end of the tale. But while already irrevocably inhabiting this gap (making or breaking the law), Bachchan's hero simultaneously looks back nostalgically to a time when law, state, and subject were all one. Neither firmly in one (modern) world nor in the (feudal) other, he can thus neither achieve romantic fulfilment nor gain the mother's approval. And while the maternal and filial love between hero and mother is never in doubt, the hero's sexual desire is always blocked, indicating that the pull towards a lineage society is greater and more legitimate than the desire for modern individuation. Mothers were very important also in Dara Singh's films, but this did not stop their hero from displaying a measure of individuated desire nor fulfilling it. That this possibility is foreclosed to Bachchan's heroes confirms that the feudal family romance remained the preferred framework against which the 'new' economy's values were to be measured. The pre-industrial rentier sector of the economy continued to determine the dominant value frame for the urbanized fusion of the feudal romance with the action film.

In the late 1980s and early 1990s other action heroes appeared in Hindi cinema who pushed this tension between simultaneously inhabited temporalities to extremes, but the perspective from which the tension is narrativized—the position from which the hero inhabits modern and pre-modern social frameworks—continued to be a backwards perspective, even more so than in Bachchan's action vehicles. In the Hindi action films of the late 1980s and 1990s, the responsibility for legal self-sanctioning—taking the law into one's hands—is pushed to its logical conclusion: a form of everyday, even mythical, individuation. But these films present that particularly positive dimension of modernity as a trauma, alienation, or madness. Nana Patekar's characters are a case in point. For instance his Anna in *Parinda/The Bird* (Vidhu Vinod Chopra 1989) and Pratap Narayan Tilak in *Krantiveer/The Revolutionary* (Mehul Kumar 1994) emphasize the psychotic dimension of individuation. In Patekar's films, as in productions featuring Sunny Deol or Sunil Shetty, an individual's social accountability, the responsibility for one's social reproduction, is fully taken on board by the heroes. But since the films tend to inhabit or stage a perspective that is infused with the ideology of a pre-modern temporality within which individuation is essentially rejected or presented as undesirable, the task of setting in place the ideal conditions for social reproduction is carried out with no consideration for one's own, the individual's, benefit. Sunny Deol's characters and many of the protagonists of N. Chandra's films are figures who have been fully instrumentalized for the management of the public sphere, vigilantes with little or no personal dimension who police a sphere that is presented as a territorialized community—such as, for instance, Munna (Anil Kapoor) in *Tezaab/Acid* (N. Chandra 1988) or the wrestler Kashi Nath (Sunny Deol) in *Ghatak/Lethal* (Rajkumar Santoshi 1996).

As I have argued in Chapter 2, in the 1920s and 1930s Bombay cinema's preferred ground for the negotiation of the terms of social reproduction was the representation of women. This was not unique to cinema, nor to Bombay stunt films. Female characters had that function also in the feudal family romance of the 1940s and 1950s. However, in those earlier decades, as industrialization triggered the disruption of pre-modern social relations and, through that disruption, redefined notions of physical energy, the cinematic representation of women moved in new directions and helped to renegotiate the criteria by which social relations were to be ideally reconfigured so that industrialization could be sustained. From the early 1960s, as in the films of Dara Singh, the prominence of industrial considerations within the production sector led, on the one hand, to the cinematic fetishization of sheer physical energy and, on the other, to a greater sexualization of female figures, like Helen in a number of Dara Singh's films, as if the strategies adopted better to sell the films, for that very reason also spoke of the perceived need to maximize the valuation of commodifiable human energy. This latter tendency persisted to varying degrees in Amitabh Bachchan's early action films. At the same time, however, Bachchan marked a point where women were called back into the house. The visibility of their sexuality as the desirable byproduct of the hero's individuation became more contained. In the mid-1980s, as Hindi male action heroes increasingly took on the burden of social reproduction themselves, images of women in action films became totally polarized.

Four instances—Helen in *Ek Tha Alibaba*, Helen again in *Sholay*, Madhuri Dixit in *Khalnayak/The Villain* (Subash Ghai 1993), and Mamta Kulkarni in *Ghatak*—will help clarify my point. I have described the opening scene of *Ek Tha Alibaba* in Chapter 4: a close-up shot of a woman's legs, walking around a pool, leads to a tracking out camera movement that, slowly, reveals the lower part of a woman's body wrapped in a towel as she walks towards the camera. The cut does not come before Helen is close enough for the camera's eye to be filled with her pelvis. The heroes' encounter with the villain in *Sholay* is marked by a similar scene, but the visibility of Helen's navel in this film is presented as far more problematic than in *Ek Tha Alibaba*. Having found Gabbar Singh's hideout, Jai and Veeru (Dharmendra) are planning to attack him. They arrive at the place to find that the bandit is holding a feast at which a gypsy woman (Helen) is performing a sensuous dance. The scene opens with a medium close-up of Helen's navel. The framing is not all that different from the one in *Ek Tha Alibaba*. However, whereas in the latter film the look at Helen's pelvis is anonymous and general, allowing the spectator a frontal and direct view of the actress's body, this is not the case in *Sholay*. In this film, the two heroes are hiding behind a rock, at some distance from the party sitting in a circle around a fire and at the centre of which Helen is dancing. The heroes are watching, but the look at Helen's sinuously moving body is always allocated to Gabbar Singh, never to the heroes, even if from where they are hiding Helen's performance is perfectly visible. As in the opening of scene *Zanjeer* (discussed later), here the heroes' desire, which would be carried by their look at the dancer, is displaced into the dynamite explosions that Jay and Veeru eventually set off in order to attack Gabbar Singh and his gang. However, this does not happen until Helen's dance is over.

By the late 1980s, a female dance number had become a regular trope and selling point of every Hindi action film. In *Khalnayak*, the controversial 'Choli ke piche kya hai' song featured Madhuri Dixit as Ganga, a woman police officer who dances in front of villain Ballu (Sanjay Dutt) in order to meet him and get him to surrender. As in *Sholay*, Ganga's dance is very sensual as a performance, but the mise en scène is designed to downplay the sexual dimension of Madhuri's movements. The camera not only stays at a greater distance from the actress: we look at her from Ballu's point of view, whose vision is constantly obstructed by other elements of the set, like other (diegetic) observers, thus emphasizing his voyeuristic desire, fusing this with that of the imagined spectator and, partially at least, frustrating both.[22] Finally, the most sexualized dance in these films is Mamta Kulkarni's 'Maara Re' in *Ghatak*. Her performance, in an alternation of black leather trousers and boots, red sari, and a tight silver sequin suit, takes place in a dark and cavernous cabaret, a den of sin that is presented as symptomatic of the evil of Katya (Danny Denzongpa), the villain ruthlessly terrorizing the small community visited by the hero (Sunny Deol). The dance is filmed frontally, as from either the front or the balcony seats of a cinema, with occasional close-ups of Kulkarni's face, projecting a (imaginary) 'lustful' look back at the viewer. By filming Mamta Kulkarni's highly sexualized performance in this way, *Ghatak* has it both ways: it can exploit the commercial potential of such a dance number and condemn, at least nominally, the public display of sexuality. Unlike in the 1920s, in *Ghatak* and, to a lesser extent in *Khalnayak*, that particular dimension of modernity which is the greater or wider visibility of women moving in ways they would not normally be seen doing, is marginalized, singled out as a selling point but extracted from the flow of the narrative, made insignificant in the very act of exploiting it commercially. The contrast between the frontal theatrical framing of the dance in this film and the frontal close-up of Helen's pelvis in *Ek Tha Alibaba* could not be sharper. When I saw *Ghatak* from a balcony seat of a provincial cinema in Uttar Pradesh in 1996, some youths sitting in the cheaper seats below marked Mamta Kulkarni's performance by pointing at parts of (the image of) her body with blue laser torch lights, as if to undo the containing effect of the theatrical mise en scène by literally inscribing onto the frame (or screen) their look of desire. Whereas in *Khalnayak* the viewer's look at the woman is quite literally blocked, Kulkarni's dance in *Ghatak* elicited a gesture of defiance the terms of which, however, remain dictated by the modality of the mise en scène: incapable of finding the space for individuation, that gesture transformed itself into an act of public condemnation turned again the woman, marked, by the torch lights, as 'the whore'. As in Amitabh Bachchan's early action films, in this and many other female cabaret dance numbers of Hindi action films, the hero (or villain) with whom the audience is asked to identify is deprived of a space for individuated desire. The libidinal energy released in and as the woman's performance is blocked, to be channelled exclusively for the regulation and reproduction of a public sphere increasingly oblivious of an individual's private dimension.

Another element of the Bachchan action films that tends to be presented in the literature as distinctive and new is the working class status of the hero.[23] Few have challenged this view, even if, as Ramjani Mazumdar observes, Bachchan's action character 'operated with the symbols of poverty visually inscribed on the body and the codes of an upper class upbringing projected through his gestures and posturing' (2000: p. 247). The problem with readings which discuss Amitabh Bachchan's action hero as a working class character is that they reduce to fixed identity labels what are in fact complex images replete with representational relays. The result is that cinematic codes are read far too literally. Characters are not fully rounded individuals, but narrative functions around which are wrapped many, often contradictory, discourses.[24] The double coding correctly identified by Mazumdar indicates, first, that written into the character of the Bachchan action hero are specific industrial considerations: the need to adapt narratives that circulated at the margins of the market to the priorities of the dominant generic ground that defined Hindi cinema until the 1960s. This pressure—the effect of a reaction against financial centralization—not only produced a character that was deemed to represent the 'underdog' or, more precisely, the migrant according to the ostensibly sensitive imagination of middle-class audiences; more importantly, it added to the already existing but, until then, marginal action narratives expectations and ambitions constitutive of notions of middle class-ness.

First among these is not class—all notions of which in the films are quite simply repressed—but the problem of how to earn a living in an urban environment, a preoccupation which surfaces in the films in a symbolic and condensed manner: a working hero. In Chapter 3 I have claimed that the question of how to achieve social mobility did not feature as a preoccupation in the mainstream Hindi cinema of the 1950s. Even in the most progressive films of the period, such as *Pyaasa*, the issue of earning a living is romanticized (in Vijay and in the figure of the prostitute Gulab). In *Andaaz*, Dilip's achievements are displaced onto a notion of romance and adultery because, no matter how good at his job, Dilip does not display the required signs of aristocratic status. As a result, the possibility of individuation—a corollary of the creation of labour power through the freeing up of human physical energy from hierarchical bonds and of self-serving energy expenditure—is presented in *Andaaz* as madness, Dilip's fate. Consider also *Aar Paar/From One Side to the Other* (Guru Dutt 1954) and *The Criminals*. The first film features a mechanic whose main use for cars is romance: Guru Dutt is primarily seen singing and dancing over and around them. By contrast, in the second film, Dara Singh is seen both fixing cars and using them as an instrument for, or as the site of, fighting, that is for the display of idealized and enhanced uses of physical energy.

Questions of social mobility began to surface in Hindi cinema in the 1960s in films that circulated around the margins of central exhibition circuits. They appeared, for instance, quite explicitly in the parallel cinema that emerged from the FFC/NFDC from 1969 onwards. A few years earlier, they had surfaced as a preoccupation in Dara Singh's films, but in a far less explicit manner. Films like *King Kong* vented notions of social mobility somewhat indirectly because they addressed a constituency defined by a set of concerns that is entirely different from those characteristic of parallel cinema: a rural population, its transformation into suburban workers, physical energy, and the most effective ways of employing it. In the so-called mainstream circuit, to which both the FFC and Dara Singh's films failed to gain access, the process of shifting from one class to another (as opposed to class markers) broke through with Bachchan's films, and not only in the ones marketed as action movies. Unlike Dara Singh's films, Bachchan's films do not emphasize notions of sheer physical energy. While containing scenes where action choreographies are displayed, on closer analysis (to follow shortly) it becomes apparent that physical energy is not what the mise en scène of these films highlights. Issues of social mobility in Bachchan's action films emerge in a manner more akin to parallel cinema, to the extent that they are foregrounded first and foremost in stories that dwell on notions of employment and trade. These are the fields in which Bachchan's hero is called upon to intervene. And while the literary, narrative- and dialogue-based manner in which this and the issue of legality are inserted in Bachchan's films may well be due to the scriptwriters' attention to the conventions of both an emerging, state-promoted genre (parallel cinema) and the then dominant melodrama, the cinematic treatment of these same tropes reveals a set of preoccupations that owes more to the nature of the capital that in the 1970s began to circulate in greater quantities within (and as) Hindi cinema.

In all of Bachchan's films, questions of legality and the accompanying fighting emerge in the context of the question: how to earn a living? Working and trading never function as pretexts for other preoccupations, as in *Aar Paar*. Indeed, modes of trade and its regulation structure the majority of the plots, triggering love interests, missions of revenge, fighting, and a lot of dancing. Never before the 1970s had the occupation of the characters been so prominent a concern in Hindi films. From *Zanjeer* to the films of the late 1980s, Bachchan's action movies all present us with a series of gradations of institutionalization (or legality) on this front. In *Zanjeer* a (female) knife sharpener sells that service but not others, a Muslim man runs gambling joints, and smugglers sell poisoned brew. Vijay's task, as a disrobed policeman, is to rally the Muslim man to his and the honest knife-sharpener's side and, with their help, defeat the smugglers. In *Deewar*, Vijay works first as a shoe-shine, then as a dockworker, and finally as a smuggler. He is in love with a call girl who dies before they can get married, while the brother, educated with young Vijay's earnings is initially unemployed. Pitted against Vijay are the mother and the brother, the latter eventually finding employment as a policeman. In *Sholay*, Jay and Veeru are first employed by the maimed landlord and ex-policeman Thakur Baldev Singh as mercenaries to free the villagers from the pillaging raids of bandit Gabbar Singh and his gang. Basanti, who helps them, makes a living as a tonga driver, while the Thakur's widowed daugther-in-law hands the keys of the family safe over to the heroes as they try to steal from it. *Trishul*'s entire story revolves around a building construction business, the task of the hero being to move from the building site, where his mother has died of exhaustion, to the director's chair, in place of the father who abandoned him and, importantly, in spite of bribery allegations. In *Shaan*, the hero and his brother make a living out of a variety of scams until their elder brother, a policeman, is killed by a really bad guy (fashioned after the character of Karl Stromberg in *The Spy Who Loved Me* [Lewis Gilbert 1977]). At which point, the two brothers abandon petty criminality and go after the psychopath. Finally, in *Muqaddar ka Sikandar*, the adult Sikandar makes a good living by turning in smuggled goods to the police and getting generous rewards. Vishal, Sikandar's best friend, is an unemployed law graduate who will end up marrying the lawyer's daughter while Sikandar is left with the love of a tawaif or dancing girl (Rekha) who kills herself to save his virtue.

The prominence in Bachchan's action films of positive, ostensibly working class, characters that break the law has led film historians to advance the hypothesis that the films articulate a critique of Indira Gandhi's regime. But this is not the fantasy actually staged by the films, if we understand films as clusters of specific narrative strategies. To begin with, even if the set of preoccupations vented in many of Bachchan films— like notions of democratization and employment—would indeed require notions of individuation to surface in the diegesis somehow, in practice the hero is never granted the ground of narration, at least not in any consistent manner. *Zanjeer* encounters enormous difficulties and ultimately fails to set in place the individuated space from which such a critique of the state would need to be articulated. Consider the opening sequence of the film, prior to the titles, which narrates the events leading to the personal development of the hero into an adult character endowed with the determination to put things right. We have been told that the hero's father has been in prison for smuggling poisoned pills. Returning home to discover that the pills he smuggled have killed his daughter, the father goes to his gang's boss to let him know that he has decided to abandon crime. The scene in question shows the killing of the hero's parents at the hands of a gang member. It is evening and the family is at home. Inserted shots of a man's legs, walking among firecrackers outside, tell us that it is Divali and that something ominous is about to disrupt the happy family scene. In a frontal shot we see Vijay, mother, and father sitting on a bed. While the mother is mending a shirt, the young boy Vijay plays hide-and-seek with his father, hiding behind the mother's back. On his mother's suggestion, Vijay hides in a cupboard (situated against the wall, next to the bed and at an angle to the main entrance of the house which is visible to the right of the frame). As the mother goes to the kitchen to make some drinks (exiting the frame to the left through a door opposite the main door), a man enters the house and shoots repeatedly at the father, who is still lying on the bed, smoking. When the mother re-enters the room, the killer shoots her too. Close-ups on Vijay's face tell us that he watches the scene by slightly opening the cupboard door. The set, furniture, and camera are arranged in such a way that he may indeed be able to catch glimpses of the killer (his hand, gun, and bracelet), but can see neither his father on the bed, nor the door leading to the kitchen, where his mother went. Yet, when she walks back into the room, we cut to a frontal close-up of her face: looking straight at the camera, her eyes and mouth wide open so as to silently urge Vijay to stay in the cupboard. Throughout, close-ups of Vijay in the cupboard are followed by shots of the event from points of view that are spatially inconsistent with Vijay's position. Moreover, the shooting is interspersed with shots of the firecrackers outside. These shots substitute for the sound of gunshots and convey, through the soundtrack, Vijay's 'blind' point of view: he can hear but not see.

The most distinctive feature of this scene is not so much the lack of spatial continuity, or the blockage of subjective narration, but the overemphatic use of the zoom. Moving from close-ups of Vijay to the other characters, fast zooming here is proposed to us ostentatiously as the point of view of a Vijay in shock. However, given that from where he is Vijay cannot possibly see what is happening, the use of the zoom deserves further consideration. Dara Singh's early films were cheap productions, but this did not prevent the filmmakers from orchestrating, however unwittingly and inconsistently, a cluster of figurations that hovered around notions of physical energy and its uses. In those films, the concern about physical energy translated as a struggle (not always successful) to convey a sense of spatial continuity, often against modes of narration, also at work in the films, that abide by other conventions, some of them quite literally obstructing the perception of the pro-filmic as organic. By the late 1960s, Dara Singh's films began to feature urban, contemporary settings, as well as fashionable clothes, scooters and cars, spacious dwellings with 1960s furniture, and expensive residential areas (Juhu beach). A few of the films were released with English titles (for instance, *The Killers* (Maruti 1969) and *The Criminals*). At the level of choreography, the shift to a modern, urban environment lent wrestling a different weight. Dara Singh films of the early 1960s were not entirely devoid of fisticuffs, but from the late 1960s these ingredients became more prominent in the choreography of action scenes. Wrestling continued to be an important ingredient, but it no longer featured as the hero's sole mode of action. These modes of fighting could be found in films that had begun to circulate in India from the late 1960s— including James Bond productions and Italian Westerns, as well as Indian versions of these. It was in order to compete with these new versions of the genre that Dara Singh adapted his wrestling formula to new fighting styles. But even in these later films, it is wrestling that is ultimately presented as lending effectiveness to the hero's fighting. One of the strategies adopted at this point to ascribe primacy to Dara Singh's main selling point was the zoom.

In the early 1960s, the zoomar lens was a new technology, but by the early 1970s, when Dara Singh's urban thrillers and *Zanjeer* were released, in India, use of the zoom was neither new nor unique. It was used quite regularly in these as well as in other cheap action thrillers of the period. *CID 909* (M. Hussein 1967), starring Feroz Khan, uses it along with other 'special' effects, such as split screen and iris. Nor is the display of technology in this film confined to the mode of address. *CID 909* centres on a gang of criminals who kidnap a 'professor', a scientist, in order to gain, access to a lethal atomic formula. Bombs and explosions, guns and, above all, technologies of transport and telecommunications, such as helicopters, motorboats, radio, and radar systems are the focus of the film. Attention to the hero's action remains, on the other hand, nominal. Feroz Khan does engage in fights, but these are brief, confined to the odd gunshot and a few punches. In contrast to Dara Singh's films, here the main preoccupation is the use and display of technology. If any sense of physical strength is at all conveyed, Feroz Khan as the hero tends to find himself at the receiving end of it, as the body that gets beaten up.[25]

In *CID 909* the zoom is used, in moderation, to draw the spectator's attention either to Helen's dance or, significantly, to the technology displayed in the diegesis. This is not the case in Dara Singh's urban thrillers. In *Kabhi Dhoop Khabi Chhaon* the zoom is used emphatically and nearly exclusively during the bouts to highlight classic wrestling holds. The zoomar lens in these moments does more than simply allow the camera to break into the ring. Breaking the theatrical space of the ring to offer a close view of the hero's body parts and moves is something that earlier

Dara Singh films achieved with a simple cut. In Chapter 4, I have shown that Dara Singh's early films are caught in a tension between, on the one hand, a pseudo-epic voice which, derivative of auditive modes of narration and characterized by theatricality and rhetorical flourishes, seeks to subjugate the wrestler's performance to its pre-given terms; and, on the other, a pressure to give full play to the wrestler's performance, to Dara Singh's skilled movements, as the films' main asset. In *King Kong* and other early films, the simultaneous operation of these two narrative layers leads to spatial discontinuities. The overemphatic use of the zoom during the bouts in later Dara Singh films stems from a parallel tension. This time around, however, as in *Kabhi Dhoop Kabhi Chhaon*, the tension is somewhat resolved: the zoom allows the filmmaker to retain the imperative mode of address of a pseudo-epic voice and, simultaneously, give full play to the wrestler's performance. With one crucial qualification: the valorization of the wrestler's performance is now under the control of a pseudo-epic voice that has fully incorporated into its authoritarian and essentially pre-modern mode of address some of the strategies of industrialized culture—not only professional wrestling as a commercial practice and the valorization of the wrestler's body as a commodity, but also industrial technology.

In an essay on the use of the zoom in popular cinema, Paul Willemen observed that

[t]o the extent that it displays a narratorial performative flourish, [the zoom] implies a recognition, within the very texture of the filmic discourse, of the presence of the audience in the same way that theatrical performances imply a recognition of this 'live' presence in, for instance, the spatial disposition of actors on the stage, the recourse to voice-projection techniques and so on. (2002: 13)

In *Kabhi Dhoop Kabhi Chhaon* the zoom does indeed acknowledge the presence of the audience, which is inscribed in the diegesis as the addressee for whom the performance is staged. At the same time, the zoom here draws attention also to itself, to the technological, narratorial entity which allows the spectator to be closer to the wrestler and his performance—the means by which the performance is not only staged, but, above all, recorded. As a result, while it enhances the perception of immediacy, the zoom in this film also channels our vision of the bout and fragments it into minute parts. These parts become replaceable, abstracting, to an extent, the performing body. Whereas in *King Kong* the mise en scène makes it very difficult to forget that the body parts we are looking at belong to Dara Singh, in *Kabhi Dhoop Kabhi Chhaon* the zoomar voice runs the risk of overriding the film's most bankable asset. It gives us the popular wrestler within closer range, but also offers itself emphatically as a narrative frame that, given other body parts and other movements, would equally be available for market exploitation.

In Dara Singh's film, display of the wrestler's performance remains a priority, and this, in turn, enables a film like *Kabhi Dhoop Kabhi Chhaon* to both use the zoom emphatically and sustain a fair degree of spatial continuity. An entirely different mode of address is at stake in the mise en scène of Bachchan's action films—a logic whereby spatial continuity is simply not a consideration. Discontinuities notwithstanding, the scene from *Zanjeer* discussed earlier hangs together somewhat because meaning is conveyed by way of punctuating diegetic elements operating like bookmarks or bold print. Emphatic images (the mother's tragic look, a gun pointed at the camera, a boy's eyes peeping through a door) and sound-images enabling iconic associations (firecrackers and gunshots) are yoked together by a narrator whose fast zooming addresses us with the imperative to look, not only at the diegetic material, but above all at the narrator's handling of the storytelling procedures. Action scenes in Bachchan's films tend to consist of an accumulation of a narrow range of more or less choreographed movements, gestures, and anatomic traits as could be found also in other films containing the action ingredient circulating in India at the time, from Italian Westerns to Dara Singh productions and Hong-Kong kung-fu films. From these, Bachchan's films borrowed stories and action ingredients, but none of these elements are assembled in the films in such a way as to convey the perception of the actor's actions as a series of movements with its own organicity. Rather, these elements are held together by a narratorial performance that points insistently and emphatically to its own qualities—the story, the type of character and his language, the sets and trendy clothes, the cinematic technology at its disposal—emphasizing their novelty and cost, their desirability as a cluster of conventions: a new genre, in the marketing-industrial sense of the term, a new brand.

Unlike in Dara Singh's films, in Bachchan's the zoom is rarely used to highlight the skills and movements of the actor. In the large majority of Bachchan's action scenes, the action is shot from medium to long distance. *Zanjeer*, a comparatively cheaper film than *Deewar* and *Sholay*, is revealing in this respect. Precisely because of its more experimental character, *Zanjeer* shows the manner in which value is ascribed to the actor, his reconstruction for future market exploitation as a new star. The climactic moment of the film shows Vijay being ambushed by a group of thugs on a bridge at night. The scene opens with a long, static shot of Vijay as he walks up the steps leading onto the bridge; the camera is behind him and at a distance. Cut to a frontal long shot of Vijay walking on the bridge, a small white figure on the dark horizon moving towards the camera. As the camera begins to track back slowly, away from Vijay as he walks along the bridge towards us, we switch, or seem to switch, to subjective narration. The backtracking movement reveals, on the bottom left of the screen, five men lying on the ground, pretending to sleep as they wait for Vijay. They get up; one of them is wearing a bright red shirt. We cut back to Vijay, who is walking towards the camera, from a medium shot to close-up. He raises his head slightly. Cut: from Vijay's point of view we see the men moving towards him. Cut to a close-up of Vijay, followed by another close-up, still of Vijay, this time from the back of his head. Nothing in the set indicates that the camera has moved to the other side of the line of action or, alternatively, that Vijay has turned and is now showing his back to a camera that did not move. The background is entirely dark and only the abruptness of the cut, as well as the logic of the sequence suggest that this is indeed what happened or what we are meant to understand to have happened. And yet, as Vijay is now seen turning around clockwise, face to the camera, we cut to the same group of men (the same bright red shirt), who still appear to the left of the screen. Had the camera actually crossed the 180 degree line, the men should not only have been different (or at least differently dressed), but they would also have had to appear to the right of the screen. If, on the other hand, it is Vijay who turned around, then his movement should have been signalled with a match on action shot. Everything suggests that the close-up shot of Vijay from the back was inserted a posteriori without, however, paying a great deal of attention to any impression of spatial continuity. The sequence continues with a frontal close-up of Vijay: he turns around again, this time anticlockwise, and turns his back to the camera once more. Cut to a frontal close up of Vijay, followed by a shot of a different group of men, again on the bottom left of the frame. They too get up and move towards Vijay. Cut to another close-up of the hero, followed by a 360 degrees movement of the camera showing the faces of the men moving towards the hero, interrupted by close-ups of Vijay as he turns on himself and looks at them.

The discontinuities and the somewhat misplaced ostentation of cinematographic wizardry that characterize this part of the sequence come to an end when the fighting begins. The confrontation between Vijay and his attackers consists of rather basic, stock wrestling moves combined with kicks, all shot entirely at a medium range by a camera that, although not entirely static, is definitely unadventurous. As in most of Bachchan's films, in *Zanjeer* continuity is eventually resumed, but at a price: the camera never breaks into the space of action. Here, it remains firmly to the left of the hero and his attackers, rarely positioning us on the side of either party. When 'partial' angles are adopted, as in *Amar Akbar Anthony* (Manmohan Desai 1977), where a similar (but better choreographed) stock of moves is used, we are nevertheless always at a distance from the action, better to see the hero's body, his characteristic features—his height, slim figure and long legs, his clothes, and above all his face. Unlike in *Kabhi Dhoop Kabhi Chhaon*, in Bachchan's films the actor's body is never fragmented to the point where it loses specificity. Spatial continuity and subjective points of view, which in many other action films are used to convey the strength and impact of the hero's blows, are here sacrificed to the need to preserve the actor in full view. In such moments, the ostentatious narratorial wizardry that characterizes other moments in the films is replaced by a mode of address relying heavily on repetition. Long action sequences shot at medium to long range display several times over a limited range of action choreographies backed up by loud sound effects that compensate for the resulting lack of a [or any] visual sense of physical impact.[26]

Repetition and (medium to long) shots of the actor's characteristic traits guarantee that the figure in action on screen is always clearly identifiable as belonging to that, and not another, actor. In this way, a figure who at the time of *Zanjeer* was barely known, within a few years was infused with value and constructed as a new star. This process involved three movements. First, it demanded that ingredients proven to sell in the marginal but larger end of the market be wrapped around a new human figure. Second, this figure was proposed to us as a constantly recognizable figure, a pressure that, in turn, prevented the actor's image from fully blending with its diegetic surroundings. Finally, the tension between these two contradictory requirements resulted in the foregrounding of the narrator, the entity that yokes together the star and the other selling points. But it would be difficult to describe the emphatic voice that characterizes Bachchan's action films as an authorial voice. Landmark Bachchan action vehicles like *Deewar* and *Sholay* invested large sums of money in their ostentatious display of narrative strategies—from cinematographic technology to the display of the star—but few of the directors, cameramen, and action choreographers employed in the making of Bachchan's films emerged from them as 'authors'.

Historically, the notion of the film author derived from a specific industrial configuration—American and European cinemas up to the late 1960s—in which film production was the priority and the dominant sector. Moreover, while in European and American cinemas the notion of author never really applied to action films, Hong Kong cinema did produce famous action film directors and choreographers, most notably from the camp of Shaw Brothers, a studio which held a near monopoly over production across Asia for a long time. This was never the case in India. From the early 1970s, the centralization of finance resulted in significantly larger amounts of money being invested in production, but this did not radically change the configuration of Bombay cinema. The Hindi action cinema that emerged at the time was not the outcome of a more cohesive production sector than before. On the contrary, well into the 1980s, action films starring Bachchan continued to be made by a diversity of small producers, in spite of the sizeable investment involved. Directors, too, continued to change. Within (and without) the action genre, prominence was ultimately given to the star because the centralization of finance presented Bombay film production with opportunities that could be exploited only by simultaneously meeting the requirements of a sector—exhibition—that was more cohesive from the start and capable of dictating how (and how fast) the larger sums of money available were to circulate also in the 1970s. This is not to say that nothing had changed since the earlier decades. On the contrary, it was precisely the financial nature of the capital which began to circulate in the 1970s also via an exhibition sector that had historically been rooted in landed interests that shaped Bachchan's films. Within and as the Hindi action film, financial capital took the form of scripts and mises en scènes designed to display the figure of the actor both as the prime site of financial investment and, through secondary elaborations, as anti-hero hero, a figure inhabiting a tension between two (pre-industrial and industrial) temporalities, pitted against a state that, having historically promoted industrialization, in the 1970s sought to extend central control over a greater share of the finances required to pursue that end.

Above all, financial capital in these films speaks in (or as) the storytelling operation of the narrator, its emphatic punctuating of quickly recognizable, quickly decodable images, loosely connected within the spatial logic of the diegesis but yoked together by authoritarian narrative strategies such as sudden and displacing zoomar movements. Whereas in the family feudal romance of the 1950s 'the star, the music, the dialogue and other component values retained an independent existence' within a weak narrative framework the coherence of which rested on the pre-modern values of a rentier class, in Bachchan's action films diagetically loosely connected ingredients are yoked together by a narrator whose operation is very similar to the address of advertising. This address became characteristic of the Hindi action film from *Zanjeer* onwards, because it was through the zoom, over-familiar images, and similar time-saving strategies that the film industry became capable of circulating larger amounts of capital in a quicker manner than had previously been demanded from its cinema.

Sholay marked the institutionalization, within Hindi cinema, of *Zanjeer*'s advertising address, not least by presenting itself as a commodity. *Sholay* was thus marketed, from the start, as a film made with expensive, state-of-the-art, foreign technology, capable of incorporating generic elements associated with foreign films and re-proposing them to the Indian, mainstream, domestic market, and thus capable of competing with imported films. But *Sholay*'s advertising potential went well beyond the circumscribed market of Indian cinema. As Anupama Chopra reminds us,

Amjad Khan became a legend—Hindi cinema's first advertising icon: Gabbar Singh, the gravelly-voiced, unwashed villain who sold both records and biscuits equally well. [S]holay has been used to sell everything from glucose biscuits to gripe water. And copywriters are still milking it dry. An Aiwa print advertisement, circa March 2000, ties prices for its electronic products with the run rate of the Indian cricket team, exhorting: '*Bhaag Saurav, mere paise ka sawaal hai*' [Run, Saurav, my money is at stake!], which echoes Basanti's command to her mare: '*Bhaag, Dhanno, Basanti ki izzat ka sawaal hai*' [Run, Dhanno, Basanti's honour is at stake!
A Channel V filler spoofs the song '*Yeh Dosti*' [/'*This Friendship*'] (2000: 3–5)

Films have been used to sell goods ever since cinema was invented. Edison's kinetoscopic record of Fred Ott's sneeze, entitled *The Sneeze* and filmed in 1894, was made for publicity purposes: Edison advertising his machinery and its possible uses. Immediately after World War II, as North American industry consolidated its foreign markets, the American government issued a series of reports on the world trade in motion pictures and equipment. Compiled by the American embassies and consulates all over the world, the reports 'made a special point of noting the influence that Hollywood films could be said to have on the sales figures of US merchandise in the countries concerned' (Willemen 2005b: 102).[27] As Willemen argues, this example 'draws attention to the fact that the US government was not simply looking at ways of selling films and film equipment: the export of films is seen as having a multiplier effect on the sale of other US merchandise' (ibid.: 102). From this perspective, *Sholay*'s advertising pull was not a new phenomenon. The difference between Edison, the American government reports, and *Sholay* lies in the industrial-financial horizon that, at any given time and place, speaks through a commodity—through the ways in which we, 'consumers', are encouraged to relate to 'it', to and by its constitutive qualities, as well as by the ancillary, marketing strategies deployed to sell it.

As far as Hindi cinema is concerned, throughout the 1980s and 1990s, the advertising address institutionalized by *Sholay* manifested itself predominantly in revamped versions of feudal family melodramas. As Rachel Dwyer has shown (2000), the romance ingredient proposed aspirational figurations of a consuming middle class. While Bachchan's films (action and romances) displayed a great deal of attention to fashion, the advertising address did not become constitutive of other Hindi action films until the late 1990s, when economic liberalization led to a new compromise between Indian industry and finance. In India, the latter had historically been tightly connected to landed interests. In the next chapter I look at the transformation of landed interests into finance as it manifested itself in the Hindi action cinema of the 1990s; at the institutionalization, in recent years, of the 1970s advertising address, and, finally, at the effects of these developments on the figuration of physical energy in contemporary Hindi action films.

NOTES

1. See, for instance, Valicha (1988: 67), Kazmi (1998: 139), and Sharma (1993).

2. See Doraiswamy (1993), Basu, Kak, and Krishen (1980), Dissanayake (1993), Dissanayake and Sahai (1992), and Dasgupta (2006).

3. For instance, Desser (2000) uses individual martial artists as distinguishing criteria between American action and martial arts films. The artist's role as the star is seen by the scholar to have an impact on the narratives, settings, and motifs of the films themselves.

4. See Mishra (2002).

5. Important work in this area has been done recently by Srinivas (2003)

who has traced the connections between Hong Kong and Telugu kung fu films. Srinivas also offers an excellent account of what he refers to as the 'B circuit', within which these films circulate. See also his essay in Morris, Li, and Ching-kiu (Srinivas 2005).

6. During the years that marked the consolidation and development of the film industry in the US and Europe, critics and publicists alike located determining agency in the film star.

7. The criteria for film funding, as stated in the *Committee on Public Undertakings Report* (1976), were: '1. Human interest in the story; 2. Indianness in theme and approach; 3. Characters with whom the audience can identify; 4. Dramatic content; 5. Background and capability of the applicant.' (Rajadhyaksha and Willemen 1999: 166).

8. The importance of the script in the production of films that, like *Zanjeer* and *Sholay*, played a central role in the delineation of Amitabh Bachchan's star persona is also mentioned in Kabir's (1999) and Chopra's (2000) accounts. However, unlike Prasad, neither Kabir nor Chopra elaborate on this development.

9. In his review of the historiography of industrialization in India, Breman (2004: 30–73) makes precisely this point, in the process identifying the problem as being the linear, historicist model of history still underpinning much economic historiography.

10. For a critical review of Prasad's approach, see Vasudevan (1999).

11. Significantly, this happened within an industry, television, which historically, in India as much as elsewhere, has been far more preoccupied with social reproduction than cinema has ever been. In attempting to break into the market and move to the centre of the film industry, the low-budget films that had made Dara Singh famous incorporated in their narratives and exploited contexts of living that had, until the 1960s, been bracketed from representation. These contexts included notions of human physical energy free from hierarchical bonds, a commodity for any person to sell. In the 1980s, national television redefined the terms by which human physical energy had to be reproduced to meet a new economic horizon. Twenty-one years after Mistri's *King Kong*, Dara Singh thus became Hanuman. By then, Hindi cinema's main generic ground had changed quite radically. As I argue in the following pages, elements of the religiously sanctioned casteist outlook of Dara Singh's mythologicals can also be found in the Hindi action cinema of the late 1980s and early 1990s.

12. 'Amitabh Bachchan walks across the screen like Alice in Wonderland.' (*Film World* 8 (3), May 1972); 'Amitabh is lifeless.' (*Film World* 8 (7), September 1972); 'Amitabh looks like a patient of insomnia.' (*Film World* 8 (8), November 1972).

13. Shortly before the release and success of *Zanjeer*, Salim Khan and Javed Akhtar approached Sippy Films, which hired them in the company's story department for Rs 750 a month each. Their four-line idea for *Sholay* was first

taken to Manmohan Desai, who was not interested, and to Prakash Mehra, who was busy with *Zanjeer*. It was eventually bought by Sippy Films, who paid the duo Rs 75,000 for its development (Chopra 2000: 17–23).

14. As was common practice for the big-budget feudal family romances that dominated the industry before its success, the release of *Sholay* was also marked by pre-release advertising. In *Sholay*'s case advertising began in May 1973 (Chopra 2000: 39), that is no less than two years before the actual release.

15. *Zanjeer* was released at the Imperial, Strand, Capitol, Jaihind, Hindmata, Rupam, Bijli, Gaiety (in Bandra), Laxmi (in Parle), Ambar-Sangam (in Andheri), Aupam (in Goregaon), Kasturba (in Malad), Akash (in Kurla), Uday (in Ghatkopar), Krishna (in Bhandup), Ashok (in Thana), Basant (in Chembur), Prakash (in Kalyan), Regent (in Ulhasnagar), and Nazrana (in Bhivandi).

16. It was not, for instance, shown at the Eros in South Bombay nor at the new Shreyas, in Ghatkopar.

17. The official revenues figure for *Zanjeer* is Rs 60,000,000 (gross). For purpose of comparison, *Deewar*'s (released two years later) were Rs 70,000,000; *Muqaddar ka Sikandar*'s, in 1978, amounted to Rs 125,000,000, while *Sholay* made Rs 350,000,000 in its first run. Source: www.imdb.com (on 20 May 2006). Although it is impossible to establish the veracity of these figures, Chopra (2000: 180) gives the same figures for *Sholay*. In addition, Polydor sold over 500,000 records and cassettes of *Sholay*'s dialogues alone.

18. The full story of these negotiations still remains to be told. There is the distinct possibility that the bargain with the MPEAA was struck in the context of US-Indian negotiations concerning the use of satellites in the context of the SITE project. In other words, the MPEAA may well have conceded certain measures in exchange for the Indian government's greater cooperation with the US State Department's conduct of the Cold War.

19. Extras received Rs 22 a day in 1975 and Rs 37 in 1985 (Pendakur 1990: 231–2).

20. The late 1960s also saw the opening of a 'New school of stuntmen [i]n Filmalaya: A school for specialized training in film stunts and in general coaching film actors in suitable physical exercises has been set up by S.A. Shah at Filmalaya Studios at Andheri in Bombay. [F]or the time being the school imparts training on fencing, boxing and judo. It is well equipped with instruments for physical exercises for body-building. Future plans include training in horse-riding.' The principal trainer of this particular school was S.A. Shah better 'known as double hero Sunder and now a fight composer.' (*Screen*, 17 June 1996: 2).

21. These figures do not include the cost of one of the film industry's main advertising strategies, the pre-release of the film's music on cassette and radio and television programmes especially designed for the task.

22. This song and dance was criticized in some quarters and condemned as vulgar. However, when compared to other dances in earlier and later Hindi films, the mise en scène simply does not hold up to the allegations. I suggest

that the negative reaction of (part of) the public owed primarily to the fact that the song-dance featured Madhuri Dixit, a star who, unlike 1960s figures such as Helen, Mumtaz, and Kum Kum, was associated with, and had worked exclusively in, big-budget box-office films circulating within the industry's central circuit, targeting also family audiences and, as a rule, more concerned with defining the appropriate terms of social reproduction than cheaper, more marginal films were as they sought to break into the market.

23. See Valicha (1988).

24. Greimas (1983) offers a seminal methodological approach to characters as narrative functions. See also Johnston (1980).

25. This masochistic dimension, which in *CID 909* is linked to the question of technology and its uses, and which, in the 1970s and after, becomes a recurrent ingredient of the Hindi action film, is entirely absent from Dara Singh's films. In *Kabhi Dhoop Kabhi Chhaon* the hero is wounded and forced to walk with stitches, but neither do we see the accident happening nor does the accident prevent the hero from taking part in, and winning, the wrestling competition. In fact, in the scene immediately following the accident, the hero appears to have already recovered.

26. Among the prominent action directors considered by Ramesh Sippy for *Sholay* was Mohammed Hussein, who had also directed several Dara Singh films. Hussein began to work on the film, but soon fell out with the crew, who, according to Chopra, objected to his 'matter-of-fact attitude' (2000: 120–1). Apparently, Hussein had little regard for the safety of the actors' doubles. I take this squabble to be symptomatic of the encounter between, on the one hand, a section of the film industry that had occupied the centre ground by relying on stars whose persona was infused with pre-modern ideals of identity—with what Prasad (1998b) calls the innate charm of the aristocracy; and, on the other hand, a mode of filmmaking that, having been relegated to the margin of the industry, displayed more radical attitudes vis-à-vis its workforce, including actors and their doubles. As a big-budget production that sought to adapt narratives that had historically been confined to the lower (and, by necessity, more exploitative) end of the market to the needs of an industry dominated by the feudal family romance, in *Sholay* the stars (and the safety of their doubles) reigned supreme. Mohammed Hussein thus had to leave, while Sippy Films decided to resort to a foreign second unit, comprising stunt director Gerry Crampton, stunt coordinator Romo Commoro, and special effects technician John Grant (Chopra 2000: 122). Although this undoubtedly added to the film's production costs, judging by Chopra's descriptions, it did not result in a harmonious understanding of how actions scenes were to be filmed. Many of the discontinuities that characterize Hindi action cinema in general have to do with post-production, that is with editing. Whatever the actual choreography of the action scene (the pro-filmic), *Sholay*, as much as *Zanjeer*, is replete with spatial discontinuities

because, as I argue here, in both films the priority, at the level of narration, was not the indexically marked cinematic rendition of human physical energy.

27. These reports gave a brief history of motion pictures in their territories, especially from the industrial point of view, listed trade restrictions and opportunities, [and] censorship issues. [T]he films were deemed to be excellent advertising for the marketing of refrigerators, cars, foodstuffs, toys, fashion products and so on. The report on the Philippines [s]tates confidently that 'as in the United States, the appearance of merchandise in the movies stimulates a desire to possess it' (US Department of Commerce and the Office of International Trade, *World Trade in Commodities*, 1948: 8). However, most of the reports admitted that there was no reliable way of quantifying the impact of Hollywood films on the sales of other commodities (Willemen 2005b: 102).

6

Contemporary Action Cinema

IN THE 1980s, AS AMITABH BACHCHAN BECAME HINDI CINEMA'S BIGGEST crowd-puller, the formula inaugurated by *Sholay* and *Deewar* produced cheaper versions of Bachchan's action films. Bengali actor Mithun Chakraborty acquired a large following through such films. His *Andhi Toofan/Whirlwind* (B. Subash 1985), for instance, borrowed narrative and musical elements from Sergio Leone's Westerns, and wrapped around those more or less explicit citations a sense of physical action that was very much centred on Chakraborty's kung fu-like use of legs. The mise en scène of action scenes, the type of physical action performed by the actor, and the borrowing from Leone's films were all mediated by the action films of Amitabh Bachchan, for these were the films that defined the Hindi film industry's dominant generic ground in the 1980s.

By the late 1980s, however, the film industry began to realize that even Amitabh Bachchan was not as inexhaustible a selling point as their marketing strategies would have him be. Action films that had been circulating on the margins of the ground defined by Bachchan's vehicles were pushing forward male action figures and preoccupations that were not addressed by Bachchan's action films. *Agnipath/Path of Fire* (Mukul Anand 1990), starring Amitabh Bachchan as an ageing, white-clad don and Mithun Chakraborty as his sidekick, marked the decline of the superstar. In the five years that followed, Chakraborty featured in some fifty productions. None of these were blockbusters or major commercial successes. Mithun Chakraborty's were B and C grade films, and the actor's market appeal had a strong local dimension. Yet, in this period and through these films, Mithun Chakraborty emerged as one of the Hindi film industry's safest assets. As producer Pawan Kumar put it:

From the investors' point of view, Mithun functions as a guarantee that the film will be ready within three months. Their interests are safe. He is an attractive proposition also for distributors and exhibitors. With a Mithun film, the distributor recovers his investment within days of release. And even if there are losses, these are minimal because the overall investment, the film's cost, was moderate to begin with. (Quoted in Grimaud 2003: 444, my translation)

This account is corroborated by Sudhanva Deshpande:

[Mithun Chakraborty] shifted to the south Indian hill of Ooty and built a hotel there. [A] producer would land up at Ooty, stay with his crew in Chakraborty's hotel at concessional rates, shoot a film with him and an aspiring or failed starlet, finish shooting in three weeks flat, do post-production in Mumbai over the next fortnight or so, and inside two months, a film would be ready with six or seven songs, several fight sequences, one rape, fiery dialogues, and a weepy mother. (2005: 193)

Kumar and Deshpande's statements suggest that, after the decline of Amitabh Bachchan, the type of economy that characterized Dara Singh's films became once again characteristic of Hindi action cinema. Mithun Chakraborty and, in the 1990s, Sunil Shetty, were part of this configuration: small but assured investments geared towards moderate profits through the production of cheap films and their circulation on the margins of the exhibition sector. However, Deshpande's account also indicates that, unlike Dara Singh's career, Chakraborty's was marked by factors that by the 1990s had become central to India's trajectory towards economic 'liberalization'. The point of interest in Chakraborty's operation is not the exploitation of well-tested selling points, such as songs, fight sequences, violent sex scenes, and Chakraborty's own physical skills, whether as a fighter or as a dancer. As we have seen, these elements also characterized Dara Singh's films. What interests me is the actor's exploitation of an economic factor that was not at work in Dara Singh's productions: real estate and its connection with film production. Whereas in the 1970s big stars such as Bachchan would get part of their fee in undeclared money, in Chakraborty's case a share of the actor's income was generated through the hotel, that is through property development. This new set of considerations, revolving around notions of space and its value, began to surface in Hindi action films in the late 1980s and early 1990s.

Landed capital had been an important player in the Indian film industry ever since its first decades. In the late 1960s it underpinned the exhibition sector's modes of operation. The centralization of finance in the 1970s led to radical changes in the generic ground of Hindi cinema: the action ingredient became once again available, this time around as one way of circulating larger amounts of capital at a faster pace than nationalized banks were capable of doing. Even so, the number of cinemas in the country did not grow at a significantly higher rate than in the earlier decades. Moreover, individual cinemas continued to offer several daily shows of the same film, often for weeks and still, in many cases, irrespective of whether a film drew audiences large enough to make a profit. Things did change in the 1970s, and speculative capital did become a far more important player in the film industry than was previously the case, but a share of exhibitors' revenues continued to derive from the rental paid by distributors to book the theatre, like a form of rent on the land and on the property leased by the exhibitor.

In the 1980s, large cities of industrializing countries suffered massive plant closures. In Indian cities, this new wave of de-industrialization went hand in hand with exponential rises in land and property prices. In Bombay, Delhi, Calcutta, and Bangalore, investment in real estate took place via the effective privatization of land and housing which earlier planning regulation had devoted to public use and industrial workers' housing. For instance, in the 1970s, Bombay's urban poor were promised new homes and jobs in New Bombay (now Navi Mumbai). Instead, within a few years, the bulk of the new housing went to civil servants and the middle class (Jacquemin 1999: 196–7). The sites of the city's once principal industry, the mills, were (and still are) closed down. While some mills were occasionally rented out to film producers as shooting sites, the long-term plan was to sell the land they occupied in the city centre to real estate speculators. Real estate investment by the upper echelons of the middle class[1] in more central areas of the city was followed, in the 1990s, by a drastic neoliberal restructing of the economy which produced a stock market bubble. Whereas during this decade India's gross domestic product grew at 6 per cent per year, 'the capitalization of the Bombay Stock Exchange doubled almost every year. One result was one million new millionaires, many of them Indian engineers and computer scientists returned from Sunnyvale and Redmond' (Davis 2006: 170–1).[2]

These developments first surfaced in the Hindi action cinema of the 1980s as a preoccupation over urban space. Urban space had featured prominently in feudal family romances of the 1950s, but the city in these films was part of a trope that hovered around a clear-cut opposition: the city and the country, modernity and tradition. Even in films that adopted a progressive stand vis-à-vis notions of modernity, or which featured specific cities, such as *Pyaasa*, the city was presented as an abstract, symbolic entity—a space of moral dissolution, at best of anomie. Arguably, among the factors contributing to this cinematic representation of the city were unreconstructed landed interests. Given that these were the interests that dominated the industry at the time, especially in the exhibition sector, it would be surprising if their priorities had not worked themselves into aspects of the cinema, including its representation of space.

Amitabh Bachchan as the action hero has tended to be seen as an urban hero, but his action films of the 1970s and 1980s incorporated important elements of 1950s cinematic ideas of urban space. Bachchan's action films customarily open with a pre-titles sequence that, showing the hero's one-way trip from the country to the city, carries that duality into the rest of the film. In *Coolie/Porter* (Manmohan Desai 1983), *Deewar, Trishul, Muqqadar ka Sikandar*, and many others, the city continued to be treated very much as a symbolic space, signalled by way of landmarks such as the station, the port, the market, and the building site.[3] These symbols mark urban space as a place of transit, somewhere to come to (for work or trade) and leave from. Although he has left the country behind, the task of Bachchan's hero is to navigate a cityscape that assumes the opposition between these two poles. Significantly, in *Deewar*, the city views that can be seen through the windows of the porters' canteen are cardboard backdrops. In *Don* (Chandra Bharot 1978), the car chase is shot following the rules of spatial continuity, but not according to the location's own geographical continuity. Different and distant parts of Bombay are used with complete disregard for continuity: one minute we are in Colaba, in south-central Bombay, and the next, as the car turns a corner, we are in the suburbs.

An entirely different presentation of urban space breaks into Hindi action cinema with the films of N. Chandra. It is not simply, as Ravi Vasudevan reminds us, that *Ankush/Goad* (N. Chandra 1985) evokes marks of urbanity such as the street-corner or the *bazaar* in a distinctive, documentary style; or that in *Tezaab* the director sought to achieve a similar degree of verisimilitude in the studio sets (2003: p. 95). More importantly, with N. Chandra's films urban *space* came to be presented as a *place*. Writing about this classic distinction between 'space' and 'place', Marc Augé explains that

[t]he fantasy [of place] is that of a closed world founded once and for all long ago; one which [d]oes not have to be understood. Everything there is to know about it is already known: land, forest, springs, notable features, religious places, medicinal plants, not forgetting the temporal dimensions of an inventory of these places whose legitimacy is postulated, and whose stability is supposed to be assured, by narratives about origins and by the ritual calendar. All the inhabitants have to do is *recognize* themselves in it when the occasion arises. (1995: 44)[4]

It is towards such a sense of familiarity or recognition that N. Chandra's films, and particularly his commercially successful *Tezaab*, work. *Tezaab* tells the story of Munna (Anil Kapoor), a former naval cadet who finds himself at loggerheads with a gang of criminals and, eventually, with the police and the law. Exiled from his city, he sets up base in the slums, where he rules. The film abounds with scenes that are choreographed to present the city of Bombay as the film's location and as a place for the spectator to recognize, including a motorbike chase and several song sequences. Although Salim–Javed scripts sought to achieve a similar effect by writing dialogues which used a particular type of Bombay Hindi, a parallel effort is not at work in Bachchan action films' urban mise en scène. By contrast, in *Tezaab*, the mise en scène literally maps the city out into distinct zones: not only the inside and outside of the city, but also its entertainment and residential areas, the slums, the docks, the promenade and so forth. Peter Wollen has written that 'protagonists appropriate the places they are "in"' (1980: 25). Munna's narrative function is precisely to draw the spectator into such zoning. The scene in which Munna is introduced takes place in the slums. As the scene begins, we do not quite know where we are; the surroundings are revealed to us gradually as 'the slums' by the eye of a camera that takes up Munna's point of view. From here onwards, it is either the protagonist's point of view or his movement through it (as seen through medium or long shots) that maps the city out into distinct zones for us to recognize, recognize ourselves in, and to 'appropriate' as 'our place'.

In N. Chandra's films, as in much other action cinema of the 1980s and 1990s, this transformation of urban space into a city place is performed by investing a space marked urban with specific values. In *Tezaab*, the zoning of the cityscape takes place by investing cinematic urban space with communal values. Much has been written about the explicit communal connotations of N. Chandra's films.[5] Here I am more interested in looking at the ideological dimension of films as one of the diegetic manifestations of the economic interests that underpinned the films' conditions of production and circulation. This is to say that reading films as historical documents, as this book tries to do, is not simply a question of mapping the political discourses or the ideology propounded by any given film. The ideological dimension of films does reveal how a film maps ideal social relations, but such ideal (filmic) social figurations are not an end in themselves: they are symptoms of the film's ideal economic horizon—the economic trajectory of which the film, as a commodity, is part, and which the film helps to reproduce by staging the social relations that would sustain that economic horizon. From this perspective, the communal content of some Hindi action films is only one of their narrative elements, one set of values ascribed to the diegetic space. As far as identifying the economic interests underpinning these films is concerned, it is not their most revealing dimension.[6] The exploitation of the action ingredient as a film's selling point and the diegetic manifestation of that commercial consideration, that is a film's foregrounding of images of physical energy, are especially symptomatic of the set of economic pressures that constitutes a film as an industrial product. Written into such images is the value a film ascribes to physical energy as the means of its own production as a commodity. From this perspective, all that appears to be required in *Tezaab* is Anil Kapoor's movement across urban space. While the type of gestures and actions performed by the actor are very similar to those of Bachchan, unlike in *Zanjeer* and other Bachchan action films, in *Tezaab* action scenes tend to be shot subjectively. Subjective narration in *Tezaab* is a function of the diegetic transformation of urban space into a distinctive place. Anil Kapoor's point of view, as he moves across this urban space, stitches the spectator into a landscape everything about which there is to know is presented as 'already known'. As one such 'known factor', religious connotations, in *Tezaab* (as elsewhere) are not an end in themselves, but, rather, a means of inscribing a sense of memory and a narrative of origins into the diegetic space. Such a marking process transforms space into a specific place. It affirms control over a share of it as a particular allotment, with an outside and an inside the value of which is absolute because it depends entirely on its internal logic.

This shift in the diegetic rendering of the hero's environment offered a new perspective on 'the city'. In N. Chandra's films we no longer look at the city from its outside, from the country, for which all space is land. We are inside the city and perceive it as a composite of familiar zones, places to occupy and defend. By the end of the decade, these all too real fantasies of land as speculative value, rather than as source of rent or a means of production, led to the phenomenon of bogus film cities: barely disguised experiments in real estate speculation like Bombay's Film City, which occupies 60,000 sq. m of effectively unused land in suburban Goregaon (Deshpande 2004). *Krantiveer*, starring Nana Patekar,[7] went a step further. This film was released at a time when, after two decades of rampant real estate speculation, what remained of Bombay's industry had moved outside the city. Suburbs continued to grow, and since so did migration to the city, unemployment and the slums also grew. *Krantiveer*'s hero inhabits a place marked if not as 'the slums', at least as something that in the Hindi cinematic imaginary is very close to it: a working class suburb. He is unemployed, but he displays a muscled, lean body that conveys a sense of sheer physical energy. Throughout the film, spatial continuity is respected. However, unlike in the films of Dara Singh, within this synthetic space the impression of physical energy derives not from the fetishization of the actor's muscle power, but from Patekar's body as he is thrown about into a built or semi-built environment. The visual impression of physical impact in such scenes is not conveyed through sound effects and the cutting and editing together of close-up shots of body parts, as it is in American action films of the same period. Sound effects are certainly a factor in *Krantiveer*'s staging of action, just as they are in all Indian action cinema. But while in most films sound tends to be used to compensate for the mise en scène's failure to convey a visual sense of physical impact effectively, *Krantiveer*'s action scenes rely on a greater degree of sensory impression—a visual sense of tactility—than is the case in most Hindi films. In *Krantiveer* the idea of physical impact is primarily signalled by showing the actor's body bumping against the confines of the place he inhabits. Whereas in *Tezaab* 'place' is defined by the protagonist's look and his movement across urban space, in *Krantiveer* the marks of 'place', its territorial boundaries, are inscribed physically into the protagonist's body. Such hammering of the zone's limits into the body is effected by placing objects within the range of the actor's gestures. Throughout the film, the diegetic appearance of such objects is not primarily another human figure, but built or semi-built structures.

As Sudhanva Deshpande (2005) has observed, slums more or less disappeared from the Hindi cinema of late 1990s and early 2000s. The look of built structures in these films changed accordingly. *One 2 ka 4* (K. Shashilal Nair 2001), an action-comedy film intended also for the family market, features Shah Rukh Khan and Jackie Shroff as two special agents. The first (Khan) is a young, attractive bachelor living in a fashionable loft, while the second is a widowed father and owner of a large house in a quiet residential area. The film opens with a fast-paced action sequence showing the two agents foiling a hold-up in a glittery shopping mall and rescuing the families held hostage inside it. Designed in such a way as to evoke the sensational openings of John Woo's films, this sequence is nevertheless predominantly preoccupied with displaying the mall's post-modern, glass architecture, and all its content in as ostentatious and as attractive a manner as possible. Among the goods and brands clearly on display as Shah Rukh Khan and Jackie Shroff carry out their duty are videogames, McDonalds, CocaCola, Pepsi, Swatch, Lakmé, and Kingfisher.

In Hollywood cinema this explicit kind of merchandizing dates back several decades, but in Hindi cinema it really took off only in the mid-1990s. It is not unique to action cinema. As the *New Indian Express* of 29 October 1999 reported, by then corporate sponsorship was leaving its mark on a range of other films:

The opening titles of Sooraj Barjatya's forthcoming film *Hum Saath Saath Hain/ We Are Together* [w]ill feature an important new player in Bollywood: Coca-Cola. The cola giant, in its bid to scramble to the very top of the Rs 3,500 crore [35 billion] soft drinks market, has spent a comparatively smaller amount, Rs 1.5 crore [15 million], on branding Barjatya's family film and ensuring its release as *Coca-Cola Hum Saath Saath Hain*. (Quoted in Rajadhyaksha 2003: 38–9)

When Dreamz Unlimited produced *Phir Bhi Dil Hai Hindustani/Still the Heart Remains Indian* (Azeez Mirza 2000), entire scenes of the film were devoted to the advertising of the film sponsors' products. The producing company was controlled by Shah Rukh Khan, actress Juhi Chawla, and Azeez Mirza, who starred in and directed the film (Deshpande 2005: 190). By then, Shah Rukh Khan was not only the biggest Hindi actor, but also a regular in commercials. To pin-point individual films, actors, or sponsors as ultimately responsible for these developments is misleading, not least because it implies too short-term and too direct a sense of cultural-historical determination. As far as action films are concerned, we can trace this tendency as far back as *Zanjeer*. Through its mode of address, *Zanjeer* advertised primarily itself, as a new genre, and its technology. With *Sholay* the same strategy was pushed to a new level, at least to the extent that concrete steps were taken to sell other products on the back of the film. *One 2 ka 4* borrowed from both.

In *One 2 ka 4*, as in John Woo's films, at the end much of the merchandise and the property on display are blown up. Explosions in this and other sequences do not undermine the desirability of the goods on display. Sound and fast-paced editing have the same effect here as the zoom in *Zanjeer*: they are part of an emphatic address the dominant constituent of which is, to use Jakobson's terminology, the conative (or imperative) function. As in advertising, the bumping up of sound volumes, fast editing, extreme close-ups on items to be presented as desirable, and other sensory effects grab the spectator somewhat unawares. The desirability of the advertised merchandise, whether foodstuffs, cosmetic products, fashion items, or property is hammered into a spectator whose defences and thought processes are inhibited by the sensory overload. In this way, the injunction to consume is quite literally inscribed into the spectator's body. The question, then, is not so much the use of films to sell other goods, as the directness and emphasis with which this is done in recent Hindi productions. Given that the means of such imperative directness have been available to Hindi cinema since at least the 1970s, why now and not before?

The immediate economic interests underpinning merchandizing in Hindi cinema have been mapped by Adrian Athique (2007), whose research into the arrival and growth of the multiplex cinema in India provides ample evidence for the connections between real estate, retail, and cinema. As Athique observes, the boom in property development and speculation has led to a

mushrooming [in Indian cities] of gated residential complexes, retail shopping malls and, alongside (or inside) them, multiplex cinemas. [T]he developers of residential colonies and shopping malls have been well aware of the pulling power of on-site cinemas for their clientele. Multiplex cinemas are said to increase footfalls in a shopping mall by 40–50 per cent. As such, multiplex operators are now able to lease floor space in these developments at relatively low cost. Indeed, the receptiveness of mall developers to their presence has foreclosed the need for them to invest in property assets, a crucial stumbling block for expansion given the soaring property prices in the major metros. Crucially, in their desire to foster prestige commercial development projects, a significant number of Indian states have given entertainment tax exemptions specifically to multiplex theatres. (ibid.: 5–6)

As has historically always been the case in India, it is the priorities of exhibitors that determine the mode of operation of the cinema's other sectors. While an emphatic address with self-advertising purposes was already at work in Hindi action cinema in the 1970s, it became a dominant dimension of Hindi films in recent years because it is only now that exhibitors have successfully established tight relations with the retail industry. As Athique points out, the link between the two is property development, a sector with which film exhibition has entertained a relationship that goes back several decades.

It did not take as long for exhibitors' new priorities to feed back into production. Among today's largest Indian multiplex operators are Adlabs Films and Inox Leisure. Founded as a film-processing laboratory in 1978,

Adlabs entered film exhibition in 2000 and began producing films two years later. In October 2005 the land investment arm of the Reliance Anil Dhirubhai Ambani Group acquired a majority stake in the company. As an exhibitor, Adlabs currently has a seating capacity of 12,742. Inox Leisure, a subsidiary of Gujarat Fluorochemicals, is planning to enter into a partnership with the leading retailer and corporate film sponsor Pantaloon Group which is intended to pursue the development of fifty-one shopping malls nationwide, thirty-five of which will contain a multiplex cinema. Its current seating capacity is 13,267 (Athique 2007: 9–11).[8] A comparison between the 1978 *Don* (Chandra Bharot) and its 2006 remake (Farhan Akhtar) reveals the extent of the pressure on producers and filmmakers to meet the merchandizing requirements of this new type of exhibitor.

Starring Amitabh Bachchan, the original *Don* featured a reasonable number of luxury items, but the film was not built around them. Cars, fashionable clothes, and fancy women in *Don* were part of the Bachchan persona and of his character. *Don*'s 2006 version, starring Shah Rukh Khan and directed by the son of the original film's scriptwriter Javed Akhtar, is a very close remake of Bharot's *Don*, except for the goods on display and their function within the narrative. While in the 1978 version the don has a meeting in a public sauna, in the remake Shah Rukh Khan's don is seen in an oversized jacuzzi (the don's own) doing business over the phone; Bachchan's 1978 hero's idea of leisure is to indulge in a glass of imported brew; in the new version, Shah Rukh Khan plays golf. Modern technology has a prominent place in the remake. When a mole inside the don's gang is found to be passing on information to the police, in the original version he is exposed by a message written on a piece of paper that is hidden inside the heel of his shoe; in the remake, the item hidden inside the shoe is a small microphone. In the 1978 version, the don forces an acrobat to help in a bank robbery; in the later version, the same character is transformed into a software engineer. In the new *Don* cars, motorbikes, motorboats, airplanes, helicopters, and a long list of other fashionable items hold the narrative together. Technology here is not treated as a means of transport or production, as it was in earlier Hindi films, but as something to display, a luxury item. Accordingly, in Akhtar's film, the body in action, Shah Rukh Khan's, is neither a muscled nor an acrobatic or agile body, as were Dara Singh, Sunny Deol, Sunil Shetty, or Amitabh Bachchan. It is a representative body, in the sense that its main function is to carry the signs of middle class-ness, much in the same way that Dilip

Kumar's was in the 1950s. As Akhtar's *Don* shows, however, the values that now inform notions of middle class-ness are no longer the same as those of the 1950s.

The personae of contemporary Hindi action heroes have internalized the advertising potential that came to be associated with Shah Rukh Khan. Actors such as John Abraham and Hrithik Roshan look like the anonymous figures of fashion shows. As Deshpande put it, Hrithik Roshan displays 'a physique so perfect, it seems somehow unreal and plastic' (2005: 197). Action heroes such as those interpreted by Roshan have muscles and show them, but their somewhat 'unreal plasticity' owes much to the fact that they do not use them. In *Dhoom 2/Blast* (Sanjay Gadhvi 2004), for instance, the hero (Abhishek Bachchan) and his sidekick, Ali, go to Rio de Janeiro, where Ali is seen dancing with a Brazilian woman of Indian extraction against a backdrop of the city's most well-known view. The mise en scène highlights Ali's well-oiled muscles, but, like the postcard image of Rio, the motorboats and the beaches, Ali's biceps are presented as yet another symbol of luxury and leisure, like the synecdoche of a gym, not as a source of energy. In *Dhoom* and *Dhoom 2* (Sanjay Gadhvi 2006), the final confrontation between the two protagonists, a policeman (Abhishek Bachchan) and a thief (John Abraham in *Dhoom* and Hrithik Roshan in *Dhoom 2*) has them facing the camera and sorting out by talking to each other, as if to evoke, although in a more light-hearted manner, the ending of Michael Mann's *Heat* (1995), with Al Pacino as the policeman and Robert De Niro as the outlaw. In both films Abraham and Roshan display a muscled chest in full, frontal view, but the function of this mise en scène is clearly to display the designer shirts and leather jackets donned by the stars. In the same way, in *Dhoom*, shots of Abraham on his motorbike reveal a great deal more about the bike's design than about the physiognomy of the male figure and its energetic potential.

Finally, in these films, action scenes demand very little actual physical strain of the actors. The type of gestures performed at the level of the pro-filmic are very much the same as in Bachchan's films—punches, kicks, and somersaults—confirming the preference, within Hindi action cinema, for acrobatic bodies.[9] In *Dhoom* and *Dhoom 2*, however, choreography of the pro-filmic is cut to the bone because each action sequence relies primarily on a combination of digital manipulation and jump-cuts. As in *The Matrix* (Wachoski Brothers 1999), where Keanu Reeves, rather than his double, can be seen performing complex kung-fu moves on a narrow plank and impossibly high somersaults, the resulting cinematic rendition of Abraham and Roshan's physical movements is visually discontinuous, as if continuous movement over time had been reduced to a few crucial temporal fragments, or a whole sequence of photograms had been cut out during post-production for the sake of brevity. At one level, this way of shooting and editing action sequences enhances the visual impression of speed; at another level it is constitutive of a very emphatic, even aggressive, mode of address. Like the deliberate use of split screen (in *Dhoom*) or of sudden shifts from colour to black and white (in *James*, Rohit Jugraj 2005), digitally shot action sequences attack the spectator's sensory system with an overload of stimuli without allowing him or her the time to process or translate them consciously into information.[10] In this respect, these image-sequences operated not only like fast-consuming comic strips, but also like the subliminal advertising techniques that are supposed to bypass conscious perception.[11]

Dhoom and *Dhoom 2* were produced by Yash Raj Films and *James* by Ram Gopal Varma, two independent producers. According to the films' titles, some funding came from Onyx Mobile, Pepe Jeans, MTV, Dainik Jagran, Sity Max, Punjab Today, and Mauj, but to ascribe the films' advertising address to these companies raises a question of direct determination which, ultimately, distracts us from the fact that no film is reducible to the goods it advertises. A historically accurate understanding of these films must first and foremost confront the fact that a film is a dimension of a configuration of which the film's sponsors are also part and from which they both derive their mode of operation. To paraphrase Walter Benjamin, this is not a question of correlating texts with the configuration in which they circulate, but, rather, of presenting that configuration, the time which knows the films, by opening it up to the multiple and unstable set of pressures that constitute it. Some of these layers are indeed synchronous with the films, others are much older, and yet others may not have quite fully materialized as a prominent dimension of the configuration that the film addresses or negotiates.

It is the task of film historians to identify as accurately as possible which socio-economic pressures work themselves out in any given film, and to show how they do so. Here, I have tried to show that it is possible to see historical processes in operation in the film texts themselves—to read films as they stage the conditions of their reproduction, impacting in this way, on our lives as one of the dimensions sustaining the specific socio-economic constellation we inhabit. From this perspective, the current rush by major multiplex operators to expand as rapidly as they are intent on doing their tight collaboration with the retail sector, and the resulting sensory overload that characterizes films produced in this context, all raise the important question of saturation—of the market and of the audience's capacity to absorb information, not to mention act on it. As Athique observes, 'the planned expansion [of multiplex cinemas] beyond major cities may require a scaling down of the grandiosity of facilities to suit local conditions in [smaller] centres'. At a broader social and political level,

[b]eyond the strength of the market itself, the continuance of a friendly tax regime remains a key factor in the *long term* profitability of multiplexes, since the majority of entertainment tax exemptions are time limited. Revenues may be reduced considerably if multiplexes become subject to similar levels of taxation as the older theatrical infrastructure. The question here is whether the states will be willing to continue giving up their revenues once the initial investment has been attracted, particularly in light of the increased agitation amongst traditional cinemas that continue to pay high taxes and remain subject to price fixing. [O]n the other hand, if their expansion plans are successful, the sheer size of multiplex operators may well give them the kind of leverage over regulators that will facilitate the negotiation of an ongoing favourable tax regime. This is the kind of critical mass that the [t]heatrical industry has traditionally lacked in India. Although the overall shortage of cinemas and their distinctly different target audiences suggest space for the continuance of both 'organized' [multiplex] and 'disorganized' [older] infrastructures, just how exactly they will cohabit is indicative of much wider questions facing a liberalizing Indian economy. (2007: 18–19, emphasis added)

Not all about multiplex cinemas is as bleak as one may be left to feel after analysing the films I discussed in these last few pages. For one thing, multiplex cinemas are an indication that the exhibition sector, historically, in India as elsewhere, always the most reluctant to change, is finally opening up. To minimize risk, many of these new venues have multiple screens and different shows depending on the time of the day. Conspicuous consumption may well be the ideal horizon of films such as *Dhoom* or the remake of *Don*, but this is not to say that this horizon will effectively materialize on a significant scale across India, or that things will indeed stay that way for long. An image is too complex an object for a viewer to obediently read within it only what he or she is instructed to by the various authorities that govern its circulation, whether the state or a corporation. If the action films produced by Sharda, by the Wadia brothers, or those of Dara Singh are anything to go by, in the long term the opening up of Indian exhibition may also enable smaller, commercially more adventurous, producers to claim a share of the market. In the 1920s, the 1930s, and the 1960s, films produced in a shoestring sought to gain a position on the centre ground of the industry by exploiting precisely a visual 'excess' that more centrally located films did not dare to touch, and then radically scooped up contexts of living and aspects of social experience that had, until then, been bracketed from representation. There is no reason why this should not happen again. As chairman Mao's second in command said when, in the 1990s, he was asked about the effects of the French Revolution: 'It is too early to tell.'

NOTES

1. Today, 'an estimated three-quarters of urban space in India is owned by 6 per cent of urban households, and just 91 people control the majority of all vacant land in Mumbai' (Davis 2006: 84).

2. For the role of the IT industry in the property-investment-led expansion of Bangalore, see Nair (2005).

3. For the representation of the city in Hindi films, see also Prasad (2001) and Mazumdar (2002) and (2007).

4. A formulation of the anthropological distinction between the two notions of space and place can be found in Marcel Mauss (1966). See also Donald (1997). Writing in 1980, Peter Wollen observed that 'whereas "space" has often been discussed as an aspect of cinema, nothing much has been said about "place". Place is a more concrete concept—this particular place, that place over there—and more "cultural", involving a complex of connotations beyond the perspective grid, the choreography of movement or the phenomenology of perception. Place implies memory, reverie [a]nd the imaginary. [P]lace also implies displacement, being elsewhere, being a stranger' (1980: 25).

5. See, for instance, Vasudevan (2003). Within the action genre, communal markers are far from unique to N. Chandra's films. They are at work, for instance, in many of Sunny Deol's and Sunil Shetty's films, where, as in *Tezaab*, they are wrapped up in well-tested narratives of heroes protecting terrorized villagers. In *Ghatak* Sunny Deol is a Brahmin from Varanasi and a pehelwan, while Katya, the villain terrorizing the neighbourhood sports all the stereotypical markers of Muslim identity. In *Raghuveer*, Sunil Shetty plays a similar 'protecting' role as the eponymous Raghuveer, meaning Raghu's brave warrior. According to Hindu mythology, Raghu was a king of Avadh, the great-grandfather of Ramchandra.

6. Nor is communal content unique to the Hindi action film. Feudal family romances such as *Hum Aapke Hain Kaun/Who Am I to You?* (Sooraj Barjatya 1994) are as replete with communalism as N. Chandra's films, even if that particular construction of Indian life is proposed differently in the two types of film.

7. The Maharashtra actor featured regularly in N. Chandra's films.

8. The other two major multiplex operators are Priya Village Roadshow (PVR), a joint venture between Priya Exhibitors and the Australian exhibition chain Village Roadshow, and Shringar Cinemas, originally one of India's biggest distributors (Shringar Films). Shringar moved into the multiplex business in

partnership with Adlabs in 2002, but soon followed with its own. In 2005 Temasek holdings, an investment arm of the Singapore government, acquired a 14.9 per cent stake in the company (Athique 2007: 8–10).

9. There are of course exceptions to this. Not only Dara Singh in the 1960s, but also films in the 1990s with Sunny Deol and Sunil Shetty, such as *Ghatak* and *Vishwasghaat/Breach of Trust* (Himansu Bhrambhatt 1995). The notion of physical energy at work in the latter film is that of energy as 'impact', not as acrobatics. I am talking here about a dominant tendency over several decades. Neither Deol's nor Shetty's films can be regarded as having being part of the industry's central generic ground.

10. For a discussion of sensory overload as a dimension of modernity, and of Walter Benjamin's idea of 'anaesthesia', see Buck-Morss (1992). In a later work, Susan Buck-Morss writes: '[Bodies defensively adapt to their environment.] Nowhere was this defensive reflex more apparent than in the factory, where (Benjamin cited Marx) "workers learn to coordinate their own movements to the uniform and unceasing motion of an automaton." Independently of the worker's volition, the article being worked on comes within his range of action and moves away from him just as arbitrarily. Exploitation was here to be understood as a cognitive category, not an economic one. The factory system, injuring every one of the human senses, paralyzed the imagination of the worker, whose labour was "sealed off from experience"; memory was replaced by conditioned response, learning by "drill", skill by repetition: "practice counts for nothing." Under conditions of modern technology, the aesthetic system undergoes a dialectical reversal. The human sensorium changes from a mode of being "in touch" with reality into a means of blocking out reality. Aesthetics— sensory perception—becomes *anaesthetics*, a numbing of the senses' cognitive capacity that destroys the human organism's power to respond politically even when self-preservation is at stake. Someone who is "past experiencing," writes Benjamin, is "no longer capable of telling ... proven friend ... from mortal enemy."' (Buck-Morss 2000: 104).

11. Broadly speaking, vision involves three processes: the registration of light by the eye, the coding of sensory stimulation by the nervous system, and the interpretation of these codes by a person's cognitive system. As Jacques Aumont explains, vision is first and foremost a spatial sense, but temporal factors play an important part in it for three reasons: because 'most visual stimuli vary across time, or are produced successively'; because 'our eyes are in constant motion, which means that the information received by the brain is constantly changing'; and because 'perception itself is not an instantaneous process— certain stages of perception are rapid, others much slower, but the processing of information always takes place in time' (1994: 16). Subliminal advertising techniques are supposed to bypass consciousness because the image of the advertised good is projected or shown for too short a time to be processed— that is decoded—as an advertisement.

Bibliography

BOOKS AND ARTICLES

Abel, Richard. 1999. *The Red Rooster Scare: Making Cinema American, 1900–1910*, Berkeley: University of California Press.

———. 2004. 'The "Culture War" of Sensational Melodrama, 1910–14', in Yvonne Tasker (ed.), *Action and Adventure Cinema*, London and New York: Routledge, pp. 31–51.

Adarkar, Neera. 1991. 'In Search of Women in the History of Marathi Theatre, 1843–1933', *Economic and Political Weekly*, 26 October, pp. WS87–WS90.

Alter, Joseph. 1992. *The Wrestler's Body: Identity and Ideology in North India*, New Delhi: Munshiram Manoharlal Publishers; Berkeley: University of California Press.

Altman, Rick. 1995. 'A Semantic/Syntactic Approach to Film Genre', in Keith Grant (ed.), *Film Genre Reader 2*, Barry, Austin: University of Texas Press, pp. 26–40.

———. 1998. 'Reusable Packaging: Generic Products and the Recycling Process', in Nick Browne (ed.), *Refiguring American Film Genres: Theory and History*, Berkeley: University of California Press, pp. 1–41.

Anandi, S. 1991. 'Representing Devadasis: "Dasigal Mosalai" as a Radical Text', *Economic and Political Weekly*, Annual Number, March, pp. 739–46.

Arrighi, Giovanni. 1991. 'World Income Inequalities and the Future of Socialism', *New Left Review* 189, pp. 39–66.

Athique, Adrian M. 2007. 'Leisure in the New Economy: The Rapid Rise of the Multiplex in India', Paper presented at the 'Asian Cinema: Towards a Research and Teaching Agenda' conference, Bangalore, February.

Augé, Marc (trans. from French by John Howe). 1995. *Non-Places: Introduction to an Anthropology of Supermodernity*, London and New York: Verso.

Aumont, Jacques (trans. from the French by Claire Pajackowska). 1994. *The Image*, London: British Film Institute.

Awasti, Suresh. 1983. *The Gift of Gods: Culture, Performance and Communication in India*, Tokyo: Institute for the Study of Languages and Cultures of Asia and Africa.

———. 2001. *Performance Tradition in India*, New Delhi: National Book Trust.

Bahl, Vinay. 1995. *The Making of the Indian Working Class: A Case of the Tata Iron and Steel Company, 1880–1946*, New Delhi and London: Sage.

Balcon, Michael, Ernest Lindgren, Forsyth Hardy, and Roger Manvell. 1947. *Twenty Years of British Film 1926–1945*, London: Falcon Press.

Bandyopadhyay, Samik (ed.). 1993. *Indian Cinema: Contemporary Perceptions from the Thirties*, Jamshedpur: Celluloid Chapter.

Banerjee, Sumanta. 1989. 'Marginalisation of Women's Popular Culture in Nineteenth Century Bengal', in Kumkum Sangari and Sudesh Vaid (eds), *Recasting Women: Essays in Colonial History*, New Delhi: Kali for Women, pp. 129–81.

______. 1998. *Dangerous Outcast: The Prostitute in Nineteenth Century Bengal*, Calcutta: Seagull.

Barnouw, Eric and S. Krishnaswamy. 1980. *Indian Film*, second edition, New Delhi: Oxford University Press.

Basu, Siddhartha, Sanjay Kak, and Pradip Krishen. 1980. 'Cinema and Society: A Search for Meaning in a New Genre', *India International Centre Quarterly*, 8 (1).

Benjamin, Walter (trans. from the German by Harry Zohn). 1969. 'The Storyteller: Reflections on the Works of Nikolai Leskov', in *Illuminations*, New York: Schocken Books, pp. 83–109.

______. (trans. from the German by Rodney Livingstone, et al.). 1999a. 'Literary History and the Study of Literature', in Michael W. Jennings, Howard Eiland, and Gary Smith (eds), *Selected Writings Volume 2 1927–1934*, Cambridge, Mass. and London: The Belknap Press of Harvard University Press, pp. 459–65.

______. (trans. from the German by Rodney Livingstone, et al.). 1999b. 'On the Concept of History', in Michael W. Jennings, Howard Eiland, and Gary Smith (eds), *Selected Writings Volume 4 1938–1940*, Cambridge, Mass. and London: The Belknap Press of Harvard University Press, pp. 389–400. Published as 'Theses on the Philosophy of History', in *Illuminations*, New York: Schocken Books, 1969.

Bharucha, Bejan Dadiba (ed.). 1938. *Indian Cinematograph Year Book 1938*, Bombay: Motion Picture Society of India.

Bhattacharya, Rimli. 1998. 'Introduction', in Binodini Dasi, *My Story and My Life as an Actress*, New Delhi: Kali for Women.

Bhaumik, Kaushik. 2001. *The Emergence of the Bombay Film Industry 1913–1936*, Unpublished D. Phil., University of Oxford.

Bhavanrao, Shrinivasrao (aka Balasaheb Pant Pratinidi, B.A., Chief of Aundh). 1931. *Suryanamaskars (Perfect Physical and Mental Culture) for Health, Efficiency & Longevity*, Third edition, Aundh State Press.

Bordwell, David, Janet Steiger, and Kirstin Thompson. 1985. *The Classical Hollywood Cinema: Film Style and Mode of Production to 1960*, New York: Columbia University Press.

Bousquet, Henri and Laurent Mannoni (eds). 1992. 'Éclair 1907–1918', *1895: Association française de recherche sur l'histoire du cinéma 12*, Pordenone: Le Giornate del Cinema Muto.

Bowser, Eileen. 1990. *History of the American Cinema, Volume 2: The Transformation of Cinema, 1907–1915*, Berkeley, Los Angeles and London: University of California Press.

Breman, Jan. 2004. *The Making and Unmaking of an Industrial Working Class: Sliding Down the Labour Hierarchy in Ahmedabad, India*, New Delhi, Oxford and New York: Oxford University Press.

Brenner, Robert. 1998. 'The Economics of Global Turbulence', *New Left Review* 229, pp. 1–264.

Browne, Nick (ed.). 1998. *Refiguring American Film Genres: Theory and History*, Berkeley: University of California Press.

Buck-Morss, Susan. 1989. *The Dialectics of Seeing: Walter Benjamin and the Arcades Project*, Cambridge, Mass.: MIT Press.

———. 1992. Aesthetics and Anaesthetics: Walter Benjamin's Artwork Essay Reconsidered', *October* 62, pp. 3–41.

———. 1995. 'Envisioning Capital: Political Economy on Display', in Lynne Cooke and Peter Wollen (eds), *Visual Display: Culture beyond Appearances*, Seattle: Bay Press, pp. 110–41.

———. 2000. *Dreamworld and Catastrophe: The Passing of Mass Utopia in the East and West*, Cambridge, Mass.: MIT Press.

Bürger, Peter (trans. from German by Michael Show). 1984. *Theory of the Avant-Garde*, Minneapolis: University of Minnesota Press.

———. 1992. 'Some Reflections upon the Historico-Sociological Explanation of the Aesthetics of Genius in the Eighteenth-Century', in *The Decline of Modernism*, Cambridge: Polity Press, pp. 57–69.

Casetti, Francesco (trans. from Italian by Francesca Chiostri and Elizabeth Gard Bartolini-Salimbeni). 1999. *Theories of Cinema 1945–1995*, Austin: University of Texas Press.

Chabria, Suresh (ed.). 1994. *Light of Asia: Indian Silent Cinema 1912–1934*, Pordenone: Le Giornate del Cinema Muto; Pune: National Film Archive of India.

Chakrabarty, Dipesh. 1989. *Rethinking Working Class History: Bengal 1890–1940*, Princeton: Princeton University Press.

Chandavarkar, Rajnarayan. 1994. *The Origins of Industrial Capitalism in India: Business Strategies and the Working Classes in Bombay, 1900–1940*, Cambridge: Cambridge University Press.

———. 1998. *Imperial Power and Popular Politics: Class, Resistance and the State in India c. 1850–1950*, Cambridge: Cambridge University Press.

———. 2004. 'From Neighbourhood to Nation: The Rise and Fall of Life in Bombay's Girangaon in the Twentieth Century', in Neera Adarkar and Meena Menon (eds), *One Hundred Voices One Hundred Years: The Millworkers of Giranagaon, An Oral History*, Calcutta and New Delhi: Seagull Books.

Chandra, Bipan. 2003. *In the Name of Democracy: JP Movement and the Emergency*, New Delhi: Penguin Books.

Chandra, Sudhir. 1992. *The Oppressive Present: Literature and Social Consciousness in Colonial India*, New Delhi: Oxford University Press.

Chatterjee, Partha. 1986. *Nationalist Thought and the Colonial World: A Derivative Discourse?* Delhi: Oxford University Press.

______. 1993. *The Nation and its Fragments: Colonial and Postcolonial Histories*, Princeton, New Jersey: Princeton University Press.

______. 1997. 'Indian Democracy and Bourgeois Reaction' and 'The Politics of Appropriation', in *A Possible India: Essays in Political Criticism*, New Delhi: Oxford University Press, pp. 35–57; 146–55.

______. 2003. 'Are Indian Cities Becoming Bourgeois at Last?', in Indira Chandrasekhar and Peter C. Seel (eds), *Body City: Siting Contemporary Culture in India*, New Delhi: Tulika Press, pp. 171–85.

Chibber, Vivek. 2004. *Locked in Place: State-Building and Late Industrialization in India*, New Delhi: Tulika Books. Originally published by Princeton University Press, 2003.

Chopra, Anupama. 2000. *Sholay: The Making of a Classic*, New Delhi: Penguin Books.

Cook, David A. 2000. *History of the American Cinema* Vol. 9: *Lost Illusions: American Cinema in the Shadow of Watergate and Vietnam 1970–1979*, Berkeley: University of California Press.

Crary, Jonathan. 1990. *Techniques of the Observer: On Vision and Modernity in the Ninenteenth Century*, Cambridge, Mass.: MIT Press.

______. 1999. *Suspension of Perception: Attention, Spectacle and Modern Culture*, Cambridge, Mass.: MIT Press.

Das, Veena. 1980. 'The Mythological Film and its Framework of Meaning: An Analysis of *Jai Santoshi Ma*', *India International Centre Quarterly* 8 (1), pp. 43–56.

Dasgupta, Chidananda. 1989. 'Seeing and Believing, Science and Mythology: Notes on the Mythological Genre', *Film Quarterly* 42 (4), pp. 12–18.

Dasgupta, Susmita. 2006. *Amitabh: The Making of a Superstar*, New Delhi: Penguin Books.

Davis, Mike. 2001. *Late Victorian Holocausts: El Niño Famines and the Making of the Third World*, London and New York: Verso.

______. 2006. *Planet of Slums*, London and New York: Verso.

Dehejia, Vidya and Daryl Yauner Harnisch. 1997. 'Yoga as a Key to Understanding the Sculpted Body', in Vidya Dehejia (ed.), *Representing the Body: Gender Issues in Indian Art* Delhi: Kali for Women, pp. 68–81.

De Mellow, Melville (ed.). 1987. *Indigenous Games and Martial Arts of India*, New Delhi: Sports Authority of India.

Derné, Steve. 1995. 'Market Forces at Work: Religious Themes in Commercial Hindi Films', in L.A. Babb and S.S. Wadley (eds), *Media and the Transformation of Religion in South Asia*, Philadelphia: University of Pennsylvania Press, pp. 191–216.

Desai, Meghnad. 1975. 'India: Emerging Contradictions of Slow Capitalist Development', in Robin Blackburn (ed.), *Explosion in a Subcontinent*, Harmondsworth: Penguin Books in association with *New Left Review*, pp. 11–50.

______. 2002. *Marx's Revenge: The Resurgence of Capitalism and the Death of Statist Socialism*, London: Verso.

______. 2004. *Nehru's Hero: Dilip Kumar in the Life of India*, New Delhi: Roli Books.

Deshpande, Haima. 2004. 'Lights, Camera, Losses!', *Sunday Express*, 14 March, p. 3.

Deshpande, Sudhanva. 2005. 'The Consumable Hero of Globalised India', in Raminder Kaur and Ajay J. Sinha (eds), *Bollyworld: Popular Indian Cinema through a Transnational Lens*, New Delhi and London: Sage, pp.186–203.

Desser, David. 2000. 'The Martial Arts Film in the 1990s', in Winston Dixon Wheeler (ed), *Film Genre 2000: New Critical Essays*, Albany: SUNY Press.

Dharap, B.V. 1978. *Indian Films*, Pune: Motion Picture Enterprises.

Dirks, Nicholas B. 1990. 'History as Sign of the Modern', *Public Culture* 2 (2), pp. 25–32.

Dissanayake, Wimal. 1993. 'The Concept of Evil and Social Order in Indian Melodrama: An Evolving Dialectic', in *Melodrama and Asian Cinema*, Cambridge: Cambridge University Press.

Dissanayake, Wimal and M. Sahai. 1992. *Sholay: A Cultural Reading*, Delhi: Wiley Eastern.

D'Monte, Darryl. 2002. *Ripping the Fabric: The Decline of Mumbai and its Mills*, New Delhi: Oxford University Press.

Donald, James. 1997. 'This, Here, Now: Imagining the Modern City', in Sally Westwood and John Williams (eds), *Imagining Cities: Scripts, Signs, Memory*, London: Routledge, pp. 181–201.

Doraiswamy, Rashmi. 1993. 'Les genres dans le cinema Indien', *CinemAction: panorama des genres du Cinéma*.

Ducrot, Oswald and Tzvetan Todorov. 1972. *Dictionnaire encyclopédique des sciences du langage*, Paris: Editions du Seuil.

Dwivedi, Sharada and Rahul Mehrotra. 2001. *Bombay: The Cities within*, Bombay: Eminence Design PVT.

Dwyer, Rachel. 2000. *All You Want is Money, All You Need is Love: Sex and Romance in Modern India*, London: Cassell.

______. 2002. 'Real and Imagined Audiences: *Lagaan* and the Hindi Film after the 1990s', *Etnofoor* 15 (1/2), pp. 177–93.

______. 2005. *Filming the Gods: Religion and Indian Cinema*, London and New York: Routledge.

Eco, Umberto. 1976. 'Articulations of the Cinematic Code' in Bill Nichols (ed.), *Movies and Methods: An Anthology*, Berkeley: University of California Press, pp. 590–607. First edition 1967.

Fazalbhoy, Y.A. 1939. *The Indian Film: A Review*, Bombay: Bombay Radio Press.

Feldman, Martha and Bonnie Gordon (eds). 2006. *The Courtensan's Arts: Cross-Cultural Perspectives*, New York: Oxford University Press.

Fernandes, Leela. 2004. 'The Politics of Forgetting: Class Politics, State Power and the Restructuring of Urban Space in India', *Urban Studies* 41 (12), pp. 2415–30.

Ferro, Marc (trans. from French by Naomi Greene). 1988. *Cinema and History*, Detroit: Wayne State University Press. (Originally published as *Cinéma et histoire* by Éditions Denoël in 1977).

Forbes, Geraldine. 1998. *The New Cambridge History of India: Women in Modern India*, New Delhi: Cambridge University Press.

Freud, Sigmund. 1976. 'The Dream-Work', in James Strachey (ed.), *The Pelican Freud Library Vol. 4: The Interpretation of Dreams*, Harmondsworth: Penguin Books, pp. 381–628.

Fujii, James. 1993. *Complicit Fictions: The Subject in the Modern Japanese Prose Narrative*, Berkeley: University of California Press.

Gabriel, Karen. 2005. *Imaging a Nation: The Sexual Economies of the Contemporary Mainstream Bombay Cinema (1970–2000)*, Maastricht: Shaker Publishing.

Gandhy, Behroze and Paul Willemen (eds). 1982. *Indian Cinema*, London: British Film Institute.

Ganti, Tejaswini. 2004. *Bollywood: A Guidebook to Popular Hindi Cinema*, New York and London: Routledge.

Garçon, François (ed.). 1992. *Cinéma et histoire: autour de Marc Ferro*, Paris: CinémAction 65.

Gledhill, Christine. 2000. 'Rethinking Genre' in Christine Gledhill and Linda Williams (eds), *Reinventing Film Studies*, London: Arnold; New York: Oxford University Press, pp. 221–43.

Godzich, Wlad and Jeffrey Kittay. 1987. *The Emergence of Prose: An Essay in Prosaics*, Minneapolis: University of Minnesota Press.

Godzich, Wlad and Nicholas Spadaccini. 1994. 'Popular Culture and Spanish Literary History', in *The Culture of Literacy*, Cambridge, Mass.: Harvard University Press, pp. 72–95.

Ghosh, Jayati. 2005. 'The Indian Economy (1970–2003)' in Dharma Kumar (ed.), *The Cambridge Economic History of India*, 2, Cambridge: Cambridge University Press; Hyderabad: Orient Longman, pp. 1027–45.

Greimas, Algirdas Julien (trans. from French by Paul J. Perron and Frank H. Collins). 1983. 'Actant, Actors and Figures', in *On Meaning: Selected Writings in Semiotic Theory*. Minneapolis: University of Minneapolis Press, pp. 106–20.

Grimaud, Emmanuel. 2003. *Bollywood Film Studio: ou comment les films se font à Bombay*, Paris: CNRS Editions.

Guha-Thakurta, Tapati. 1988. 'Artists, Artisans and Mass Picture Production in Late Nineteenth- and Early Twentieth-century Calcutta: The Changing Iconography of Popular Prints', *South Asia Research*, 8 (1).

______. 1991. 'Women as "Calendar Art" Icons: Emergence of Pictorial Stereotype in Colonial India', *Economic and Political Weekly*, 26 October, pp. WS91–9.

______. 1992. *The Making of a New 'Indian' Art: Artists, Aesthetics and Nationalism in Bengal, c. 1850–1920*, Cambridge: Cambridge University Press.

Hansen, Kathryn. 1983. '"Sultana the Dacoit" and "Harishchandra": Two Popular Dramas of the Nautanki Tradition of North India', *Modern Indian Studies* 17 (2), pp. 313–31.

______. 1992. *Grounds for Play: The Nautanki Theatre of North India*, Berkeley: University of California Press.

______. 2004. 'Language, Community and the Theatrical Public: Linguistic Pluralism and Change in the Nineteenth-Century Parsi Theatre', in Stuart Blackburn and Vasudha Dalmia (eds), *India's Literary History: Essays on the Nineteenth Century*, New Delhi: Permanent Black, pp. 60–86.

Hansen, Miriam. 1983. 'Early Silent Cinema: Whose Public Sphere?', *New German Critique* 29, pp. 147–84.

______. 1995. 'Early Cinema, Late Cinema: Transformations of the Public Sphere', in Linda Williams (ed.), *Viewing Positions: Ways of Seeing Film*, New Brunswick: Rutgers University Press, pp. 134–52.

Harvey, David. 1999. *The Limits to Capital*, London and New York: Verso.

Hjelmslev, Louis. 1953 [1943]. *Prolegomena to a Theory of Language*, Baltimore: Indiana University Publications in Anthropology and Linguistics. Second English edition published by Madison: University of Wisconsin Press, 1961.

Hozic, Aida A. 2001. *Hollyworld: Space, Power and Fantasy in the American Economy*, Ithaca and London: Cornell University Press.

Hughes, Stephen P. 1996a. *Is There Anyone Out There? Exhibition and the Formation of Silent Film Audiences in South India*, Unpublished D. Phil., University of Chicago, pp. 39–64.

______. 1996b. 'The Pre-Phalke Era in the South Asia: Reflections on the Formation of Film Audiences in Madras', *South Asian Studies* July–December, pp. 161–204.

______. 2000. 'Policing Silent Film Exhibition in Colonial South India', in Ravi Vasudevan (ed.), *Making Meaning in Indian Cinema*, New Delhi: Oxford University Press.

______. 2003. 'Pride of Place', *Seminar*, 25 May 2003.

Hunt, Lynn. 1993. *The Invention of Pornography: Obscenity and the Origins of Modernity 1500–1800*, New York: Zine Books.

Iampolski, Mikhail. 1998. *The Memory of Tiresias: Intertextuality and Film*, Berkeley and London: University of California Press.

Indian Cinematograph Committee 1927–28: Evidence. 1928. Calcutta: Government of India Central Publications Branch.

Jacquemin, Alain. 1999. *Urban Development and New Towns in the Third World: Lessons from the New Bombay Experience*, Aldershot: Ashgate.

Jain, Rikhab Das. 1960 *The Economic Aspects of the Film Industry in India*, Delhi: Atma Ram and Sons.

Jakobson, Roman. 1988. 'Linguistics and Poetics', in David Lodge (ed.), *Modern Criticism and Theory: A Reader*, London: Longman.

Jeffrey, Robin. 2000. *India's Newspaper Revolution: Capitalism, Politics and the Indian-language Press 1977–1999*, London: C. Hurst.

Johnston, Claire. 1980. 'Double Indemnity' in E. Ann Kaplan (ed.), *Women in Film Noir*, London: British Film Institute, pp. 100–11.

Joshi, Chitra. 2003. *Lost Worlds: Indian Labour and Its Forgotten Histories*, Delhi: Permanent Black.

Joshi, Heather and Vijay Joshi. 1976. *Surplus Labour and the City: A Case Study of Bombay*, Delhi: Oxford University Press.

Kabir, Nasreen Munni. 1999. *Talking Films: Conversations on Hindi Cinema with Javed Akhtar*, New Delhi: Oxford University Press.

Kakar, Sudhir. 1989. *Intimate Relations: Exploring Indian Sexuality*, Chicago: University of Chicago Press.

Kapur, Anuradha. 1993. 'The Representation of Gods and Heroes: Parsi Mythological Drama of the Early Twentieth Century', *Journal of Arts and Ideas*, 23–4, pp. 85–107.

Kapur, Geeta. 1987. 'Mythic Material in Indian Cinema', *Journal of Arts and Ideas* 14–15, pp. 79–109.

_____. 1993. 'Revelation and Doubt: *Sant Tukaram* and *Devi*', in Tejaswini Niranjana, P. Sudhir and Vivek Dhareshwar (eds), *Interrogating Modernity: Culture and Colonialism in India*, Calcutta: Seagull Books, pp. 19–46.

Kaul, Gautam. 1998. *Cinema and the Indian Freedom Struggle*, New Delhi: Sterling Publishers.

Kaviraj, Sudipta. 1997. 'A Critique of the Passive Revolution', in Partha Chatterjee (ed.), *State and Politics in India*, New Delhi: Oxford University Press, pp. 45–88.

Kazmi, Fareeduddin. 1998. 'How Angry is the Angry Young Man? "Rebellion" in Conventional Hindi Films', in Ashis Nandy (ed.), *The Secret Politics of Our Desires: Innocence, Culpability and Indian Popular Cinema*, New Delhi: Oxford University Press.

Kesavan, Mukul. 1994. 'Urdu, Awadh and the Tawaif: The Islamicate Roots of Hindi Cinema', in Zoya Hasan (ed.), *Forging Identities: Gender, Communities and the State*, New Delhi: Kali for Women, pp. 244–57.

Khatri Pahalvan, Shrikrishna. 1920. *Malkhan Samar*, Kanpur.

Khote, Durga (trans. by Shanta Gokhale). 2006. *I Durga Khote: An Autobiography*, New Delhi: Oxford University Press.

Kosambi, Meera. 1986. *Bombay in Transition: The Growth and Social Ecology of a Colonial City 1880–1980*, Stockholm: Almqvist & Wiksell.

Kothari, Komal. 1980. 'Myth, Tales and Folklore: Exploring the Substratum of Cinema', *India International Centre Quarterly* 8 (1), pp. 31–42.

Kracauer, Siegfried. 1974. *From Caligari to Hitler: A Psychological History of the German Film*, Princeton: Princeton University Press.

Lele, Jayant. 1995. 'Saffronisation of Shiv Sena: Political Economy of City, State, Nation', *Economic and Political Weekly*, 24 June, pp. 1520–8.

Lent, John A. 1983. 'Heyday of the Indian Studio System: the 1930s', *Asia Profile* 11, pp. 465–74.

Lutgendorf, Philip. 2003. '*Jai Santoshi Maa* Revisited', in *Representing Religion in World Cinema: Filmmaking, Mythmaking, Culture Making*, New York: Palgrave Macmillan, pp. 14–42.

Mandave, Suryakant. s.d. Master Vithal: Hero of the First Talkie, Pune-Kolhapur: unpublished monograph (mostly in Hindi).

Mani, Lata. 1985. 'The Production of an Official Discourse on 'Sati' in Early

Nineteenth-Century Bengal', in Francis Barker (ed.), *Europe and its Others: Essex Conference on the Sociology of Literature*, July, Colchester: University of Essex, 1985, pp. 107–27.

———. 1989. 'Contentious Traditions: The Debate on Sati in Colonial India', in Kumkum Sangari and Sudesh Vaid (eds), *Recasting Women: Essays in Colonial History*, New Dehli: Kali for Women, pp. 89–125.

Mauss, Marcel. 1966. *Sociologie et anthropologie*, Paris: PUF.

Majumdar, Neepa. 2001. *Female Stardom and Cinema in India: 1930s to 1950s*, Unpublished D. Phil., Indiana University.

Mazumdar, Ranjani. 2000. 'From Subjectification to Schizophrenia: The "Angry Man" and the "Psychotic" Hero of Bombay Cinema', in Ravi Vasudevan (ed.), *Making Meaning in Indian Cinema*, Delhi: Oxford University Press.

———. 2002. 'Ruin and the Uncanny City: Memory, Despair and Death in *Parinda*', in *Sarai Reader 2*, http://www.sarai.net/journal/reader2.html

———. 2007. *Bombay Cinema: An Archive of the City*, Minneapolis: University of Minnesota Press.

McKeon, Michael. 1987. *The Origins of the English Novel 1600–1740*, Baltimore: Johns Hopkins University Press.

Meduri, Avanthi. 1996. 'Nation, Woman, Representation: The Saturated History of the Devadasi and Her Dance', Unpublished D. Phil., New York University.

Mehta, Suketu. 2005. *Maximum City: Bombay Lost and Found*, London: Headline Review.

Metz, Christian. 1974. *Language and Cinema*, The Hague: Mouton.

Mishra, Vijay. 2002. *Bollywood Cinema: Temples of Desire*, London: Routledge.

Mittal, Ashok. 1995. *Cinema Industry in India: Pricing and Taxation*, New Delhi: Indus Publishing Co..

Morris, Morris D. 2005. 'The Growth of Large-Scale Industry to 1947' in Dharma Kumar (ed.), *The Cambridge Economic History of India*, 2, Cambridge: Cambridge University Press; Hyderabad: Orient Longman.

Meaghan Morris, Siu Leuing Li and Stephen Chan Ching-kiu (eds). 2005. *Hong Kong Connections: Transnational Imagination in Action Cinema* Durham: Duke University Press; Hong Kong: Hong Kong University Press.

Mujawar, Isak. 1969. *Maharashtra: Birthplace of Indian Film Industry*, New Delhi: Maharashtra Information Centre.

Mukherjee, Meenakshi. 1984. *Realism and Reality: The Novel and Society in India*, Delhi: Oxford University Press.

Mukhopadhyay, Urvi. 2004. *The Perception of the 'Medieval' in Indian Popular Films: 1920s–1960s*, Unpublished D.Phil., School of Oriental and African Studies.

Mulvey, Laura. 1975. 'Visual Pleasure and Narrative Cinema', *Screen*, 16 (3).

Murphy, A.D. 1972. 'Film Trade Sanity Asserts Itself', *Variety* 12 April, p. 3, 20.

Musser, Charles. 1990. *History of the American Cinema, Volume 1, the Emergence of Cinema: The American Screen to 1907*, Berkeley, Los Angeles, London: University of California Press.

Nair, Janaki. 1994. 'The Devadasi, Dharma and the State', *Economic and Political Weekly*, 10 December, pp. 3157–67.

_____. 1998. *Miners and Millhands: Work, Culture and Politics in Princely Mysore*, Delhi: Sage.

_____. 2005. *The Promise of the Metropolis: Bangalore's Twentieth Century*, New Delhi: Oxford University Press.

Neale, Steve. 1980. *Genre*, London: British Film Institute.

_____. 2000. *Genre and Hollywood*, London: Routledge.

Nevile, Pran. 1996. *Nautch Girls of India: Dances, Singers, Playmates*, New York: Ravi Kumar Publishers; New Delhi: Prakriti India.

Ohmann, Richard. 1996. *Selling Culture: Magazines, Markets and Class at the Turn of the Century*, London and New York: Verso.

Oldenburgh, Veena Talwar. 1990. 'Lifestyle as Resistance: The Case of the Courtesan of Lucknow, India', *Feminist Studies* 16 (2), pp. 259–87.

Oommen, M.A. and K.V. Joseph. 1991. *Economics of Indian Cinema*, New Delhi: Oxford and IBH Publishing.

Orsini, Francesca. 1999. 'Domesticity and Beyond: Hindi Women's Journals in the Early Twentieth Century', *South Asia Research* 19 (2), pp. 137–60.

_____. 2002. *The Hindi Public Sphere 1920–1940: Language and Literature in the Age of Nationalism*, New Delhi and Oxford: Oxford University Press.

Parasher, Aloka and Ushan Naik. 1986. 'Temple Girls of Medieval Karnataka', *The Indian Economic and Social History Review* 23 (1), pp. 63–78.

Patnaik, Prabhat. 1975. 'Imperialism and the Growth of Indian Capitalism', in Robin Blackburn (ed.), *Explosion in a Subcontinent*, Harmondsworth: Penguin, in association with *New Left Review*, pp. 51–78.

Pierce, Charles S. 1977. *Semiotic and Significs: The Correspondence between C.S. Peirce and Victoria Lady Welby*, Bloomington and London: Indiana University Press.

Pendakur, Manjunath. 1985. 'Dynamics of Cultural Policy Making: The US Film Industry in India', *Journal of Communication*, 4, pp. 52–72.

_____. 1989. 'New Cultural Technologies and the Fading Glitter of Indian Cinema', *Quarterly Review of Film and Video*, 11, pp. 69–78.

_____. 1990. 'India', in John Lent (ed.), *The Asian Film Industry*, London: Christopher Helm.

_____. 2003. *Indian Popular Cinema: Industry, Ideology, and Consciousness*, Cress Hill, New Jersey: Hampton Press.

Pinney, Christopher. 2004. *Photos of the Gods: The Printed Image and Political Struggle in India*, London: Reaktion Books.

Pinto, Jerry. 2006. *Helen: The Life and Times of an H-Bomb*, New Delhi: Penguin Books.

Prakash, Shruti. 1995. 'The Bajrang Brigade', *Pioneer on Sunday*, 10 September, pp. 1–2 Pulse supplement.

Prasad, Madhava M. 1994. *The State and Culture: Hindi Cinema in the Passive Revolution*, Unpublished D. Phil., University of Pittsburgh.

_____. 1998a 'Back to the Present', *Cultural Dynamics*, 10 (2), pp. 123–32.

———. 1998b. *Ideology of the Hindi Film: A Historical Construction*, New Delhi: Oxford University Press.

———. 2001. 'Realism and Fantasy in Representations of Metropolitan Life in India', *Journal of the Moving Image*, 2, pp. 127–39.

Rahman, P. and Anup Katiyar. 1993. 'Bombay Film Industry: Underworld Connections', *India Today*, 15 May, pp. 114–22.

Rajadhyaksha, Ashish. 1980. 'Wrestling: Sport or Racket?', *Sport World*, 30 April, pp. 6–10.

———. 1986. 'Neo-Traditionalism: Film as Popular Art in India', *Framework*, 32–33, pp. 20–67.

———. 1987. 'The Phalke Era: Conflict of Traditional Form and Modern Technology', *Journal of Arts and Ideas*, 14–15, pp. 47–78.

———. 1993. 'The Epic Melodrama', *Journal of Arts and Ideas*, 25–26, pp. 55–70.

———. 2003. '"The Bollywoodization" of the Indian Cinema: Cultural Nationalism in a Global Arena', *Inter-Asia Cultural Studies*, 4 (1), pp. 25–39.

———. 2004. 'Rethinking the State after Bollywood', *Journal of the Moving Image*, 3 (June), pp. 47–90.

———. 2007. 'The Curious Case of Bombay's Hindi Cinema: The Career of Indigenous Capital', Paper presented at the Asian Cinema: Towards a Research and Teaching Agenda conference, Bangalore: February.

Rajadhyaksha, Ashish and Paul Willemen (eds). 1999. *Encyclopaedia of Indian Cinema*, London: British Film Institute; New Delhi: Oxford University Press.

Rajhans, P. 1992. 'That's Entertainment: Director Manmohan Desai Flashbacks to *Amar Akbar Anthony*', *Cinema in India*, 3 (6), pp. 10–15.

Ramasubban, Radhika and Nigel Crook. 1995. 'Spatial Patterns of Health and Mortality', in Sujata Patel and Alice Thorner (eds), *Bombay: Metaphor for Modern India*, New Delhi: Oxford University Press, pp. 143–69.

Report of the Film Enquiry Committee. 1951. New Delhi: Government of India Press.

Reuben, Bunny. 1999. *Mehboob ... India's DeMille*. New Delhi: HarperCollins India.

Rosen, Phililp. 2001. *Change Mummified: Cinema, Historicity, Theory*, Minneapolis and London: University of Minnesota Press.

Ryall, Tom. 1998. 'Genre and Hollywood', in John Hill and Pamela Church Gibson (eds), *The Oxford Guide to Film Studies*, Oxford: Oxford University Press, pp. 327–38.

Salmi, Markku (ed.). 1982. *National Film Archive: Catalogue of Stills, Posters and Designs*, London: British Film Institute.

Sarkar, Sumit. 1983. *Modern India 1885–1947*, Madras: Macmillan India.

Schulze, Brigitte. 2003. *Humanist and Emotional Beginnings of a Nationalist Indian Cinema in Bombay*, Berlin: Avinus Verlag.

Sharma, Ashwani. 1993. 'Blood Sweat and Tears: Amitabh Bachchan, Urban Demi-god', in Pat Kirkham and Janet Thumin (eds), *You Tarzan: Masculinity, Movies and Men*, London: Lawrence & Wishart, pp. 169–71.

256 Bibliography

Shoesmith, Brian. 1987. 'From Monopoly to Commodity: the Bombay Studios in the 1930s', in Tom O' Regan and Brian Shoesmith (eds), *History on/and/in Film*, Perth: History and Film Association of Australia.

Singh, Dara. 1993. *Meri Aatmakatha*, New Delhi: Pravin Prakashan.

Somaaya, Bhawava. 1999. *Amitabh Bachchan: The Legend*, Delhi: Macmillan.

Sorlin, Pierre. 1977. *Sociologie du cinéma*, Paris: Albatros.

———. 1980. *The Film in History: Restaging the Past*, Oxford: Basil Blackwell.

Srinivas, S.V. 2003. 'Hong Kong Action Films in the Indian B Circuit', *Inter-Asia Cultural Studies* 4 (1), pp. 40–62.

———. 2005. 'Hong Kong Action Film and the Career of the Telugu Mass Hero', in Meaghan Morris, Siu Leuing Li and Stephen Chan Ching-kiu (eds), *Hong Kong Connections: Transnational Imagination in Action Cinema*, Durham: Duke University Press; Hong Kong: Hong Kong University Press, pp. 111–25.

Srinavasan, Amrit. 1984. 'Temple "Prostitution" and Community Reform: An Examination of the Ethnographic, Historical and Textual Context of the Devadasi in Tamilnadu, South India', Unpublished D. Phil., Cambridge University.

———. 1985. 'Reform and Revival: The Devadasi and Her Dance', *Economic and Political Weekly* 20 (44), pp. 1869–76.

Stahlberg, Per. 2002. *Lucknow Daily: How a Hindi Newspaper Constructs Society*, Stockholm: Stockholm Studies in Social Anthropology.

Thapar, Romila. 1987. *Cultural Transaction and Early Modern India: Tradition and Patronage*, New Delhi: Oxford University Press.

———. 1988. 'Imagined Religious Communities? Ancient History and the Modern Search for a Hindu Identity', *Modern Asian Studies* 23, pp. 209–31.

———. 2000. 'The Historian and the Epic', in *Cultural Pasts: Essays in Early Indian History*, New Delhi: Oxford University Press, pp. 613–29.

Thomas, Rosie. 2005. 'Not Quite (Pearl) White: Fearless Nadia, Queen of the Stunts', in Raminder Kaur and Ajay J. Sinha (eds), *Bollyworld: Popular Indian Cinema through a Transnational Lens*, New Delhi and London: Sage, pp. 35–69.

Thompson, Kristin. 1985. *Exporting Entertainment: America in the World Film Market 1907–1934*, London: British Film Institute.

Todorov, Tzvetan. 1973. *The Fantastic: A Structural Approach to a Literary Genre*, Ithaca, New York: Cornell University Press.

Tudor, Andrew. 1974. *Theories of Film*, London: Secker and Warburg and British Film Institute.

Vachani, Lalit. 1989. *Narrative, Pleasure and Ideology in the Hindi Film: An Analysis of the Outsider Formula*, Unpublished MA, University of Pennsylvania.

Vaidyanathan, A. 2005. 'The Indian Economy since Independence (1947–70)', in Dharma Kumar (ed.), *The Cambridge Economic History of India*, 2, Hyderabad: Orient Longman, 2nd Edn, pp. 947–94.

Valicha, Kishore. 1988. *The Moving Image: A Study of Indian Cinema*, Hyderabad: Orient Longman.

Vanaik, Achin. 1990. *The Painful Transition: Bourgeois Democracy in India*, London and New York: Verso.

Vasudevan, Ravi S. 1996. '"You Cannot Live in Society and Ignore It": Nationhood and Female Modernity in *Andaz*', in Patricia Uberoi (ed.), *Social Reform, Sexuality and the State*, Delhi: Sage, pp. 81–108.

———. 1999. 'Review: 'Ideology of the Hindi Film: A Historical Construction"', *Journal of the Moving Image* 1, pp. 117–27.

———. 2002. 'The Exhilaration of Dread: Genre, Narrative Form and Film Style in Contemporary Urban Action Films', *Sarai Reader* 2, http://www.sarai.net/journal/reader2.html

———. 2003. 'Selves Made Strange: Violent and Performative Bodies in the Cities of Indian Cinema, 1974–2003' in Indira Chandrasekhar and Peter C. Seel (eds), *Body City: Siting Contemporary Culture in India*, New Delhi: Tulika Press, pp. 84–117.

Verma, R.K. 2000. *Filmography Silent Cinema 1913–1934*, Dehradun.

Visaria, Leela and Pravin Visaria. 2005. 'Population (1775–1947)', in Dharma Kumar (ed.), *The Cambridge Economic History of India*, 2, Cambridge: Cambridge University Press; Hyderabad: Orient Longman, pp. 463–532.

Vitali, Valentina. 2000. 'The Families of Hindi Cinema: For a Historical Approach to Film', *Framework: The Journal of Cinema and Media*, 42.

———. 2002. 'The Politics of Film Historiography', *Southern Review: Communication, Politics & Culture* 35 (2), pp. 131–5.

———. 2005. 'Hong Kong—Hollywood—Bombay: On the Function of "Martial Art" in Hindi Action Cinema', in Meaghan Morris, Siu Leuing Li, and Stephen Chan Ching-kiu (eds), *Hong Kong Connections: Transnational Imagination in Action Cinema*, Durham: Duke University Press; Hong Kong: Hong Kong University Press, pp. 125–50.

———. 2006. 'Not a Biography of the "Indian Cinema": Historiography and the Question of National Cinema in India', in Valentina Vitali and Paul Willemen (eds), *Theorising National Cinema*, London: British Film Institute, pp. 262–73.

Wadia, J.B.H. [1978]. *Those Were the Days*, Bombay: unpublished autobiography.

Wenner, Dorothee (trans. from German by Rebecca Morrison). 2005. *Fearless Nadia: The True Story of Bollywood's Original Stunt Queen*, New Delhi: Penguin Books. Originally published as *Zorros Blonde Schwester: das Leben der indischen Kinolegende Fearless Nadia*, Berlin: Ullstein Buchverlage, 1999.

Wilkins, W.J. 1975. *Hindu Mythology: Vedic and Puranic*, Calcutta: Rupa.

Willemen, Paul. 1991. 'Negotiating the Transition to Capitalism: The Case of *Andaz*', *East-West Film Journal* 5 (1), pp. 56–66.

———. 2000. 'Of Mice and Men: Reflections on Digital Imagery', *TwoNineTwo: Essays in Visual Culture* 1, pp. 5–20.

———. 2002. 'The Zoom in Popular Cinema: A Question of Performance', *New Cinemas* 1(1), pp. 6–13.

———. 2005a. 'Action Cinema, Labour Power and the Video Market', in Meaghan

Morris, Siu Leuing Li, and Stephen Chan Ching-kiu (eds), *Hong Kong Connections: Transnational Imagination in Action Cinema*, Durham: Duke University Press; Hong Kong: Hong Kong University Press, pp. 223–48.

______. 2005b. 'For a Comparative Film Studies', *Inter-Asia Cultural Studies* 6(1), pp. 98–112.

Wollen, Peter. 1998. *Signs and Meaning in the Cinema*, London: British Film Institute, 1998. Originally published by Secker and Warburg in 1969.

______. 1980. 'Introduction: Place in the Cinema', *Framework* 13, p. 25.

Yogendra, Shri. 1956. *Yoga: Physical Education*, Bombay: The Yoga Institute.

Zarrilli, Philip, B. 1995. 'Repositioning the Body, Practice, Power and Self in an Indian Martial Art', in Carol Breckenbridge (ed.), *Consuming Modernity: Public Culture in a South Asian World*, Minneapolis: University of Minnesota Press, pp. 183–215.

______. 1998. *When the Body Becomes All Eyes: Paradigms, Discourses and Practices of Power in Kalarippayattu, a South Indian Martial Art*, New Delhi: Oxford University Press.

MAGAZINES AND NEWSPAPERS

Bombay Chronicle
Cinema (Lahore)
Cinema Advance
Cinema in India
Cinema Samsar
Cinema Vision, Special Issue 'Pioneers of Indian Cinema: the Silent Era', 1 (1), (1980).
Citrapat
Film Art Supplement
Filmfare
Film India (Mother India)
Filmland
Filmland Pictorial News
Film World
Kiran
Madhuri
Modern Review
Motion Pictures Monthly
Mouj Majah
Movie Land
Picture Post
Ranjit Bulletin
Screen
Talk-A-Tone (Madras)
The Times of India
Variety Weekly

WEBSITES:

D'Essence Consulting, 'Industry Overview' at <www.dessenceconsulting.com/
    pdf/multiplex%20industry%20in%20India.pdf>
Dodona Research at <http://www.dodona.co.uk/bollywood.htm>
Price Waterhouse Coopers, 'The Indian Entertainment and Media Industry:
    Unraveling the Potential', at <www.businessworld.in/APR1706/
    frames_pwc_2006.pdf>

Index